The Making of V&A East

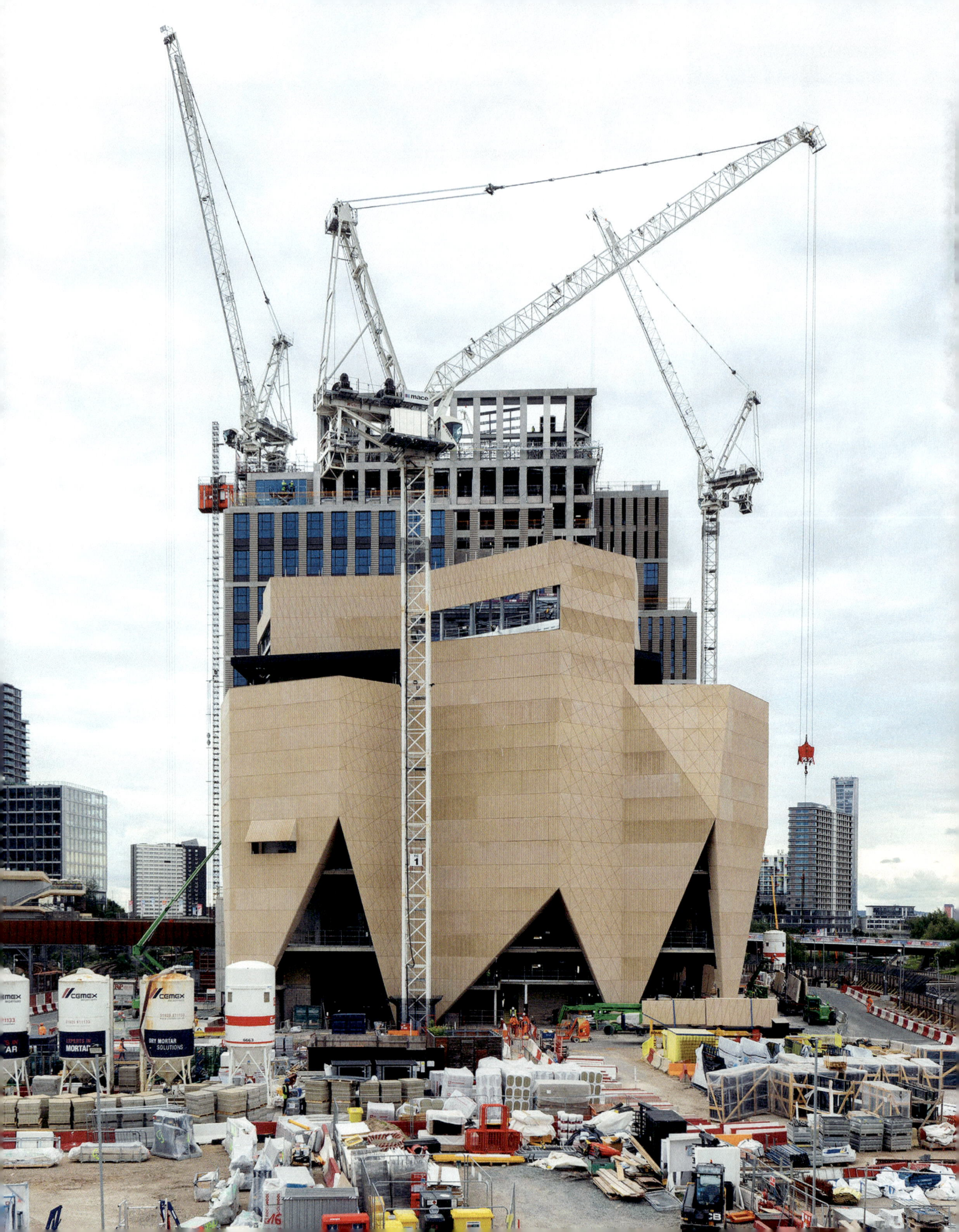
mace
CEMEX
CEMEX
DRY MORTAR SOLUTIONS

The Making of V&A East

Edited by Tim Reeve and
Gus Casely-Hayford with
Brendan Cormier

V&A Publishing

People and Place

What a Museum Can Do

What a Storehouse Can Do

Global Narratives

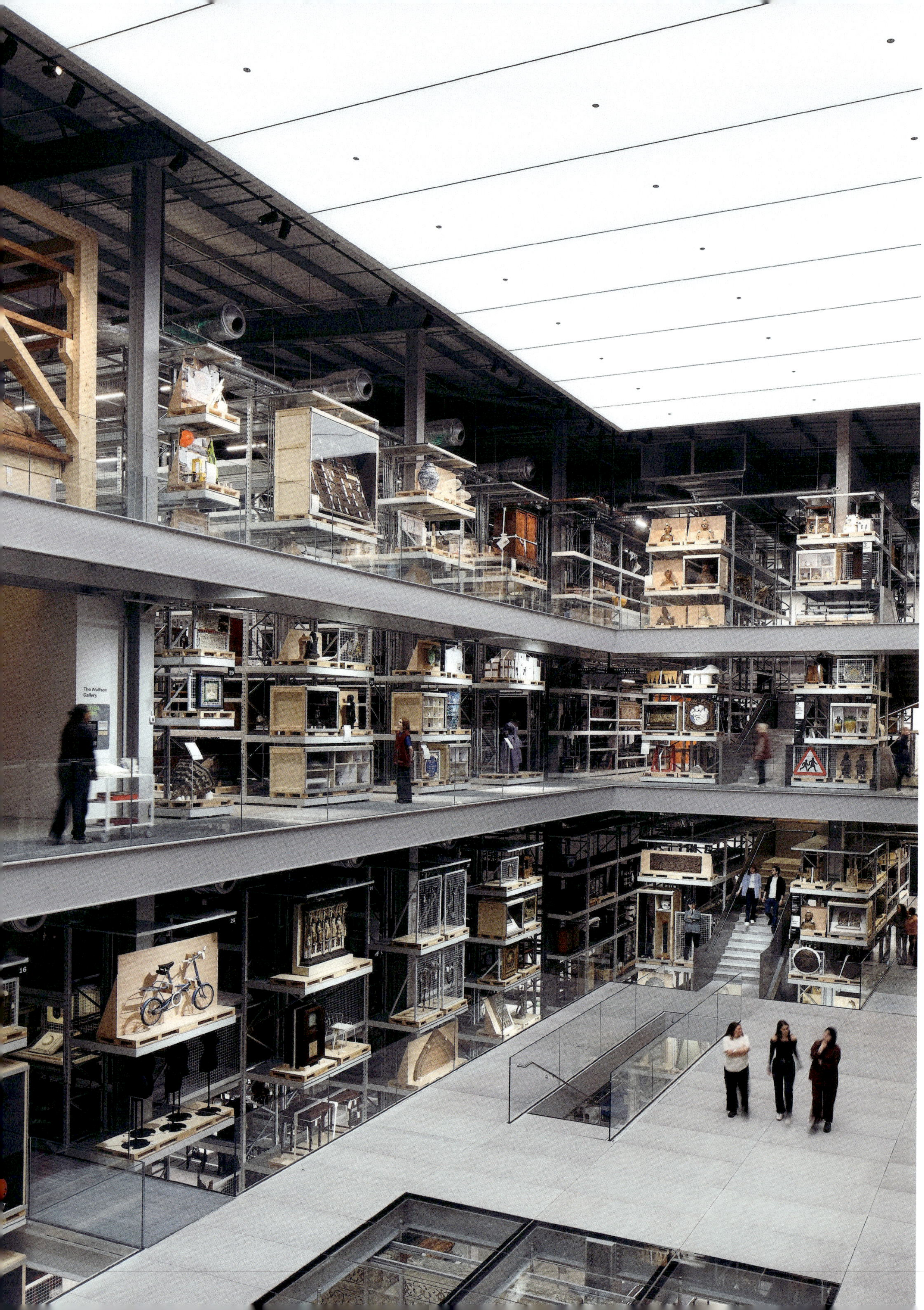

Weston Collections Hall, V&A East Storehouse, 2025

Foreword
Tristram Hunt

In welcoming visitors to its two new spaces in east London, V&A East builds on the V&A's commitment to the principles of art and design for all, inspiring the artists and designers of today and tomorrow. Our abiding mission is to encourage local communities to access this phenomenal collection – *their* phenomenal collection – while also supporting creative industries locally.

The Storehouse, which opened in May 2025, is a walk-in *Wunderkammer*, a real-life cabinet of curiosities, which takes the idea of V&A's founder, Prince Albert, of a storehouse of learning and display into the era of popular, democratic access. Across 16,000 square metres, it immerses visitors in over half a million works spanning every creative discipline from fashion to theatre, streetwear to sculpture, design icons to pop pioneers. A busy and dynamic working museum store, it has allowed visitors to get up close to their national collections on a scale and in ways not possible before.

The Museum, opened in Spring 2026, offers new ways of interpreting our collections with a contemporary spin. The Why We Make Galleries, encompassing two floors of the building, foreground makers and their motivations for engaging in arts and culture, with the intent to inspire younger audiences to pursue a creative discipline. They are both global in outlook – with projects from around the world – and locally rooted, following themes that resonate with young Londoners today. Meanwhile, our temporary exhibition space and commissions programme offer countless opportunities to platform and promote some of the most exciting and leading-edge contemporary artists, performers and designers.

This book provides an opportunity to explain our aspirations and motivations for this pioneering new cultural hub. The opening section, on east London, is told via many perspectives, from V&A East Director Gus Casely-Hayford's reflection on the region's global manufacturing and artisanal history and Chief Curator Brendan Cormier's exploration of the role that place and context play in both artistic practice and cultural institutions to testaments from local young people and creatives who are inspired daily by the energy of the community they call home.

Chapters on the Storehouse and Museum, from Deputy Director Tim Reeve and curators Georgia Haseldine and Zofia Trafas White, highlight not only the architectural evolution of these exciting, dynamic and welcoming buildings but also the creativity and ingenuity that animates them, spotlighting a small cross-section of objects that might be encountered on a visit and hearing from the staff who make it all possible.

The book concludes by looking out, as east London has done for centuries, to an interlinked global community. Curator Madeleine Haddon brings together insights from museum leaders who are doing things differently across the world, from Hong Kong to Nairobi. Together they present a hopeful paradigm – for museums that evolve in dialogue with their audiences, whilst pushing the boundaries of scholarship and learning.

We are hugely grateful to our many funders, public and private, charitable and corporate, who have made this transformational development and act of meaningful access possible.

Tristram Hunt, Director, V&A

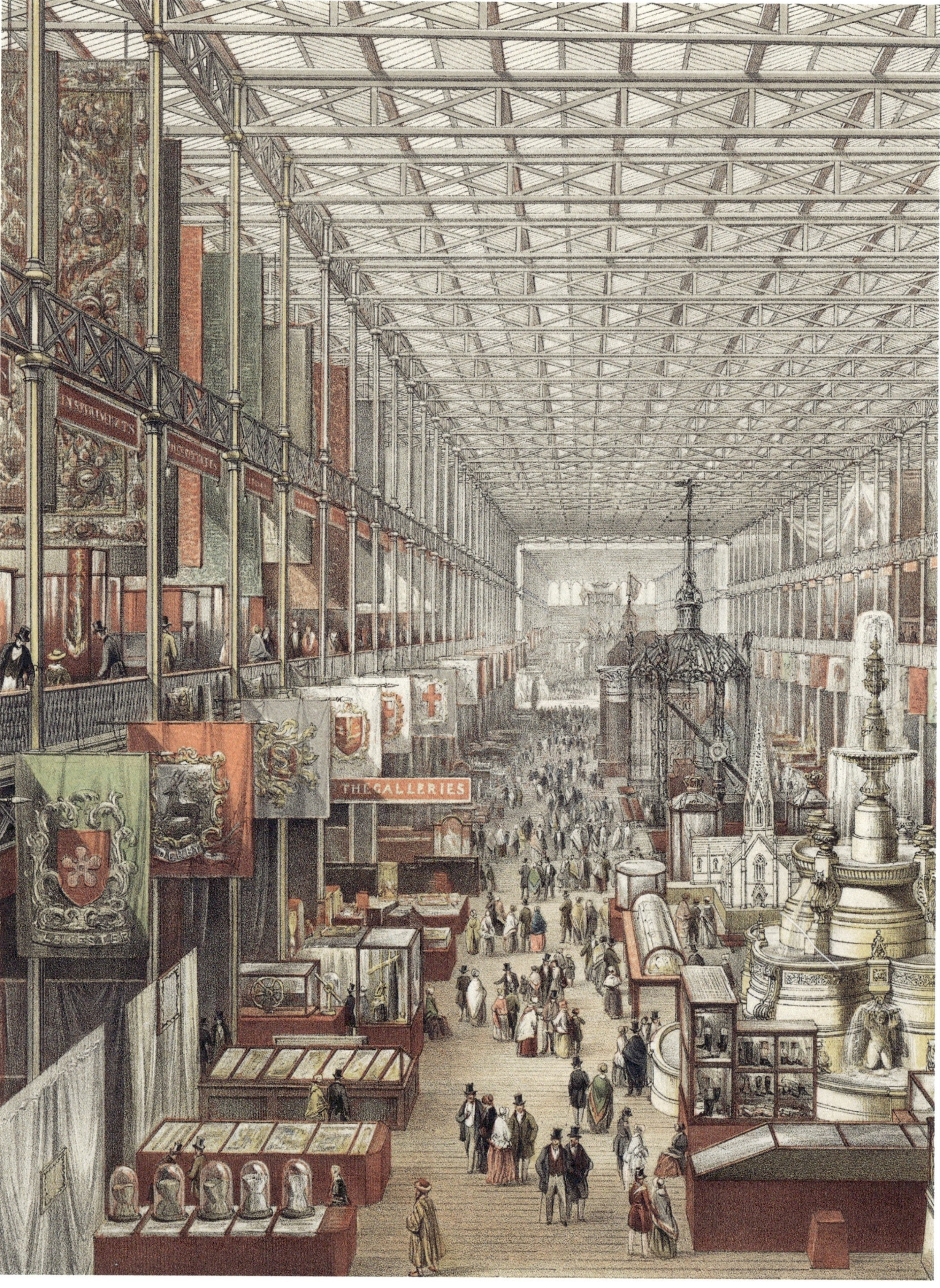

Hand-coloured lithograph by Ackermann & Co. of the British Department at the Great Exhibition, Hyde Park, London, 1851

Making V&A East
Tim Reeve

The founding story of the V&A has been well rehearsed, and maybe even embellished over the many decades of its existence. It is still much told, both within the V&A and across the community of applied arts and design museums who take their inspiration from the founding of Albertopolis – the world's first cultural district – in the mid-nineteenth century. Since that date, the V&A has been a home for design and creativity, responding to the rapidly changing world as it was, and as it is, always looking to innovate, experiment and evolve.

In its earliest days, the V&A had gas lighting and evening openings to ensure after-hours access for working people. Between 1857 and 1883, over 6.5 million of the total 15 million visits were made during the evenings, once the working day had finished. We recall that the V&A's founding director, Henry Cole, campaigned for cheaper and more regular public transport links to the then more remote area of Kensington. These are reminders of an institutional duty and purpose to understand, respond to and make sense of the world in which we exist, and to promote the power of creativity to impact the world for the better.

Cole was indisputably a progressive, a moderniser and a reformer. His vision was formed around an instinct that through a stronger interrelationship between design and making, function and style, and simplicity over ornamentation, Britain would remain prosperous and relevant. In that sense, the Great Exhibition of 1851 was not simply a showcase of the best and brightest from the wider world of making, but a site of contention, effecting a paradigm shift in attitudes about the sustainability of Britain's place as manufacturing superpower.

The subsequent creation of what became the V&A was not planned; rather, it was the result of events, momentum, happenstance, politics and money, which enabled a legacy of education through exhibition. The parallels between the Great Exhibition and the Olympics, and the creation of the V&A (and Albertopolis) and V&A East (and East Bank) are imprecise, but what they share are roots in a great global gathering. Both examples highlight the power of creativity and the creative industries as a British success story, while also reminding us of the ongoing deficit of opportunities for all, and the value of radical access to national collections as a source of contemporary inspiration – as important now as it was in the mid-nineteenth century.

As was the case with the Great Exhibition and the V&A in South Kensington – responding to the existential crisis of Great Britain falling behind in designing and making, and then investing in the original cultural quarter through the windfall profits – so too the creation of V&A East was born out of absolute necessity and a tantalising opportunity. The opportunity came through an invitation by the Mayor of London, Boris Johnson, to be the founding cultural partner – along with University College London as the founding educational partner – of an Olympic legacy development in east London, with culture, education and innovation as its heart and soul – what the Mayor called 'Olympicopolis – an Albertopolis for the digital age'. Here we would be joined by a constellation of new and existing east-London creative practitioners and partners, collaborating to engineer a new type of catalysing legacy in boroughs that had endured decades of underinvestment in cultural infrastructure. The necessity stemmed from the need to vacate our home of nearly 50 years at Blythe House, requiring a new home to be found for 250,000 objects and over 1,000 archives of art, design and performance.

Although these two drivers remained entirely separate for the first three years of our involvement in the legacy programme, that push from Blythe House, allied to a political pull to east London, developed into a vision for a new type of audience-centred museum experience in the Olympic Park, which became V&A East Museum and Storehouse.

To construct a new museum building, with permanent galleries, a cafe and an exhibition gallery, would not have represented museological innovation. But, to combine it with a unique

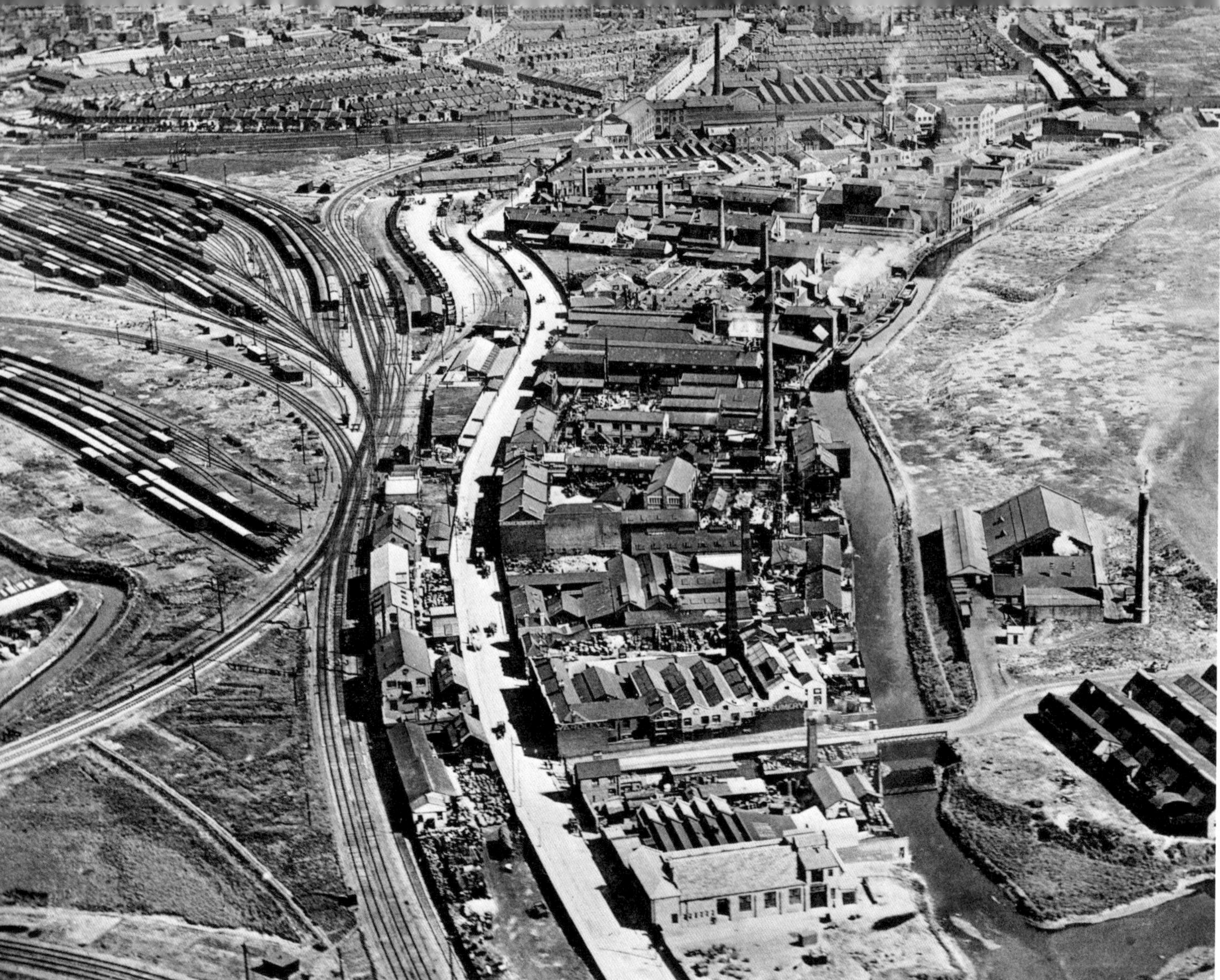

View of Carpenters Road, the Waterfront site where V&A East now sits, pre-1914

cultural experience designed around the 'stored' collection from Blythe House – a new type of building, as part of a new district, for a new and underserved audience – was to rediscover that radical mission and entrepreneurial drive to place these collections as a sourcebook to inspire the next generation of artists and designers.

The V&A is fortunate to have been able to build a collection of collections over many decades, representing human creativity and ingenuity over millennia, covering almost any material type, design and making discipline we are able to imagine. It is not alone in having long ago run out of space to make these collections fully and meaningfully accessible, and to have more objects in storage than on display. While this long-standing problem had been visible for some time, the solution was far from obvious. With V&A East came the extraordinary opportunity to create public access to these collections in a new and innovative way.

The industrial story of east London long predates the Olympic Games, with a rich creative heritage still evident across the four boroughs. In that sense, the legacy is not the creation of a new place but the rediscovery and renewal of a *sense* of place, with the repurposing of land that had been left to degrade, but which housed vibrant, diverse and creative communities at its margins. People speak of the 'Carpenters Road Fridge Mountain' as evidence of a perpetual industrial wasteland, but there is different testimony to the exact site of the new V&A East Museum's place in the history of east London. This very road was named for the purchase of land by the Worshipful Company of Carpenters in the eighteenth century. They turned it from marshland into agricultural land, and then leased it for small-scale industrial use – from match making to linen manufacturing, and latterly from pies to fish to fur. This is historically a place of making and commerce, although one that needed a grand national investment of the scale of the Olympic Games to make up for decades of neglect.

On the park itself, the seeds for the V&A's eventual commitment to east London, through the development of the museum and storehouse concept, were sown with the competition in early 2012 – before the Olympic Games themselves – to secure a viable future use for the Broadcast and Press Centres on the Hackney Wick side of the park. The winning pitch – from a shortlist said to include an indoor snowdome – was for the creation of Here East as a vibrant technology and innovation campus, with tenants including BT Sport, Wayne McGregor Studios, Loughborough University and the Bartlett School of Architecture. In a building large enough to fit Canary Wharf's One Canada Square building, the Broadcast Centre had room to spare, keeping alive the possibility of a V&A presence as part of this new campus.

The starting point for the Stratford Waterfront project on the Westfield side of the park was a 'think-piece' concept by Bureau Ole Sheeran, commissioned by the London Legacy Development Corporation (LLDC) in 2014, for an ambitious series of interconnected and hybrid boxes, set on the Waterfront and intended for cultural collaborations. In parallel, Her Majesty's Government had confirmed that – should the V&A wish to commit as a founding partner in this new cultural district – the required revenue support would be found to make it happen. The line-up of potential partners evolved; joining UCL and the V&A as founding partners would be a consolidation of the London College of Fashion into a single new 'factory' building, a new Sadler's Wells performance venue featuring a hip-hop academy, and even the possibility of the Smithsonian Institution to add some transatlantic heft. Briefs were written, funding packages negotiated and partnerships began to form, both among the new arrivals and, crucially, with the communities who we all hoped to serve, inspire and collaborate with.

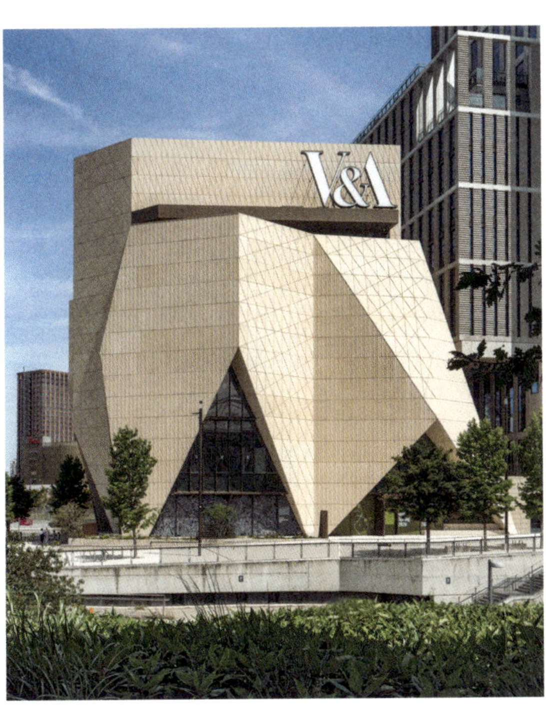

V&A East Museum from across the River Lea, 2025

The next challenge? To mould this constellation of possibilities into a coherent brief for the international design competition launched by LLDC in 2015. The team, led by Allies & Morrison supported by Royal Gold Medal-winning Dublin-based practice O'Donnell + Tuomey, was announced in 2016 and offered something for everyone. Certainly, a new V&A building designed by a practice responsible for the LSE's Saw Swee Hock building and Dublin's Lyric Theatre was an exciting prospect. At this point, a boxy V&A East Museum building of some 20,000 square metres would provide the gateway to the culture and education district, with enormous residential towers at the far end of Stratford Waterfront to make the funding model work, but with no new home yet secured for the Blythe House collections.

A change of administration at City Hall, and new mayor Sadiq Khan's redrawing of a financially unviable masterplan – prompted in large part by the need to shorten those residential towers to preserve the views of St Paul's Cathedral from Richmond Hill – gave the V&A the time and space to recraft our proposition, placing the collections at the very heart of our east-London commitment. For the first time, the possibility of V&A East as a 360-degree window into the full wonder and complexity of contemporary museum life, through two new experiences on each side of the park – V&A East Museum on the Stratford Waterfront and V&A East Storehouse in Here East on the banks of the canal at Hackney Wick – came to life. Together, under a single operating model, these new cultural institutions tell the story of design and making for new audiences, using the V&A collections to reflect the creative heritage of east London but also as inspiration for contemporary makers locally, nationally and internationally. The newly designed and located O'Donnell + Tuomey Balenciaga-inspired building would now sit at the crossroads between the International Quarter and a maturing Olympic Park – the 'stage'

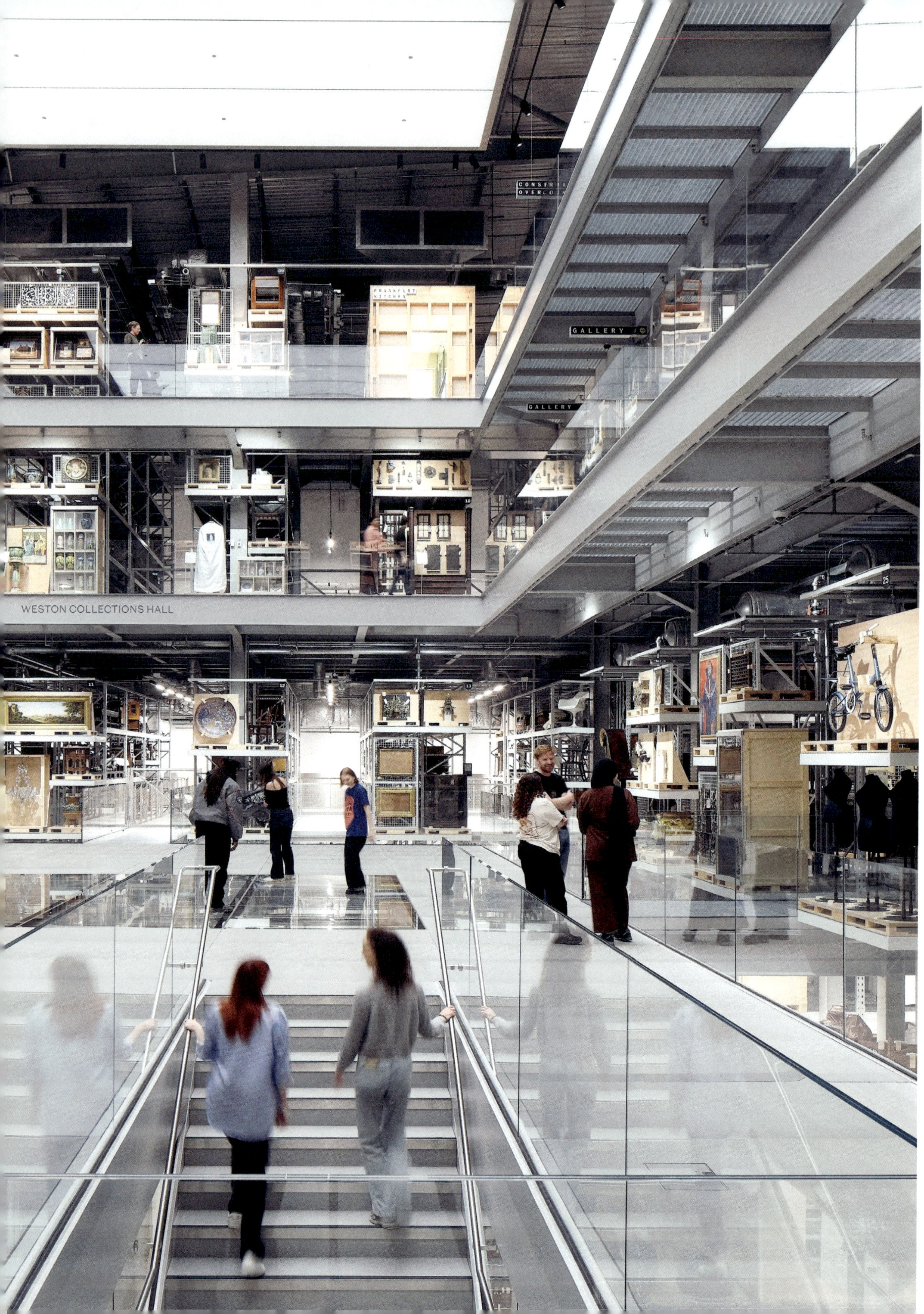

Weston Collections Hall, V&A East Storehouse, 2025

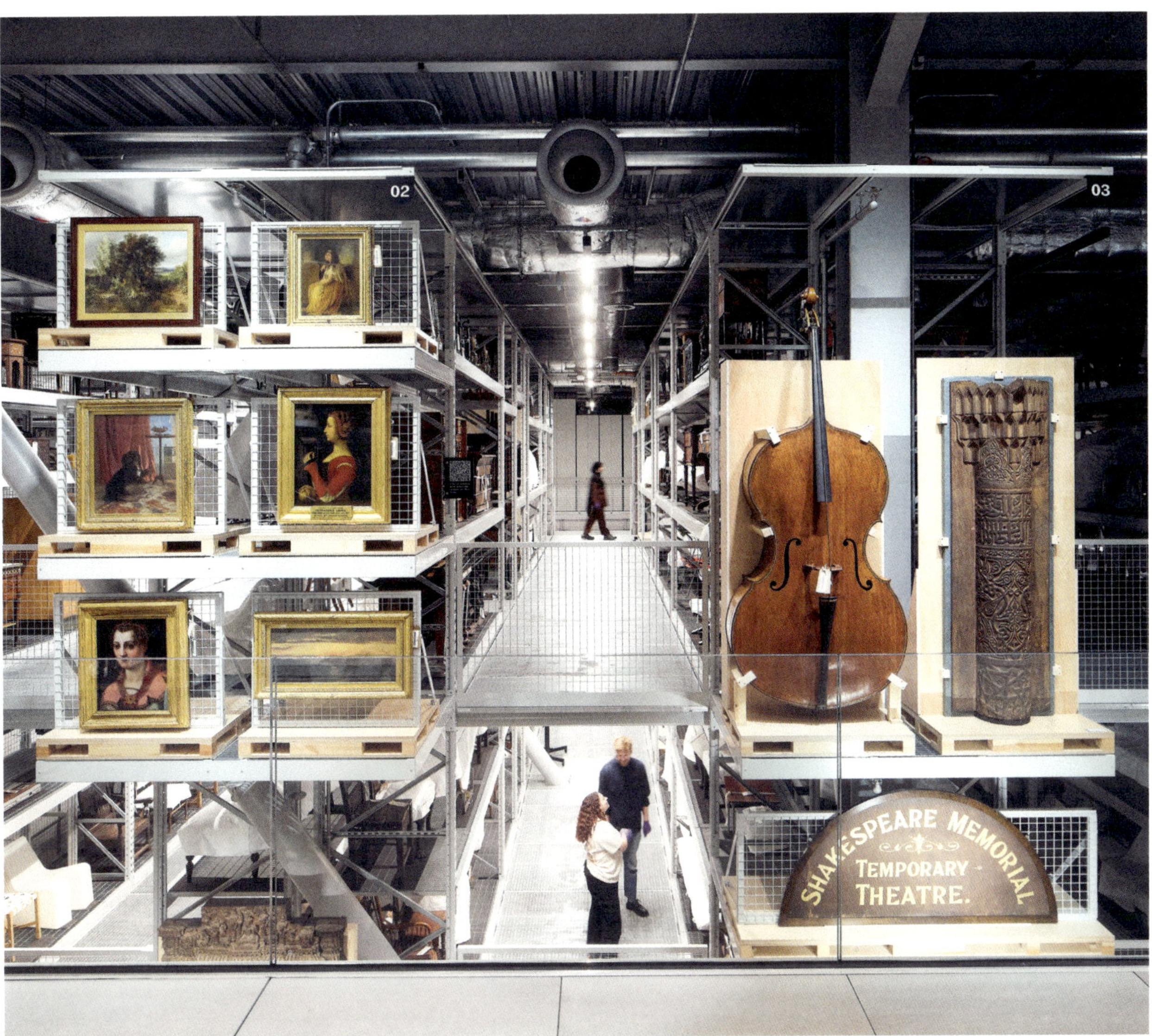

Stacked ends, V&A Storehouse, 2025

for new galleries, exhibitions and commissions. This would be complimented by the brilliantly conceived design by Diller Scofidio + Renfro for V&A East Storehouse, with a self-guided public network woven within the V&A's stored collection, to create a new paradigm for free public access to national collections. This is the 'studio': the working building, always a work in progress and provisional, designed for maximum transparency, with an entirely new atmosphere, mode and rhythm as a retrofit project within a warehouse building.

That V&A East now exists as part of East Bank in the Queen Elizabeth Olympic Park is a minor miracle, hanging by a thread as it was in the early years. Testament to the commitment and sheer will of so many who saw this as a moment to make good both on the opportunities lost through underinvestment in arts and culture, and the opportunities gained through an Olympic legacy imagined beyond commercial development, in this very special place. Ultimately, though, V&A East and East Bank are not about buildings and operating or funding models, but about an idea and a mission, about people and place, and about opportunities to create and innovate.

It is an interesting thought experiment to consider where a new institution of art and design, committed to access for all, and to the opportunity and inspiration that great works of art and design can provide, would fit best and create the greatest impact, if the V&A didn't already exist in South Kensington. East London wouldn't be a bad place to start that particular shortlist. Thankfully, this is a choice we don't have to make. The creation of V&A East is part of a long-overdue investment in cultural infrastructure and creative opportunity for communities that deserve it, and we tell that new V&A story with pride and humility.

Tim Reeve, Deputy Director and Chief Operating Officer

People

and

Place

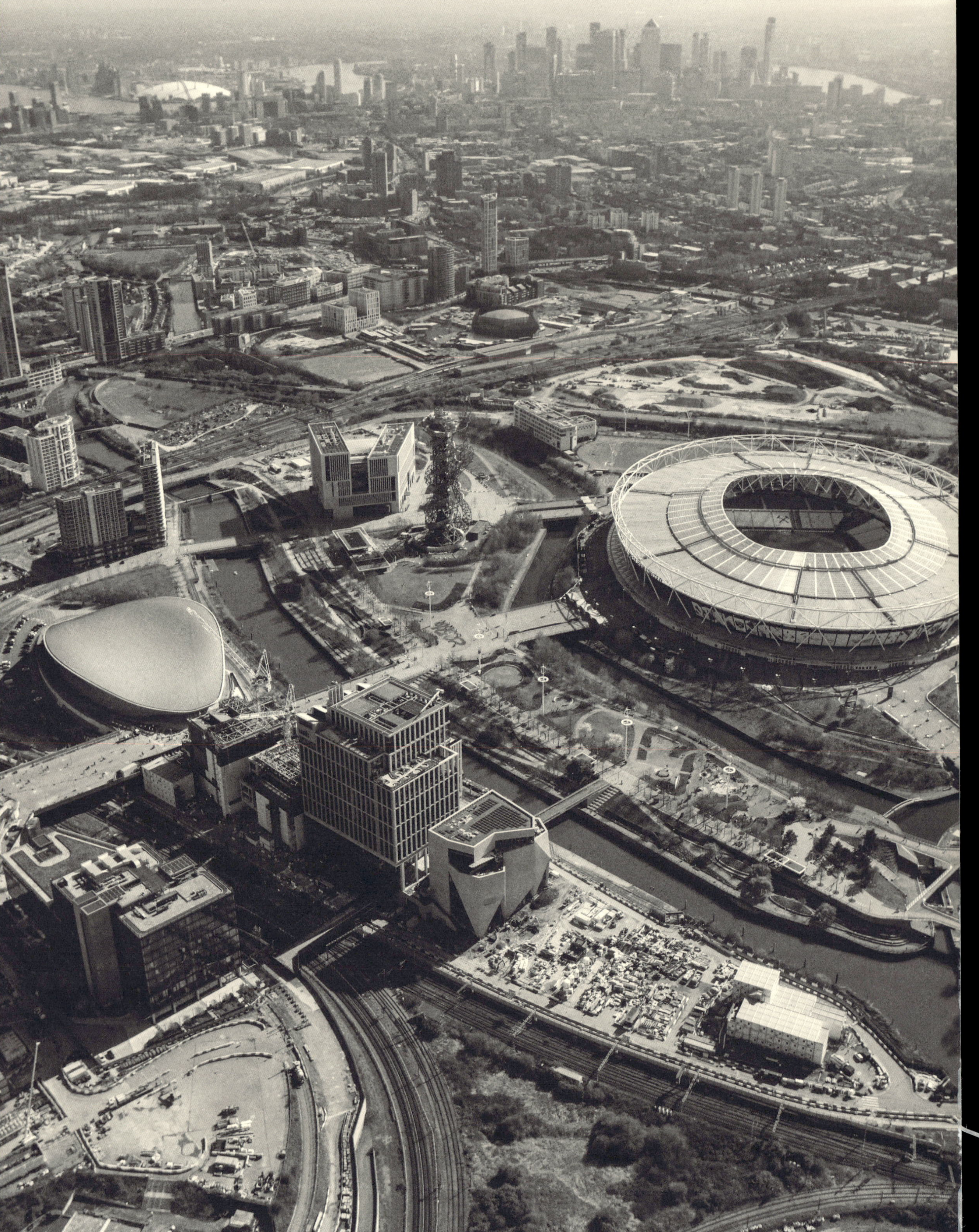

View of the Queen Elizabeth Olympic Park looking south, with V&A East Museum at the lower centre, 2024

New museum projects are shaped by the places they inhabit. In this case, east London offers a potent mix of historic and contemporary realities to respond to. Historically affected by poverty, pollution and exploitation, the area was a flashpoint for urban reformers, seeking novel ways to improve the city and its social life. At the same time, this part of London has seen several different waves of migration, making it a testing ground for cohabitation and ways of living together.

This raises many opportunities and challenges for a cultural institute and cultural practitioners, with both inspiration and responsibility to consider. On the one hand, east London provides a wealth of lived experience and knowledge from which to foster new partnerships and drive cultural projects forward. On the other, there is the responsibility to local communities to ensure a positive impact. This section explores the commitment to place in building a new cultural agenda.

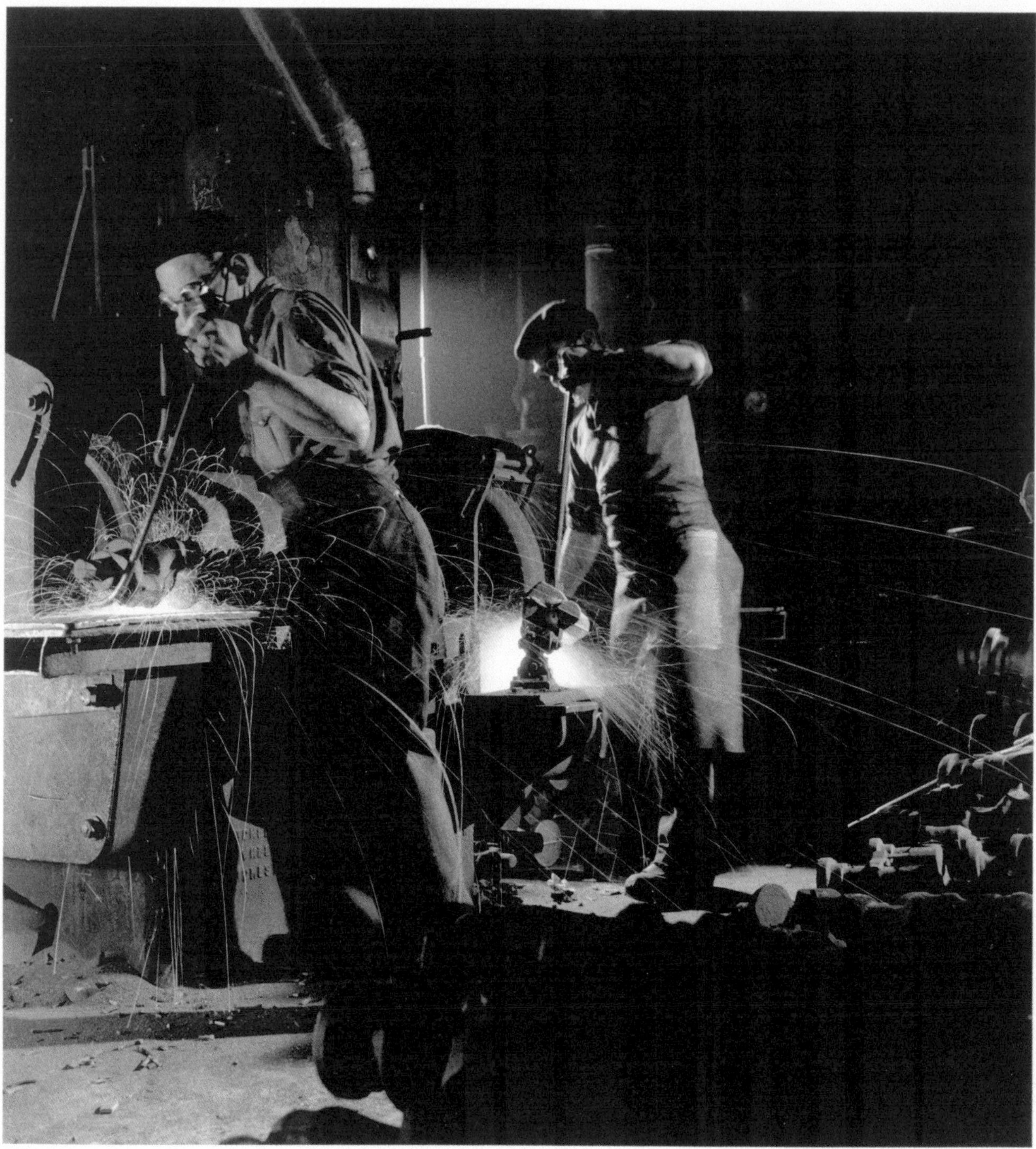

Fettlers, Dagenham, by Maurice Broomfield, 1953, V&A

Makers of the World
Gus Casely-Hayford

Long before Yinka Shonibare set up his studio in Hackney, before the young Alexander McQueen began a fashion course at Newham College, before David Bailey took those era-defining, unflinching photographs on its streets, east London was already a place of makers, of artists, of poets and creatives. That history, that ever-evolving web of creative tissue, connects east Londoners over generations and across eras, through waves of migration and cycles of demographic churn. It is a history that is characterised by a particular creative spirit, a dynamic and resilient energy, that had the potency to take flight upon the zeitgeist, to transcend locality and to deliver irresistible global innovation in formidable ways.

It was no accident that this area of London saw the manufacture of the world's first electric light bulb and the invention of the first diode. No coincidence that the earliest solid-state colour television was crafted in Enfield by communities whose antecedents had manufactured the armaments that made possible the most ambitious campaigns of empire. No quirk of fate that Hackney Wick produced the world's first plastics in its Parkesine Works and refined the first petrol to spur the early British automotive industry. Not just incremental innovation, this area delivered consistent, uncompromising invention that changed the way that British people saw themselves in the world – and it remains a crucible of resourcefulness and creativity that continues to shape the way that the world sees Britain.

But that narrative of creativity and innovation does not really capture the full story of east London. Even though it sits a stone's throw from what was, for much of the last two centuries, one of the wealthiest square miles on earth, east London is perhaps better defined by the lives of its majority, as a place that has endured sustained underinvestment and economic challenge. Against many of the accepted metrics of success, this area has, over generations, fallen short of the wider London story of growth. It sits downriver of the City, beyond London's walls and its bridges, outside of convention and expectation. It nurtured a culture of gentle rule-bending and creativity, but the everyday realities were often challenging for its residents. Its locality meant that this was the part of London where chemicals could be processed for the tanning industries, where the toxic dyeing, and the industrial washing and drying of clothes could happen, where lethal lead-making and fetid bone-processing, and the manufacture of and trade in almost everything caustic, dangerous and unpleasant could occur. From soap making to the fashioning of fine china, east London became the home of 'the stink-industries'. Sir William Petty, the seventeenth-century economist bemoaned 'the fumes, steams, and stinks of the whole Easterly Pyle'. And yet while he and his generation stood aghast at the malodourous and toxic mess of east London, they revelled at so much of what the 'Easterly Pyle' produced. Although it sat to many beyond geography, it was, in its own way, the very centre of many worlds and, in so many ways that mattered, it was the future.

In 1851, as Britain invited the world to London to see the Great Exhibition, one of its earliest visitors, Henry Mayhew, a *Punch* journalist and social reformer, set out to see east London for himself. He understood that while the Great Exhibition was a platform for international practice it was also a fantastic advert for the very best of British creativity. The journalist in Mayhew wanted to uncover the communities that were the engines of this national transformation, so he travelled east to the least fashionable area of the city. His description of east London, written at the time, is an affecting condemnation of Victorian urban and civic management, but through the crippling poverty and deprivation he also defined it as a proud place of makers: of tailors, shoemakers, sawyers, carpenters, cabinet makers and silk-weavers. Dickens, who walked the same streets in the same era, described it similarly as a place of oil boilers, gut spinners, varnish makers, printers and ink makers. Like other chroniclers of Victorian London, they were shocked at how, in this period of growth and advance, those who were making some of the biggest sacrifices, were shockingly enjoying the

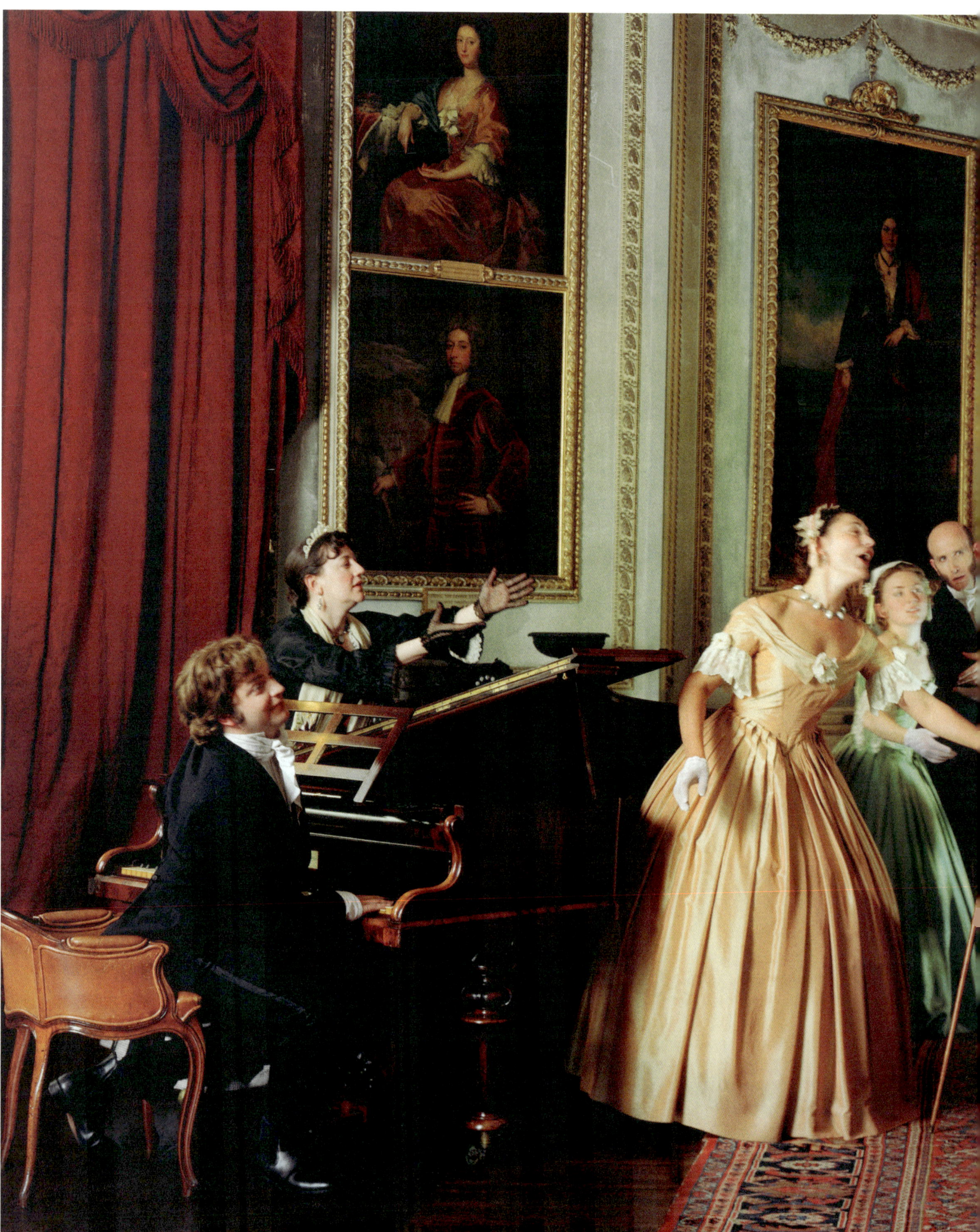

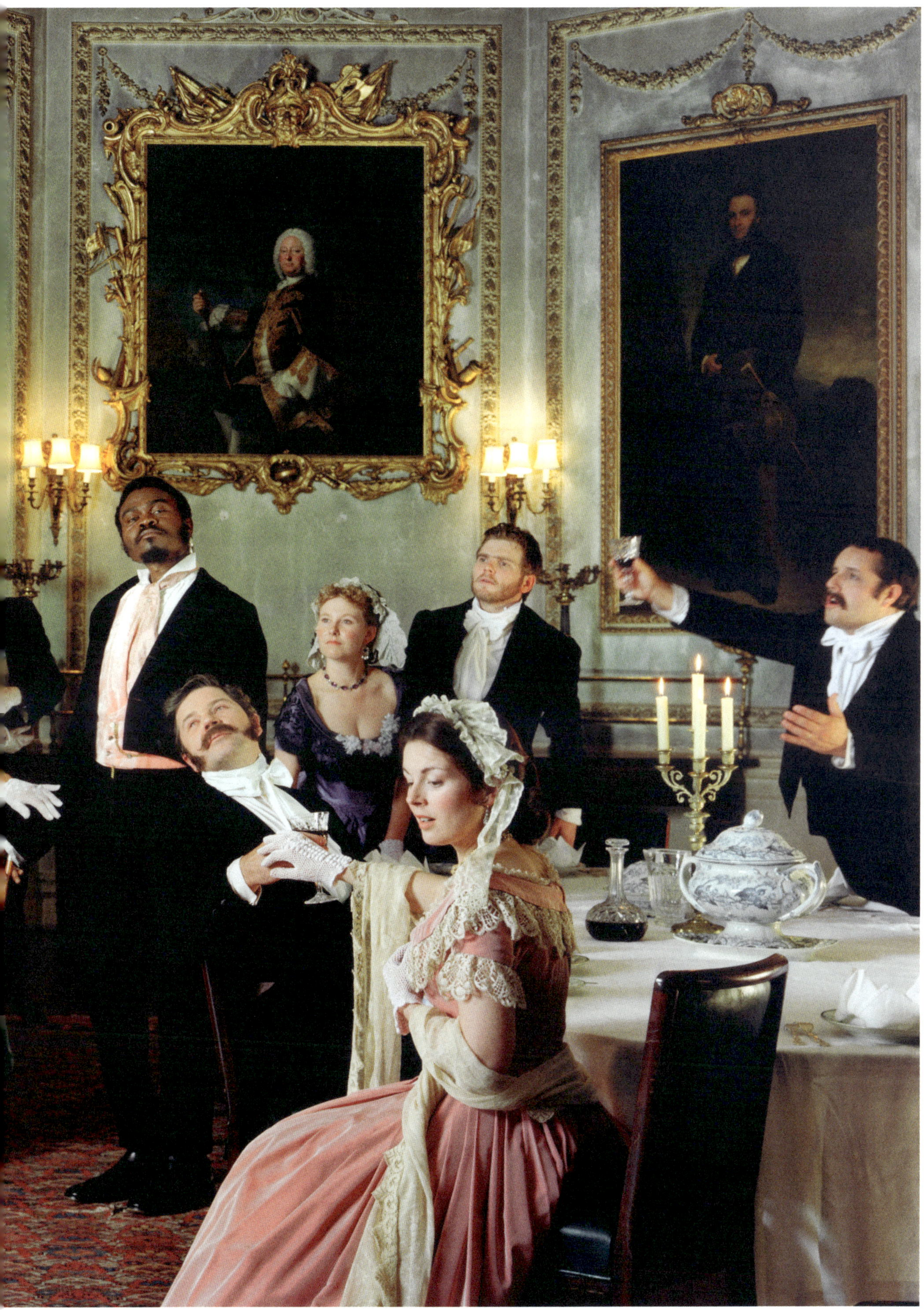

Diary of a Victorian Dandy, by Yinka Shonibare, 1998 (photograph), 2012 (printed), V&A

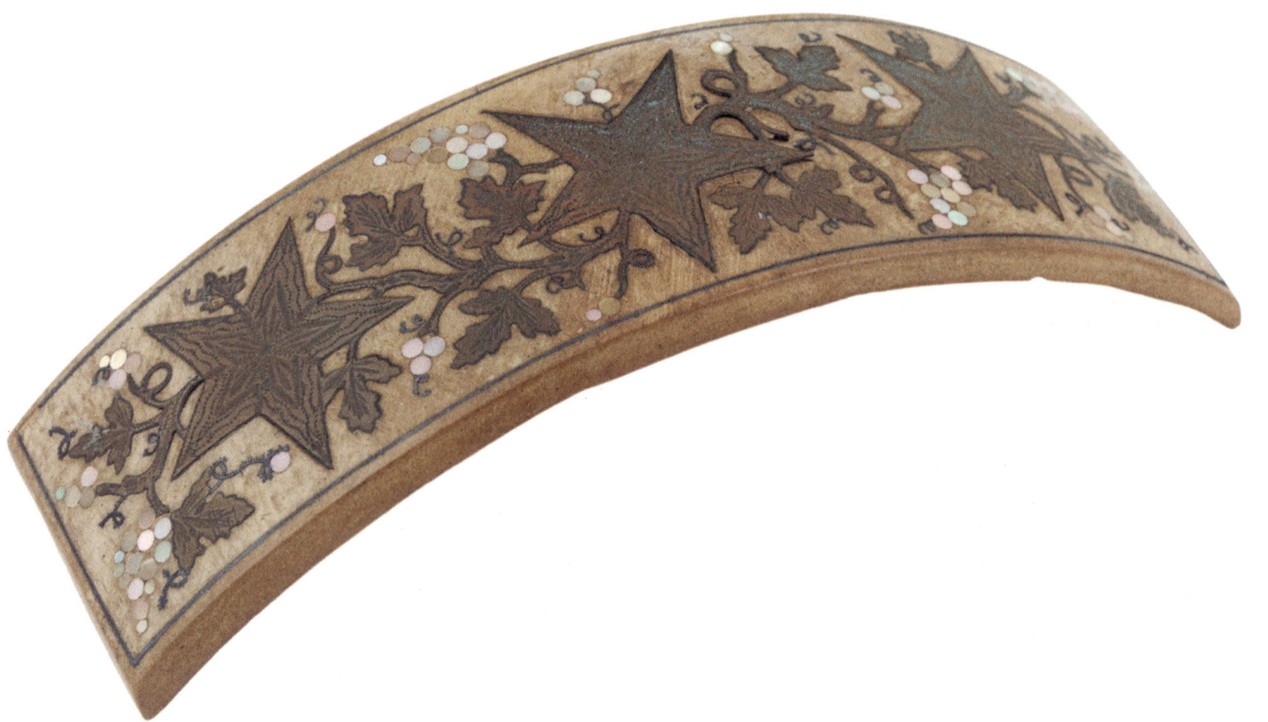

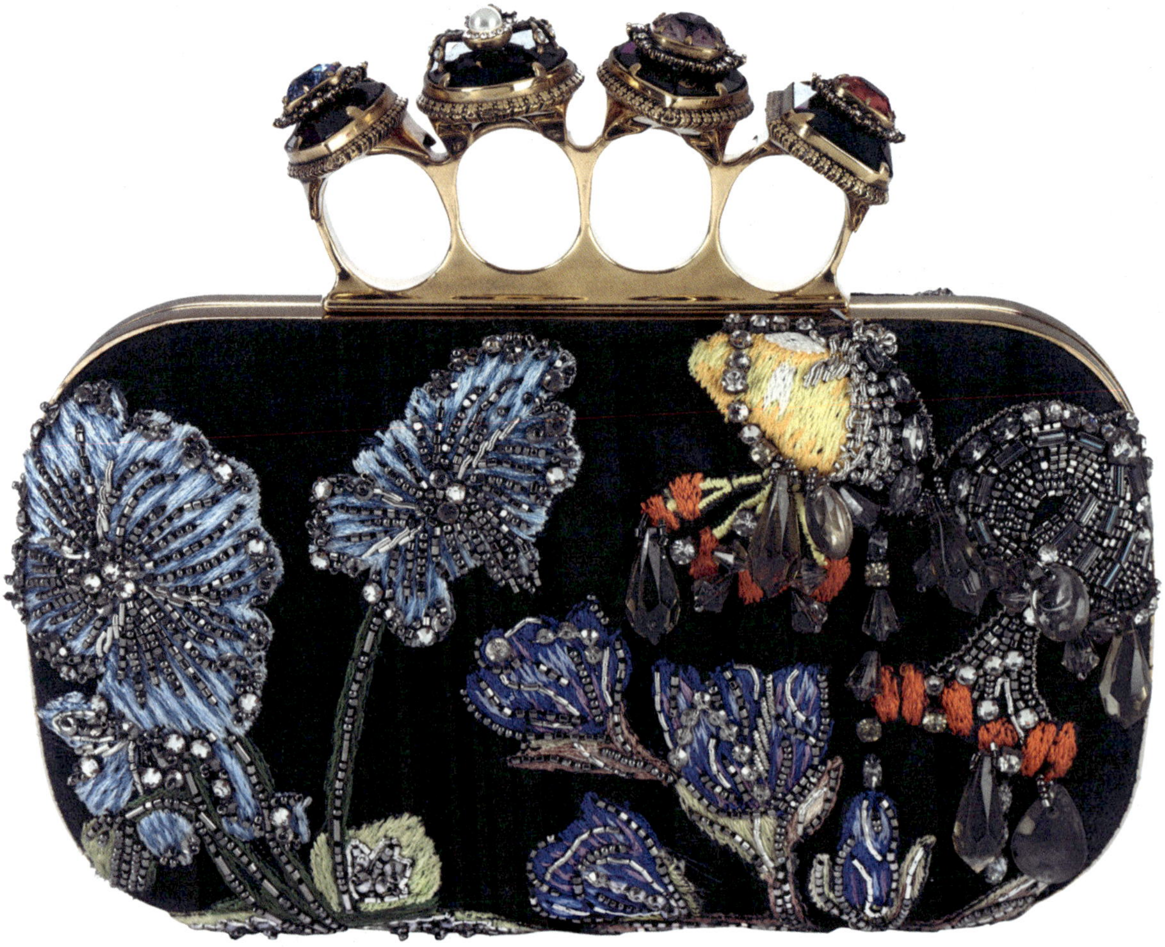

above Hairslide, Parkesine coloured to simulate pale wood, about 1860, Science Museum
below *Spider Jewelled Four Ring Box Clutch*, bag by Alexander McQueen, 2020, V&A

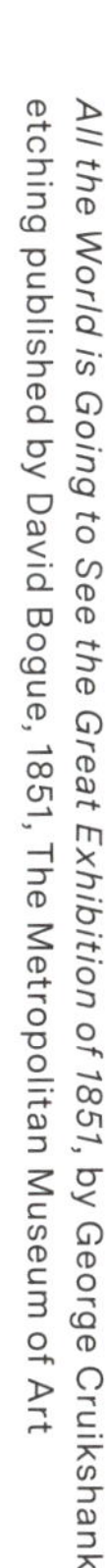

All the World is Going to See the Great Exhibition of 1851, by George Cruikshank, etching published by David Bogue, 1851, The Metropolitan Museum of Art

least benefit. It would be a pattern that would repeat itself across the history of east London, as the region again and again rose to deliver the substantive manufacturing and making responses to the big challenges of each epoch, yet rarely saw what might be considered the just rewards. Nevertheless, east London continued to make and create and invent. And although there has been a constant churn of population and culture, coded deep into the regional DNA is that drive to deliver innovation and invention. Today, one can still see that spirit of radical making – you can still trace that heritage playing itself out in the communities of artists, designers and creatives who build their lives and practice here.

In so many ways this project is dedicated to that history, to this part of London and its unique and endless energy. V&A East is a love letter to the ever-changing east-London communities, to the region's creatives and makers, to its very particular artistic drive and irrepressible invention, to its generations of complex overlapping and interdependent communities of indefatigable innovators and makers. It is a celebration of some of the best global creative practice and to the waves of creative migrants and the demographic complexity that made east London what it was, is and may become. And it is an acknowledgement of the growing lure of east London, of how this area has helped reset the axis of London's cultural geography, drawing ways of thinking that once lay beyond the periphery into the centre – pulling our capital eastward and, with that shift, making our city more equitable and unashamed to celebrate its diversity.

It feels right that, amongst these communities, the V&A should site a national storehouse and museum, two exquisitely crafted buildings whose contents tell the story of, and are dedicated to, the makers of the world. V&A East is a glorious celebration of our shared human drive to make, to craft, to build, beautiful and effective things – and to improve our lives by being in close proximity to them. It is an industry-redefining platform for the research and propagation of our understanding of histories and traditions of making; a toolbox that might be deployed to tell new stories and be used to inspire innovation in making. We hope that V&A East might become a compass to be deployed to inspire and orientate future generations. A place where we can expose visitors to the very finest global practice. Where we can offer them the tools and expert support to learn, to observe and maybe to fall in love with what they find, but perhaps also to interrogate, to ask questions and to re-imagine our world.

Gus Casely-Hayford, Director, V&A East

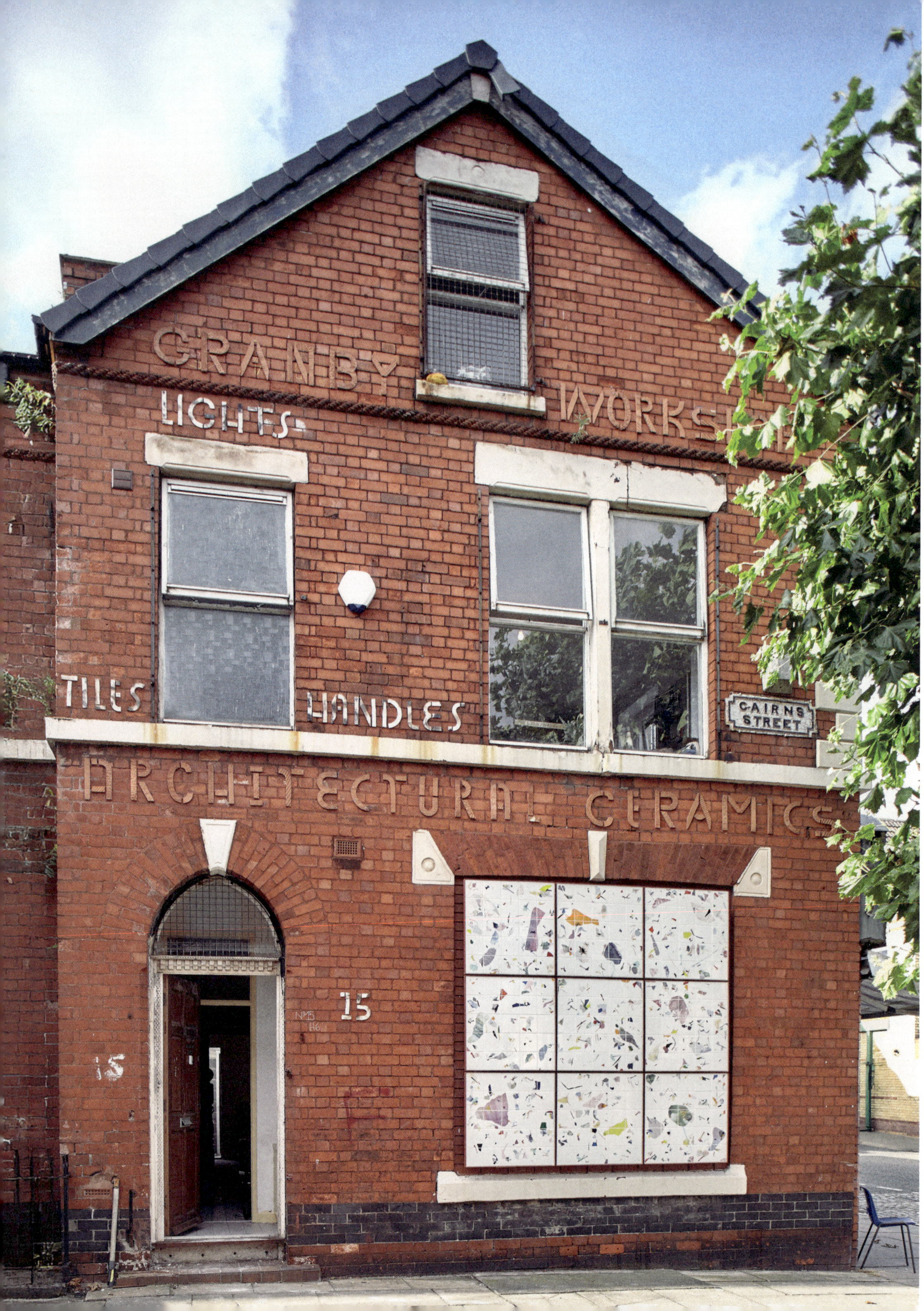

Granby Workshop, Cairns Street, Liverpool, 2019

What Place Can Do
Brendan Cormier

Does 'place' really matter anymore? Over the past half century, we have been awash with clichés about its imminent death. In the 1960s, Marshall McLuhan heralded the concept of the 'global village' to describe a new mass audience, from every corner of the earth, consuming the same types of content and literate in the same cultural trends, nuances and lingo. It prophesised our current condition of universal streaming and global blockbuster film and television series, with phones and laptops – assuming good data and WIFI connections – becoming ersatz cultural hubs. No need to brave a new city and explore what the local bookshop or theatre has to offer when you've got a world of content in your pocket. Gone are the haphazard discoveries from a random stroll, or an unexpected conversation, when a centralised algorithm and carefully curated friend circle populates your feed.

From a production sense, too, over the past century there has been a consistent move away from the vernacular and the situated quality of what we produce. The art critic Clement Greenberg influentially shaped the art world by pushing for an ideal in art that moved increasingly towards abstraction and universality. The invention of the white cube gallery – a now ubiquitous device whereby a room is removed of all architectural qualities (i.e. vernacular) to focus solely on the work – was a direct manifestation of the art world's push towards this notion of autonomy: that an artwork speaks for itself, regardless of the context in which it sits. In consumerist terms too, products are designed to be as generic and unassuming as possible, denuded of any character that might reveal the hands that made them (with notable exception to craft, where the hands are the key selling point), all with the goal of capturing the largest market share.

Even the way we build cities – arguably where the notion of 'place' should have the most currency – the tendency is towards the formulaic: developments designed to be the most palatable to the largest number of people and reproduced the same way around the world. The French anthropologist Marc Augé hit on this tendency in his 1995 essay 'Non-Places', when looking at new developments such as airports and shopping centres, bemoaning the erasure of history and identity.

The museum world too is complicit, starting with the very notion of a collection. To collect and preserve is to uproot something from its place of creation, and to maintain it in a suspended state of placelessness for as long as possible (no dust, no light, no pests). But there is also a homogenising effect on what we collect and the stories we tell, which can render one collection indistinguishable from another. In the same way cities compete for premiere architect commissions, museums – through the continuous construction of a canon of masterpieces and blue-chip artists – have even more so been locked in a global race to acquire the same handful of works, at the expense of celebrating and supporting local practitioners.

And yet, this is all a gross characterisation. While, yes, at many levels, this loss of place rings true, everywhere we look we can see cracks. On virtually every front of critique that shapes our modern world – around ecology and the climate crisis, around social justice and equity, around mental health and well-being – a renewed focus on place and locality seems to be the common call. Indeed, a sea change seems to be underway in creative practice, pushing back against the flattening and universalising tendencies of globalisation, promising to open up new modes of practice, production and presentation, in which place plays a central role.

Much of this work is being spearheaded by artists and designers. In the 1980s, for example, Dolores Hayden founded the non-profit Power of Place in Los Angeles. Her drive was to revive and celebrate unique local histories, diasporas and communities shaping the city, and yet whose stories were being erased by urban planning developments. More recently, Cuban artist Tania Bruguera has advocated strongly for 'useful art', borrowing the term *'arte útil'* from Argentine artist Eduardo Costa's *Manifesto de Arte Útil* written in 1969. Through her Useful Art

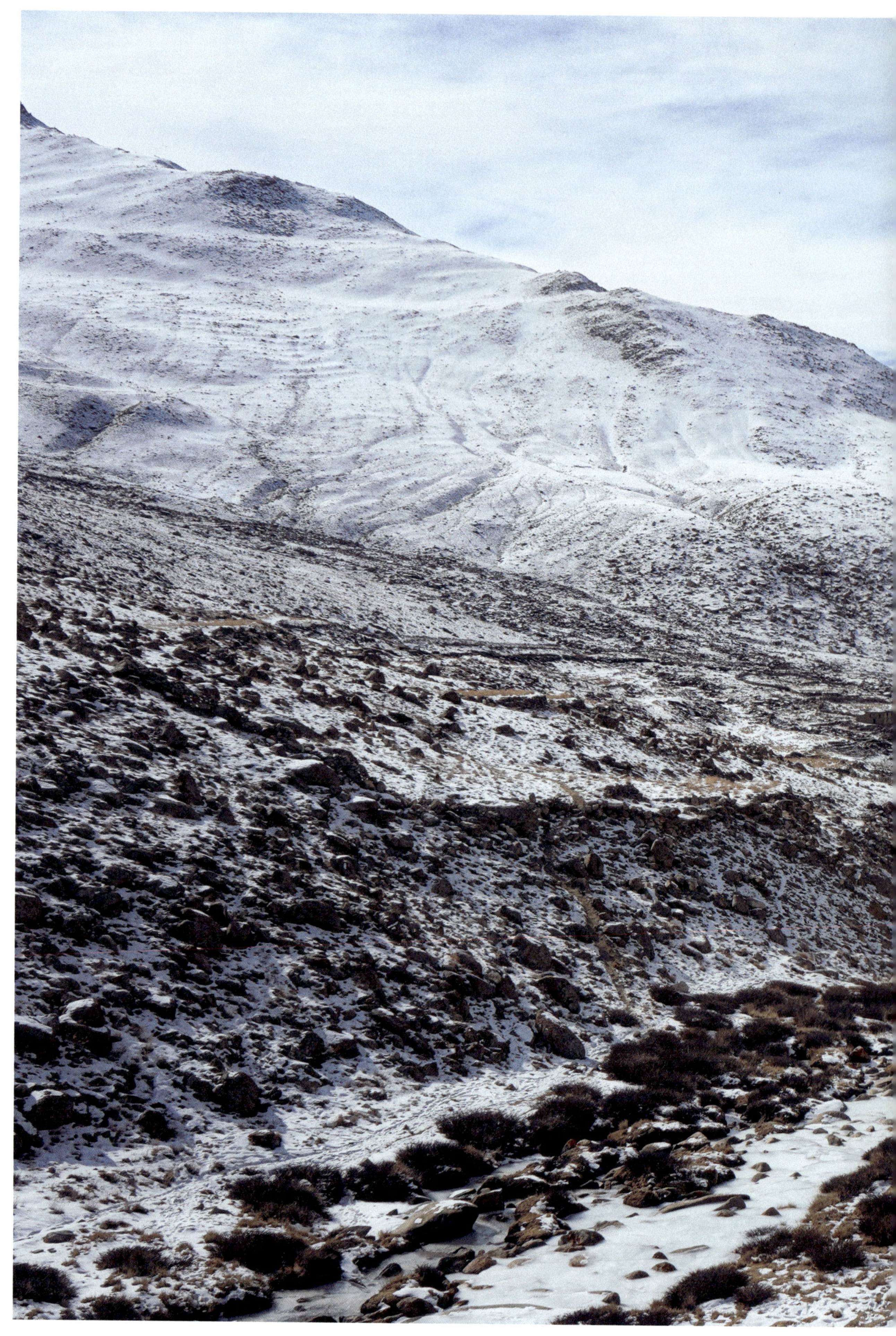

One of two ice stupa prototypes developed by the Himalayan Institute of Alternatives Ladakh to supply the Ladakh region of India with fresh water

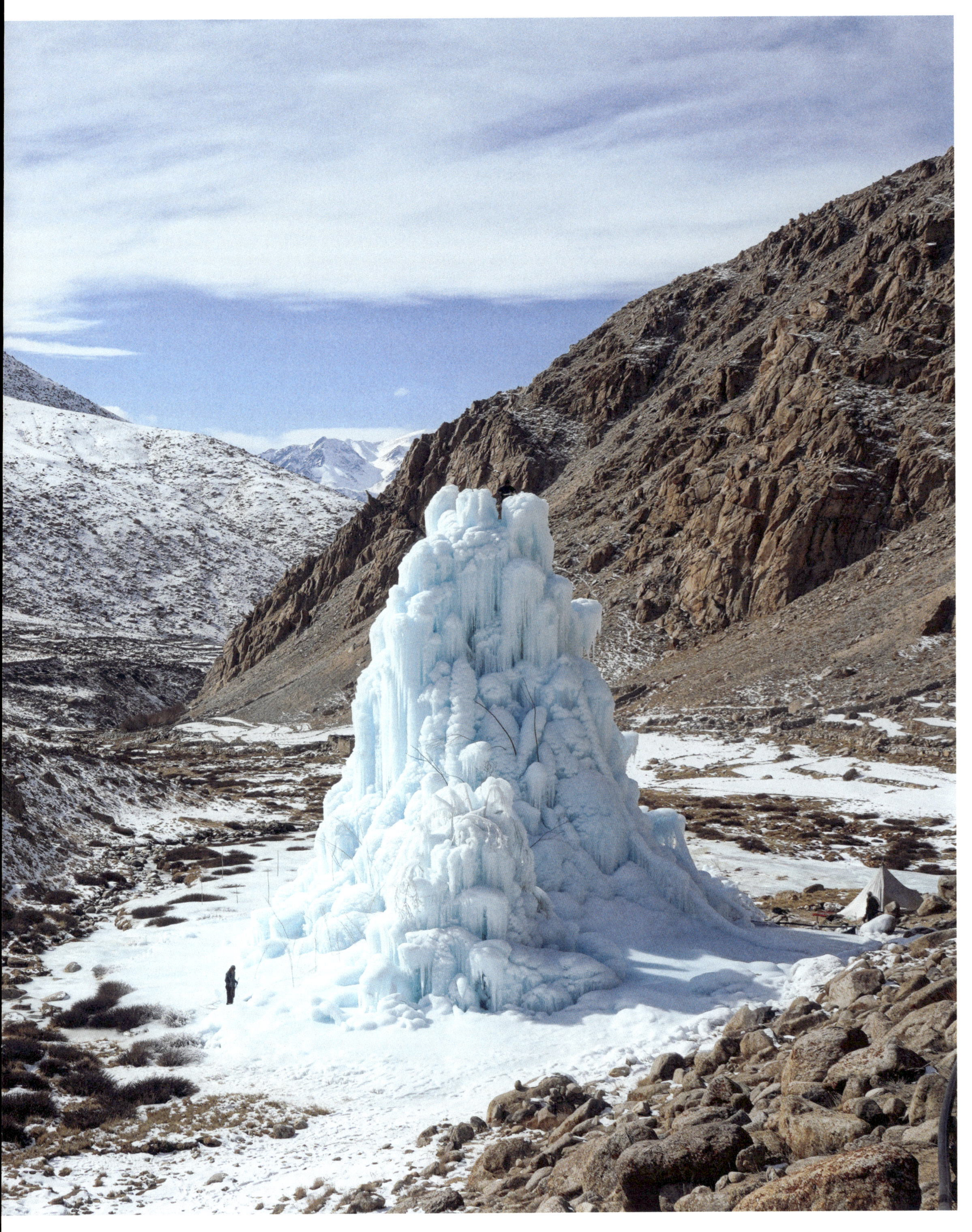

Association, Bruguera has both led art projects and amplified and encouraged the work of others, which explicitly engages in practices and problems of everyday life and place, to create positive change. In a complete reversal of the notion of the white cube and the autonomy of art, many practitioners today – particularly those concerned with ecological and social movements – believe rightly that there is no way to divorce work from context, and that indeed context itself should be the primary creative force for new creation.

A significant moment came in 2015 when the architecture collective Assemble was awarded the Turner Prize. Not only was it unprecedented for an architecture practice to be included in a prize traditionally designed to celebrate artists, but the work being presented by Assemble was framed more as a process than a final work. Centred in the Toxteth neighbourhood of Liverpool on a community-led renovation plan for 'Granby Four Streets', the ongoing work has resulted in several spin-off projects, including the refurbishment of 10 derelict houses, a winter garden and a ceramics workshop, called Granby Workshop. The work is durational, collaborative, situational and open-ended, with the site of intervention being the main catalyst for what gets produced.

This type of art (and architecture) practice has existed on the margins throughout the twentieth century, but it is now gaining greater traction in the mainstream, as evidenced by celebrated practitioners like Bruguera and Assemble. It is difficult work, not least because it tends to operate against market logics and is economically precarious. Yet, for many young practitioners who see the world as one being increasingly squeezed by multiple crises, pursuing creative work that is grounded in place and context, in collaboration with a community of stakeholders, is one of the clearest paths to meaningful impact.

Place, indeed, does matter, more than ever. Museums too are wrestling with their commitment to locality. As Madeleine Haddon points out later in this book, the definition of what a museum is and questions around what and who it should serve are currently in a state of flux. Increasingly, museums are being called upon to provide an expanded set of public services that go well beyond the preservation and display of collections. In cities, particularly those that pursue neo-liberal agendas, basic community services, educational infrastructure, public space and access to shelter feel in

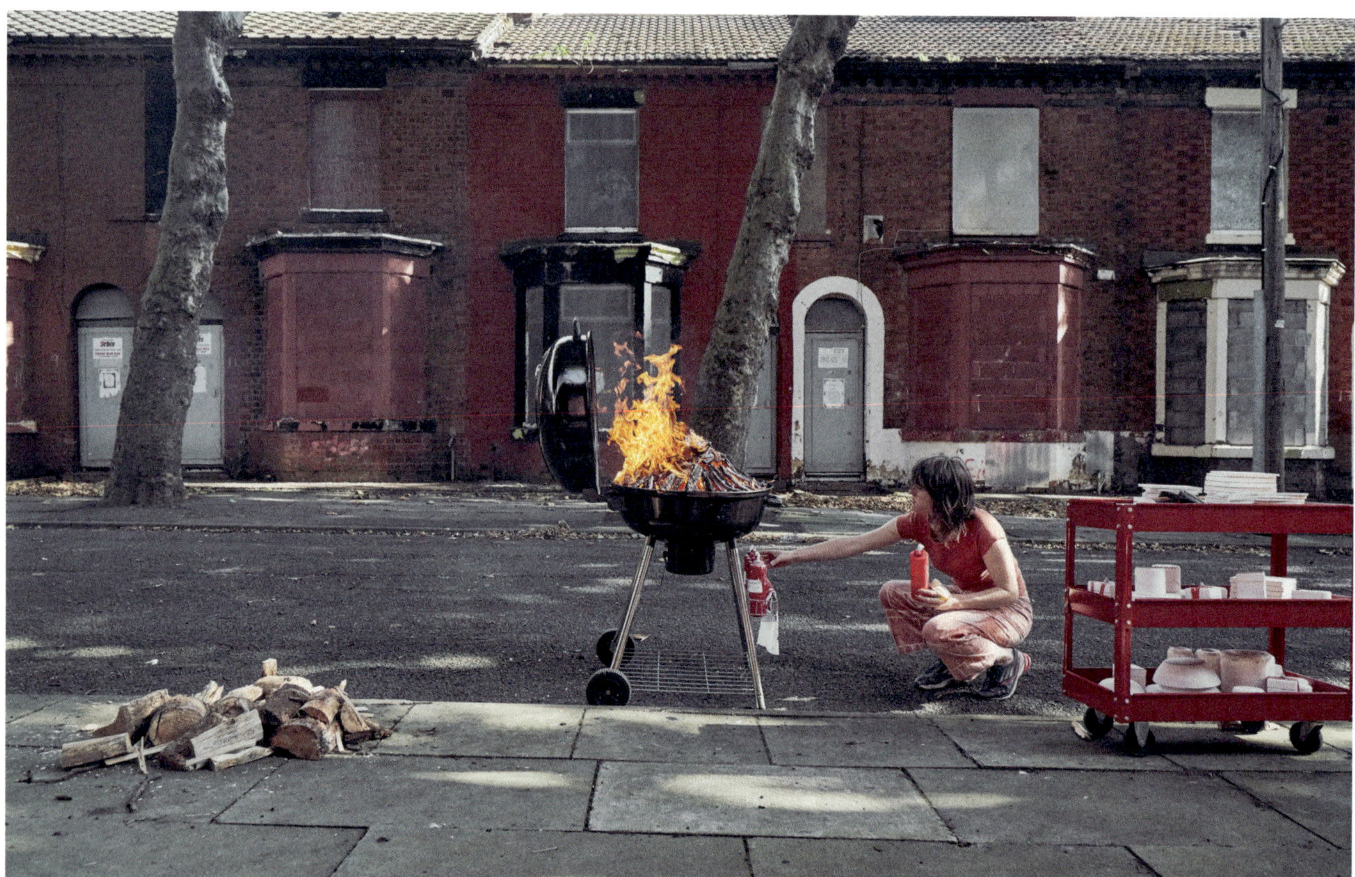

Tile-making by Assemble collective on the Welsh Streets, Liverpool, 2016

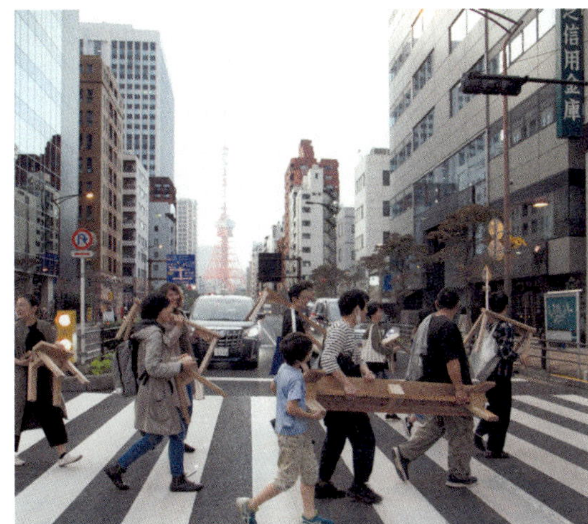
Ishinomaki furniture being carried by hand by participants in Open! FURNITURE, organised by Shibaura House, Tokyo, 2019

increasing short supply. Museums are being called upon to fill this gap as a social and community service, while at the same time, being rightly critiqued for accelerating processes of gentrification, which have negatively impacted local communities. It is a tricky paradox. But museums can no longer ignore their place in a local geography, and need to be prioritising the health and well-being of the local communities they serve.

V&A East is charged with the challenge of doing right by the local community, many of whom are made insecure by the massive waves of development and gentrification currently trans-forming east London. But it is also an opportunity to lead a conversation about place-based practice, championing creatives who engage deeply with context, and who have ecological and social well-being firmly embedded as an ethic that informs everything they do. For the Why We Make Galleries, we've drawn from inspiring projects around the world: a monumental 'ice stupa' prototype, developed by the Himalayan Institute for Alternatives Ladakh to deliver fresh water to the Ladakh region of India; sustainable bamboo architecture in Bali, from the design collective IBUKU, derived from centuries of craft knowledge; or the Ishinomaki Laboratory in Japan, founded in response to the 2011 Tōhoku earthquake and tsunami, as a workshop to engage locals in furniture making in an effort to rebuild the local economy.

Through programming, installations, activations and workshops, the museum should be using the case of east London to ask the big questions about how we want to live together in the future, and how design and creativity can forge a pathway. It should be able to capitalise on east London's illustrious making history, as Gus Casely-Hayford has highlighted in his essay, introducing new audiences to the opportunities that this legacy provides. While Young V&A opened recently with the mission of spurring and encouraging creative young minds, V&A East can take that baton and empower younger genera-tions with the creative tools to impact positive change, both locally and further afield.

The V&A started off as an applied arts museum. The term 'applied arts' has since fallen out of favour, with design, art and craft being variously used in its place. Perhaps now is the time to revive it. Afterall, 'applied arts' always connoted a context – you were always applying something to something else. A statue adorned a building façade or sat in a public square, a painting added symbolic depth to a church or palace, potters and glassmakers elevated every-day wares and households through their skill and artistry. Context mattered. For me, the creatives today who are working with communities and localities, engaged deeply in unpicking problems over a period of time, are the new applied artists. And in that sense, V&A East is an opportunity to champion this unique brand of applied art for the twenty-first century.

Brendan Cormier, Chief Curator

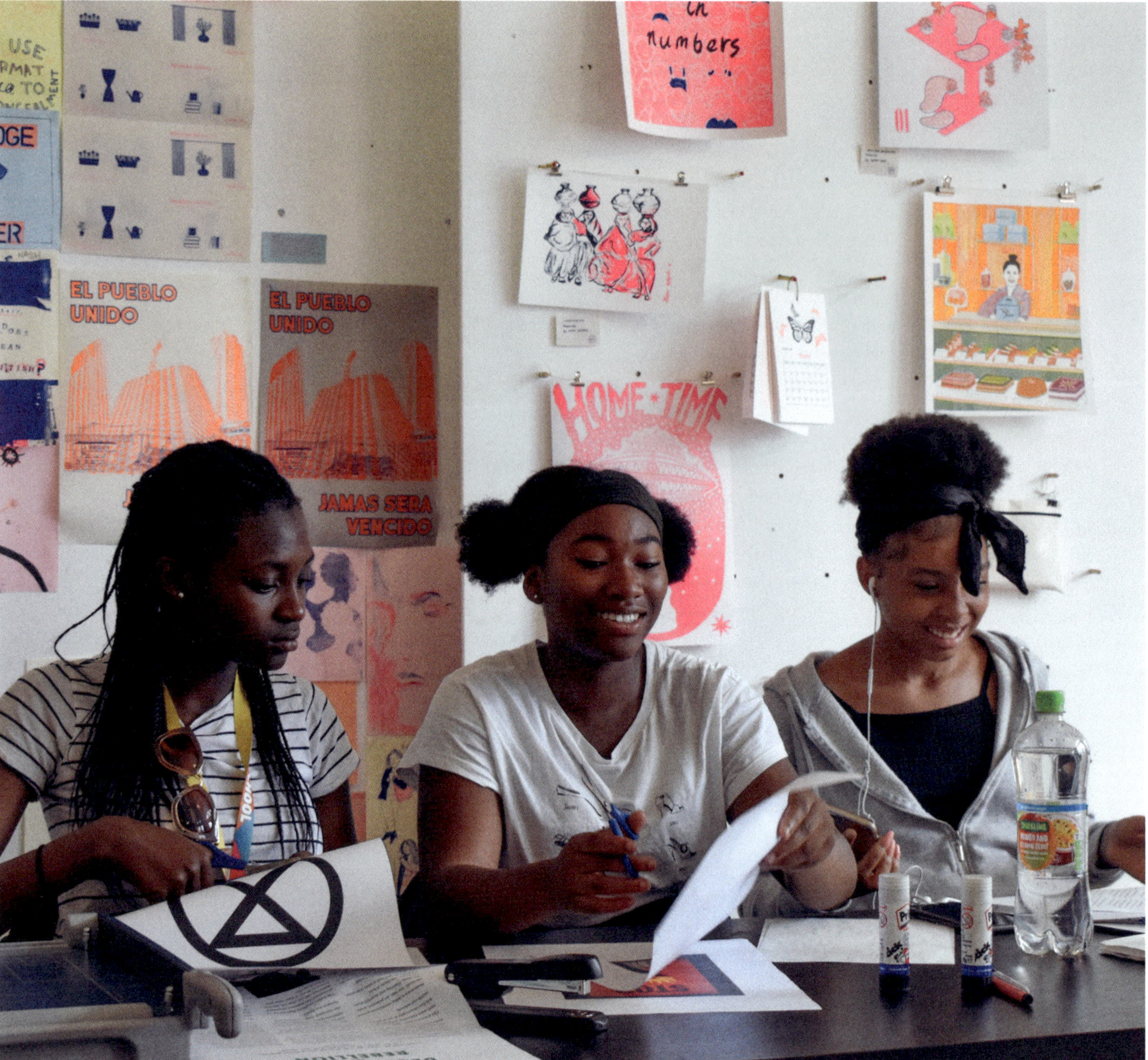

East Education Summer School with Sahra Hersi, Rabbits Road Press, 2019

Working in East London
Afia Yeboah and Komal Khetia

It is almost impossible to ignore the rapid gentrification of east London over the past 20 years. Accelerated, in part, by the legacy of the 2012 Olympics, places that would have been overlooked in previous decades have become highly sought after by individuals and developers eager to make their mark on the capital. While in many ways this shift is perhaps unremarkable – a by-product of an often-told story of 'regeneration' – in the boroughs of Newham and Hackney, it brings a new cultural quarter to east London, with the V&A East Museum and Storehouse as prominent contributors to the Olympic legacy.

For those witnessing these changes first-hand, an understandable sense of wariness prevails. Allaying these concerns is an ongoing process. There is work to do, building trust with local communities and acknowledging the place of the V&A as the newcomer in town. In turn, teams at V&A East need to understand how the local area operates and to consider how we can contribute and become part of the existing ecology.

From the inception of the V&A East project, engagement has meant getting out of the office and into the community. Over a number of years, we have been connecting and consulting with local youth groups, including Hackney Quest, Elevate Youth Voice and Spotlight, and creative practitioners and educators, as well as visiting social spaces and hubs to introduce ourselves to our new neighbours, to better understand the community make-up and to discover what they are expecting from V&A East. This outreach provided opportunities to look at new ways of engaging with local communities and embedding their voices into the infrastructure of the buildings through the development of collaborative projects, partnerships and programmes in direct response to consultation feedback. As well as learning from the insights of our new neighbours, we also hoped that this early engagement would act as a good way of introducing ourselves, a housewarming of sorts, before we officially opened our doors. Informed by the people who know east London best, who hold a rich knowledge and tacit insights into the area, we developed projects and programming to reflect local interests and priorities. Through initiatives such as Lund Point – a creative photography project led by Brendan Barry in partnership with Beyond The Box Consultants, offering a unique perspective from a 23-storey tower block on the edge of the Olympic Park (p. 41), and the Lansbury Micro Museum, with its series of locally inspired changing exhibitions (p. 36), we have been able to successfully engage young audiences, giving them a platform to produce creative outputs inspired by the museum's collection, but which also have a distinct and uniquely east-London feel.

Meanwhile, the V&A East Youth Collective, which started as a pilot in 2021, is still going strong. Young people from across the Olympic boroughs take a seat at the decision-making table through the year-long programme and have worked on live projects including gallery co-design with Jayden Ali Projects and co-production for London Design Festival with creative youth worker residents RESOLVE Collective. Significantly, these collaborative working opportunities empowered participants to use their local environments as sources of inspiration for the creative outputs. The wider success of the Youth Collective, and their continued involvement through the alumni network, attests to a shift away from institutional reticence in relation to youth voices towards the embedding of such voices across every aspect of the V&A East project.

The desire is to continue to work in this collaborative way, meeting people where they're at and actively listening and developing a methodology that gives a voice, and agency, to local communities. V&A East Make Space, which was developed in response to a call to action through consultation with young people and their youth workers in 2019, is a good example of this. The programme is designed to allow young people to come together to make, develop their creativity and access advice and guidance on careers and opportunities in the creative sector. Delivered with partner organisations in the Olympic boroughs, we have created an open

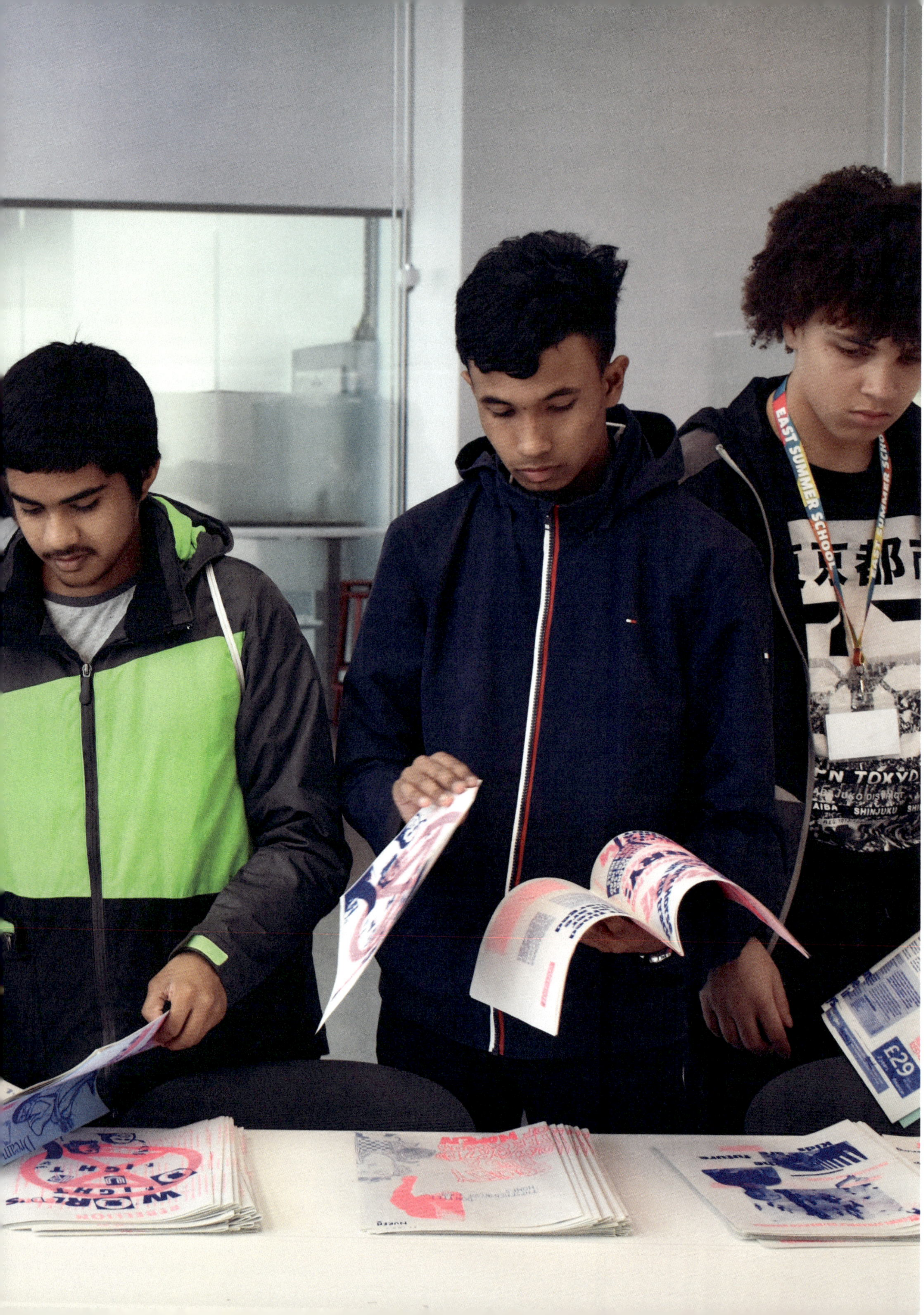

East Education Summer School with Sahra Hersi, Rabbits Road Press, 2019

studio environment that acts as a safe space for participants with light-touch facilitation, inspiration from local creatives and signposting to further opportunities provided by workshop assistants and youth workers. The iterative approach of the programme allows for intergenerational participation and are part of the regular portfolio of programmes at V&A East Storehouse.

Through partnership work with local organisations, we can cultivate a community to foster the next generation of artists, designers and makers and, in doing so, actively work to address the disparity of diversity and representation within the creative industries. We hope to gain better understanding of local interests and needs, bridging the gap between the individual and the institution and drawing on the wealth of the collection to facilitate participation. There is so much potential to celebrate people as well as to celebrate the collection with the V&A East site, and that is exciting.

Yet, the success of V&A East hangs on the acceptance of, and continued engagement by, our audiences. If we can't engage with local young people as our primary audience, or retain them as repeat visitors, can we really say V&A East is successful? The work continues to ensure that V&A East is both maker-centric, showcasing the ways that making can positively impact and allow further enjoyment of everyday life, and remains east-London-centric. Museums and galleries must stay ahead of the curve if we are to be truly relevant to the next generation of creatives; we have to expand the definition of what it means to be a museum and encompass a people-centred way of being.

There is no doubt that, to many people in east London, V&A East will seem like just another manifestation of the ongoing gentrification of the area. However, we are actively working to address this, even if at times this means acknowledging the uncomfortable and wrestling with the unknown. Our endeavour is to centre the voices of our communities within the institution. We invite and encourage local residents and partners to enter into a dialogue with the museum, and with the collection. Through such collaborative working new knowledge and fresh perspectives can be generated, enriching our museum for all users. For us, this is only the beginning of the conversation about how we work. Evolving and being flexible are key if we are to welcome future generations into V&A East.

Afia Yeboah and Komal Khetia, Senior Producers, Community Engagement

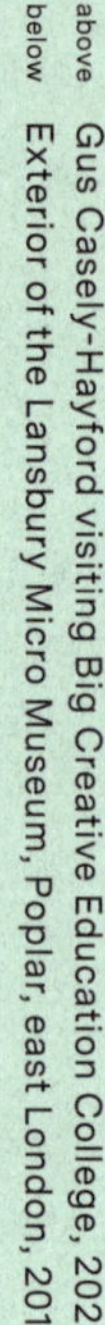
above Gus Casely-Hayford visiting Big Creative Education College, 2022
below Exterior of the Lansbury Micro Museum, Poplar, east London, 2016

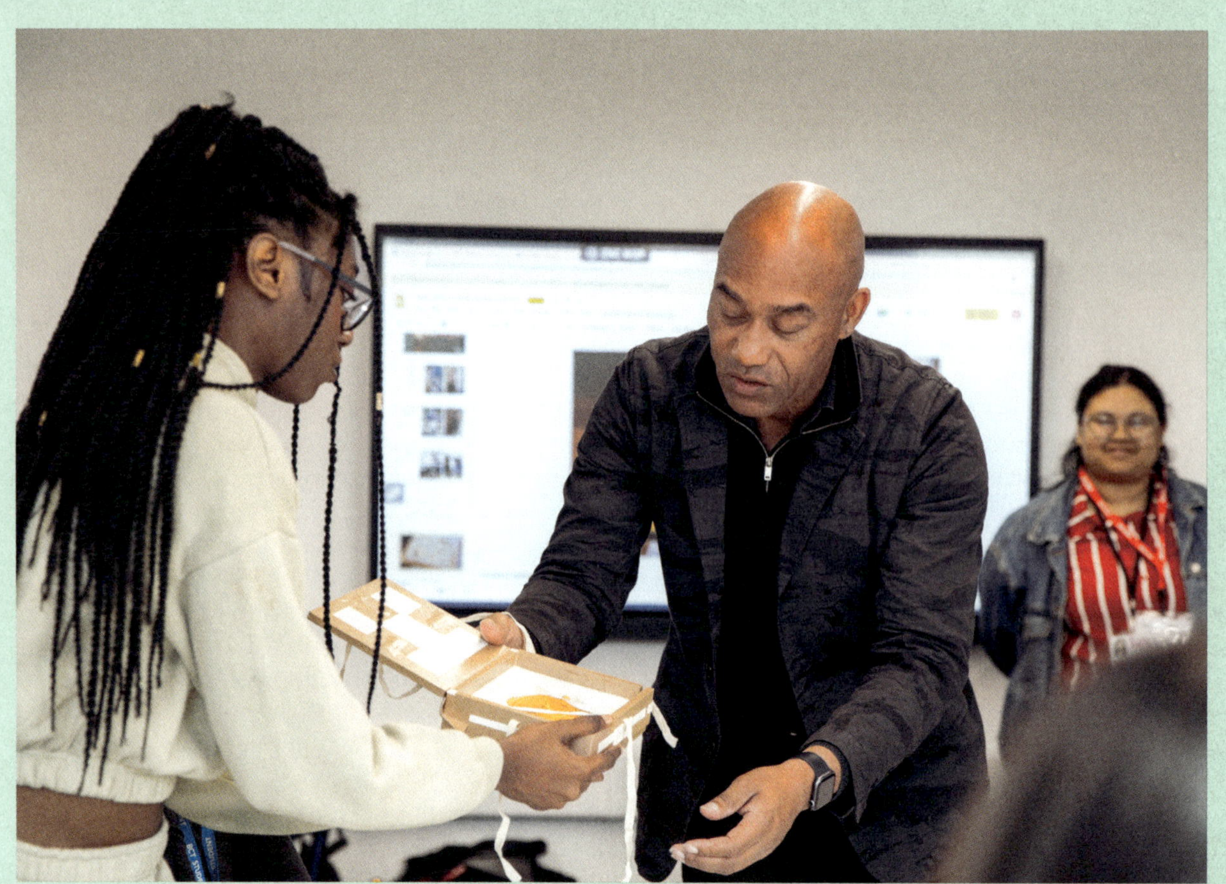

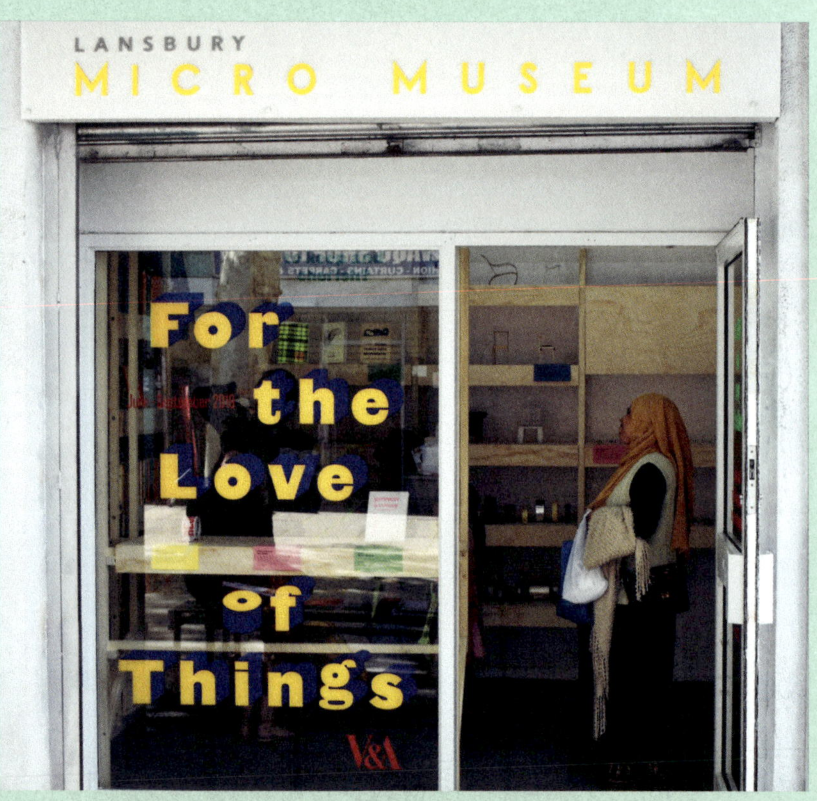

Your Collection: V&A East in Schools
Kamal Hussein, Community Engagement Coordinator

Conceived by Gus Casely-Hayford, Director of V&A East, 'Your Collection: V&A East in Schools' ran from June 2022 to March 2025. The programme aimed to provide young people, schools and other educational institutions across east London with access to objects from the museum's collection.

By collaborating with educational institutions, forging partnerships with cultural and creative organisations, and expanding to include all learning provisions, the programme has continually adapted and evolved since its inception.

Developed in consultation with teachers across east London, the programme began by selecting three objects to travel to the schools we visited. In total, six objects were featured throughout the programme, including a silver-gilt 'Free Zulu' pendant, a cast gold badge from Ghana and an open pomander from seventeenth-century Germany. Gus Casely-Hayford engaged pupils by discussing the complex histories of these objects while introducing them to the two new V&A East sites in east London.

A partnership with the organisation Art Matters further enriched the programme, enabling a collaboration on a competition where pupils were invited to create jewellery from recycled materials inspired by the objects featured in Your Collection.

Expanding on the success of Your Collection, optional workshops were incorporated into the sessions, including a 'behind the scenes at the museum' workshop focusing on careers in museums. Visiting 80 schools and engaging with over 8,000 students, this project has been instrumental in helping young people feel connected to the arts and in raising awareness of the new cultural sites on the doorstep of young east Londoners.

Lansbury Micro Museum
Zofia Trafas White, Senior Curator

Based in a former shop in Chrisp Street Market on the Lansbury Estate in Poplar, east London, the V&A's Lansbury Micro Museum was an offsite project space in the early years of making V&A East.

From 2016 to 2019, it played host to a series of changing exhibitions exploring the history of the neighbourhood and its communities, each developed in close collaboration with local residents, historians and invited artists and designers. Displays were accompanied by public events and making projects with local schools, creating a valuable space to meet and learn from future audiences.

The Museum's opening programme, 'Neighbourhood Number 9', was a three-part exhibition exploring the significance of the estate as a microcosm for planning ideas for London. Displays brought together archives, V&A Collection objects and residents' oral histories to explore stories behind the architecture and the lives of the community – from the founding ideals of the Lansbury Estate and the role it played as a 'model' neighbourhood during the Festival of Britain in 1951, to periods of rapid change from 1950 to 1980 that saw industrial modernisation, declining docklands and the relocation of communities to New Towns outside of the city. The closing programme addressed topical debates about local regeneration plans, offering a platform for resident voices.

In 2018, the UK centenary of women's suffrage served as a starting point for the Micro Museum's second chapter, exploring histories of women's rights and local community activism. An exhibition of posters by the See Red Women's Workshop, a feminist screen-printing collective from the 1970s, piloted new oral history formats co-developed with Museum in a Box.

The Museum's closing project, 'For the Love of Things', brought Lansbury residents into dialogue with developing plans for V&A East Storehouse through an open-call exhibition that put the personal collections of its visitors on display.

RESOLVE Collective

Jasmine Sarkodee-Adoo, Brands and Campaigns Officer

Set within the classical surrounds of the Cromwell Road entrance of the V&A South Kensington, in the autumn of 2021 an assemblage of upcycled materials, sourced from east-London market stalls, were used to adorn the museum's main atrium, sparking interest amongst visitors. With materials draped across discarded museum drawers and strung up on graffitied scaffolding beams, this bracing artwork, entitled *Made on Location*, marked the culmination of interdisciplinary design practice RESOLVE Collective's year-long residency as V&A East's first Creative Youth Workers in Residence.

Created in collaboration with the V&A Research Institute (VARI) and east-London youth groups, including Blackhorse Responders, Hackney Quest and the V&A East Youth Collective, *Made on Location*'s central placement signalled the regenerative future of the V&A, marking it as a place of exploration in which the voices of its young audiences are empowered to use their local environments and influences as valid sources of inspiration.

Founded by brothers Akil and Seth Scafe-Smith and Melissa Haniff, RESOLVE's design approach falls at the intersections between architecture, art, technology and engineering to platform new ideas of creative practice that incite equitable socio-economic change.

During their residency, RESOLVE leant on the needs and aspirations of their young co-collaborators, devising a rich programme of creative workshops and activities across east London and South Kensington. These sessions included their 'Starting from the Ends' workshop, where the young respondents drew on their distinct experiences to create personalised maps of east London. RESOLVE's dynamic approach to programming prompted open conversations questioning the museum's capacity to remain inclusive amid rapid urban change.

This innovative collaboration between RESOLVE and V&A East has proven vital in piloting youth-led consultation to encourage outdated institutional practices to be more polyvocal and accessible in their remit.

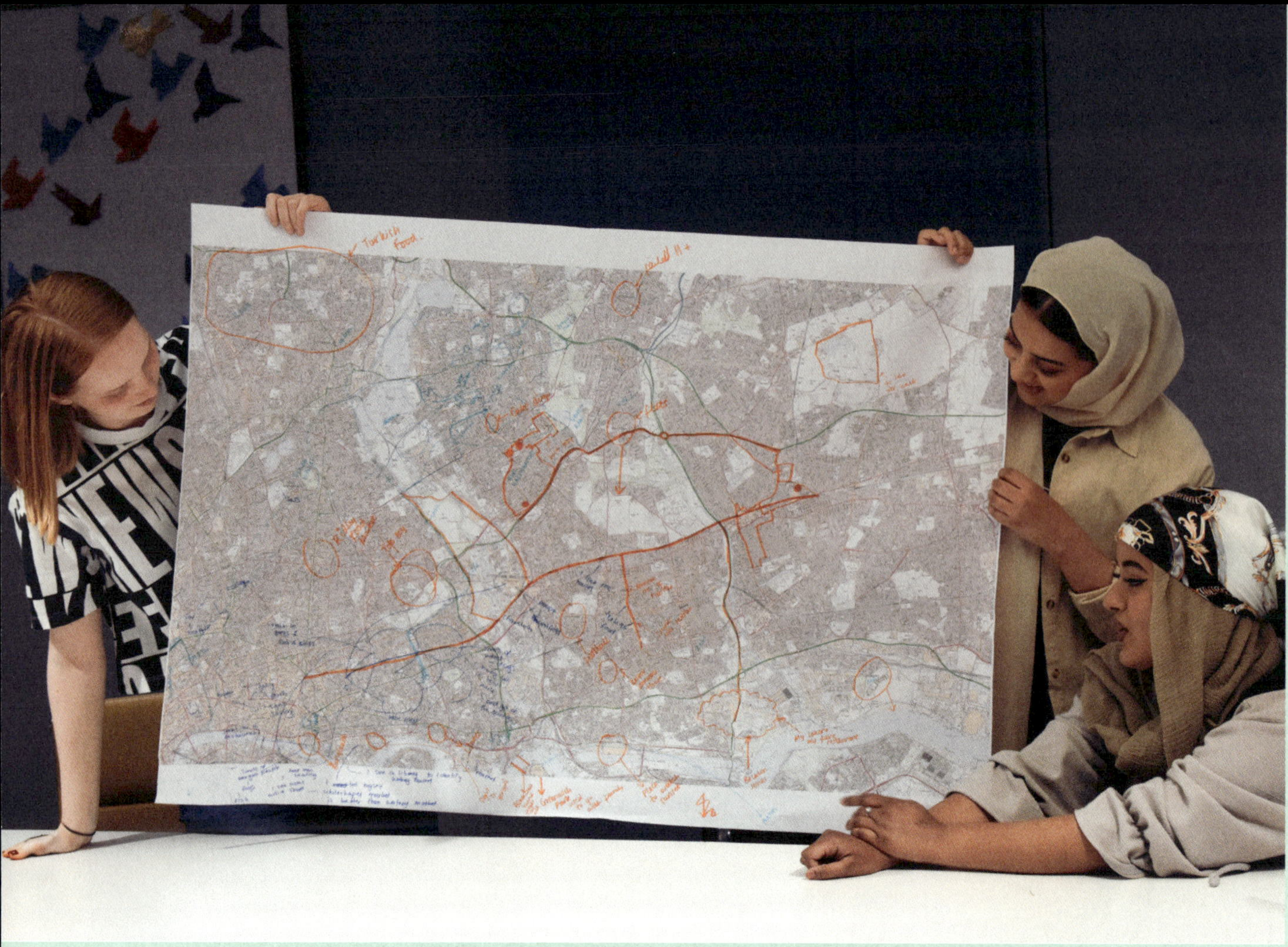

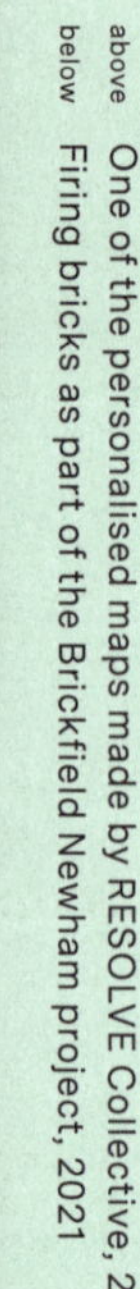

above One of the personalised maps made by RESOLVE Collective, 2021
below Firing bricks as part of the Brickfield Newham project, 2021

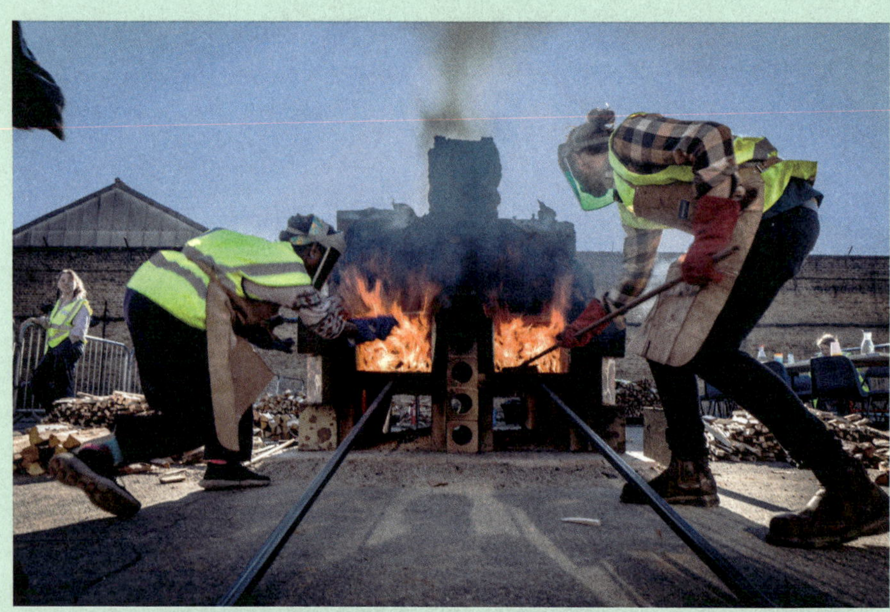

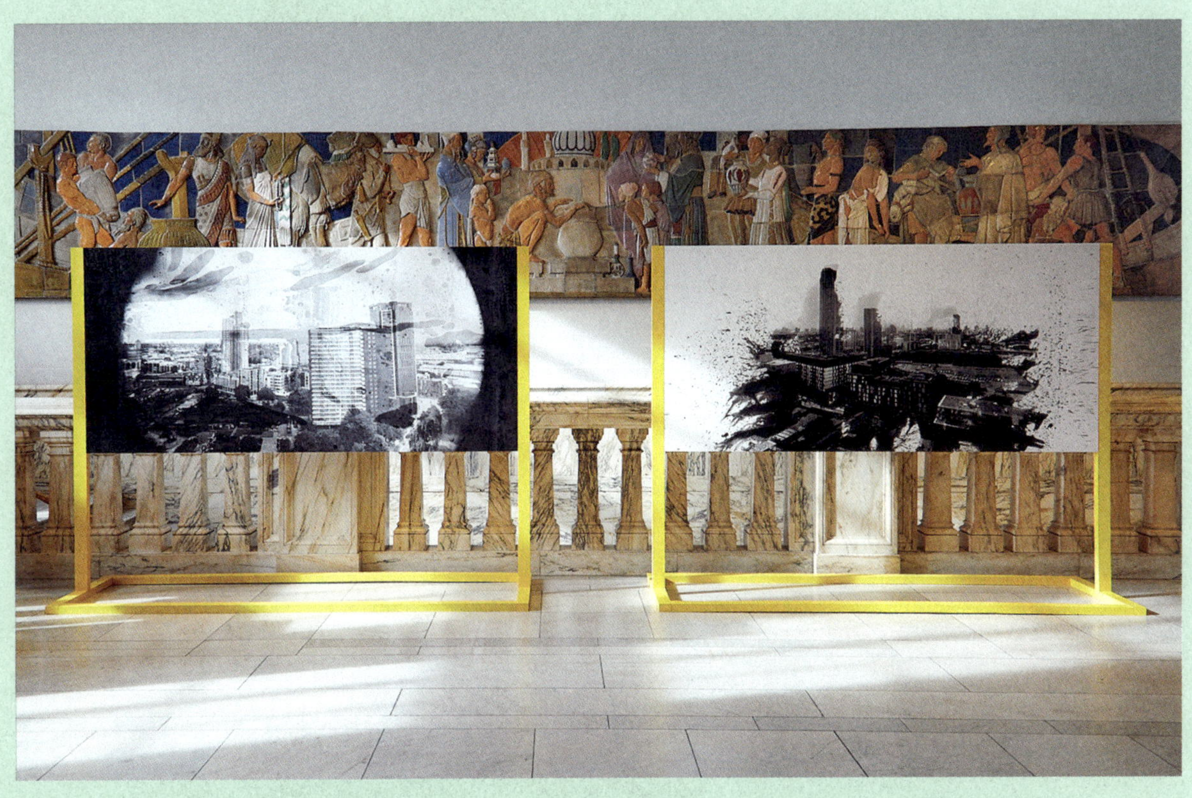

Lund Point Camera Obscura project, large-format prints on display, 2021

Brickfield Newham
Georgia Haseldine, Senior Curator

Brickfields were ubiquitous in nineteenth-century east London, springing up to satisfy a demand for the construction materials needed to house a rapidly growing population. Whole families worked the brickfields, living in wooden shacks on site. The bricks of the Victorian homes that Londoners walk past every day are pieces of their labour.

Responding to this local history, community research project Brickfield Newham set up a brickworks and a performance space on a construction site in the Royal Docks as part of Newham Heritage Month in May 2021. Through theatre and craft, hundreds of local people questioned clay and its importance to the urban landscape by connecting to the earth beneath their feet. It was V&A East's largest off-site pre-opening commission.

At the heart of the project were the Brickfield Makers, a group of local people passionate about brick, ceramics and housing activism convened in collaboration with Newham Council's Youth Empowerment Team. The Brickfield Makers exchanged their knowledge and lived experiences, as well as building a spectacular kiln.

Led by artist Rosanna Martin, founder of Cornish-based Brickfield, communities from across the borough came together to make bricks from local industrial waste materials, including clay dug during the excavation work for two new social housing projects in Plaistow and the Royal Docks. Once lit, the kiln was fired with wood continuously for 27 hours, restoking around every seven minutes to ensure it reached at least 1,000 degrees. The bricks fired to a beautiful range of colours, some bearing 'kiss marks' from the kiln and others the patina of rain on the drying surface.

Students from the University of East London created performances that gave a voice to histories of labourers that are now hidden from us, as well as developing tools to advocate for housing justice and imagine better places for us all to live as part of a co-taught MA Theatre and Directing programme with the V&A. The many linked events included the development of a new play, which told the story of a squatted Newham house, tracking backwards through time to its creation, as well as the delivery of clay and sand to the brickworks by the traditional Thames barge *Blue Mermaid*.

Lund Point Camera Obscura
Maia Ardalla, Producer for Schools and Young People

The Lund Point Camera Obscura project took place in August 2021 on the Carpenters Road Estate, Stratford, as part of a collaborative project between V&A East, the V&A Research Institute (VARI) and Beyond the Box CIC. The project, initiated by Matilda Pye, was an iteration of V&A East and VARI's Show+Tell+Share action research and presented a unique opportunity for the museum to explore co-creation models with young people.

Through a partnership with Beyond the Box CIC, young people aged 14 to 25 were recruited as cultural producers for a two-week intensive project, which involved working alongside photographer Brendan Barry to create analogue photography.

Inhabiting and transforming unoccupied flats at the top of the large tower block, with guidance from Barry participants developed hands-on making skills through the construction of photographic dark rooms, and by contributing to the preparation of chemicals and materials, ensuring each of the elements were optimum for the photographic process. It was a rare opportunity to blur curatorial, learning and social practice, with photography, community and young people.

The large-format analogue prints that were produced during the project were later displayed in three locations including V&A South Kensington, London Design Festival and Here East as part of Beyond the Box's People's Pavilion 2021 Community Festival.

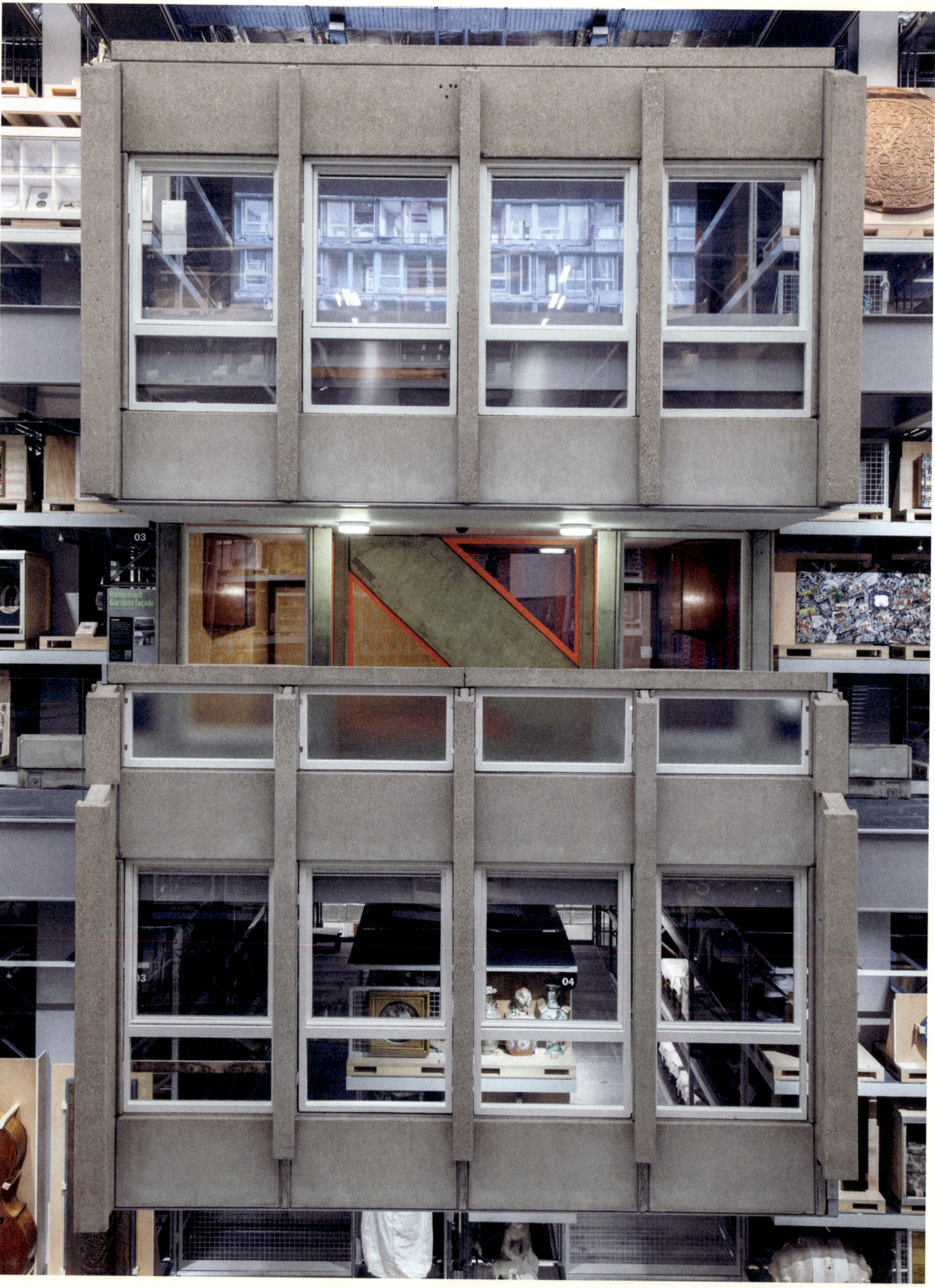
03
04

Robin Hood Gardens installed in V&A East Storehouse, 2025, V&A

Robin Hood Gardens is an estate located in Poplar in the London Borough of Tower Hamlets. Over the course of its 50 standing years, the estate became home to thousands of residents. In 2017, the decision was made to demolish it and, at the time of writing in June 2023, one block has yet to be taken down, and 20 residents are yet to be re-housed. In his 2008 survey, resident Darren Paulling showed that out of 140 surveyed Robin Hood Gardens households, 130 wanted the estate to be renovated, not demolished. Paulling's survey contradicted the council's poll from the previous year that had been used as supporting evidence for the estate's demolition. The council's poll concluded that demolition was the favoured outcome for the estate, despite the poll representing less than 40 per cent of the estate's households and failing to include renovation as an alternative option. The demolition decision became a flash-point in wider debates about the eradication of council housing and the responsibilities of heritage and cultural sectors within this context.

Architects Alison and Peter Smithson designed the homes of Robin Hood Gardens to blur the boundaries between inside and outside.[1] Arranged over two blocks of seven and 10 storeys, with a park encased between them, 213 well-proportioned flats and maisonettes opened onto horizontal street decks with views over London. The street decks, known as 'Streets in the Sky', were designed to be wide enough so that 'two women with prams can stop and talk without blocking the flow', and with pairs of doorways turned to face each other, aimed to combat the isolation of post-war vertical living, as well as providing shelter from the noise of the nearby Blackwall Tunnel.[2] The sharp citrusy aroma of coriander or the red fruits of a Naga Morich chilli plant attested to the use of the gardens and balconies by many first-generation British Bengali residents to grow herbs and spices. Summer Fun Days and days where children, parents, teachers, residents and volunteers 'dug hundreds of holes and planted hundreds of trees and shrubs' revealed a togetherness in the community that elevated the concrete-reinforced structure of Robin Hood Gardens into one that represented beauty and joy.[3]

In 2007, English Heritage approved a Certificate of Immunity from Listing for Robin Hood Gardens by Blackwall Reach Regeneration project. This meant that the estate could not be listed for five years. Residents, campaigners and the architectural community battled for years to keep the estate alive, but a second Certificate of Immunity from Listing was instated in 2012, paving the way for its demolition, which began in 2017.[4]

In 2018, without consulting residents, the V&A acquired a three-storey façade from the Western Block of Robin Hood Gardens, raising concerns that residents' voices would be over-shadowed by the architectural significance of the estate. Residents feared that, in the process of transforming their homes into a museum object, their memories may be forgotten and their experiences misrepresented. The façade is now embedded in the Weston collections hall at V&A East Storehouse. Here visitors can walk across the street deck and gaze into flats 93 and 94 to catch a glimpse of the Smithsons' vision. But the legacy of this façade extends far beyond the architectural. It expands into the turmoil of today's housing crisis. It highlights the tension between, on the one hand, families who migrated from Bangladesh, the Caribbean and East Africa and proudly made Robin Hood Gardens their home, and on the other, stigmatising narratives in popular discourse that branded them 'sink estates' seeking to validate their destruction. It speaks to the systematic demolition of hundreds of social housing estates in favour of regeneration schemes that displace families and irreversibly fracture communities. And it throws a spotlight on the way in which, when renovation has been an alternative, it has been conditional upon middle-class integration into working-class housing areas to fulfil the social potential of the Brutalist vision.

Ben Selig, Curatorial Fellow

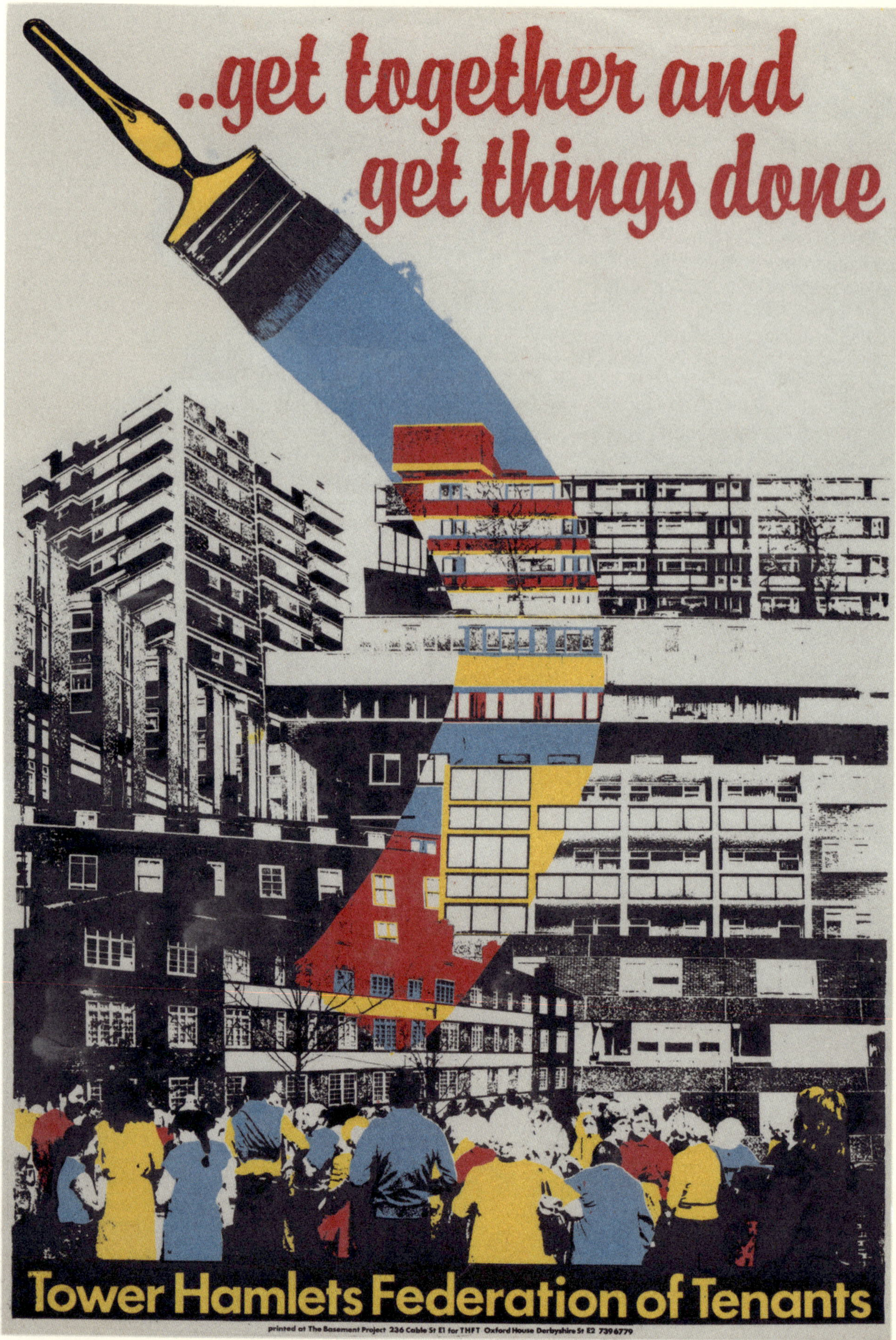
..get together and
get things done
Tower Hamlets Federation of Tenants
printed at The Basement Project 236 Cable St E1 for THFT Oxford House Derbyshire St E2 7396779

Basement Community Arts Workshop poster for Tower Hamlets, by Tony Minnion, 1984, V&A

In 1984, Tony Minnion, a young artist who worked for the Docklands Community Poster Project assembling wooden billboards for their photomurals, was commissioned by the Tower Hamlets Federation of Tenants Association to produce a poster to spearhead a campaign to increase tenant involvement in local housing decisions. In the poster, a paintbrush sweeps through a montage of photographs taken by Minnion of local housing demonstrations outside the Burdett and Samuda Estates, 'transforming a colourless environment into one of colour, a place where people live'. Around 200 copies of this design were screen printed as posters in the Basement Community Arts Workshop and distributed around Tower Hamlets.

In the late 1970s, the Tower Hamlets art scene was beginning to bubble. If you walked down the steps underneath St George's Town Hall on a weekday evening you might stumble across an architect distributing technical drawings to a group of school children, interrupt an oral history recording or radio broadcast, or turn and see Tony Minnion arranging photographs from the most recent housing demonstration for a new poster campaign. Underneath St George's Town Hall lived an inky world of printing workshops, alongside film studios and drama rehearsal spaces, known as the Basement Community Arts Workshop. Established by schoolteacher Chris Searle, film director Maggie Pinhorn and local councillor and artist Dan Jones, the Basement Community Arts Workshop distinguished itself among a sea of new community arts projects that, by the early 1980s, had transformed the landscape of Tower Hamlets into one that flourished with art and activity.

Affordable housing in east London was, however, under increasing threat from commercial developers as Margaret Thatcher's pursuit of privatisation and centralisation enabled the newly formed London Docklands Development Corporation to override local authorities and their accountability to communities. Supported by the Greater London Council, the Docklands Community Poster Project was formed to assist local tenant action groups in their campaign against the London Docklands Development Corporation through the production of large photomurals, posters, banners and photographic documentation. Concerned about facing 'a chaotic situation' if the government was successful in its 'declared aim of taking away the right to raise and spend money locally on locally determined priorities', individuals, action groups and arts workshops came together, conscious that battling these changes required a collective effort. In 1984, the Tower Hamlets Federation of Tenants Association, Docklands Community Poster Project and Basement Community Arts Workshop collaborated to construct an extensive campaign that reflected on Tower Hamlets' 'chronically understaffed' housing services. The pamphlet outlined an opportunity for the council to establish an improved staffing structure in which tenant participation would provide a 'crucial element to ensure that the system responded to consumer needs and preferences'.

Emerging from the turbulence wrought by destruction and change, *... get together and get things done* encapsulates, within east London's working class, a community mobilised by arts projects, workshops and action groups in a process that promoted both individual self-expression and community solidarity. Ben Selig, Curatorial Fellow

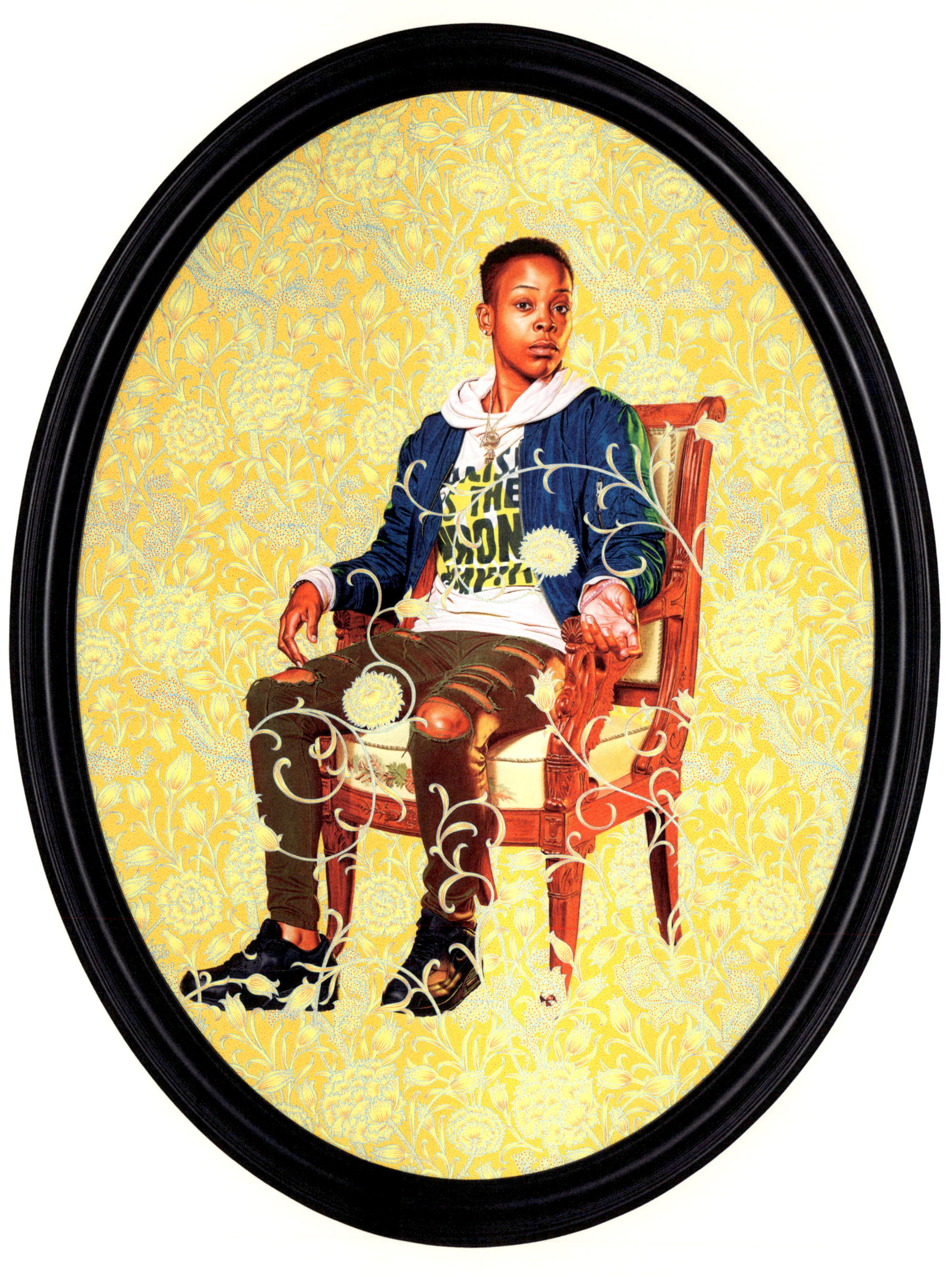

Portrait of Melissa Thompson, by Kehinde Wiley, 2020, V&A

In 2020, American artist Kehinde Wiley painted this portrait of Melissa Thompson, a young woman from Hackney. Wiley met Thompson while looking for sitters in Dalston's Ridley Road Market for a new body of work created for his first solo exhibition in the UK, *The Yellow Wallpaper*, at the William Morris Gallery in Walthamstow. This portrait is reflective of Wiley's practice, which transforms and subverts the typology of historic Global North portraiture, responding to the absence of figures of colour within our art historical canon by proudly placing Black subjects within this iconography. Here, inside this large oval canvas, Thompson sits in a Regency-style chair, angled in a three-quarter pose typical of historic portraiture. She looks out at the viewer with a look of determination and defiance.

Wiley's signature focus, on hyperrealist detail and vibrant, saturated colour, invokes a sense of the baroque and ornate in Thompson's style of dress. A pink bracelet with the word 'Respect' encircles her left wrist. Through her expression and the position of her arms on the chair, Thompson exudes power and authority. However, upon closer inspection, the seemingly innocuous ornate floral background, painted in shades of yellow, white, blue and red, reaches out its tendrils to encircle and grip her legs and chest, as if to keep her immobile and confined in the chair and canvas.

Wiley's exhibition, *The Yellow Wallpaper,* takes its title from the 1892 feminist text by American novelist Charlotte Perkins Gilman, a semi-autobiographical story of a woman who is confined to her bedroom after being diagnosed with hysteria. Here, the torturous pattern of the room's yellow wallpaper winds its way into the recesses of her mind, symbolising her imprisonment. Gilman's story has haunted Wiley as a metaphor for 'the sense of powerlessness and ... invention that happens in a person who's not seen, who's not respected and whose sense of autonomy is in question', often due to race, class or gender.[1] Wiley's painting invokes this tension in its struggle between the figure and her surroundings: a powerful woman being restrained by her environment.

In commemoration of his exhibition at the William Morris Gallery, Wiley's portrait also engages with the work of British designer, writer and social reformer William Morris. Morris was born in Walthamstow, and his work shaped the interiors and collections of the South Kensington Museum. His designs have been a constant reference for Wiley for the organic decorative backgrounds found in his portraits. The yellow wallpaper in *Portrait of Melissa Thompson* is a contemporary reimagining of a pattern designed by Morris and produced by Morris & Co. in the 1880s as part of its project to create beautiful art and design on a mass scale for the middle classes.[2] Wiley has said of his practice that 'the starting point of my work is decidedly empathy ... It's about seeing yourself in other people'.[3] Wiley's painting radiates empathy for Thompson, Morris and Gilman, and speaks to how we can understand ourselves through others and the unique capacity of the maker to bring all of these experiences into dialogue with a single creation. Madeleine Haddon, Curator

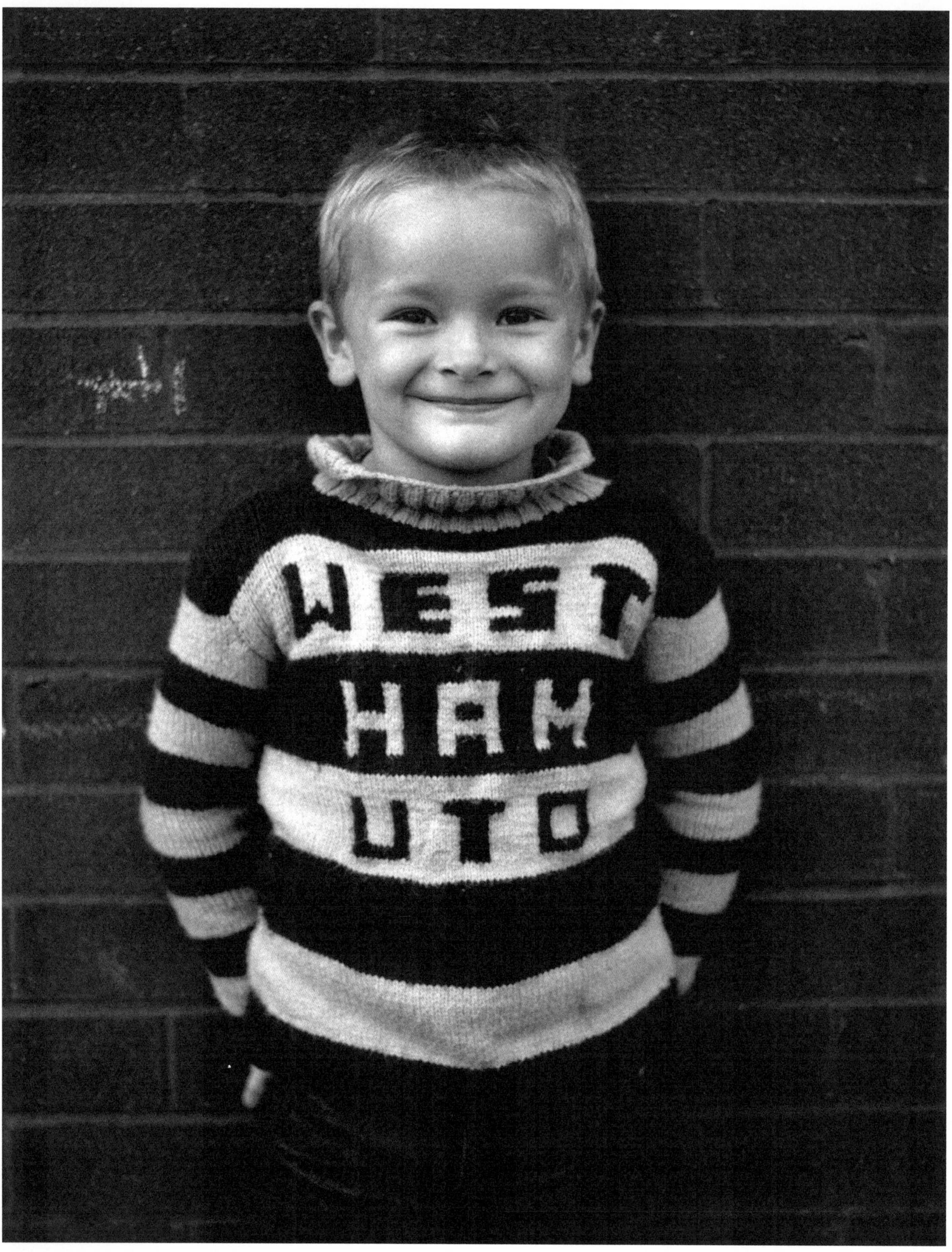
WEST
HAM
UTD

Designer Sportswear, by John Heywood, 1983, V&A

In this portrait, a young boy with his hands in his pockets is depicted standing in front of a simple brick wall. Despite the everyday nature of the background, photographer John Heywood has skilfully captured a heartwarming scene. The child's pose and cheeky expression leave us wondering if he is hiding something, feeling shy in front of the camera, or displaying a roguish confidence. Additionally, the hand-knitted jumper with 'West Ham Utd' emblazoned across the front suggests that the boy's parents shared their passion for their beloved local football team with their children. Moreover, the mischievous title of the photograph, *Designer Sportswear*, emphasises the pride of the wearer in his jumper, a departure from the 1980s trend of donning commercially branded sportswear. This interplay between the title and content of the photograph reflects the photographer's sense of humour, much like the cheeky smile captured on the child's face.

Heywood, an English photographer based in Northampton, stands out from his contemporaries. Unlike many photographers working in the 1980s, who were predominantly middle-class university graduates, Heywood was a self-taught working-class photographer. Heywood pursued his passion for photography while juggling various other jobs. He sought employment opportunities related to his interest in photography and eventually found work as a hospital record-shot photographer, and later as a darkroom technician at a local newspaper. At this time, he also captured moments during his walks through the park or on his way back home from work.

With the birth of his oldest daughter in 1979, Heywood shifted the focus of his work, beginning to portray children. This was to become a significant moment for him. His photographic series, 'My Family and Other Children', candidly documented the everyday lives of working-class children from infancy through to adolescence. Through his lens, Heywood offered sociological observations on how children interacted, had fun and shaped their identities. The series was displayed at the Bethnal Green Museum of Childhood as part of the exhibition *Childhood, Inward and Outward View*, from 16 May to 15 July 1990. Following the exhibition, Heywood donated his series - which spans a 40-year photographic study of childhood - to the museum.

Heywood's photographs focus on portraying endearing moments of childhood - a lone girl sat on a bench talking to her invisible friends; two boys barefoot in the mud; a group of friends climbing a tree; a baby asleep amid a miscellany of toys. They have a beautiful intimacy and convey the pure affection and joy of the photographer, as well as his desire to share these emotions with others. By closely capturing the ordinary lives of children, Heywood's photographs have become a source for cultural memories and a valuable record of the history of urban and domestic spaces in modern Britain. His work also invites introspection, reminding us that we all share memories of joy and friendship that transcend our differences. Just as John Heywood's affectionate gaze captured the care-free moments of his subjects, so too here the child's captivating smile beautifully encapsulates the inherent charm of childhood.

Miri Ahn, Curatorial Coordinator

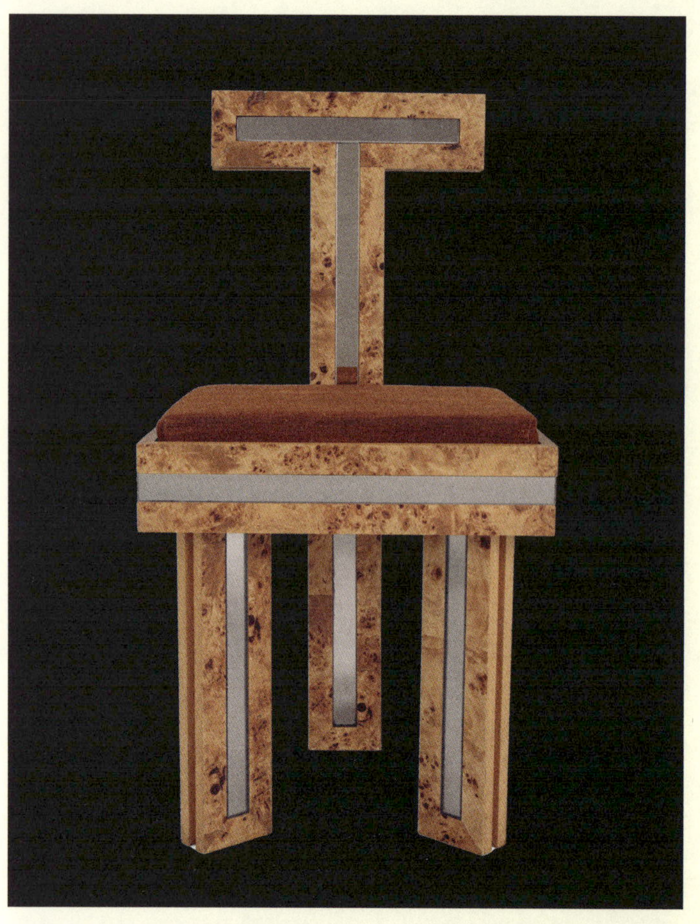

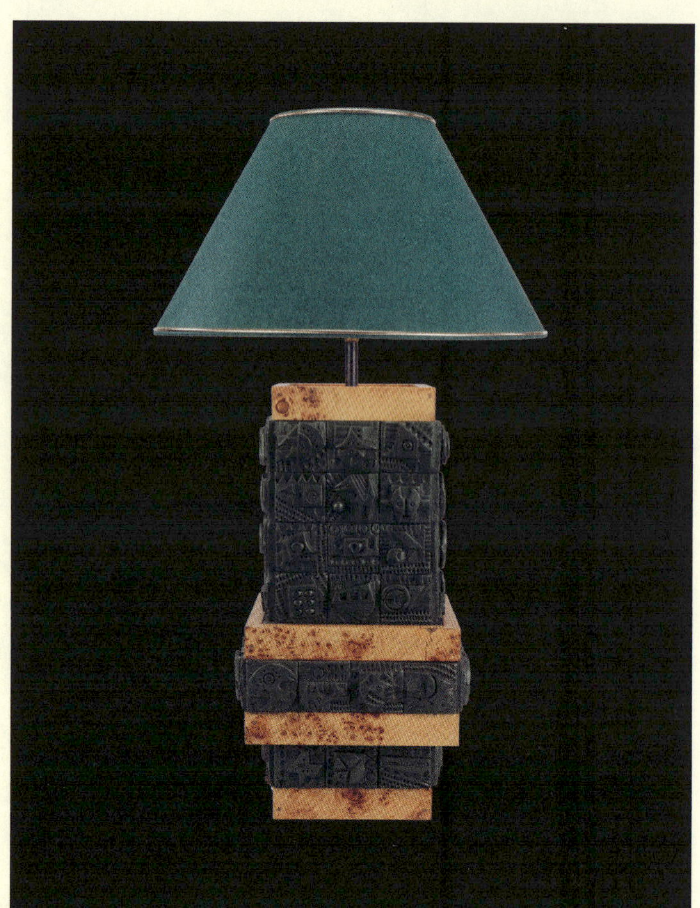

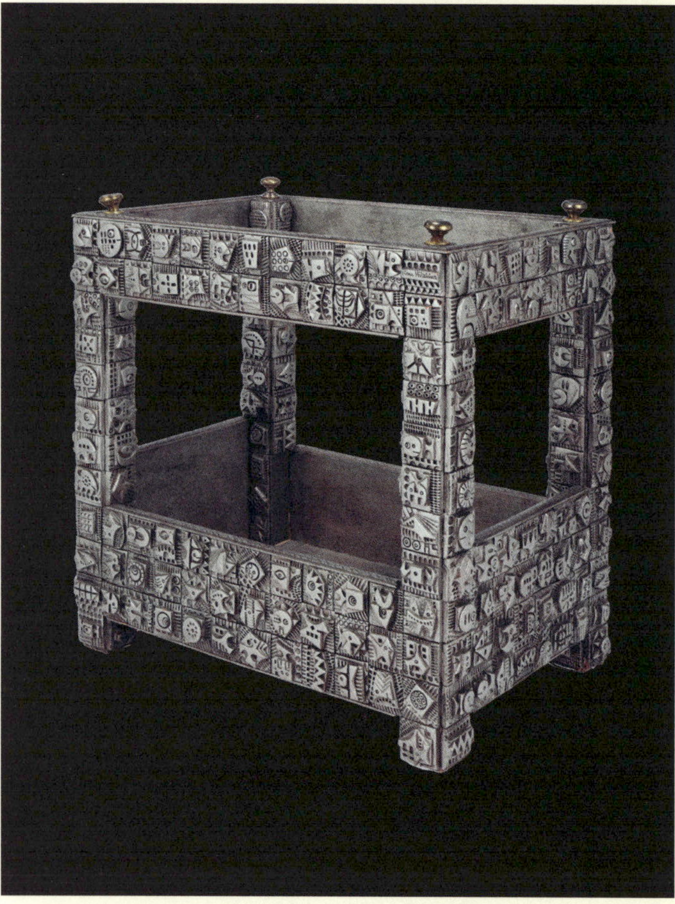

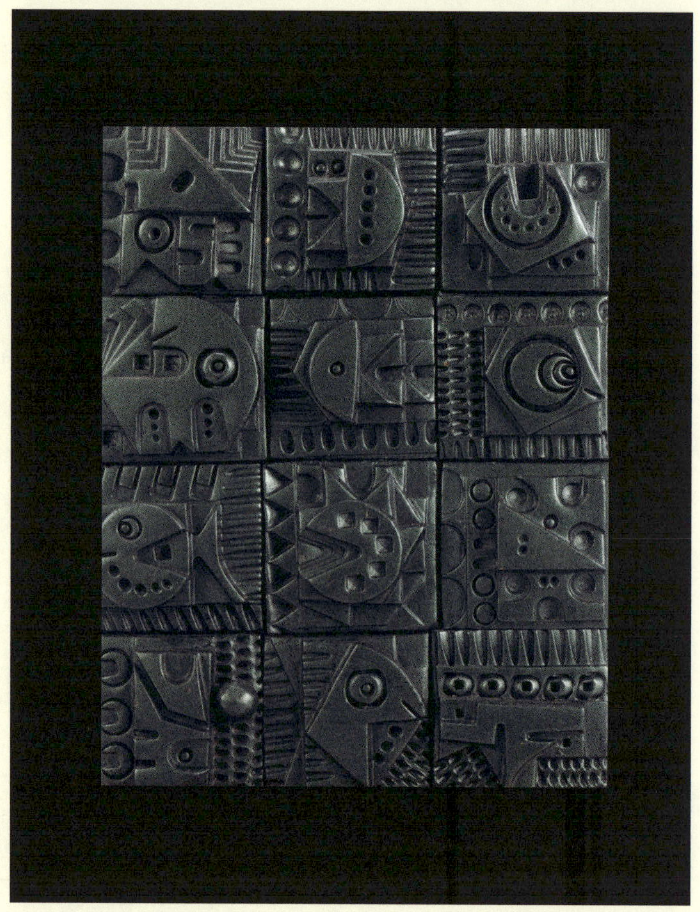

Furniture and ceramics by Ron Hitchins from his Hackney home, 1950–2000, V&A

After a fruitless search for bathroom tiles to decorate his Hackney home, Ron Hitchins decided to make his own. It was a DIY solution that would spark decades of making. Inspired by Aztec designs, the tiles combine layers of expressive mark making and abstract forms. Glimpses of faces and outlines resembling animals emerge across the dynamic surface – and no two tiles are the same.

Over many decades, Hitchins crafted every aspect of his home; from joinery and bespoke furniture, including a tiled four-poster bed (along with a pet-friendly version for his cat, Kipper) to three-legged maple-veneer chairs, and from kitchen cupboards to statement table lamps and picture frames. Hitchins worked with curiosity, experimenting with materials including clay, resin, metal and wood, and with finishes from boot polish to car spray paint. In addition to traditional implements, in the resourceful spirit of The Waste, a market on the Kingsland Road at which he was once a stallholder, he used improvised tools from household debris, such as Biro tubes, paperclips and ice-lolly sticks.

Born in 1926, Hitchins was from a generation whose life can be mapped onto east London's changing landscape through two World Wars, witnessing the impacts of gentrification first-hand. In 1926, Pennyfields in Poplar, where he was born and grew up, was known as the Limehouse Chinatown. From the late nineteenth century, a community of Chinese Londoners, of whom Hitchins' father was one, had settled in this area due to its proximity to the Docklands.

Hitchins' guiding philosophy was that life should be enjoyed. Nowhere was this more apparent than in his home, a pink Georgian terrace at 43 Malvern Road, Hackney, which he purchased in the late 1950s. It was here that Hitchins, a burgeoning professional Flamenco dancer, installed a parquet dance floor and created two studios, one for dance and the other for craft.

Hitchins briefly sold his tiled homeware through retailers like Liberty and Heal's, and held his first exhibition at the Whibley Gallery, London, in 1966. Despite positive reviews and offers of gallery representation he moved away from the commercial art world. He felt these circles disregarded him for his working-class roots, and he was also conscious of protecting his creative independence. Instead, he sought to preserve the fun of making for himself, working only on his own projects and selective commissions.

Over the 65 years that Hitchins lived at 43 Malvern Road he embraced design as a means of self-exploration and expression. He even installed a kiln in his basement so he could fire tiles from the comfort of home. This was a space that could shape-shift, as workshop, studio, stage and, above all, his ultimate artistic project. Through his prolific making and genuine spirit of innovation, Ron Hitchins crafted his own world in a Hackney terrace that grew with him in the way that homes do; both shaped by, and instrumental in shaping, the lives of those that call them home.

Chloe Kellow, Assistant Curator

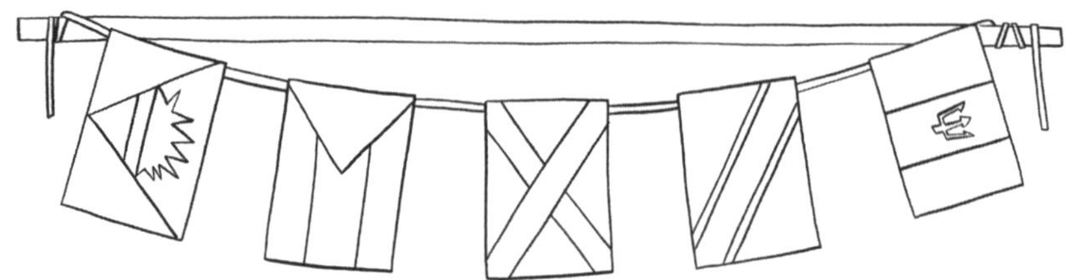

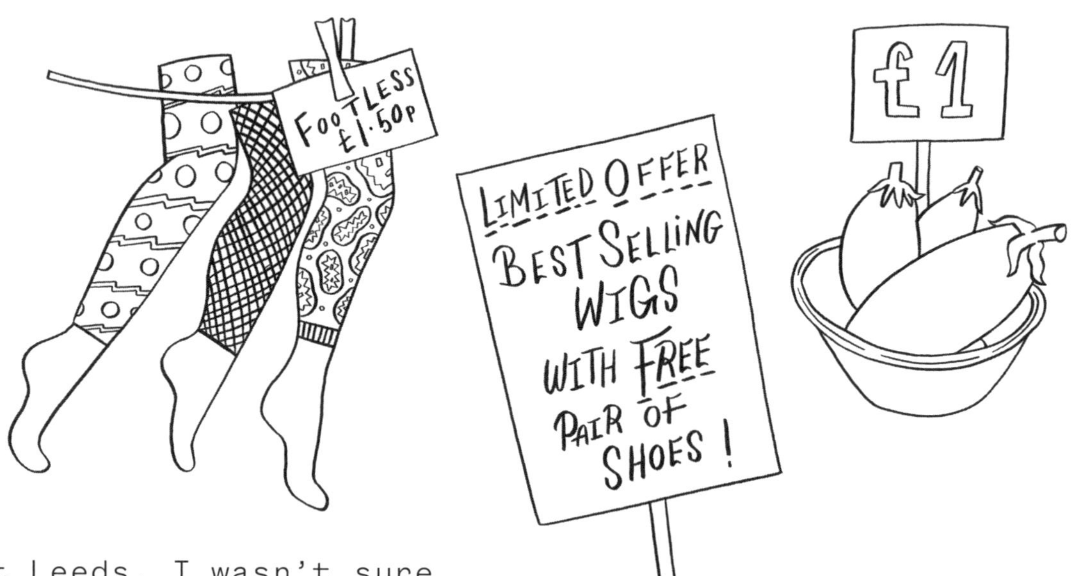

Dear East,

When I first left Leeds, I wasn't sure about where in London I would fit in. It's such a busy maze of a city; a universe of its own. But I remember when I found you. I remember the first time I saw your crowded markets and cycled the lengths of your parks. I remember the first time I smelt your aromas and tasted your food.

You have never made me feel odd or like an outlier. You embrace all who enter and, although I might be small and insignificant, when seen against the backdrop of your vast history and endless days and nights, you have always filled my heart and given me a special sense that it mattered I was here.

Suhaiymah Manzoor-Khan, Nourishing Ourselves

East London, it's just a part of me. By the age of six, half my dialect was cockney and maybe half my spirit too. From Redbridge to Hackney and further, so many experiences have poured into me. Now I see mini versions of me running around, and older role models slowing down. I know they need us to pour back into them so I will show them what their love meant to me.

Soji Sonibare, Co-founder of Nourishment

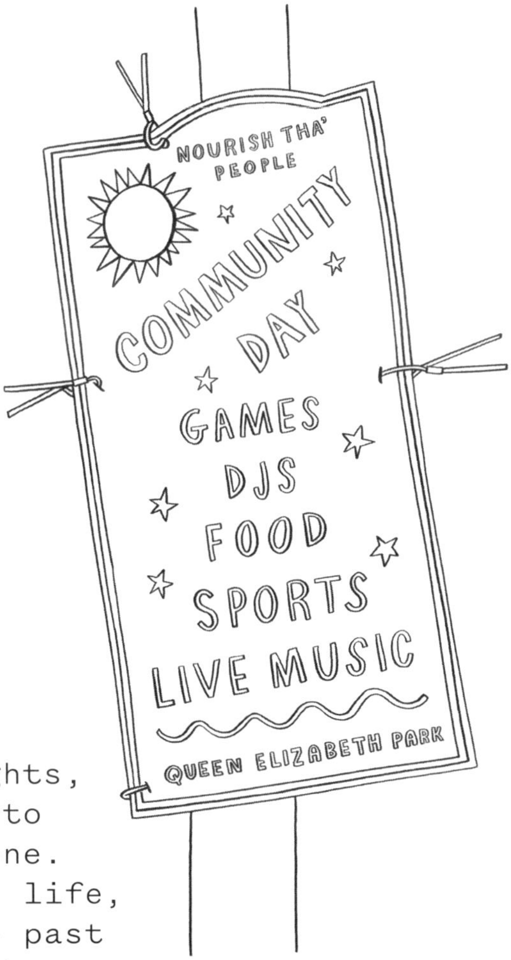

I have memories all over east London. Some remain lodged in parts that have changed and no longer remember me. The creativity and chaos, the love and lights, the diversity and the details. Second to so many, but a spirit replicated by none. How my hometown of Barking pulses with life, laughter and music. My memories of the past are my hopes for the future. Let east be the birthplace of new ideas that we can fondly remember.

Tito Mogajie, Co-founder of Nourishment

From overlooked to adored, east London's evolution weaves a tale of resilience and revival.

It boasts a vibrant tapestry of voices and dreams. It is a place where cultures converge and where stories are woven into the very fabric of its streets.

East London's charm, as I see it, emanates from its unwavering spirit, from the pulse of its markets to the rhythm of its creative souls. It is a place that holds dear its roots yet adapts to change, whether good or bad. Here, I find inspiration and hope. I am inspired to continue to drive for social change and I am hopeful for the boundless opportunities to engage and make a difference.

East London welcomes me with open arms, inviting me to add my voice to the chorus of transformation.

East London is my home. It is my purpose.

Lola Martinez-Rufete, Elevate Youth Board

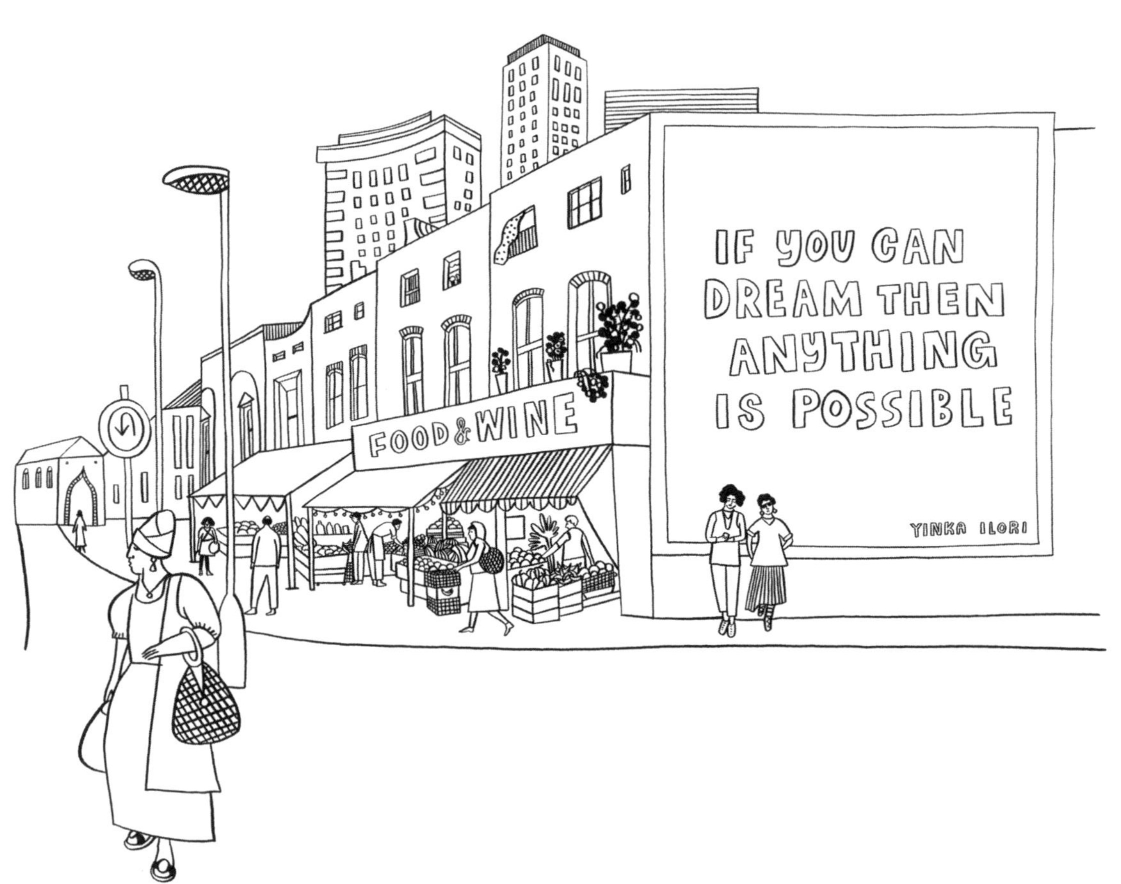

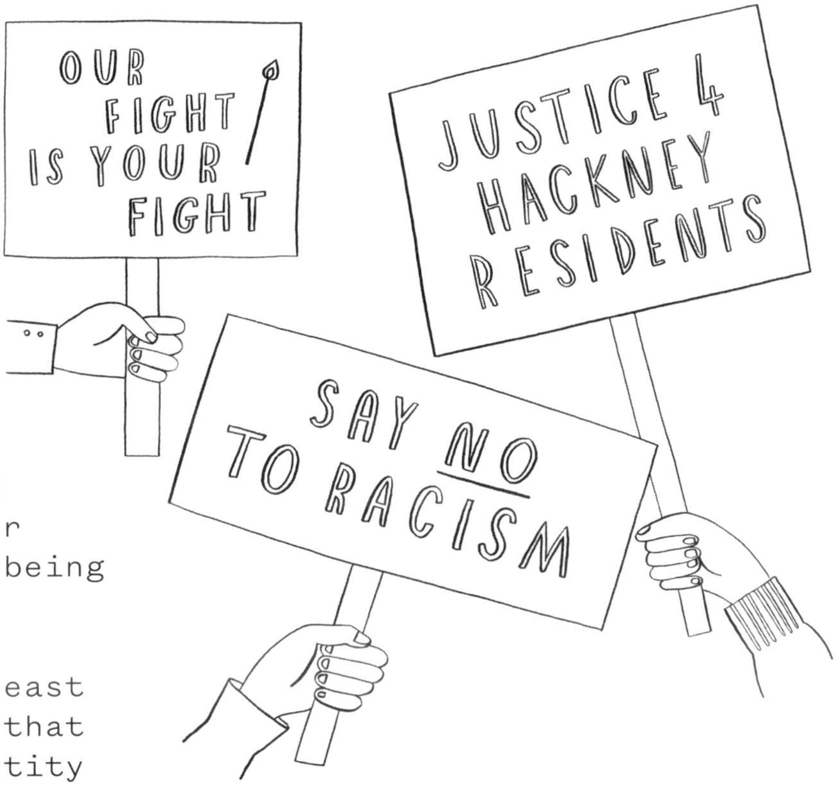

Hackney is my home,
it's my community.
I was born in Hackney,
grew up in Hackney and
now I am a youth worker
here. I can't imagine being
from anywhere else.

I am proud to be from east London; proud of what that wider east-London identity stands for. It's an identity that is the product of people from different backgrounds and from all corners of the globe, and we celebrate that fiercely.

To me, east London evokes the idea of solidarity. I think of the past – of the Matchgirls' strike, the Battle of Cable Street, or Rock Against Racism in Victoria Park. But in the present, too, we can still see and feel the fight against racial discrimination, oppression, exploitation, poverty and inequality. It is there in the struggle against gentrification, and in the efforts to make the Olympic legacy mean more than just unaffordable housing, and shops and leisure venues for the rich. V&A East must be on the right side of those struggles.

Luke Billingham, Hackney Quest

I do what I do now because I'm from east London. I needed to be born here in 1987 to Jamaican parents, to grow up on pirate radio, which introduced me to local sounds like Jungle and Garage. To become a teenager while Grime was emerging in the early 2000s.

My experience of living here, of documenting it through music and art, has taken me around the world several times. People often ask me, 'Where else would you want to live? Tokyo? New York? Berlin?' But I know that if I didn't live here, I couldn't do what I do. And nowhere remains vibrant organically; that vibrancy is generated by the people who stay and continue to make art, both for now, and for the next generation. So as long as I'm here I'll be making the ting.

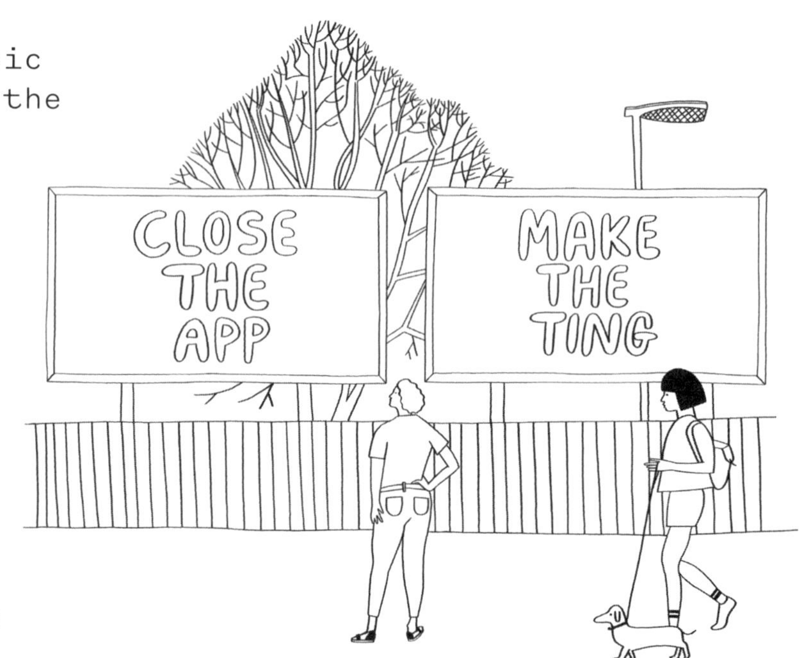

Elijah, Writer, DJ and Founder of Make The Ting

Dear East,

What can I say about you? You are full of contradictions, always changing, always morphing. But you always let me in.

You are warm, and so big, and at the same time, like a village. You let me grow roots and expand. You make me feel like I belong.

Thank you, dear East.

Alaa Alsaraji, Visual artist and creative facilitator

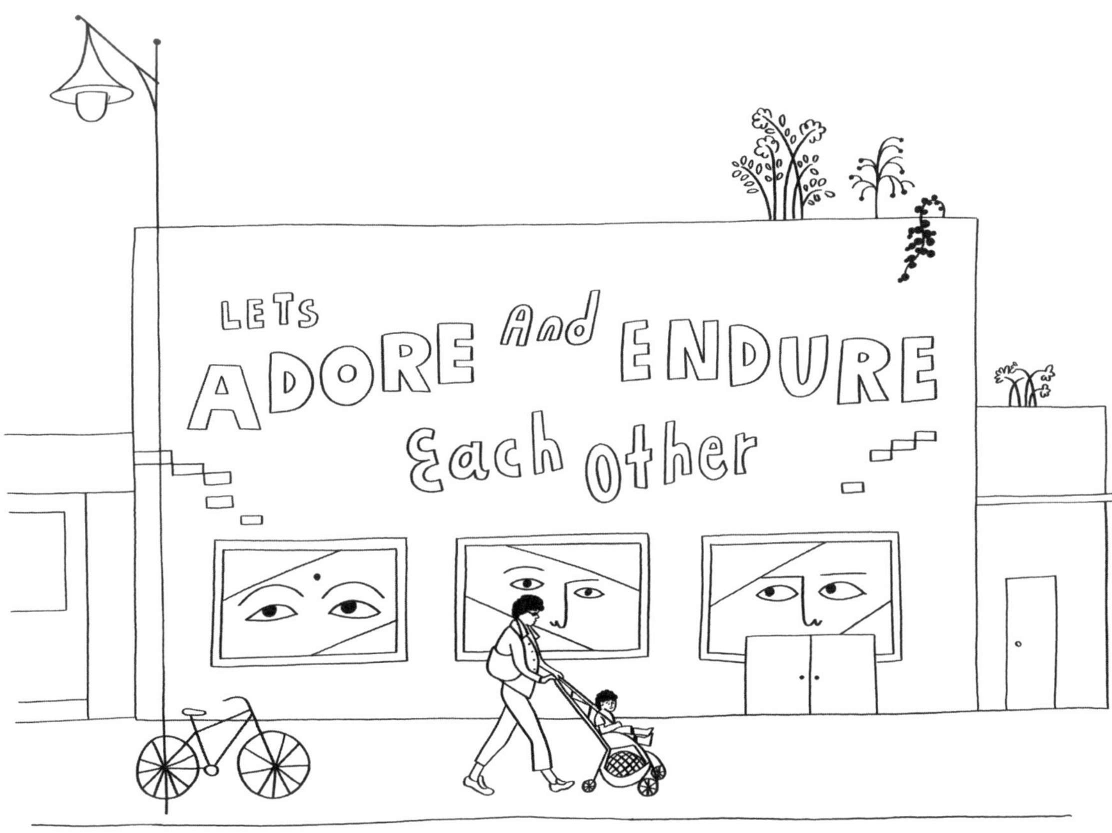

My affection for east London is profound. It is where I embarked on my artistic journey. I graduated from a foundation course in art and design at Newham College in 2007, a crucial stepping stone in my career. Rabbits Road Press, nestled in Old Manor Park Library, was where I joined a community of like-minded creators. Their influence was pivotal, deeply embedding my work in the area's diverse cultural tapestry.

During my time at the Royal College of Art, while studying for an MA in architecture, I explored the origins of renowned institutions, including V&A East. This research enriched my understanding of the cultural importance of east London.

East London is not only my childhood home, but also the place I choose to live and love now. It is a constant wellspring of inspiration and opportunity. As V&A East emerges, I anticipate it will add to the vibrancy of our community, which remains at the core of my creative endeavours.

Sahra Hersi, Rabbits Road Press

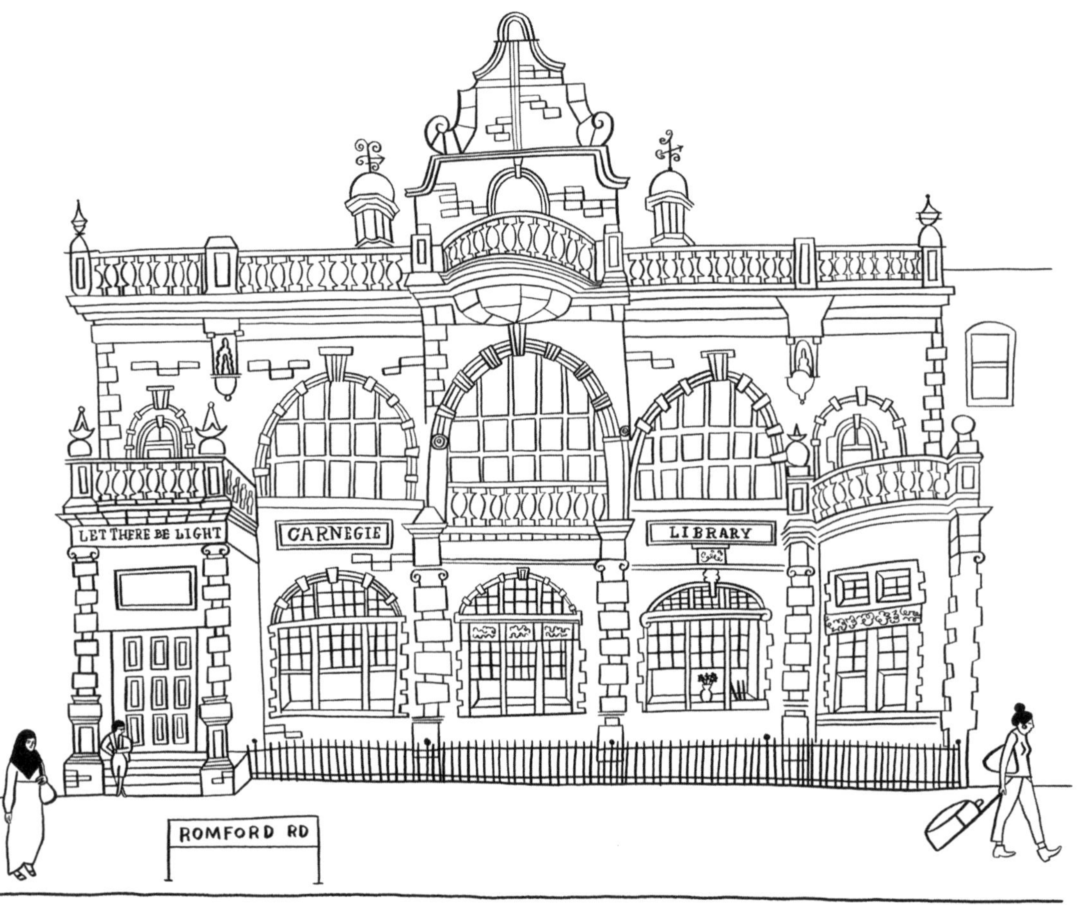

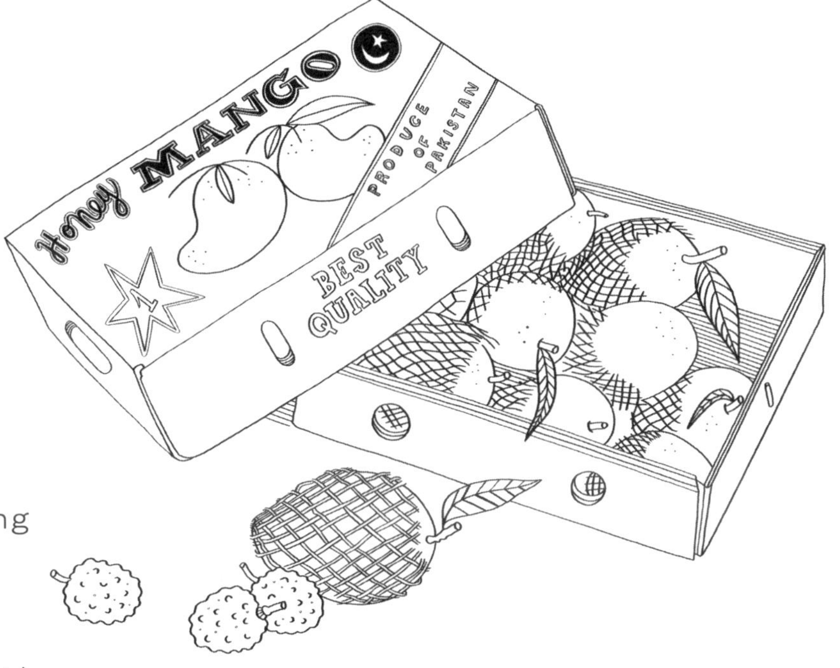

Things I love about you: the best honey mangoes imported from Pakistan, halal food in abundance and bidet culture of course. The chaotic energy in the lead up to Eid, catching up with old school friends at taraweeh prayers and neighbours looking out for each other.

Exhibiting my paintings has allowed me to travel from LA to Seoul, but east London will always be my grounding place. Here I can be re-energised by newer galleries, like Rose Easton, conveniently within walking distance of the Whitechapel Gallery, one of the first publicly funded galleries in the UK.

Muslim Sisterhood, the creative agency I've built with Lamisa and Sara, thrives in the richness of your tapestry. We started our collaboration to reflect our community authentically. You are not just a place; you are a living entity that pulses with the dreams and resilience of those who call you home.

Zeinab Saleh, Artist and Co-founder of Muslim Sisterhood

What

a Mu

Can

seum

Do

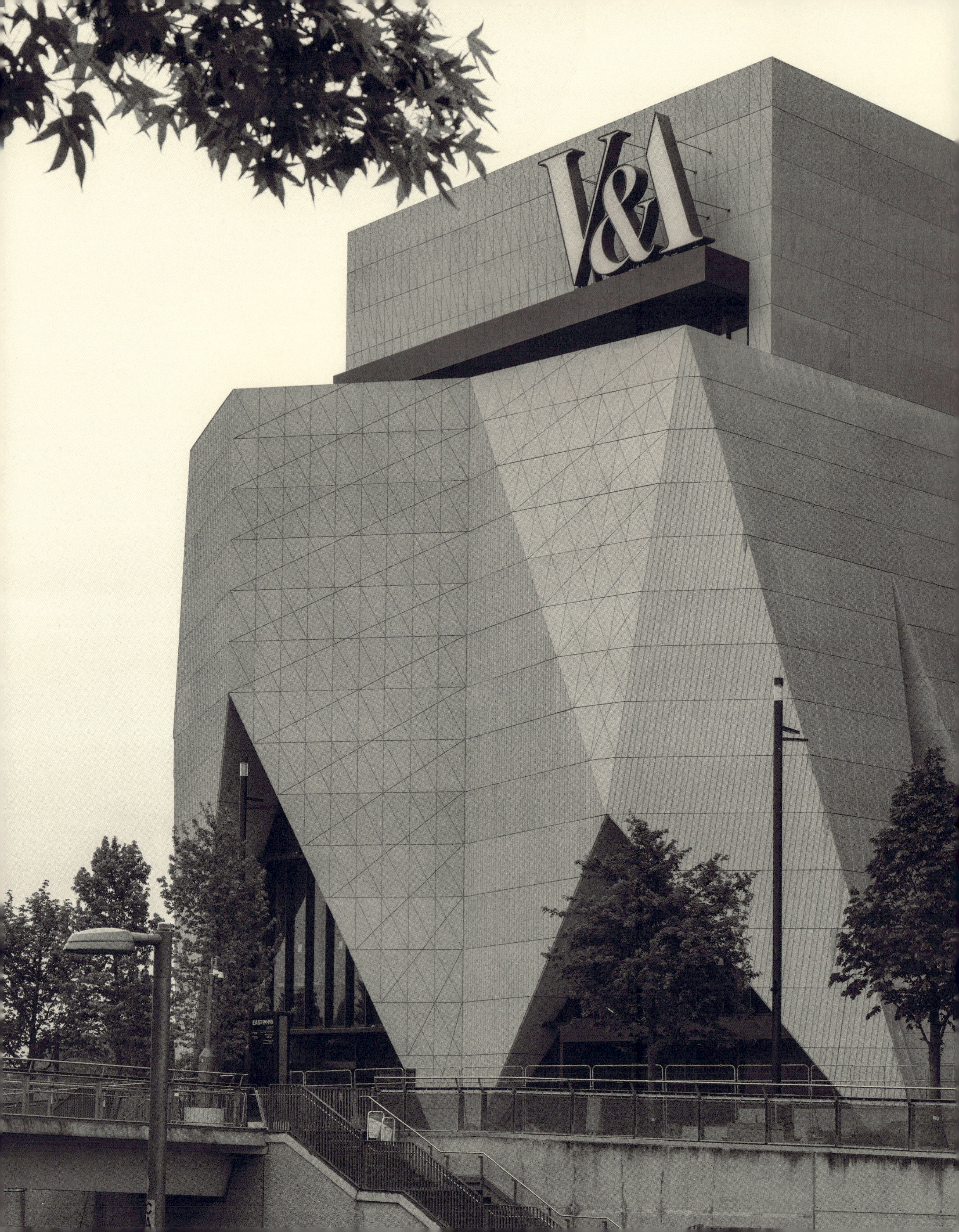
V&A

A new museum is an opportunity to reboot and refresh, to reconsider old narratives and insert new ones. In the case of V&A East, it has been a chance to explore new ways of displaying our collections and new narratives that can link our historical holdings to contemporary themes, thoughts and concerns. In particular, it has been a chance to rethink what making means in the twenty-first century and the Why We Make Galleries bring a new urgency and intentionality to the term. Making is not neutral, and many young practitioners are especially driven to engage in creative and material practice with an aim of making a positive mark on the world. This section explores in greater detail the V&A East Museum, its buildings and its galleries; it also shares conversations with young people and makers about what motivates them to make.

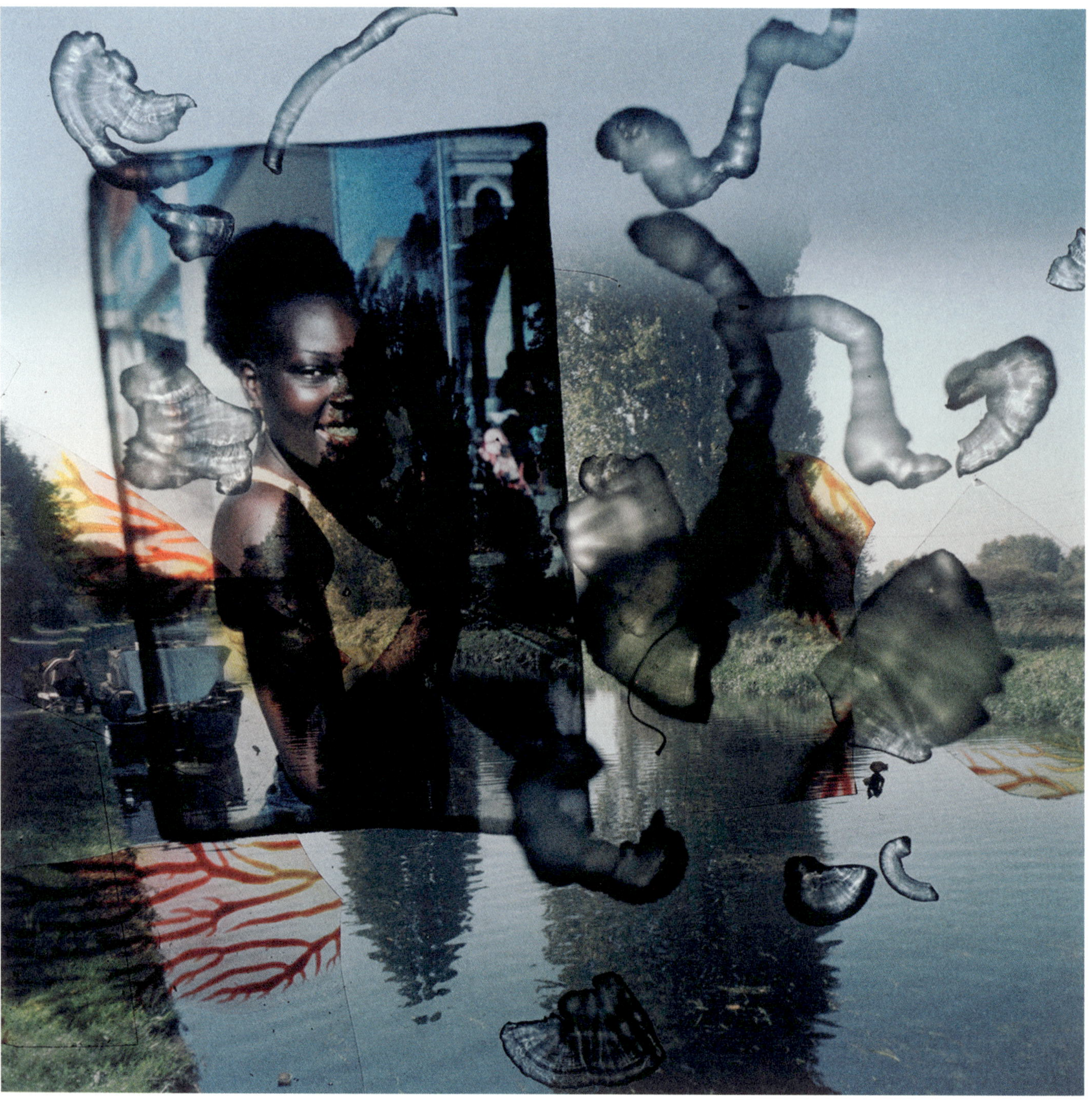

Lady in yellow vest with trees in background from the series 'Talking to Ants', by Stephen Gill, 2009–13, V&A

New Dialogues with Collections
Zofia Trafas White

The opportunity and challenge of creating a new museum raises important questions about what a museum can be. In the 10-year process of developing V&A East, several such questions stimulated our thinking and debates. How can a museum project be a test bed for innovative ways of curating collections? How can a museum serve as a meaningful civic platform? How can it be experimental and future-facing, exploring new ways for museums to act in the world? From rethinking traditional canons and disciplinary boundaries to addressing topical issues, the Why We Make Galleries propose a response to these fundamental questions. At their heart are new conversations with and around V&A collections. Shaped through discussions with young people, educators, artists, designers and fellow curators, Why We Make considers the urgency of *why* making matters and how a museum collection can speak to the world today.

Situated across two floors, the Why We Make Galleries explore attitudes, agendas and motivations for making, tuned to the major issues of our time. They consider how creative practitioners give purpose to their work and seek to change the world for the better by championing equity, collective action and environmental responsibility. The stories and voices of makers are at the centre of the galleries, and it is their collective narratives that define the 'we' of Why We Make. A thematic gallery structure brings together practitioners and V&A objects from different geographies and eras; these themes explore individual and collective motivations for making, from the restorative power of artistic expression to collaborative efforts to design for social and ecological needs.

Context matters

The curatorial approach at V&A East is rooted in context: from the project's unique urban locality to urgent, wider debates about the state of art and design education in the UK.

Why We Make draws inspiration from the histories and distinctive multicultural character of east London and the four boroughs of Hackney, Tower Hamlets, Newham and Waltham Forest that are home to the Olympic Park. With over a hundred languages spoken locally, east London is a unique microcosm of the world, home to a myriad of global communities who have made England's capital city their home. It is also the site of rich histories of manufacturing and technological innovation, the legacy of which continues today with growing networks of creative studios and making spaces. Interwoven into these histories are also stories of creative practices of the many immigrant communities who have settled in east London over the centuries. Always in flux, east London has been transformed by difficult forces of change: from Second World War bombardment to waves of rapid urban redesign delivered through post-war architectural planning and, more recently, housing development and gentrification.

Beyond its histories, east London today is home to some of the youngest and most diverse communities in the UK, making it a vital context for conversations about the future of creative education. In the years of V&A East's development, the UK witnessed a steady decrease in funding for creative subjects in state schools, leading to growing gaps in who can access related careers, particularly when coupled with increasing economic and social disparity and rising university fees. Conversations with educators made the stark situation clear: 'Making is very important. We're at a crossroads now where making is not on the agenda … it's being taken away from schools and we're in danger of losing it.'[1] With this perceived decline in the value of art and design in education, a lot is at stake.

The Why We Make curatorial agenda speaks directly to this layered context. Through the voices and politics of diverse makers, the galleries champion the social value of art, design and making, and its enduring potential to be

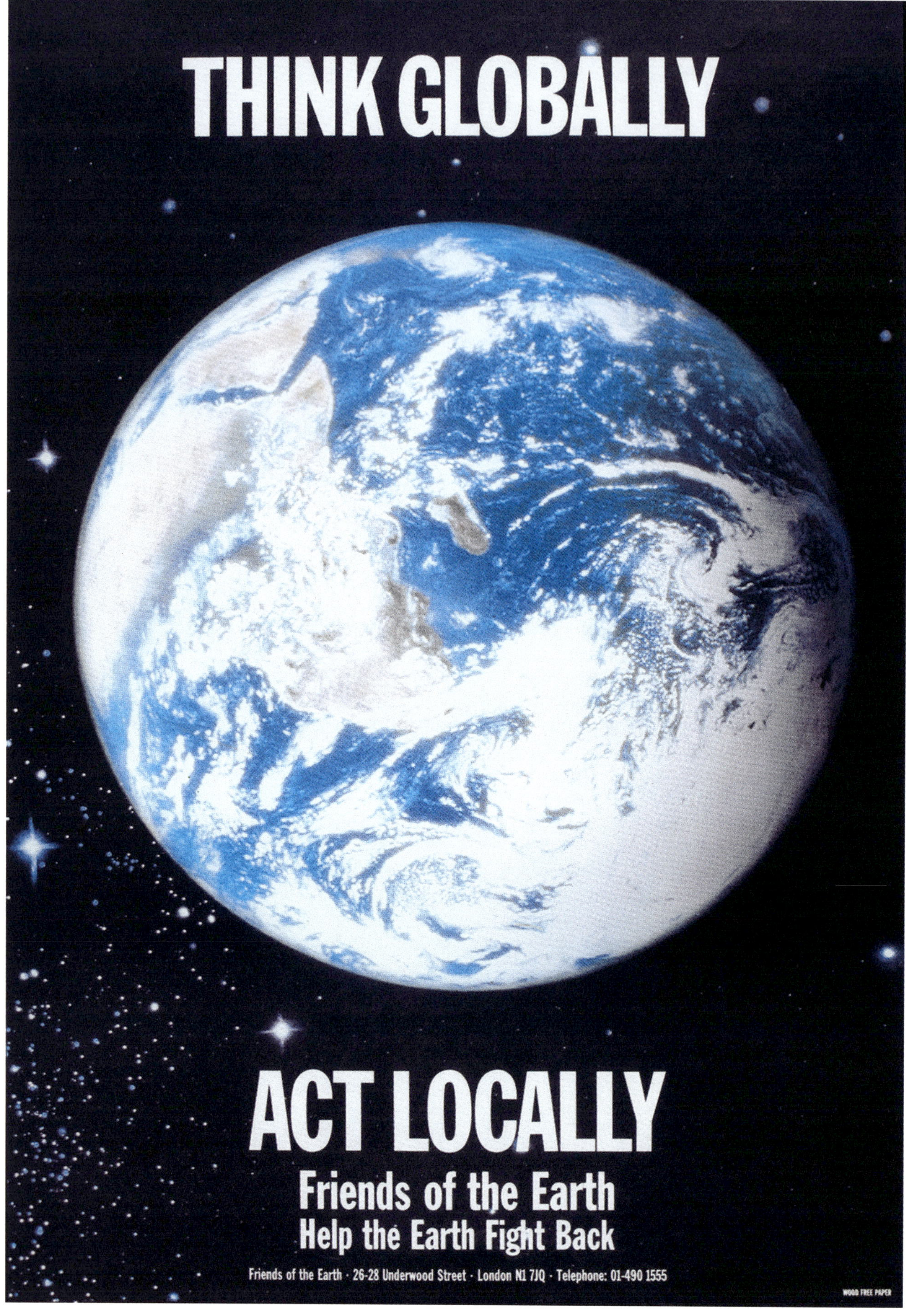

Think Globally, Act Locally, poster issued by Friends of the Earth, about 1990, V&A

a transformative, civic act. Through the mix of global and local practitioners featured in the galleries, Why We Make echoes the communities and creative histories of this part of the city: from designer and socialist visionary William Morris, who grew up in Walthamstow, and Newham-born fashion designer Alexander McQueen, to the many cross-cultural practitioners who for decades have adopted east London as their home. Today's thriving landscape of creative studios is woven into Why We Make: from fashion designers Molly Goddard and Nasir Mazhar to studio ceramicist Bisila Noha and photographers Stephen Gill, Tom Hunter, Jamie Hawkesworth and Hassan Hajjaj, to name just a few. Beyond individuals, local issues inform many of the galleries' topical themes – from post-pandemic concerns about urban well-being to pressing conversations about gentrification and the voice of communities in these debates. Transcultural and polyvocal, the galleries echo the multicultural spirit of east London itself.

Drivers of museum practice

Responding to this context, Why We Make foregrounds new models of curating that de-centre traditional canons of knowledge and put the perspectives of audiences first. Four curatorial drivers define this approach.

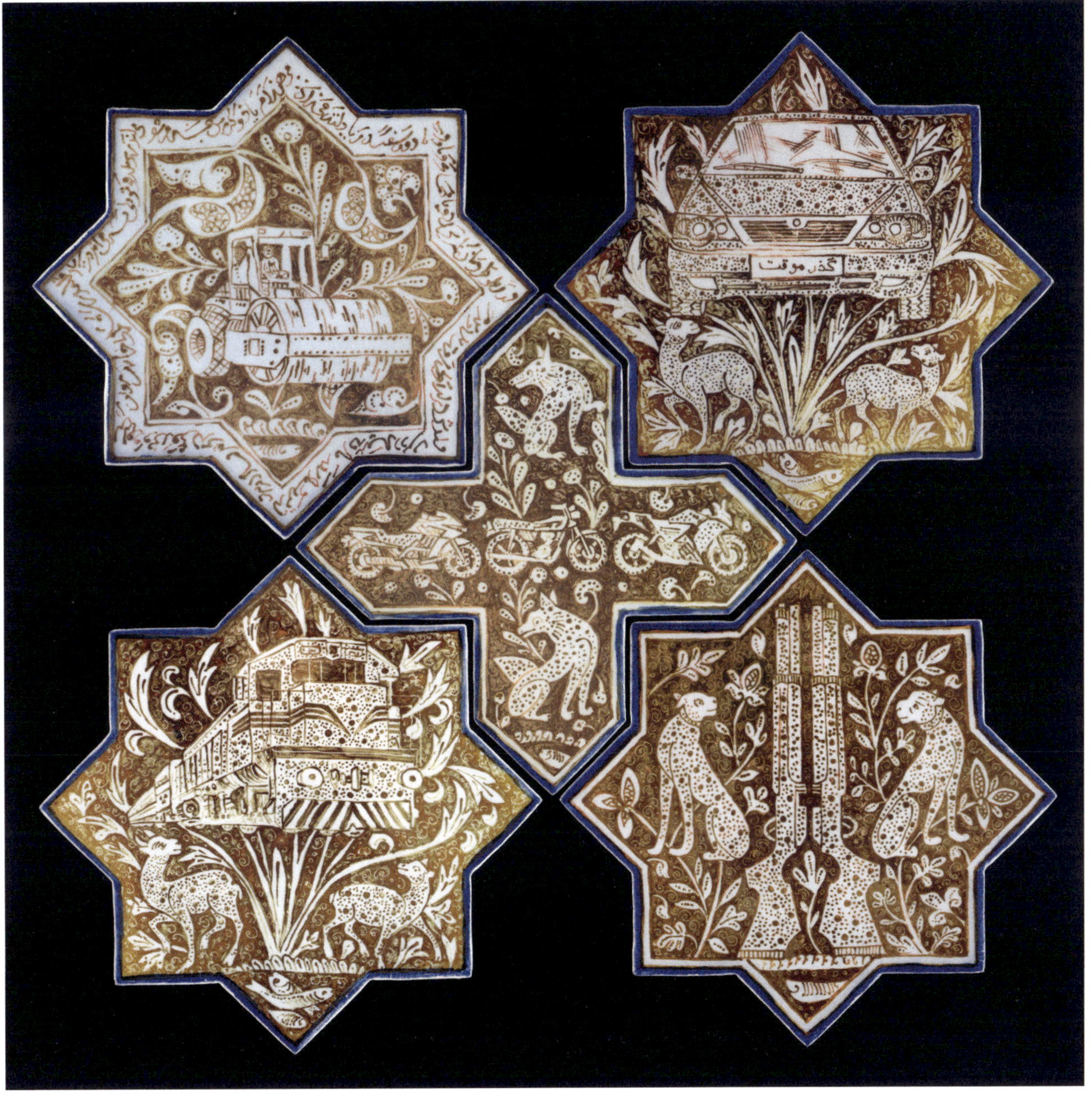

Tiles from the series 'Kashi and Kashan', by Abbas Akbari, 2019, V&A

A contemporary lens

The first driver explores the V&A collection though a contemporary lens, focusing on the issues that matter to audiences most. Nigerian curator and educator Okwui Enwezor argued that exhibitions cannot escape the context of the 'messy world' they inhabit, and ultimately need to serve a role in civic discourse 'as a forum of public discovery of art's potential in the face of difficulty'.[2] It is not without significance that critical research years for these galleries coincided with moments of turbulent global upheaval, from the Covid-19 pandemic and Black Lives Matter protests to armed invasions, escalating displacement and looming evidence of an advancing climate crisis. Why We Make responds to this rapid flux of world events and the bigger picture of living in 'the critical decade' for mitigating damage to our planet's climate.[3] V&A East Museum opened in 2026, beyond mid-way on the road to the 2030 goals for drastically reducing global carbon emissions, as set out in the 2016 Paris Agreement. Climate policy negotiators Christiana Figueres and Tom Rivett-Carnac have poignantly called this a pivotal decade for 'the future we choose'.[4] The narratives of Why We Make speak to questions about possible futures.

A transhistorical approach

The second driver is a transhistorical approach that connects objects from diverse geographies and periods and explores their relevance for the concerns of today's world. Over its 170-year history, the V&A's holdings and displays have been shaped by shifting priorities and collecting strategies focused on materials, geographies and chronologies of design and style. Why We Make has its starting point in the premise that these collections can be a repository for *new* stories. By foregoing traditional art-historical chronologies and disciplinary taxonomies, collection objects are brought into fresh dialogues. These thought-provoking juxtapositions highlight continuities in the agendas of practitioners across time. In 2015, Dutch designer Hella Jongerius and educator Louise Schouwenberg launched the 'Beyond the New' manifesto – a rousing call for designers to recognise the enduring relevance of historic making practices. In their words:

> We advocate for an idealistic agenda in design, as we deplore the obsession with New for the sake of the New, and regretfully see how the discipline lacks an intimate interweaving of the values that once inspired designers, as well as the producers of their ideas.[5]

Echoing this call, Why We Make tests the possibilities for 'a transhistorical museum' and invites exploring pertinent continuities – from early modern models of ecological making to pioneering statements on identity politics that go back hundreds of years. As argued by cultural theorist Mieke Bal, rather than causing a loss of understanding of historical difference this invites seeing historic objects anew, 'not as a heritage from the past but as partners in a discussion of what matters in contemporary culture'.[6] As starting points for new conversations, museum objects live a life in front of constantly changing audiences.

Expanding canons

The third curatorial driver expands traditional canons to centre global and diverse creative practices. Why We Make actively foregrounds people, places and practices marginalised by hitherto dominant canons of Western art and design history, while strategic acquisitions made through V&A East projects support ongoing work to diversify the V&A collection – from under-celebrated women practitioners and self-trained makers to traditions of global ecological architecture not previously collected by the V&A.

As highlighted by American curator Maura Reilly in her writings on curatorial activism, the quest to widen representation is far from over.[7] Broadening the sourcebooks for creative

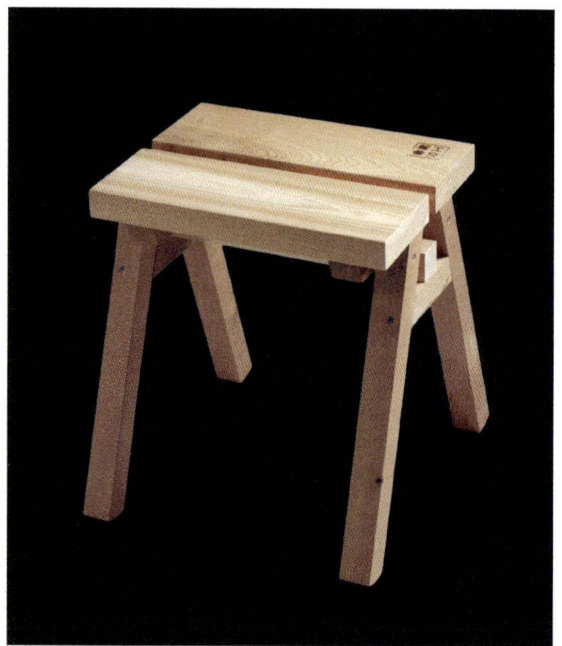

Ishinomaki stool, designed by Keiji Ashizawa, 2011, produced by the Ishinomaki Laboratory, 2015, V&A

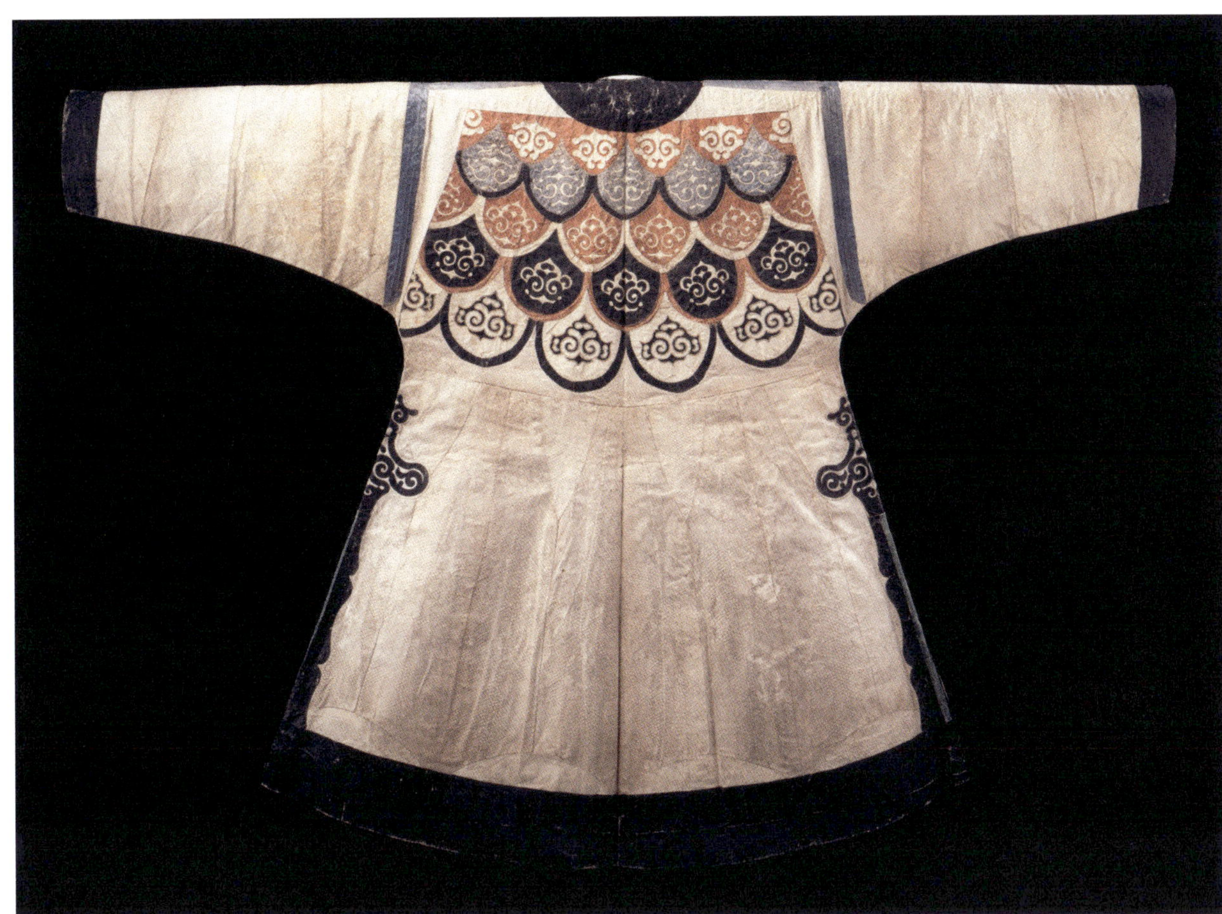

Salmon skin coat, Amur River estuary, eastern Siberia, by unrecorded Nivkh woman maker, about 1900, V&A

practice is urgent in a globally connected world that needs to find pathways to a more equitable and environmentally balanced future. Past calls for socially responsible practice from 1970s design critics like Victor Papanek remain relevant but need updating.[8] As argued by anthropologist Arturo Escobar in his writings about 'designs for the pluriverse', de-centring Western progressivist histories of functionalism and technology is a vital step in the transition to more relational, ecologically minded forms of making.[9] Educator, activist and designer Julia Watson has proposed the notion of 'design by radical indigenism' as a movement that rebuilds understanding of traditional ecological knowledge systems to generate climate resilient designs.[10] Such projects are among many in the field calling for the broadening of canons. Why We Make seeks to serve as a platform for expanded, plural sourcebooks for making practice.

Thinking through practice

The fourth driver considers how a museum project such as V&A East can create and learn from new models of institutional working and test curatorial strategies with fellow staff. Creating these galleries has inspired important reflections on the V&A's institutional history as a museum founded in the nineteenth century, bound up in legacies of colonialism and the optimism of the Industrial Revolution – eras with consequences for the social justice and environmental agendas that are pressing today. Why We Make has been attuned to conversations around museum strategies addressing environmental responsibility and inclusivity, alongside ground-up initiatives such as staff reading groups exploring decolonisation and the Anthropocene. The design of the Why We Make Galleries, by JA Projects and A Practice for Everyday Life, together with sustainability consultants URGE Collective, extends reflective practice further into V&A East through a radical scheme rooted in salvage, local material sourcing and carbon footprint tracking. As a testing ground, Why We Make is ultimately an invitation for new conversations through museum collections.

Zofia Trafas White, Senior Curator

Visualisation of views inside Gallery 1, V&A East Museum, JA Projects, 2025

A Journey Through the Why We Make Galleries
Zofia Trafas White

The Why We Make Galleries bring together over 500 objects from the V&A collection, drawn from diverse geographies, disciplines and time periods, from the 1100s to the present day. The narrative is shaped by the voices and stories of practitioners, both known and unrecorded, who are brought together into thematic dialogues that explore their shared motivations for making. Over 220 makers from 50 countries are featured, intermixing global stories with those local to east London. The galleries are subdivided into 10 thematic sections that collectively speak to attitudes and agendas for making in the twenty-first century. Creative disciplines are brought together within this thematic structure: from photography, fashion, textiles, architecture, furniture, product and performance design to painting, graphics, sculpture and ceramics. The juxtapositions of diverse practitioners and objects are deliberate, but also invite serendipitous connections and new narratives to be shaped by visitors.

The first set of five themes, occupying Gallery 1, explores personal and collective stories of identity, creative careers and community endeavours. The second set, occupying Gallery 2, expand into a bigger picture of political and ecological systems, exploring works that inspire reflection and action around topical issues today.

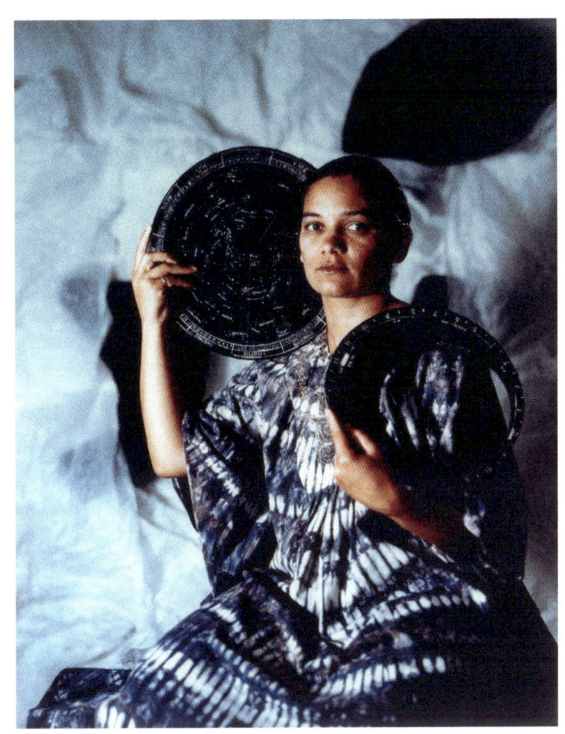

Urania (Portrait of Lubaina Himid) from the series 'Zabat', by Maud Sulter, 1989, V&A

Gallery 1

Our Place in the World

'It's important for me as an individual, and obviously as a Black woman artist, to put Black women back in the centre of the frame – both literally within the photographic image, but also within the cultural institutions where our work operates.'[1]

Maud Sulter, photographer

From portraiture to diverse imaginings of the Earth, the opening section, 'Our Place in the World', explores the power of creativity to make people and systems visible. Tuned to topical agendas around representation, identity politics and environmental consciousness, it considers experiments in portraiture and fashion over centuries that assert diverse identities: from the work of pioneering women photographers like Ghanaian Scottish Maud Sulter and Iranian Shadi Ghadirian to statement dresses by British designer Molly Goddard and monumental portraits by American artist Kehinde Wiley. Beyond the personal, collective understandings of our place in wider ecosystems are explored through cosmological maps and pioneering photographs of our planet taken from space.

Breaking Boundaries

'To create, one must first question everything.'[2]

Eileen Gray, furniture designer and architect

'Breaking Boundaries' considers the careers of trailblazing pioneers who redefined their professions and advanced inclusive and transcultural trends, from fashion to theatre.

Golden Harvest furnishing fabric for Hull Traders Ltd, by Althea McNish, 1959, V&A

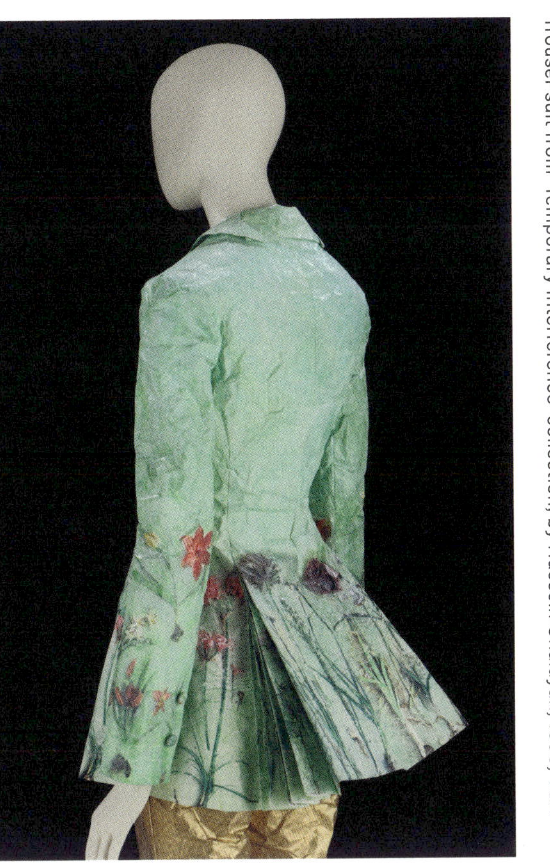

Trouser suit from 'Temporary Interference' collection, by Hussein Chalayan, 1995, V&A

Daring subversions of style in eighteenth-century silk dressmaking and 1980s punk by British designers Anna-Maria Garthwaite and Vivienne Westwood are considered alongside genre-defying designs for opera and dance from cross-disciplinary artists like Derek Jarman, Leigh Bowery and Mr Pearl. The influential role of émigré figures is celebrated through stories of pioneering businesswomen such as Irish-born Eileen Gray and British Trinidadian Althea McNish.

Crafting Stories

'You have to push forward and realise the power of fantasy and escapism.'[3]

Alexander McQueen, fashion designer

'Crafting Stories' celebrates the transformative power of the imagination. This section considers how creative practitioners are motivated to produce works of art and design beyond function, in which humour and symbolism come together to enable escapism, critique or thought-provoking speculation. Examples of catwalk couture from British Cypriot fashion designer Hussein Chalayan and Japanese streetstyle from Takuya Angel consider storytelling through clothes, while playful postmodern chairs meet early modern cabinets in an exploration of crafting narratives in the realm of the home. Dark humour and works of critical design by British duo Dunne & Raby offer comment on topical debates, while fantastical drawings and carnival costumes in the work of British artists Hew Locke and Keith Khan confront troubled histories of colonialism. Experimental works across ceramics and digital art reveal new forms of personal storytelling.

Building Creative Communities

'Through our activities, the belief is that DIY and design can energise people and communities – and life as a whole – in any situation or environment.'[4]

Ishinomaki Laboratory

'Building Creative Communities' brings together a roster of visionary practitioners from across the globe to explore how artists and designers can drive social change. From socialist visions for textile factories from William Morris and Indian designer Asha Sarabhai to innovative homeware-producing community enterprises led by collectives like the Ishinomaki Laboratory in Japan and the British Assemble studio, this section showcases diverse projects committed to creative education, empowerment and worker welfare. Case studies of training centres like the

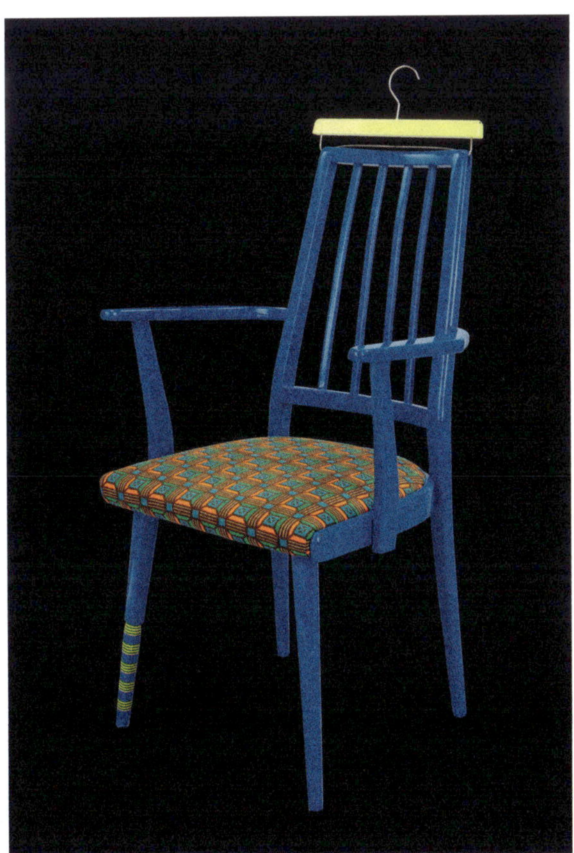

Captain Hook armchair from the series 'If Chairs Could Talk', by Yinka Ilori, 2015, V&A

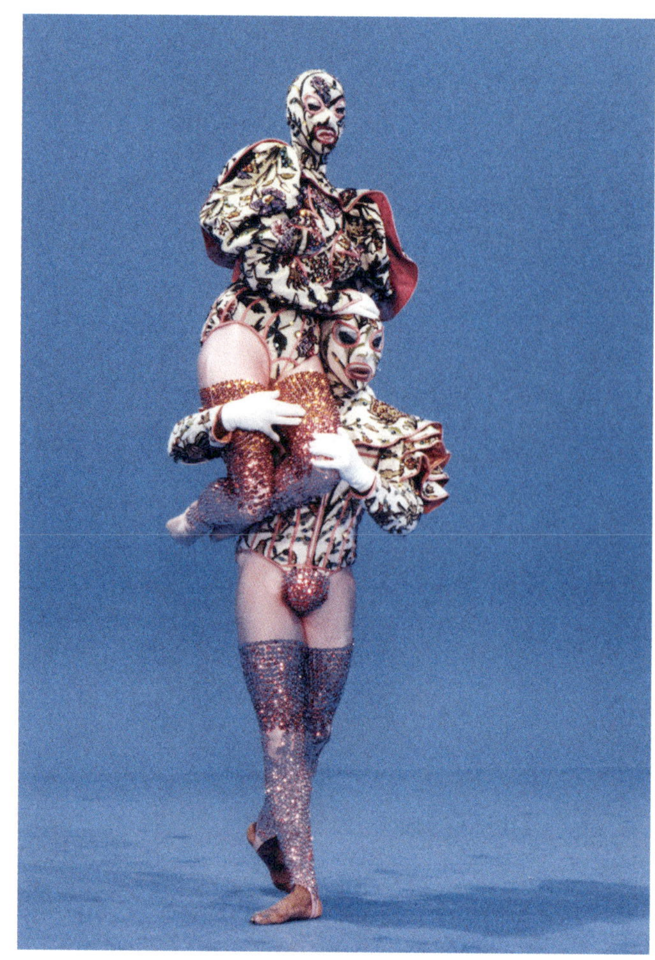

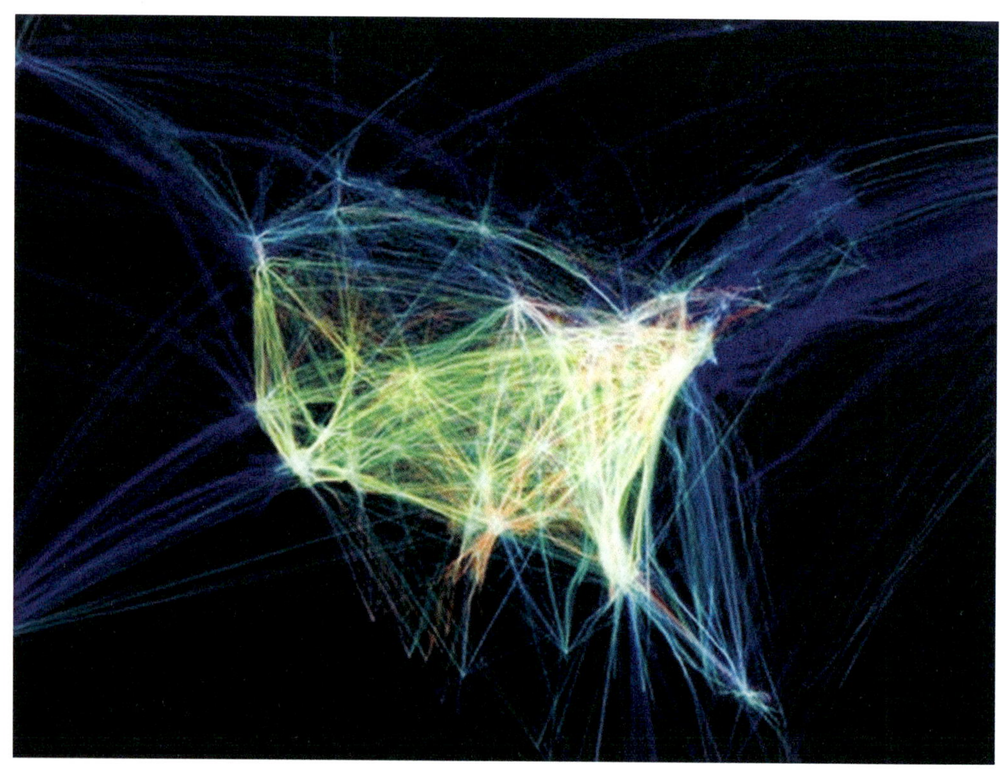

above Costumes for Michael Clark's ballet *Because We Must*, by Leigh Bowery with corset-maker Mr Pearl (Mark Erskin Pullen), 1987, V&A below *Flight Patterns*, digital animation, by Aaron Koblin, 2009, V&A

Nigerian Abuja Pottery and Egyptian Wissa Wassef Art Centre reveal how, through objects, knowledge is passed on through generations of students and apprentices, fostering longstanding communities of making.

Caring for Ourselves

'My intent is to express human endurance and deliver a message of reassurance: that human suffering can be healed.'[5] Lawson Oyekan, sculptor

'Caring for Ourselves' responds to contemporary concerns with well-being by considering design and material culture for healing. In the ceramics of Lebanese potter Nathalie Khayat, the photographs of British artist Jo Spence and the collaborative needlework projects of the charity Fine Cell Work, diverse stories of craft reveal how making provides solace in adversity. Designs for urban green space alongside therapeutic interiors demonstrate how, across centuries, cultures of making have harnessed the restorative powers of the natural world. Preoccupations with empowering the human body are explored through a global range of ritual artefacts, from protective talismans to therapeutic wearables that navigate human experience across physical and spiritual life.

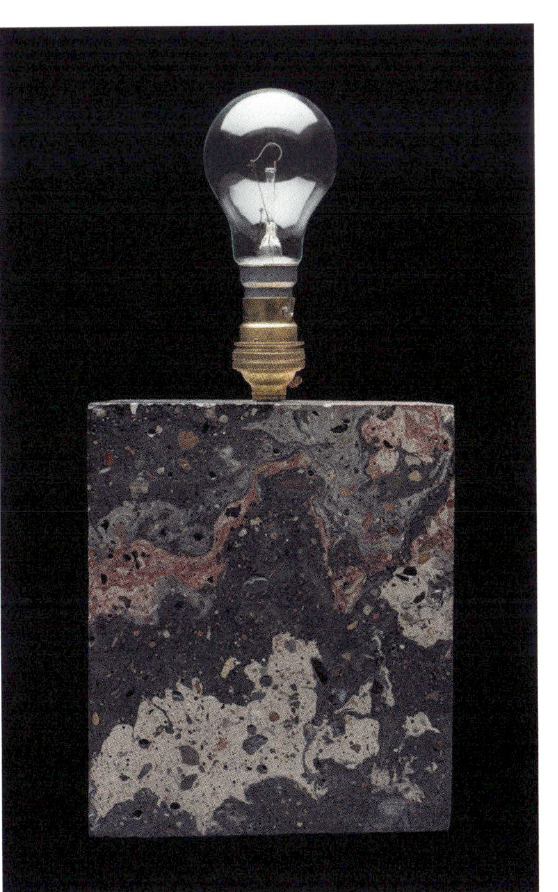

Table lamp made from Granby Rock, by Granby Workshop, 2015–16, V&A

Gallery 2

Revealing a World in Flux

'In the past it has been the job of artists to reflect on the choices being made by society, in this age of technology and global issues I see this as one approach to that task.'[6] Aaron Koblin, digital media artist

'Revealing a World in Flux' considers the long-standing role of creative practitioners as observers, bearing witness to significant events and places, drawing on their lived experiences and making sense of the world through visual means. Complementing 'Our Place in the World', this section presents projects that expose hidden systems, political events and broader forces of social and ecological change. From painting and photography to new forms of digital mapping, it explores how artists and designers have pushed the tools of making to develop new understandings of the world – from traditional decorative textiles reimagined as secret documents of civil uprising in the work of Cairo tentmaker Hany 'Abd al-Kader to pioneering visualisations of flight data by American digital artist Aaron Koblin, whose work invites reflection on the impacts of human activity.

Voicing Dissent

'My aim was to capture in a simple form what I was witnessing: the birth and spread of collective rebellion against injustices and the desire for freedom.'[7] Jerzy Janiszewski, graphic artist

Moving from reflection to response, 'Voicing Dissent' considers the power of making as a tool of resistance and solidarity. Exploring stories of protest on issues of politics, climate crisis, racism and inequality, this section brings together subversive graphic design and rebellious accessories from across centuries. From logos that defined political campaigns to private acts of defiance through craftivism and secret jewellery, and from nineteenth-century anti-slavery reticules to a 2010s pussy hat, the unique power of objects to make political statements is considered.

Rethinking Systems

'Repair-Making is social as well as material: a field of exciting actions, communities and politics, changing objects, mindsets and habits.'[8] Bridget Harvey, maker

'Rethinking Systems' champions the power of designers to drive systemic change, tackling

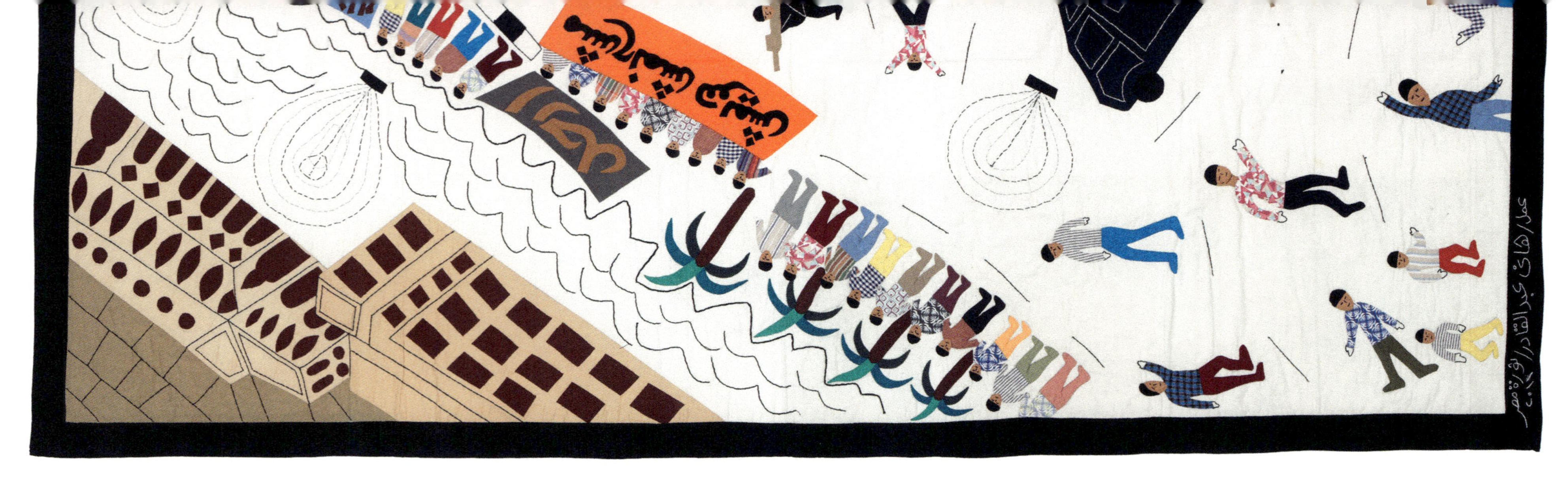

Second Revolution Khayyamiyya, textile panel, by Hany ʻAbd al-Kader, 2011–12, V&A

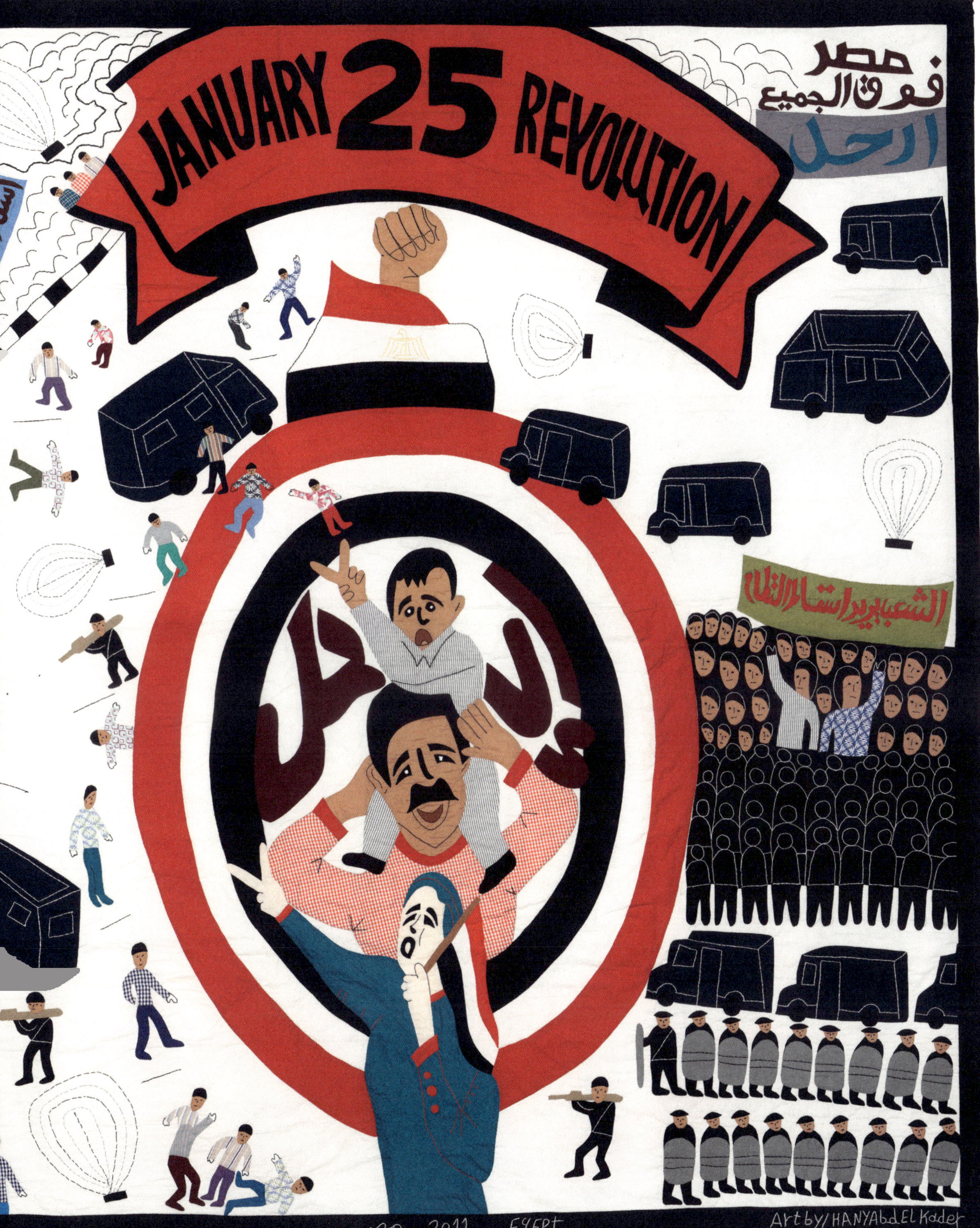
JANUARY 25 REVOLUTION
مصر فوق الجميع
ارحل
الشعب يريد اسقاط النظام
ارحل
مصر 2011 EYEPT
Art by/HANYAbdEl Kader

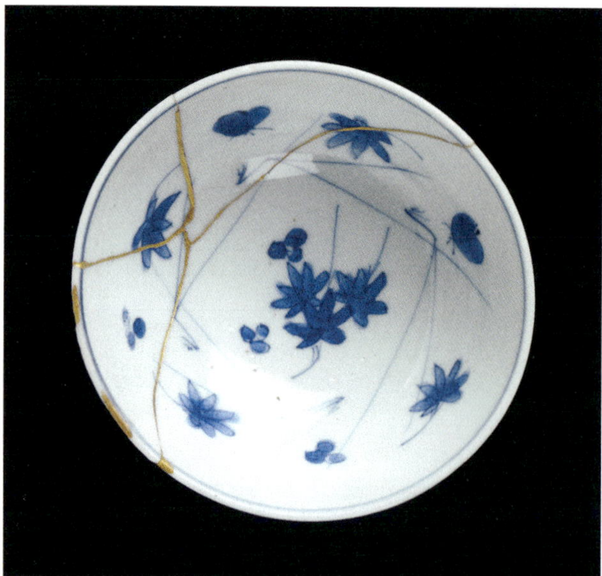

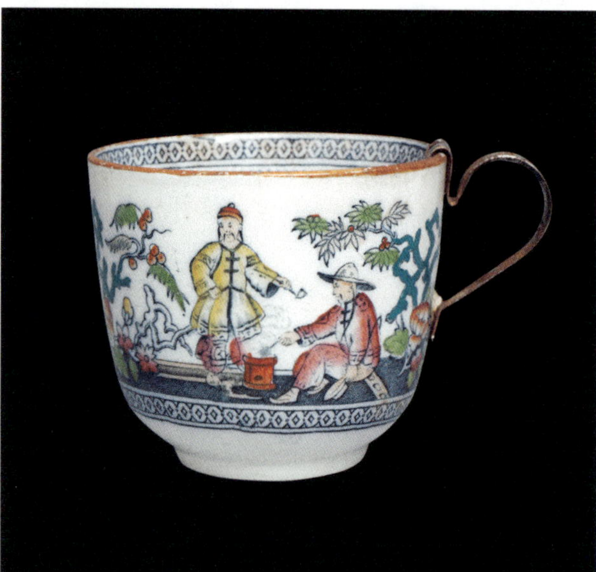

above Porcelain bowl, China (Jingdezhen), Ming dynasty, about 1550–1650, broken and repaired with gold lacquer (repair date unknown), V&A below Earthenware cup, Staffordshire or Sunderland, about 1880, with clip-on metal replacement handle designed by Frederick Warren Wilkes, about 1920, V&A

urgent agendas around environmentally responsible and resilient making practices attuned to the limits of our planet. This section brings together transhistorical projects and prototypes across furniture, fashion and products to explore the potential of circular design and manufacturing. Contemporary practitioners like British fashion designers Richard Malone and VIN+OMI and Berlin-based Chinese product designer YUUE Studio propose ways of rethinking the entire life cycle of objects, from materials origin to strategies for disposal, while historic examples of textile and ceramic repair offer pertinent models of object re-use. New forms of cross-disciplinary practice, bridging the fields of design and science, consider natural systems as a model of resource efficiency, while innovative bio-textiles lay pathways for avoiding waste.

Empowering Through Design

'To create a canvas on which communities can participate as equal partners, making every structure unique using their own innovations, and not to give them a finite product.'[9]

Yasmeen Lari, architect

'Empowering Through Design' considers how, by sharing design tools and expertise, makers can empower each of us with creative agency. Examining a diverse range of socio-economic contexts around the world, this section considers campaigns for 'access to tools' that have proved groundbreaking. From the feminist causes enabled by community printing, such as the See Red Women's Workshop, and east-London-based Rabbits Road Press run by collective One of My Kind (OOMK), to post-war do-it-yourself guides for furniture making and contemporary humanitarian projects by Pakistani architect Yasmeen Lari, the civic potential of accessible making is revealed. Stories of designer-user collaboration behind inclusive, accessible products also consider the potential of mass production to serve equitable design solutions.

Reimagining Traditions

'We wanted to integrate traditional practices and beliefs with innovative technology, because climate change cannot be handled by engineering alone.'[10]

Sonam Wangchuk, co-founder of the Himalayan Institute of Alternatives Ladakh (HIAL)

'Reimagining Traditions' brings together past and contemporary makers to explore how vernacular and indigenous traditions from across the globe can inspire future-facing, environmentally responsible practice. This section draws into dialogue diverse projects from around the world that take inspiration from historic crafts and Traditional Ecological Knowledge (TEK). From the revival of ancient food systems in the work of Fernando Laposse in Mexico to teaching programmes that revisit Indian earth-building traditions at the Himalayan Institute of Alternatives Ladakh, and bamboo architecture by Ibuku in Bali, indigenous materials knowledge is seen as vital in tackling the climate challenges of today. Artists and designers can be central in reimagining traditions, making these practices relevant in new and unexpected ways.

Zofia Trafas White, Senior Curator

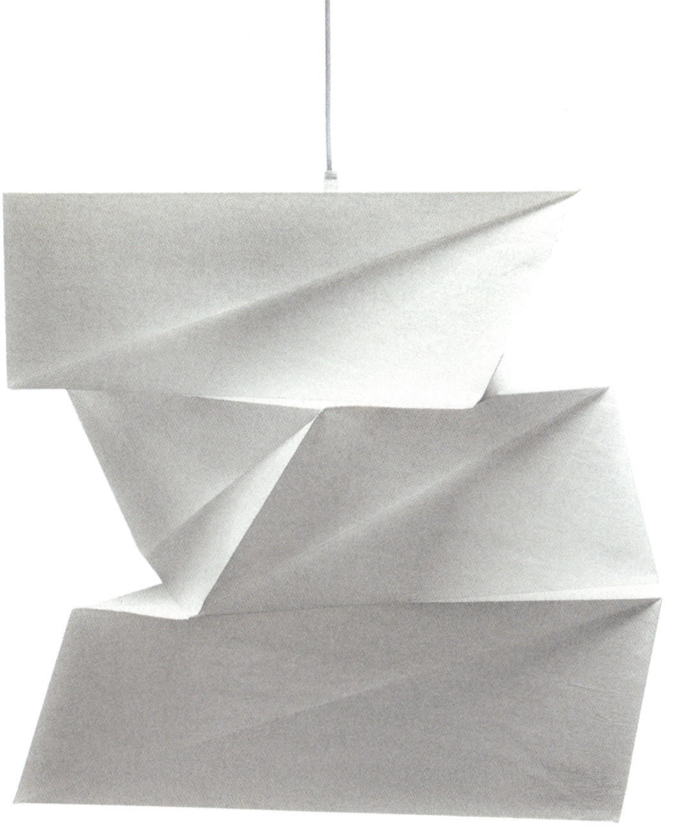

above *Katatsumuri* light from the 'IN-EI' range, Issey Miyake / Reality Lab for Artemide in collaboration with Teijin Limited and Jun Mitani, 2012, V&A below Architectural student study model for HIAL Staff Quarters, by Himalayan Institute of Alternatives Ladakh (HIAL), 2022, V&A

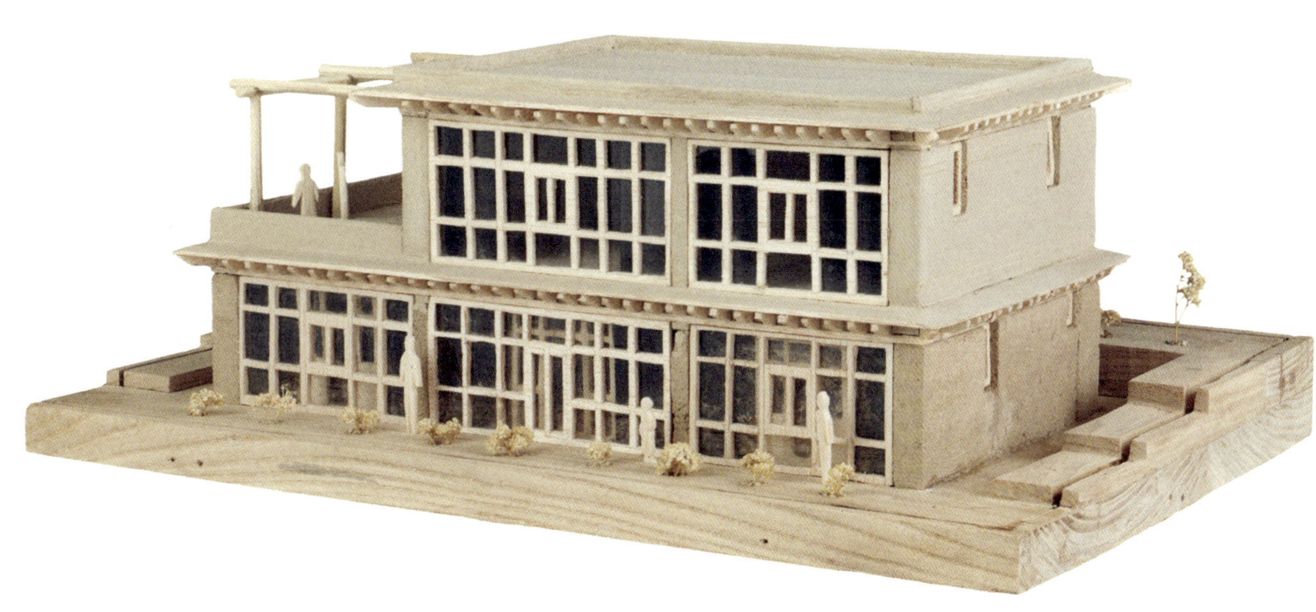

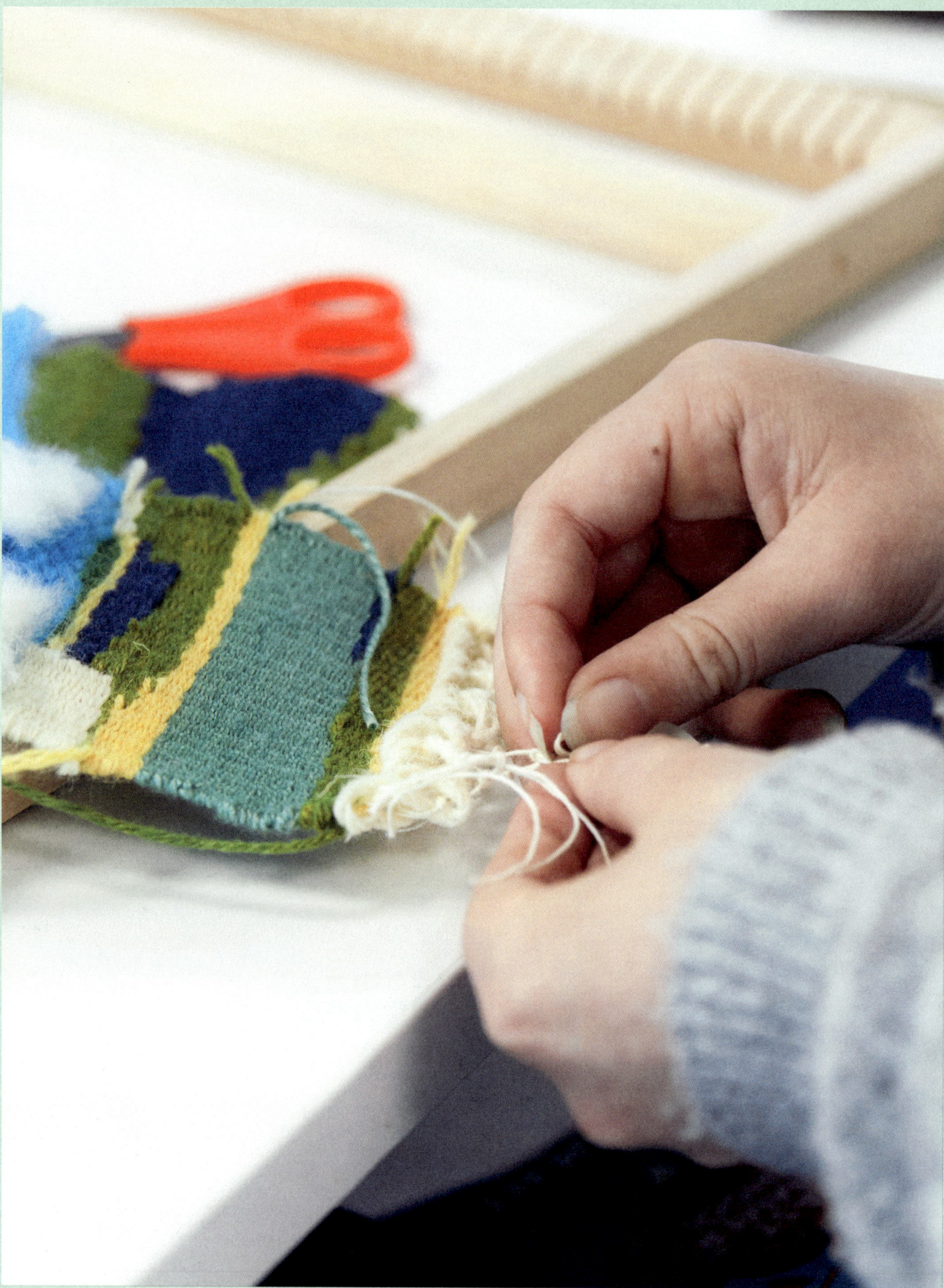

V&A East Summer School with Dalia James, 2023

Why Do You Make?

The Why We Make Galleries explore the underlying agendas that motivate artists, designers and creative practitioners from around the world to engage in making and creative processes. Making is not neutral, and behind every project there are underlying goals, ambitions and intentions. For a more granular snapshot of these motivating forces, members of our V&A East Youth Collective sat down with local London creatives to discuss their careers in the creative sector, to dissect why they do what they do, and what happens when you apply creativity as an ethos to everyday life.

All photographs in 'Why Do You Make?' by Abiola Remi-Lawal

Bisila Noha and Ruqaiya Asim

Ruqaiya Asim Why do you make?

Bisila Noha I love the process of working with clay; it is a fantastic material. I also make because I think crafts and arts have a lot of power to help us engage with difficult topics, to raise awareness about different issues and to make the world a better place.

RA Is the material of clay important to your process?

BN It is, but I am also discovering other materials with which I can have that interaction. When I make, generally I make a shape that would be the canvas. It starts as a big flat piece or a vessel. Then, when I come to the decoration, I have all these ideas in my head that I want to achieve, but I don't know exactly what is going to come out with each piece. So, it's about the first line that I make and then it's a conversation with the material. Its tactility allows me to experiment as I make.

RA How did you get to where you are now?

BN I didn't study art; I studied translation and then international relations. I moved to London and a friend recommended that I did pottery, so I went on a course and I loved it. I started going to more courses and then I did a residency and an apprenticeship; I travelled to Mexico. After six months I came back and I started making and selling. At the beginning I made tableware, plates, mugs, smart orders for shops and restaurants etc. But I always wanted to make differently; I never really enjoyed making lots of things in one day and everything looking the same. I wanted to develop a bigger project, and once I had I felt this is the way I need to work, I want to work.

RA Do you have a personal manifesto or approach that drives your work?

BN For me, the main thing is to challenge the norm in terms of what historically has been considered art. So, I apply that to the type of clay that I use and the type of vessels that I make. Also, I have been focusing on Black women from the Global South, who to me are the first makers, and how the work they have been making, because it's domestic and handmade, has been completely ignored and erased from history.

RA Can you describe the pieces that will be on display at V&A East?

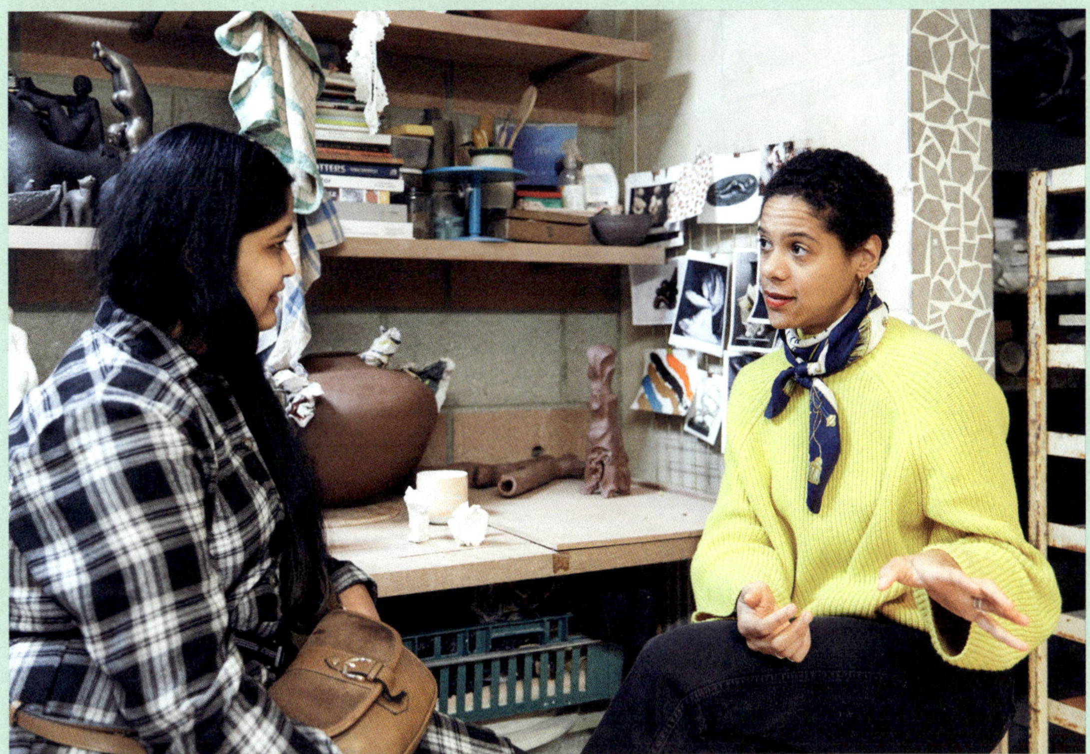

Ruqaiya Asim and Bisila Noha, 2024

BN There are two, and both are two-legged vessels. They are part of a collection of 25 pieces, and each piece is different. The shape comes from the work of a woman from Tanoh Sakassou in Ivory Coast; her name is Kouame Kahahá. This is a piece that she's been making for a long time. I developed this collection to give her work visibility. I went to her village and spent 13 days with her.

RA Can you tell me more about that?

BN There's this cooperative in the village and there's around 30 people making there. It's a village of around 800 people, in the middle of the Ivory Coast, and every morning I would sit at the pottery making pots along with them. Kahahá is still making, but mostly inside her house. It was just like a day of work at the studio but surrounded by all these people speaking in French and Baulé. I had an interpreter, and I learnt a lot: this is the way they make, the way they see the world, understand the world and the way they interact with their work.

RA You've mentioned Black women and heritage. I'm a fine art student, and my background is from Pakistan. I've been raised here, and I feel disconnected from my heritage. Do you have any advice for someone who feels a bit disconnected from their culture but wants to bring it into their practice?

BN For me, the main thing that has helped me connect is actually the material. This journey started by working with clay from Baney, which is my dad's village in Equatorial Guinea. I made two collections with that clay and I started talking about the place. Then I went to Baney for the first time in 12 years, and when I arrived I realised I felt there the connection that I had developed with the clay and with the producers by talking about it.

RA It's interesting how you're taking materials from your culture and heritage and using them, and that's how you've connected with it. Has that informed your practice since?

BN Since that, I've mainly only worked with terracotta. Going back to my manifesto, terracotta is not a material that you will necessarily see in exhibitions, galleries and museums unless it's something about ethnographic research. I use it on purpose because to me it's equally valid as a material and it is extremely beautiful as well.

RA When I was looking at the V&A East pieces you're going to display, I was interested in how you came up with the title.

BN The main title is *Reunion* because these pieces are from the 'Searching for Kouame Kahahá' project. They have been a way of connecting with this woman in particular, but, to me, she also represents all the other women throughout the history of pottery who have been ignored. It was me coming together with these women and with this heritage.

RA On your website, you refer to topics like the forgotten and the ignored. Could you talk more about that?

BN I co-direct an art and activism organisation, Lon-art Creative. Our main project is called 'Sheroes' and it's about women artists. In 2019, we started a project called 'Sheroes Revoluciones'. It was inspired by all the revolutions, mainly in South America, started by women to fight for their rights. We hosted an exhibition with 30 artists from all over the world to talk about violence against women and girls, not just domestic violence, but in the broader sense. The special thing about that exhibition was that most of the artists were talking about their own experiences of violence over the years. They used their art practices to share it openly. These women were speaking up not only to process their own journeys but also to empower other women to do this and to raise awareness about the topic. That's when I started to focus on the forgotten and the invisible.

RA What stories have you learned about women of colour that have inspired your work?

BN My next body of work is about is Pearl Primus; she was an American dancer, choreographer and anthropologist, and she changed contemporary dance in America by bringing in elements of dance from the Caribbean and

Africa, particularly West Africa. She travelled to different countries to get really embedded in those cultures. That's something that I find extremely inspiring, the element of immersing yourself in an environment to embody it.

RA Is there anything in particular that you've learned about your own heritage by incorporating all of this into your artwork?

BN I think the fact that I come from a mixed heritage is a very important part of my practice. I'm always mixing things and putting together things that at first might be controversial, like how I mix clays or how I make materials with plaster and clay. I think that's part of who I am.

RA How does your own personal story come through in your work, and how does London come through?

BN My own personal history has come through because it's been through working with clay that I have embraced my Blackness. Being in London is having access to so many people and all the exhibitions, and access to culture and knowledge. I wouldn't be able to make the work that I make if I was in Spain. I sometimes struggle to talk about certain topics in Spanish because I don't have the language because I've learned or developed my own thinking in English. I am who I am because I've lived in London.

RA You went from making cups and plates and then you brought in your identity and Black women. Were you afraid to make that transition or did it come naturally to you?

BN It came naturally because I was going through that transition personally. Before I moved to London, I grew up in Spain, in white culture. I was the only Brown person everywhere except for in my house. I grew up thinking I was white and then I came to London and then I got into Black feminism. I remember reading Angela Davis and realising all the internalised racism that I had, everything that I had been missing, how I didn't know who I was. Then by using clay from my dad's village, everything came together.

VIN+OMI and Joanna Afroozi

Joanna Afroozi Why do you make?

VIN+OMI We both have a deep-rooted desire to make and always have multiple projects on the go at any time. When we started making as a brand in 2000, however, we had to put a stop to just producing. The overwhelming principle of not wanting to do the wrong thing for the planet became paramount. There was a turning point when we thought about how we had to curb the urge to just make and shift our creative thinking to the wider process. We see VIN+OMI, the brand, as a large making project. Every day, we craft the way we move forward. Creating our dresses and interiors is hands on, tactile making. The crafting of VIN+OMI is more nebulous, but we feel the same way about its development, as if it were a dress.

JA At what point did eco-activism find its way into your designs, and when did your work evolve from fashion into consultancy and other forms of art?

VO When we started out, our focus was on how we could get hold of materials that had been made ethically, hadn't been through 10 different people and didn't cost a fortune. We started with latex from Malaysia. We went to look at the plantations and they were terrible. The workers weren't being looked after and there were no educational programmes for the villages. We thought, 'We can do better than this.' We got some investment and put it into a plantation. The people needed to be treated right. The trees needed to be treated right. It was also about shipping the latex with other things to reduce the carbon footprint. Through that first project we learned a lot; that was 23 years ago.

We never set out to be in the fashion industry. It was blue-sky thinking, and a crazy idea of where sustainable design could go. In design, there is the frivolous idea that you can manufacture anything you want without thinking about the impact on the planet. We wanted to counter this attitude, so we started a manifesto. At the start, we were very naïve; we thought we could change the world.

When we started to realise the mess that the fashion industry was in, we wanted to challenge it. We don't like being part of a group where we have to go along with what everybody else thinks. The fashion world is about saying everything's wonderful and everyone's amazing, and that's not true. They've got their own way of dealing with things, which can be quite cutting, and they don't care a lot about the planet. We thought, 'We're nothing like these people so why should we join a group with them? Why should we be part of an industry we don't believe in?'

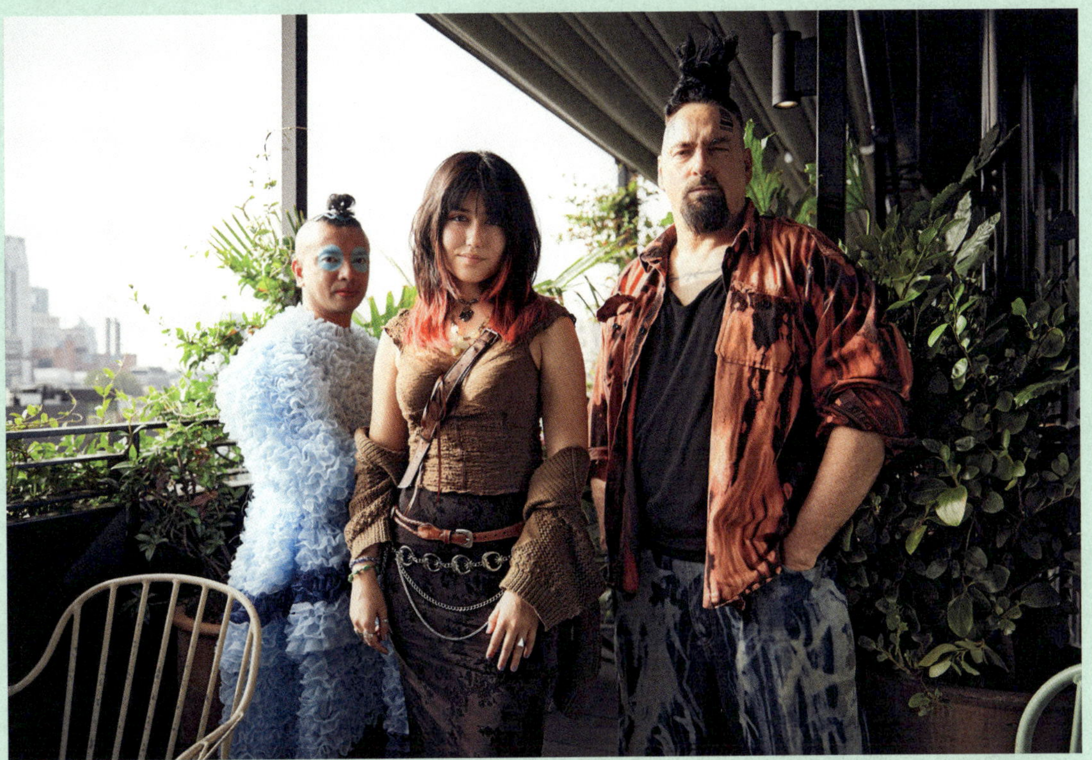

Joanna Afroozi and VIN+OMI, 2023

JA That's really inspiring, especially considering it was 23 years ago.

VO We were called hippies by the British Fashion Council and had lots of doors shut in our faces. But it was also a time when new scholarship allowed us to really understand about sustainability. Fashion became our tool in conveying that message; it's a language more universal than English. Everybody wears clothes so we thought they could be our canvas. We could write a million manifestoes and they would never be translated, but if we put something out on the catwalk, something innovative combining environmental, social and educational elements, that would create a conversation.

JA Knowing that your work is going to be archived at the V&A, what do you hope people will take from it?

VO We want to inspire young people to see that they can do things their own way and a major museum will recognise that.

The items going on display at V&A East originate from our engagement with the wider making process. The outfit made from the Team GB sailing equipment wasn't just a case of reworking discarded sailing materials. That project originated from a conversation with Olympic gold-medal-winner Hannah Mills, who we contacted due to her passionate work in recycling plastic and helping save the oceans. She donated materials from Team GB and walked in the show.

The nettle pieces stem from our exploration of the UK countryside and the questions of what large estates do with their organic waste.

This led to our meeting King Charles and discussions about what we could take from his estates.

We work 75 per cent of the time on paper, drawing every seam and figuring out how much electricity is going to be used. We ask what sort of educational programme we can inject into a garment and the innovations we can create around that. Once we have all of that, then we create the piece. Our practice plays with so many factors: the zeitgeist, popular culture, technology, social culture, diversifying of gender. Design is secondary.

JA Your work is political, but it stays at grassroots and is people and community orientated. Have you considered speaking on a global level?

VO There are a lot of institutions who ask for your opinions and then nothing is implemented. They like the idea of us sitting there, but I think we learnt that the way forward is working with people at the grassroots level and really understanding what communities need. That is where the power is. Not in Westminster. And all of our work is a rebellion. It's a statement, a manifesto. Every piece has a story.

It's not about the design; it's about the cause. We believe that in the future people will really think about the origins of their clothes. For example, in Summer 2023 we were at King Charles's private residence in Sandringham. In the grounds there is quite a rare plant, which grows out of control on the side of a lake. They gave us permission to wade into the lake and just take some of this plant. We made the world's first dress out of that plant and put it on the catwalk in September that year. We want people to see that process and think, wow, that plant had never been used before in a dress or textile. We developed something new and that's what we really enjoy doing.

We are powered by nature and our collaborators – be it King Charles, Debbie Harry, Michelle Obama, or whoever – all align with us on one thing: the environment. It's not about giving celebrities free clothes. It's about getting people to buy into our ideology.

JA I really like that, because there's been an explosion in looking aesthetic, which removes the meaning behind the creation of different garments. How do you feel about this and the disconnect it creates from the making process?

VO I hate it. Recently we were in Paris and decided to go to The Ritz. We were all made-up – Vin had a Mohican; I had my face painted and was in a dress – and we walked up to the door and were refused entry. Right next to us there was somebody who looked exactly as you described, that aesthetically perfect look that has no soul or meaning to it, and they walked straight in.

It's sad that design has gone down that road and has taken away the very essence of what makes someone creative, because commerciality has taken over.

JA What are your opinions on fast fashion?

VO Trends come and go in clothing; fast fashion may just be a trend and in 10 or 15 years there won't be fast fashion. Nor will there be really expensive designer brands, because they're obscene. Perhaps there will be a new way of looking at things; hopefully it will be smaller businesses that can make wonderful stuff for the right reasons.

JA People are programmed to buy as much as possible and to look as good as possible, and it removes meaning from clothing and from design. How do you deal with that when your work counteracts and encounters it every day?

VO I used to be so angry, but then I reached a point when I looked around and thought, 'We've created this wonderful community and that's enough.' Backstage at our shows it's all our friends working together, and it's fun. It's sad because a lot of our peers were wonderful, creative people, but the industry sucked the life and creativity out of them. When Vin and I started out we decided we couldn't go down that road.

JA Is all the meaning in your work translated through the making process, or do you also implement meaning through the words, colours and shapes you use?

VO When we start, process is king and where we get our raw materials from dictates what we make. What is wasted and left around is what we're working with for that season. For example, if they need to cut down the plants in a field to create a pathway, we get those plants, so we're working with them to develop fabric.

When we put words onto our clothes it's often when we're angry about something political. We did a show called 'Opinions', where all the models were asked to think of something that they really wanted to say. When you see 60 models come out at the end, all carrying signs, placards and posters, it gives a powerful message.

Shahed Saleem and Glenda Gaspard

Glenda Gaspard Why do you make?

Shahed Saleem I've always made, since I was a little kid. For me it's not just about seeing my ideas become some form of reality; it's also a way of exploring those ideas and taking them further. There is an impulse to make; an impetus to interpret the world as you experience it through making.

GG In your work we see a lot of plurality and seeking insights from others. Have you always been someone who has known how to navigate conversations into your creative journey, or has that come over time?

SS I think that has come along the way. When I was studying architecture there was still very much the idea of the architect as the single author. Thankfully now the designer is seen as much more a part of a wider conversation, but this was learned for me through working on projects. As an architect you are always working with clients who have ideas that you need to respond to. By incorporating their ideas, you often find that it leads to better solutions; through collaboration comes a better outcome.

GG You've mentioned an architect as an author and a collaborator. How would you define your practice?

SS My practice is quite multipolar; I move between making, teaching, research, exhibition work and writing. Sometimes these elements seem quite disparate, but gradually I've started to bring them together, so they overlap and feed into each other. Making feeds into teaching, teaching might feed into making and research comes out of practice work.

GG Could you tell us more about that research?

SS It started with researching the history of the mosque in Britain, looking at the ways in which mosques have been built and the processes by which this architectural typology has emerged. It was very much a community-driven process; these buildings were generated, built and designed by their users. This type of architecture is so important to migrant communities as a means of finding and creating their own cultural and religious spaces. So, while my research is fundamentally about the mosque as a building type, the bigger story is about how migrant communities settle in new places and create spaces they can inhabit.

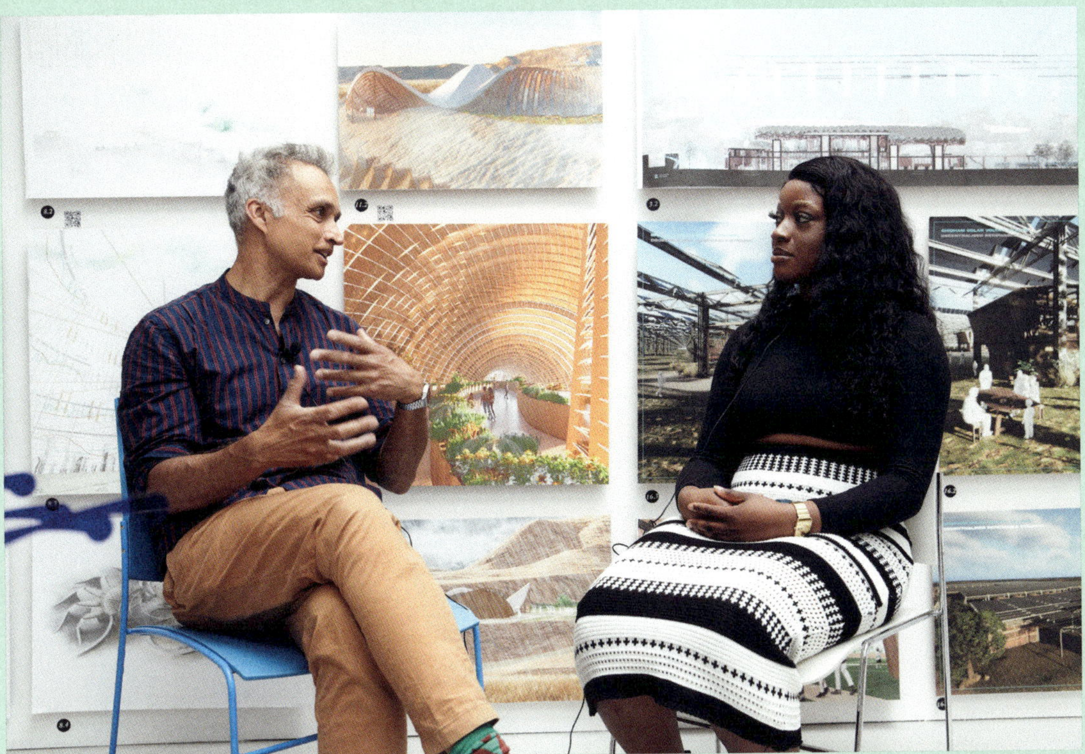

GG Why has that strand been so important to you?

SS It's important because it's my lived experience. My parents are from India; I grew up as child of a migrant family. It's partly about unpacking that experience. My parents were involved in setting up a mosque in South London as well, so I saw that whole process as a child.

GG What would you say are the main design drivers that inform your approach?

SS I tend to design step-by-step, working iteratively. I might have a broad concept for something but then I see how it evolves, letting the work inform the next steps.

GG That's such an interesting way of approaching design. With something like your pavilion at V&A South Kensington, how did your approach translate to a project like that?

SS Initially, I made a sketch of a pavilion in the courtyard of the V&A. It was the first thing that came to mind, capturing my feelings at that moment. Then I had something I could check back on throughout the process, because the sentiment in that drawing was the thing I didn't want to lose, wherever the design went.

The design language for the pavilion comes from drawings of mosque elements combined with features of domestic architecture. Those elements are arranged in a disparate way, connected within a structure, reflecting the way I feel mosques have been made in this country, the way migrant people make spaces, which is through different histories and memories combined into new compositions. There was also the idea of it making a statement to Muslim and other communities of diasporic backgrounds that they have a presence.

GG Your identity shines through in your work. You show up as your full self and invite people in to understand and experience glimpses of what the real identity of Muslim architecture is. How has your faith, your identity and your heritage shaped your practice?

SS My practice is about telling the stories of communities who have had a big impact, but that impact is largely unrecognised. What I've found is that in order to tell the stories of underrepresented communities you need a new methodology by which to tell them. Part of what I do is find new ways of uncovering and telling these underrepresented narratives.

GG It sounds like your making is a lot about challenging the way we make in general.

SS At university, we are pushed into this disconnect from our heritage by traditional narratives, which are important on one level, because it's all about learning. But we should also think, 'Where is this learning taking me? Is it taking me further from what I am or where I've come from?' That's what I've tried to do through my work and to look to more instinctive way of making as well as a return to self.

GG Being a Londoner, and with London being so personal to your work, are there any significant spaces that inspired you to explore that return to self?

SS Probably a lot of the mosque spaces I've visited through my research, because what you see in many of the self-built mosques, or adapted spaces, is a huge amount of creativity that comes from the people themselves.

GG It's the role of the maker in the hands of the community, it's very democratic.

SS Yes. For example, for some of the things we put in the Venice Architecture Biennale in 2021, which remade parts of three mosques in London, we don't know who made those pieces. For example, the calligraphy that decorated the Old Kent Road Mosque, which we recreated for the Biennale, we don't know who the artist was. And the *mihrab* in Harrow, which is going into V&A East, again, we don't know who made it. They are all things that are made as a result of being part of a community.

GG How does your work translate on the global stage? Do elements of your approach change when interacting with different people?

SS My approach does change because the audience is always reading things in a certain way. Earlier this year, I did a couple of presentations at the Islamic Arts Biennale, and I've often wondered, how does my work go down in a Muslim country where they don't have these issues of being minorities and having to make their own spaces? I still don't know exactly how it gets interpreted, but what I think is important is to try and take Muslim communities in the diasporas and connect them to the bigger history of Islamic art and architecture, because they often get left out of the traditional histories, which tend to focus on the Muslim world.

GG Given the groundwork that you and your peers have laid in relation to Islamic architecture in Britain, what do you think the impact will be for the next generation of makers who have that culture in common? I find it really inspiring to see people navigating and exploring their identity, and the way you bring the two worlds together, being a Londoner and exploring Islamic architectural typologies, it almost gives us more language to do that in our own remit.

SS It's amazing to think that the next generation are using the work that I, and my generation, do as a way of enabling them. I hope then that they take it further. What would be great is if people would do more work uncovering and documenting unrecorded histories; histories that would otherwise disappear. My work is only really a beginning; there's a huge amount to do and if people could find a way of continuing that it would be a really positive outcome for me.

GG Having explored all these points, I want to ask you the first question again: why do you make?

SS I was having a conversation with a curator, and she was talking about my work and how it destabilises and subverts dominant power structures in very subtle ways. I said to her that there is an anger inside all of us, a quiet anger, which drives what we do as migrants, as diasporas, as people who have experienced the Western world as outsiders and have seen our parents experience it. The reality is that that experience is not benign. There is a sense that things aren't right and haven't been right and at some level we're trying to redress that wrongness, and, in a way, making is one way of doing that.

Andu Masebo and Victoria Famoriyo

Victoria Famoriyo Why do you make?

Andu Masebo There's a simple answer to that question and a more complicated one. When you're young you feel good about the things that people congratulate you on. People said I was good at making and that made me feel good about myself, so I followed that route.

I guess a deeper answer is that as you get further along in your career you need to understand on a more profound level what you're trying to do. What I've realised is that, when I'm designing things, I think about the experience of making and the experience of using things. I'm always trying to shorten that gap between why something is made as it is and the person who has made it; thinking about how the person who made it might have felt and how the story of the object translates into the life of the person who lives with it. That's why I make.

VF That makes me think about how we consume and the gap between the producer and consumer; how we are often dissociated from the reality of production and consumption, that consumption requires resource and production requires sacrifice.

AM When you think about production, there are interesting stories to find in everything and if you can bring people into those stories then maybe they will care more about the objects themselves.

VF Who or what inspired you to start making?

AM Anyone who makes goes through different stages – there is the first person who inspires you at school; there is the gallery you go to when you're 15 and your mind is opened up; there is the person who mentors you through your first job – so it's hard to think of just one person who initially inspired me to start making. The person who inspires me now is the furniture and product designer Enzo Mari, who was arguably one of the godfathers of early modern design. He made things in his studio as well as manufacturing on a huge scale, but while he was doing all of that he was also very involved in politics, not in canvassing or political debate, but in how political decisions affect the way society is structured and how people's lives are impacted. He found an amazing way of weaving his politics into the products he made so that they held those values and, in my view, in some ways changed the world that they were in.

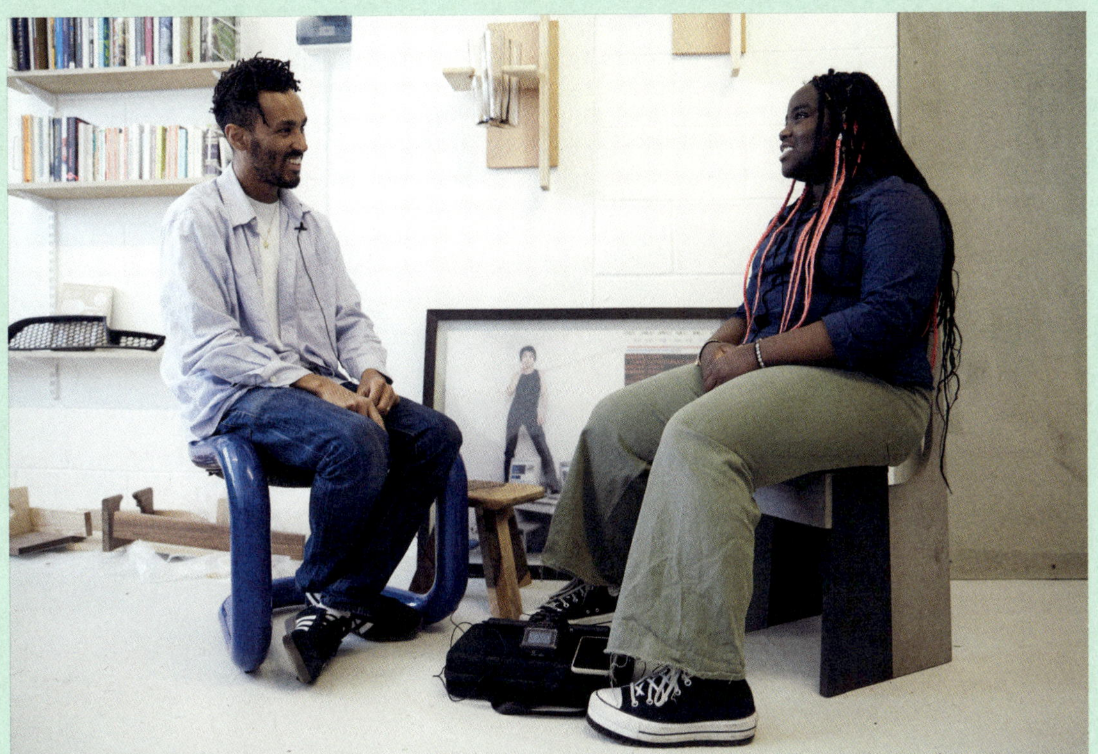

Victoria Famoriyo and Andu Masebo, 2023

VF How have you developed artistically throughout your career, and how do you hope to develop further?

AM I spent a lot of time when I was younger working as a maker so by the time I got to do my Master's I was quite disillusioned about making things, because it's not glamourous, working on a factory floor. So, I went to do my Master's with that mindset and I actually struggled to make anything that I thought was particularly interesting. But what I came to realise was that I wasn't making interesting work because I was ignoring a big part of who I was and how I worked. I realised that by embracing that part of me I didn't need to be a passenger on the narrative of what it was meant to be to be a maker; I didn't have to be the 'archetypal maker' to engage with the fact that I knew how to make.

I'd say to anyone that you are going to make the most interesting work, and the most meaningful connections with people in the world, if you spend a little less time thinking about how *they're* doing it, and a bit more time thinking about what's going on for you here and asking, 'What is interesting in this space?'

VF What are your thoughts on the importance of having young people in the art world?

AM There are two different things here: there is being in amongst the art world and there is having a voice in the art world. If we are talking about young people as being an agency for change then it is about mindset, and

I think there is a misconception that young people alone have to be that voice for change. I think that young people should feel less pressured to be the finished article, or to pretend like they know all the answers. But they need to be in the room, to absorb that experience and have time to figure out who they are and the voice they want.

VF How can we get young people in the room or improve access for young people?

AM I'm always really keen to share as much as I can. If somebody comes to me and says they want to learn to make something, I'll say, 'Come to my workshop.' I've come to realise that I also benefit from that kind of conversation; if someone is excited and enthusiastic, I vibe off that. And I think you can draw that analogy to much bigger companies, who should be encouraged to be a bit less protective and a bit more giving.

VF With V&A East you worked on the Upstart Workshops with young people. What was your favourite thing about doing that?

AM I guess it's like I said about inviting people into my studio. You can have a clever idea, or spend a long time trying to create something, but if you bring people into the conversation, you can step back from it and begin to see things you wouldn't have seen if you were just working on it alone. I felt that the workshops were as much for me as the people in them. I had this idea that you can make more beautiful objects if they originate from a deeper level of people's lives and stories. I invited people into the room, and they brought their stories and made the objects. I came up with this idea of a way of making more meaningful objects and they all proved it.

VF In what ways do issues of sustainability present themselves in your work?

AM I think there should be an inherently sustainable approach to what we do, but it's not something I will talk about specifically. Quite often I talk about shortening the gap between the person who makes a thing and the person who buys it, or I try to create objects that have a more resonant meaning to the person that lives with them. I guess these are tactics to make things that stick around longer. If you care more about why something was made and who made it, or if the object resonates deeply with a story that is part of your life, then you won't be so quick to replace it.

VF What's the biggest piece of advice you would give to a person who wants to become an artist or begin to make?

AM Recently I've engaged with people in a mentorship role and the first thing I say to mentors is that you have to listen to the mentee, because there isn't one piece of advice for everyone. It's nuanced. You have to ask, 'What do you want from life?' and 'How do you want to get there?' All of these things shape the advice you give to someone.

VF What kind of legacy or impact do you want to leave on the art world?

AM I'm mixed-race and there has been a moment in the design world where suddenly people in a position of power have realised that they need to mix things up a little bit. And what that's meant is that I've probably got opportunities as a result of that that I wouldn't have had 10 years ago. And that's great. But at the same time, I've been quite purposeful about not making work about my race. There is an amazing space for it, and it's needed, but it's not what I'm choosing to do. Personally, I'd love people to look at my work and, regardless of my race, I want them to think that my work is good. I want to be the proof that if you give people opportunities that they make good work.

VF In that sense, you want to be the evidence that diversifying the space is a good thing because diversity can bring actual talent; it's not just for the sake of diversifying?

AM Exactly. That's just my view. I think there should be lots of people doing lots of things to bring progress.

Seetal Solanki and Nabiha Qadir

Nabiha Qadir How would you describe your work?

Seetal Solanki I'd describe myself as a 'materials translator'. My practice, Ma-tt-er, helps people to find a relationship to material and advises them on how to implement this in the real world.

NQ Why do you make?

SS There are many layers to why I make. I trained in textiles, a subject that is all about making and trying to understand the root of something – how it's constructed, what it's constructed from and the origins of those fibres. It helped me to understand the making process end-to-end and formed the foundation of my work: the question of what we are made of.

Why I make is also to understand myself. Part of that is having an understanding of how fibres are connected to different cultures, how they get made into cloth and how they communicate messages. We have a relationship with material, and I'm interested in understanding and using that connection to help me understand my own identity. I'm of Indian heritage, my parents were born in Kenya, my grandfather in Uganda, and then they moved to the UK, so when I make, I navigate many worlds, and it helps me to understand what I'm made of.

NQ Could you tell me more about your personal interaction with materials and textiles?

SS There are parallels between making with textiles and cooking. I was cooking from a very young age, and it began my fascination with how to make something. We would buy things from the market, and I would think, 'Where does this actually come from?' We would be told off if we wasted anything, something very much based on respecting the ingredients and what they could provide. And we'd learn how to reinvigorate a dish from leftovers, turning it into something completely new (a sort of 'upcycling'). That became such a fundamental approach to everything I made from then on.

NQ Could you talk a bit more about the idea of upcycling and how that fits in with your approach?

SS I grew up in an intergenerational household and the first language I spoke was Gujarati, then English, so we didn't really have words connected to recycling or upcycling, it was just something we did: there was the act

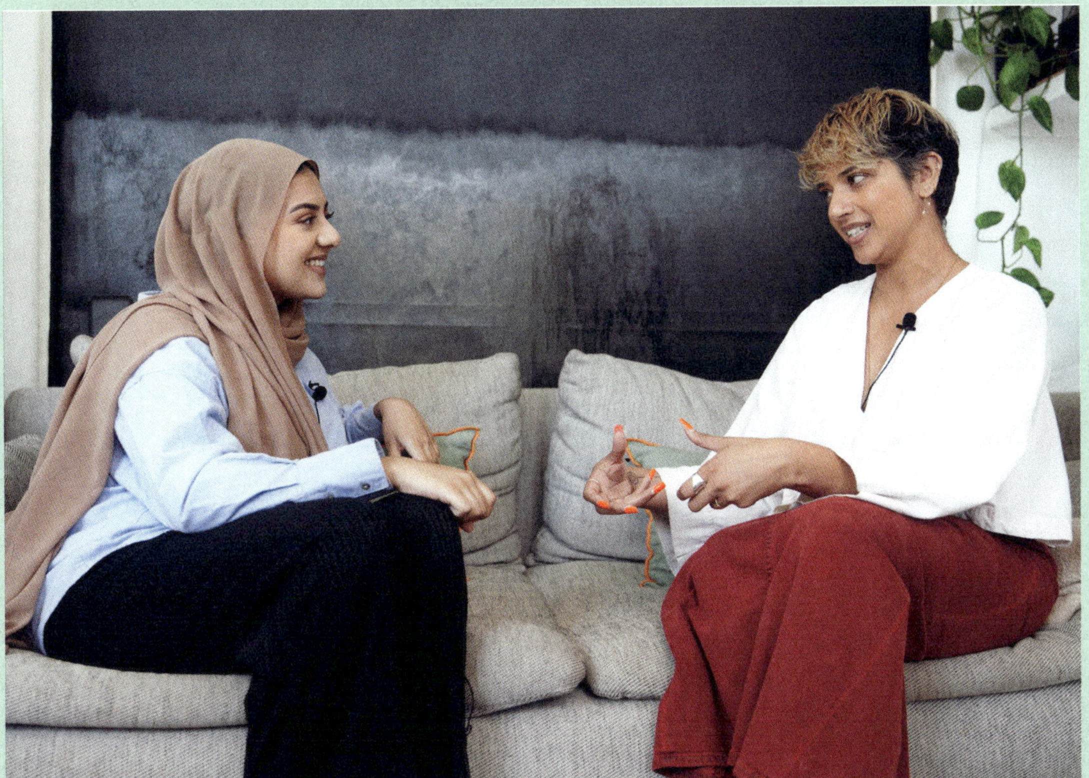

of it, rather than the speaking of it. On the other side, is the labelling and naming of these processes, or acts, which is very Western. I feel like the origins of a lot of terms have been considered in a Western context but don't necessarily translate to somewhere like India. The idea of upcycling, or recycling, is helpful in the context of the UK, because people want to understand it through words, whereas in a lot of Eastern cultures it is done through embodiment. I'm trying to bring it all together, because I think we are losing our connection to our bodies and our minds and the whole thing needs to connect.

NQ I can relate as in Pakistani culture we have similar practices, and when people talk about being more sustainable or upcycling, you realise you've already been doing it automatically.

SS I would add the example of the clay teacup in India, where tea is sold on the street, but the cup isn't disposable, it's thrown back into the pile and then used again and again. That's down to the properties of the material, it's fired in a way that means we can reuse it.

NQ So, it's made in a way that's always been intended for reuse? It's interesting this notion of the intention of the material. When you look at something like fast fashion, which is not intended to be reused, versus, say, generational dresses that have been made to be passed down in the family, it highlights these two sides of the intention of fabric.

SS Yes, but the materiality of those objects is very different. The disposability of those pieces of clothing may be linked to their affordable nature, making them 'throw-away'. And it comes back to the way that you treat and respect things. If we're not making things in way that they are respected, and we plan for their obsolescence, then it isn't just down to the customer buying them to take responsibility for what happens to them. We didn't make that object; we made the choice of *buying* it, but we didn't make the choice of *making* it. The onus can't just be on one individual. The intention behind the making needs to be more meaningful and for that we need systems to change, which means change from the top.

NQ What do you think is at the root of the issue? Is it about tackling the fashion industry and how fabrics are produced? Or is it about consumerism and changing the narrative of fashion?

SS All of the above! But the education system needs to account for a lot of these things, and I feel like the environmental side is a big part of education that can happen early on. How are we supposed to do our bit if we don't have exposure to the knowledge of what we can do? I'm trying to make a place where it feels that it's possible; where we all get to do our bit, together. I don't want to do this on my own and it isn't going to make a difference if it's just me. That's why education is key.

NQ Could you tell me more about your role as a tutor at the Royal College of Art? What would you like your students to take away from what you deliver?

SS My intention is to help students understand who they are. At MA level, they're there to go on a journey of self-discovery. I'm there to guide them and it's a dialogue, like we're having now. I'm curious about who they are and how textiles can facilitate their journey. I always want to know the 'why' of what they're doing and who it's for. They are two simple questions, but they can be the most difficult answer.

I also try to get students to be more accepting of change and not to feel too fixated on forever, because I think a lot of fear is based on that. For me, it's the most rewarding thing to see a student grow into themselves, to hold space for that and let them go out and make change in the world.

NQ I feel like empowering students as agents of change is the first step to highlighting how important they are to the next generation. That look to the next generation links to your book *Why Material Matters* (2018). What were the thoughts behind that book?

SS When the publisher approached me, I had to really think about the key message I wanted people to engage with. I felt like people needed to see that everything is a material, or at least to expand their vision of what material can be. There are things like blood, air and bacteria in there.

We are exposed to a material library that categorises things by typologies: wood, metal, plastic, glass, textiles, etc., but in a textile, you have multiple types of material, so why are we pigeonholing these materials in a way that doesn't allow them space to be more than just that? It's like humans. If I call myself a textile designer, I'm very limited in what people see me as, but also in what I feel I can do. So, it's about not limiting our own potential, as well as not limiting the potential of those materials.

NQ Thinking about your own education, do you think that your tutors did the job that you want to do with your students?

SS I started with textiles GCSE, and I loved it. It was a form of expression that I couldn't release any other way. My first degree was in jewellery and silversmithing. I learnt about form using a variety of materials as well as about technique, which was incredible, because I could make something from nothing. Then I moved into multimedia textiles and made a lot of three-dimensional forms. It was very architecturally inspired. After that I took some time out and worked in the fashion industry making 'versions of'.

Later, I applied to do an MA at Central Saint Martins, Textile Futures, and that course changed the game for me. I realised that I could do all these things that I'd been thinking about for so long and didn't know were possible. During that period, I was also working for many different types of organisations. That journey of working for 13 years really allowed me to understand what was missing for me, and that was a lack of respect towards materials. I decided to do something about it and that's how Ma-tt-er was born.

Making the Why We Make Galleries
JA Projects, A Practice for Everyday Life and Larry Achiampong

V&A East's mission is to be a home for young east Londoners. As east Londoners ourselves, we set out to understand where young people feel most at home. Working closely with the V&A Youth Collective, we developed concepts, content and finishes shaped by their lived experience.

Through a series of workshops, visits and walks, we found ourselves drawn to the effervescent high streets and tranquil parks that stitch the four Olympic boroughs together – places to meet, exchange, play and just be.

The galleries take their form from this everyday urban landscape: conceived as a collection of streets, neighbourhoods and cityscapes. Showcases with illuminated fascias draw on the language of shopfronts; cabinetry is crafted from London Plane trees; and displays of fashion, textiles and ceramics echo those encountered in markets and stores. Illuminated and kinetic titles at the entrances pay homage to the city's electric nightscape; easily changeable, characterful labels recall those found in local shops, while a new typeface – developed with the Youth Collective – guides visitors through the galleries.

Working closely with URGE Collective, the design embraces circular principles – for example, innovative use of waste materials – and prioritises the flexibility needed to continuously tell new stories.

Our shared ambition has been for our design to answer the question implied by the title of the galleries – Why We Make. Our answer: to inspire, care, commune, and to celebrate the stories, places, people and cultures we hold dear.

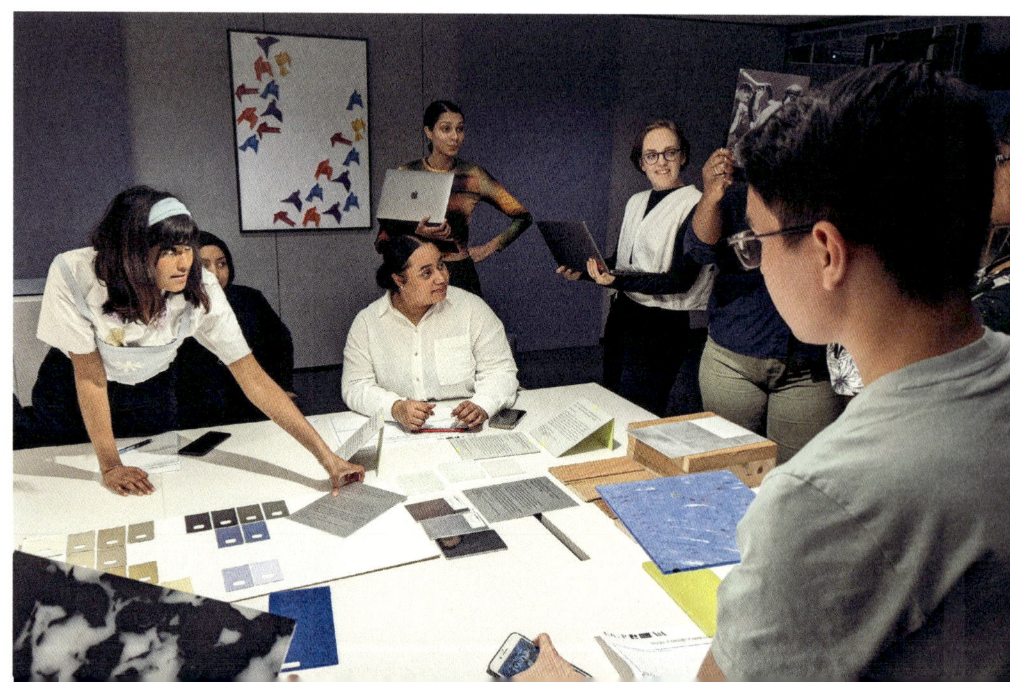

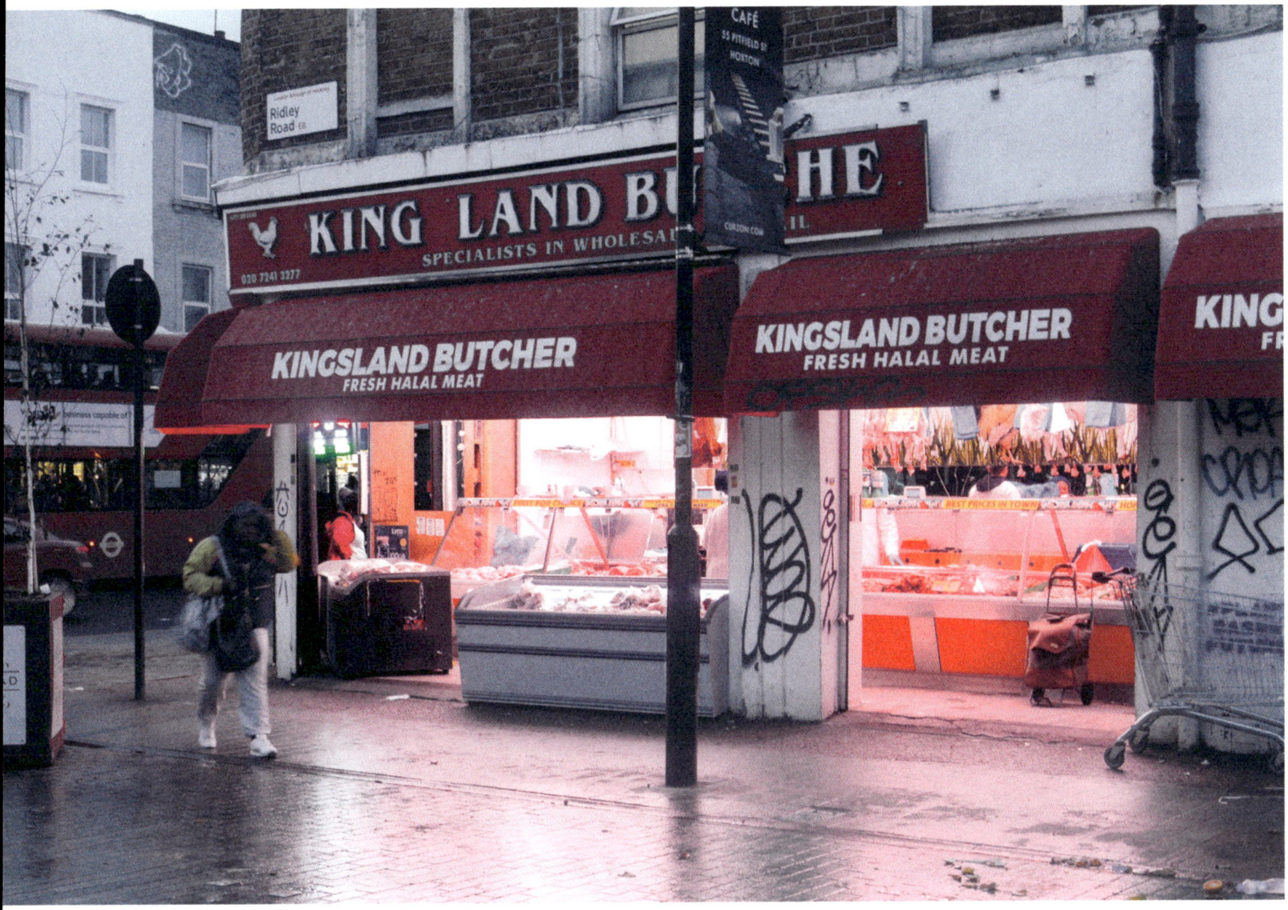

Workshops informed the use of shopfront displays as inspiration for the design schemes of the galleries.

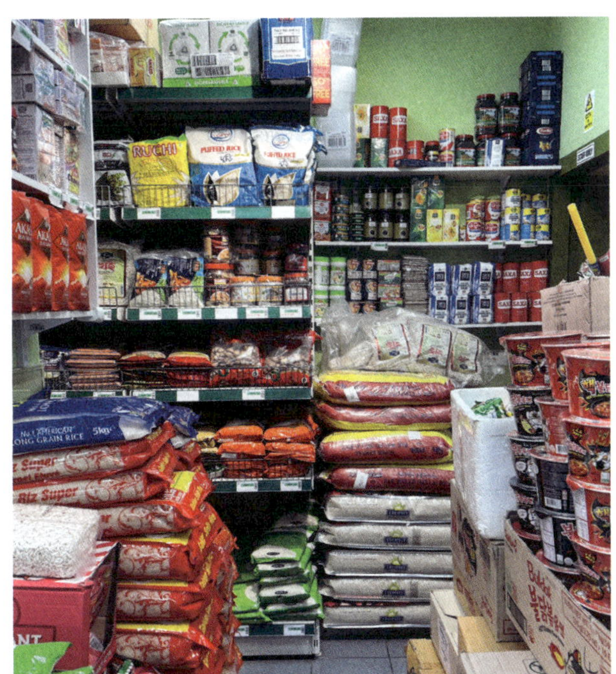

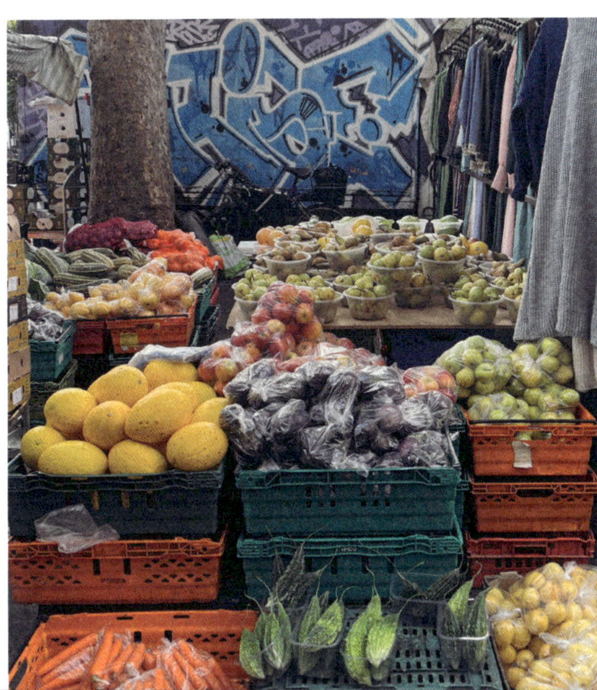

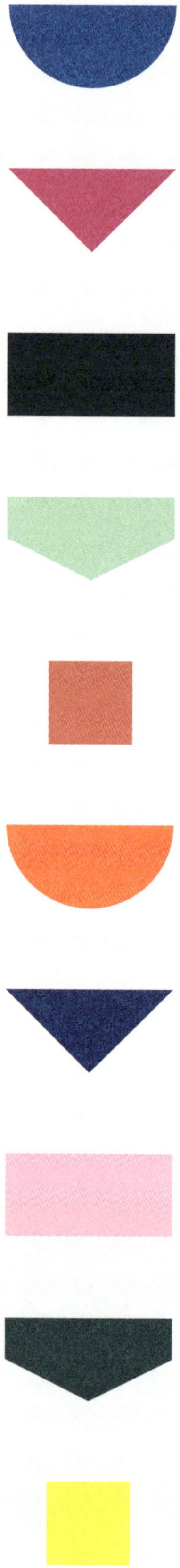

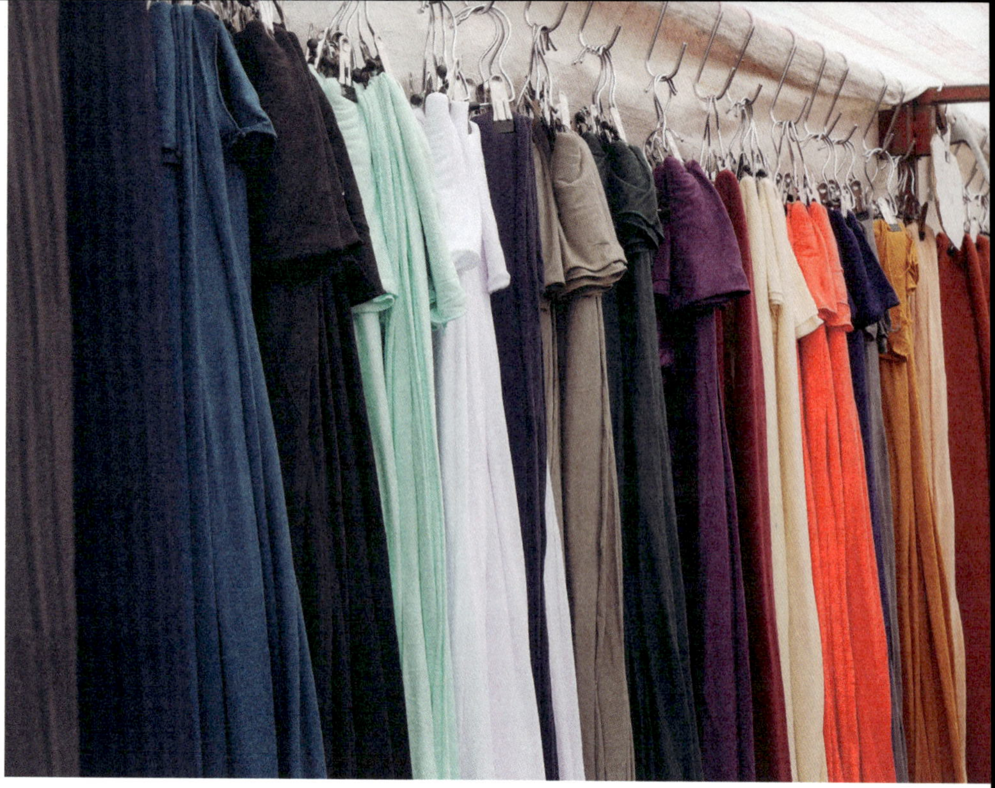

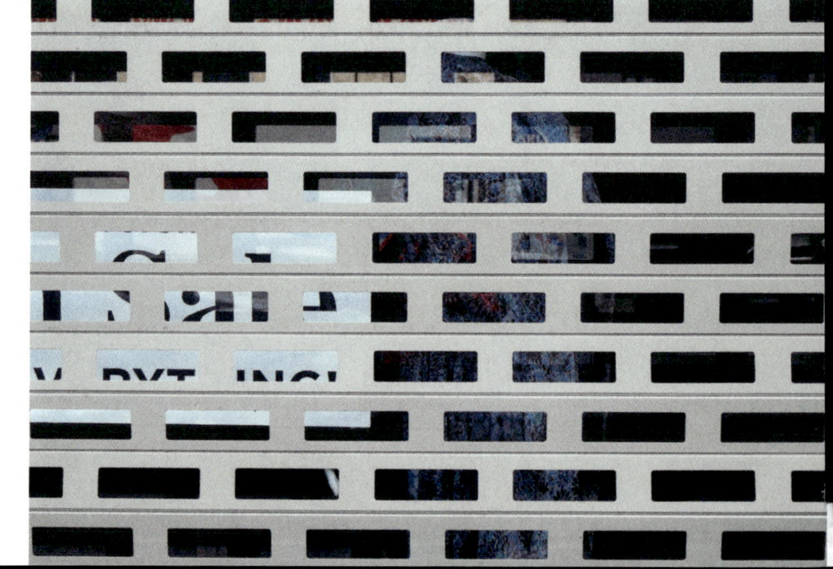

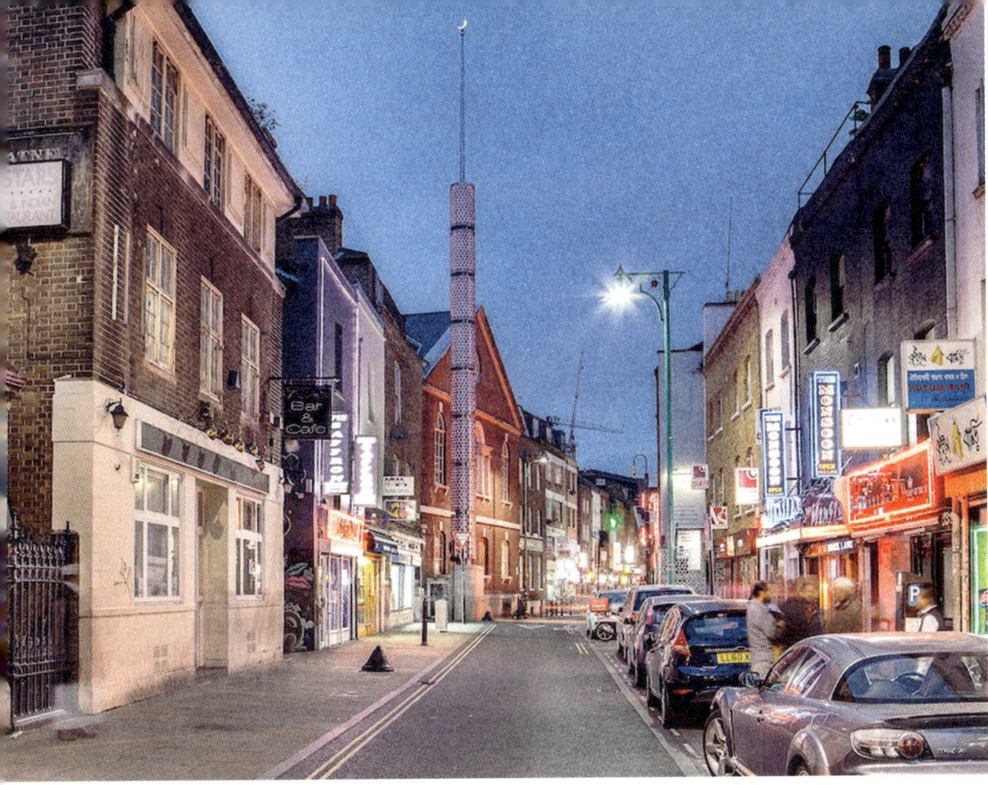

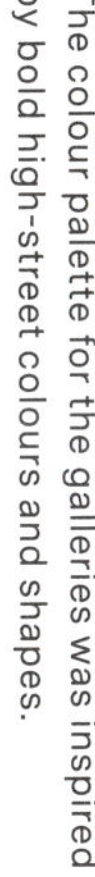
The colour palette for the galleries was inspired by bold high-street colours and shapes.

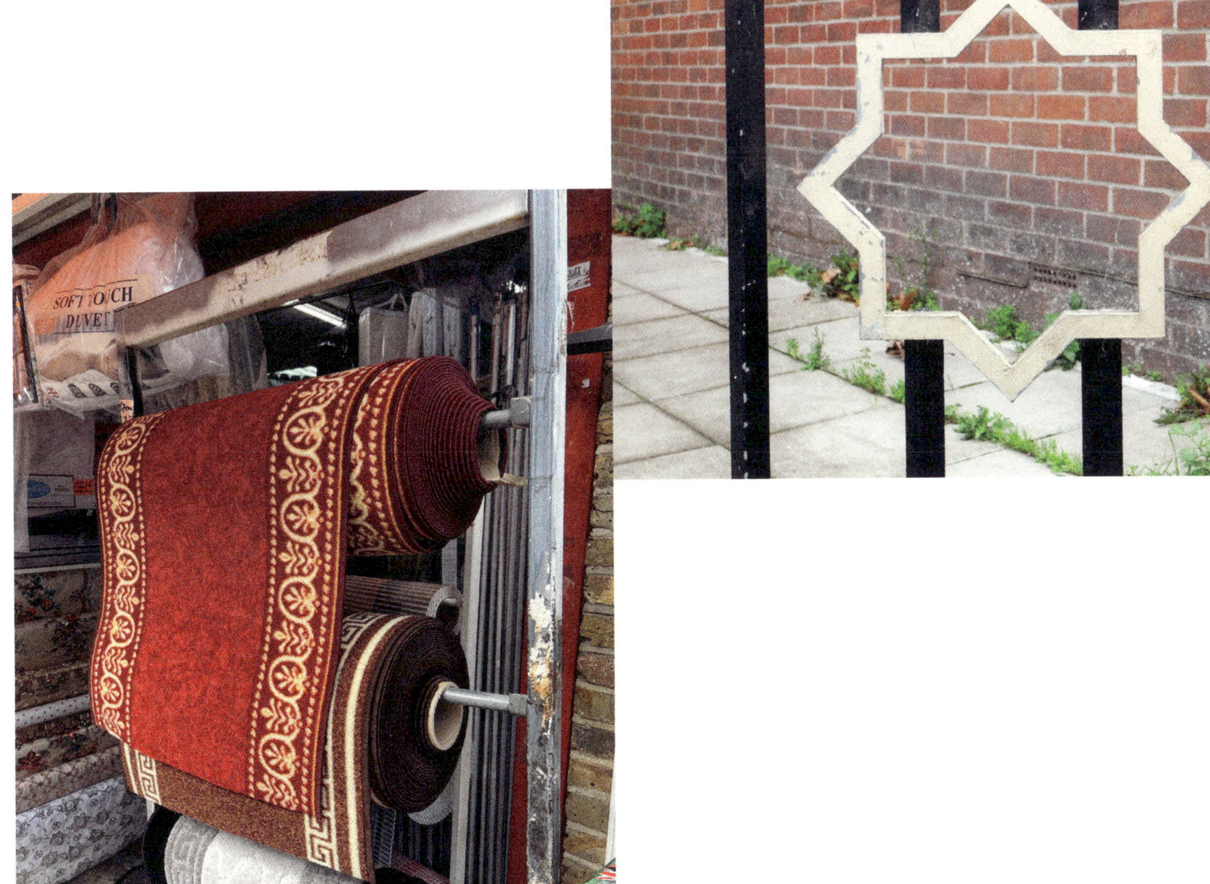

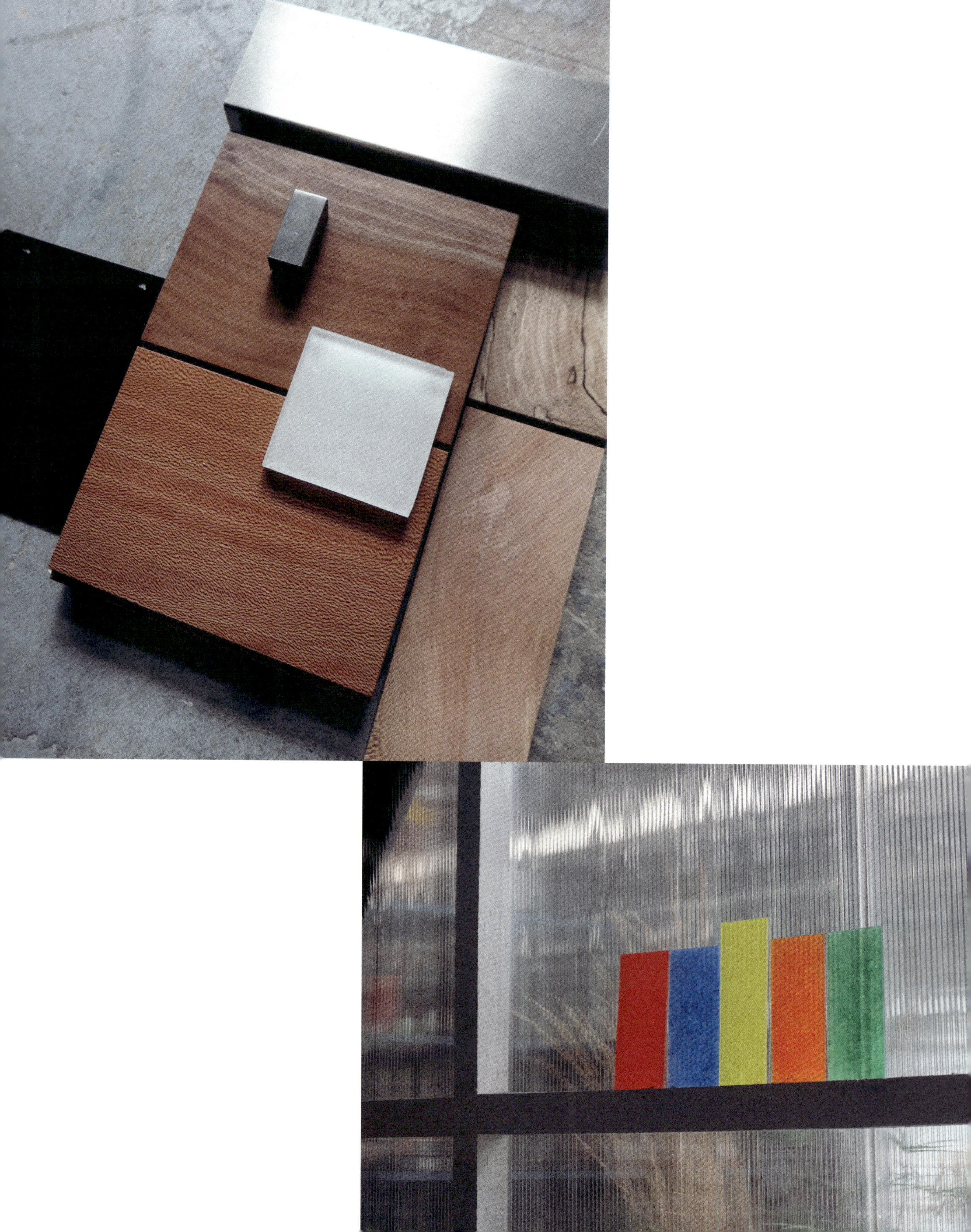

The materials palette for the gallery build was inspired by the textures, materials and urban nature found in high streets, from glass and metals to London plane trees.

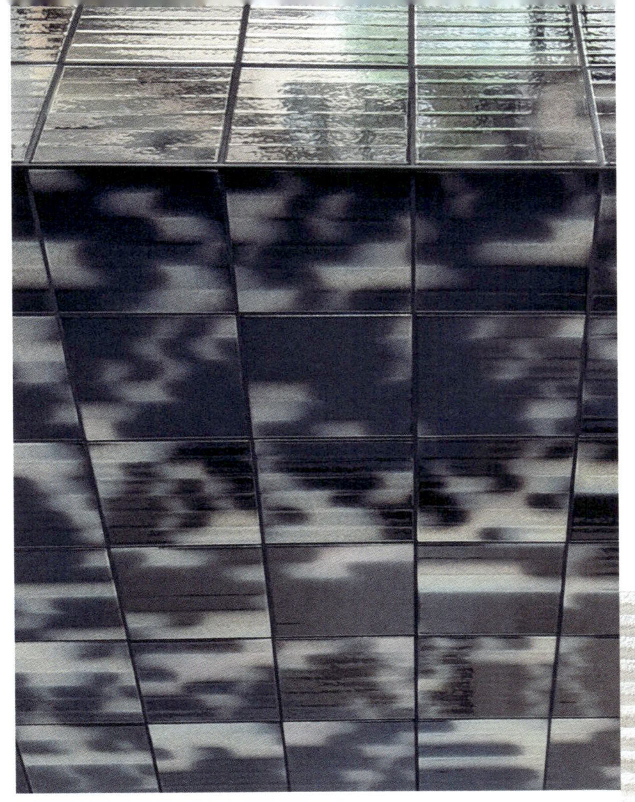

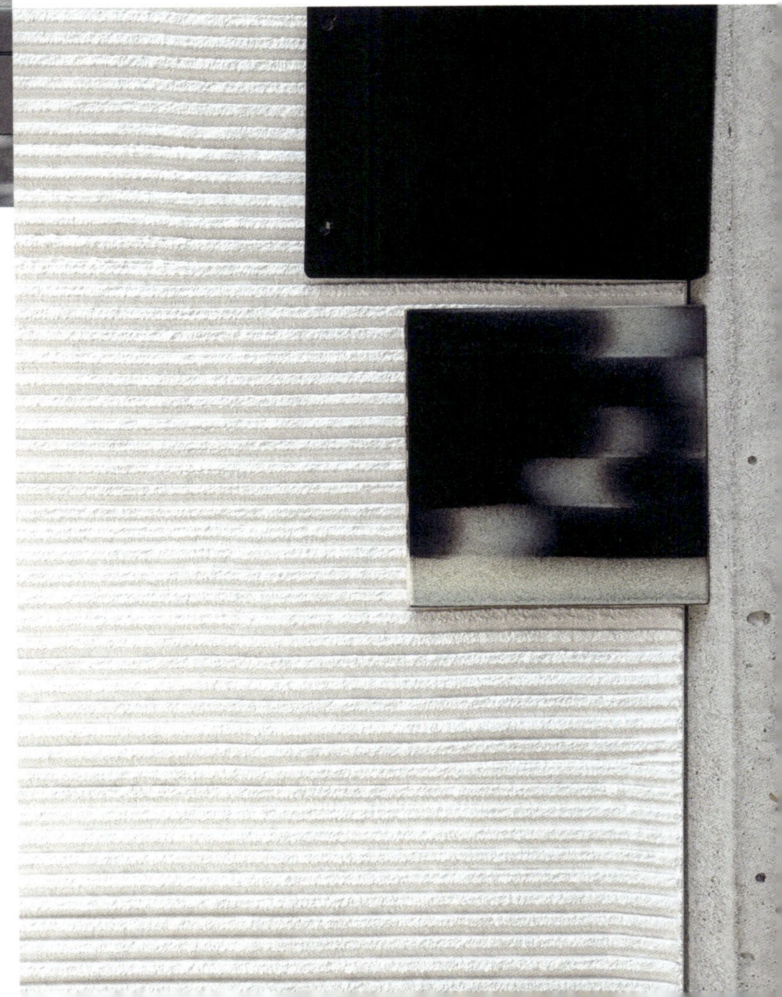

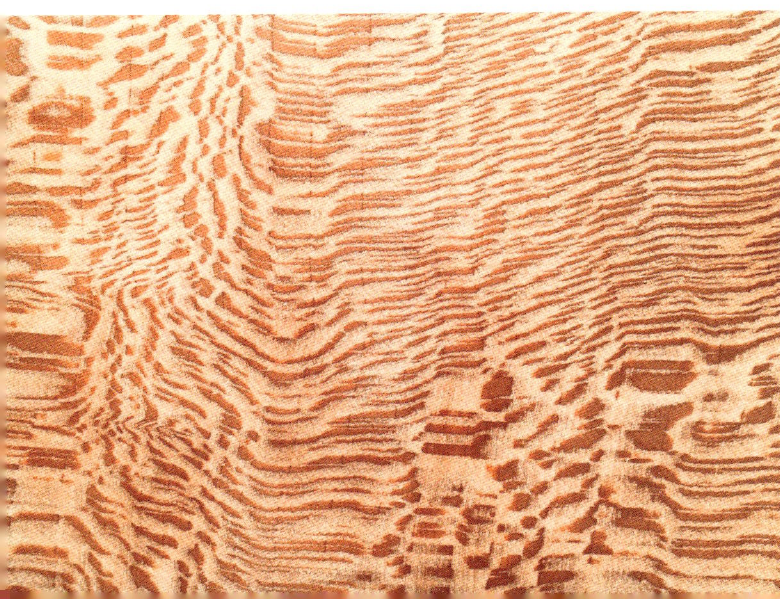

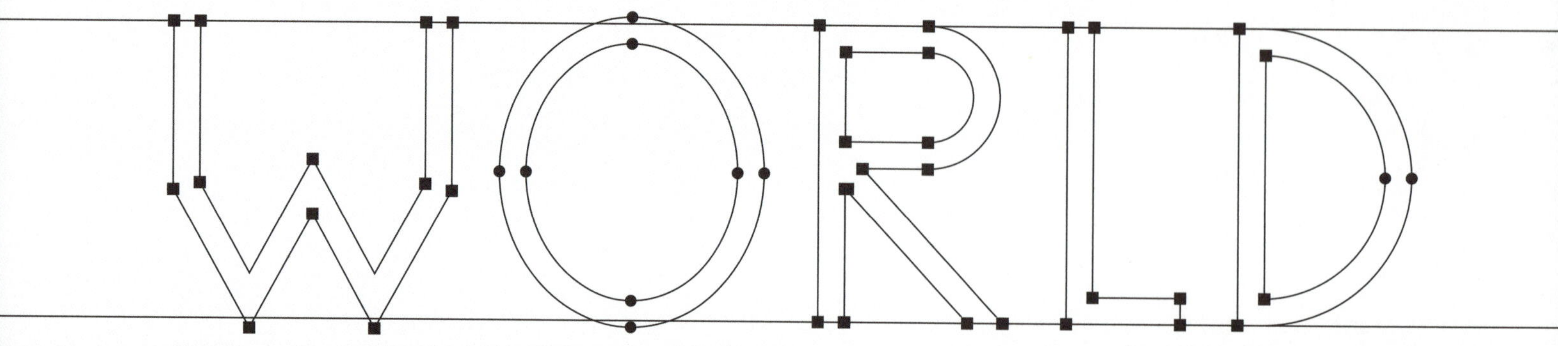
WORLD

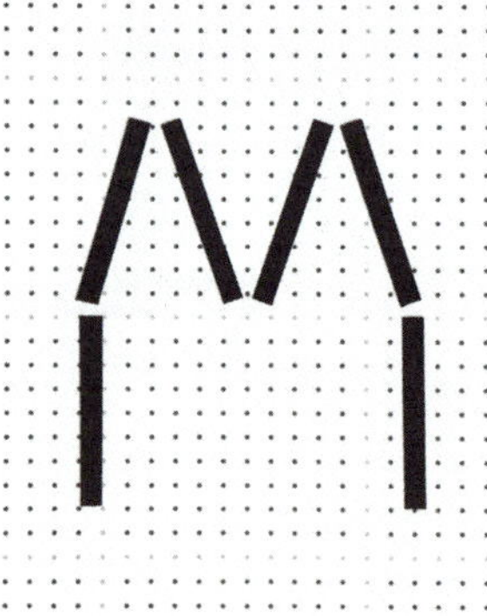
M

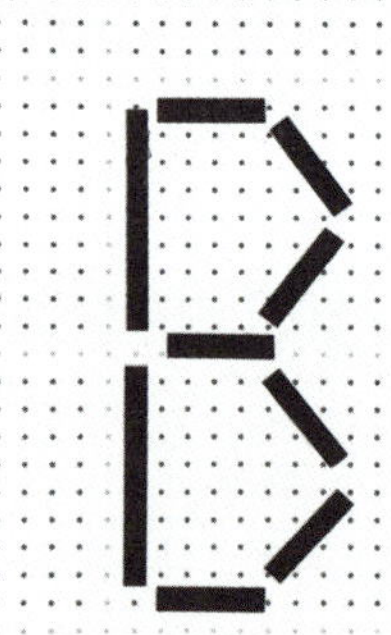
B

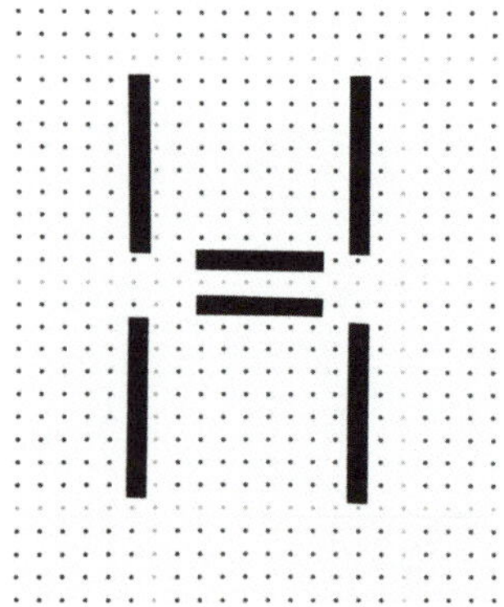
H

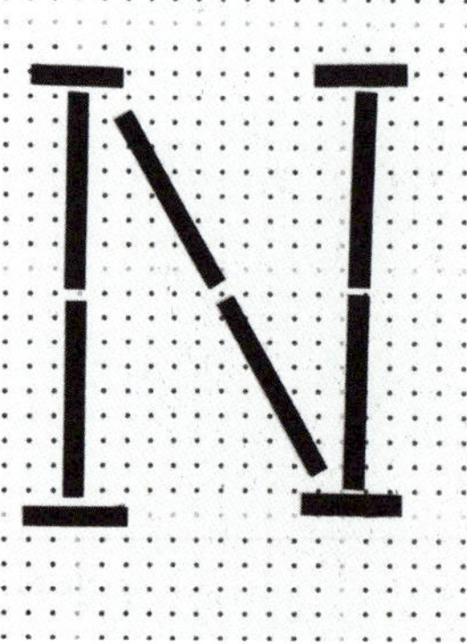
N

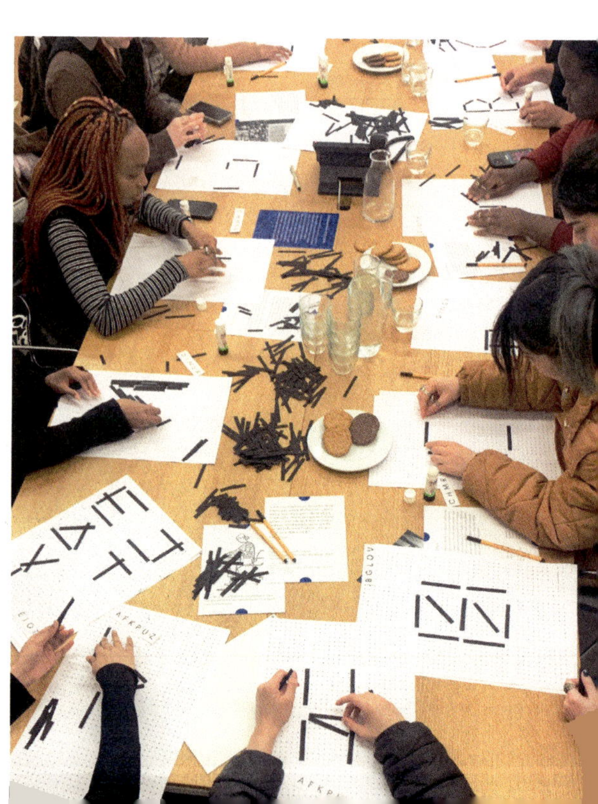

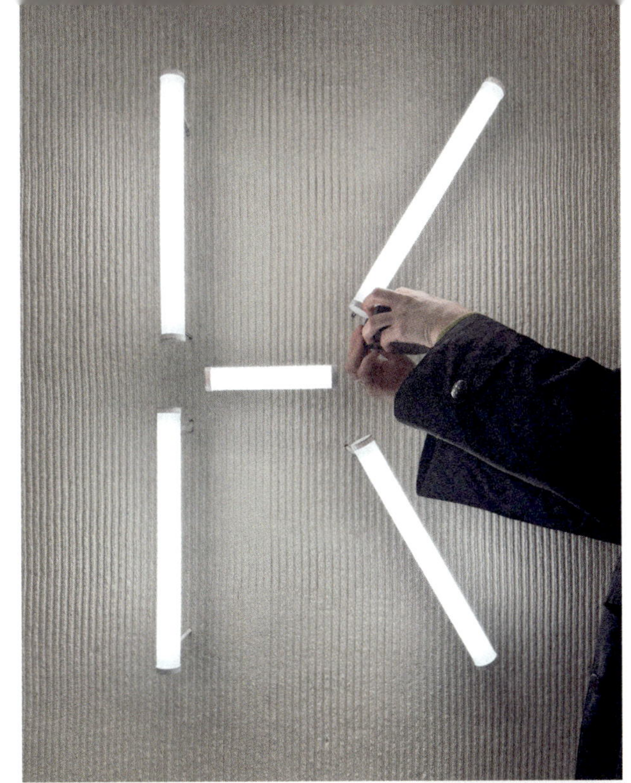

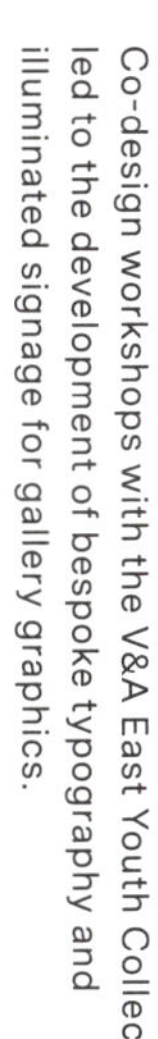

Co-design workshops with the V&A East Youth Collective led to the development of bespoke typography and illuminated signage for gallery graphics.

OUR PLACE IN THE WORLD

BREAKING BOUNDARIES

CRAFTING STORIES

BUILDING CREATIVE COMMUNITIES

CARING FOR OURSELVES

VOICING DISSENT

REVEALING A WORLD IN FLUX

REIMAGINING TRADITIONS

RETHINKING SYSTEMS

EMPOWERING THROUGH DESIGN

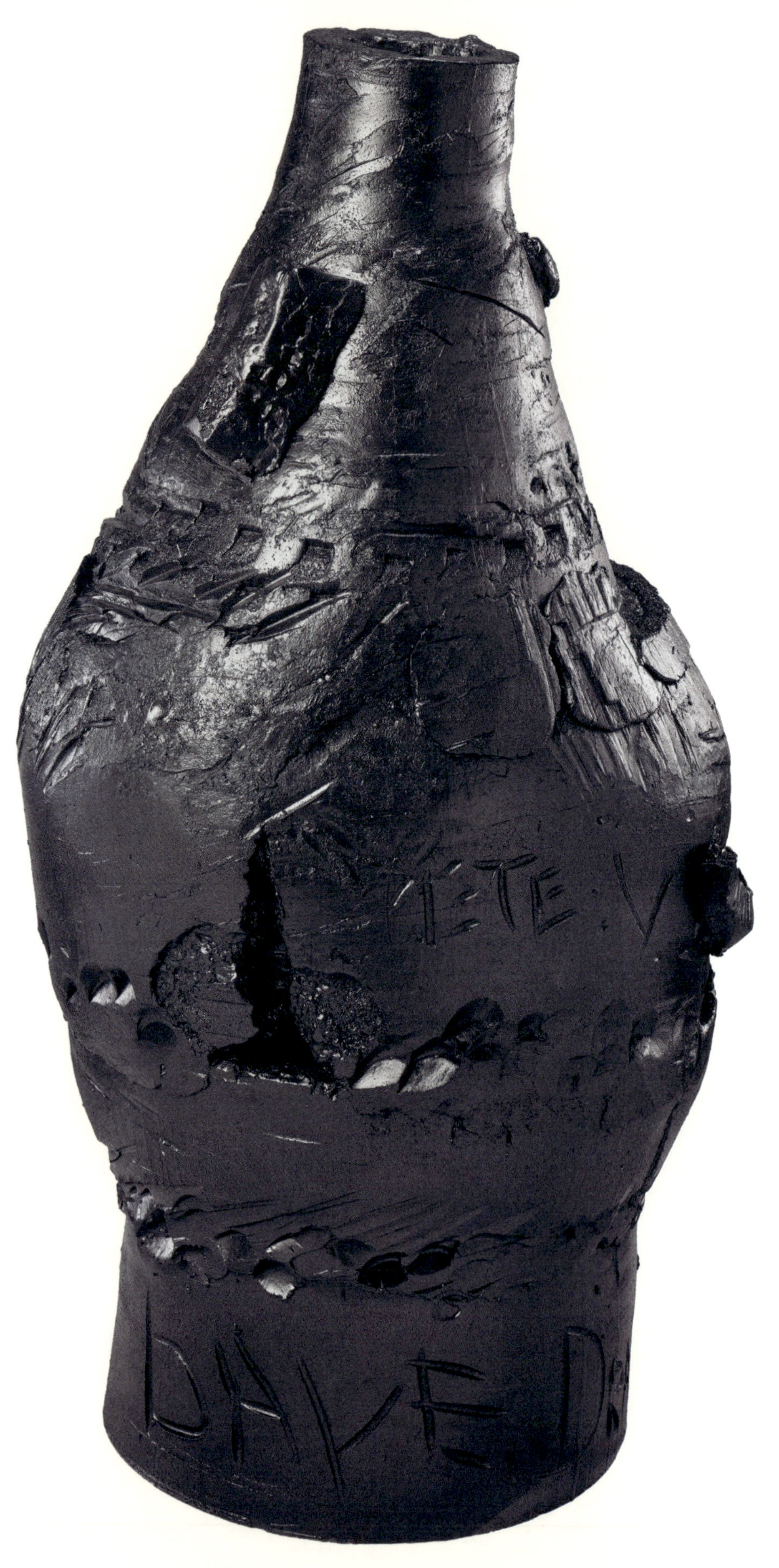
DAVE

Voulkos #1, by Theaster Gates, 2021, V&A

Scratched in foot-high letters into the vessel's clay body are the names 'Pete V', 'Dave Drake' and 'Theaster'. It was sculpted and fired by Chicago-born artist Theaster Gates in the snowy depths of a Montana winter in 2021, but the three signatures on the vessel raise the question of whether this tells the whole story of the object's creation. Gates explains that he is 'the carrier of other people's technologies and efforts, of countless lessons and reprimands and research', and that it is with 'tremendous pride' that he 'can say that my hands are the least present on my works, and hands too innumerable to count, have shaped my hands'.[1] *Voulkos #1* is the product of the transmission of multi-layered, cross-cultural craft know-how from maker to maker across time and geography.

'Pete V', Peter Voulkos, was an American studio potter who created large, abstract, stacked sculptures using a mixture of wheel-thrown and hand-built components. He instructed many US potters in his style and philosophy including Paul Soldner, who in turn trained Gates's teacher Ingrid Lilligren. Inspired by Voulkos's *Pinatubo* in the V&A's collection, Gates set about wrestling with his craft genealogy. As an act of 写 (*utsushi*), which means replication as a spiritual practice in Japanese, Gates loaded his body with the same cocktail of intoxicants Voulkos relied on, recreated his special mix of local clays and worked through the nights in Voulkos's studio at the Archie Bray Foundation for the Ceramic Arts in Montana.

But this vessel isn't just about Voulkos. It also honours the work of the potter named 'Dave Drake', a nineteenth-century enslaved African American man who produced large stoneware vessels in South Carolina. The technologies for making and firing alkaline-glazed stoneware had only recently been transmitted to the US when slave owner Abner Landrum read an early eighteenth-century French Jesuit monk's account of Chinese porcelain anagama kilns.[2] Landrum's successful experimentation led to many individuals being forced to labour in the industrial production of stoneware. Unlike many, Dave was allowed to sign his pots, perhaps due to his staggering talent, and this is why we know his name. At this time, it was illegal for enslaved persons to read or write in South Carolina and yet Dave also inscribed lines of his own poetry onto many of his pots. Often opaque or multi-faceted, it is likely that these poems embody a concealed form of resistance. For example, one vessel made on 16 August 1857 bears the lines: 'I wonder where is all my relation / Friendship to all – and every nation', which could allude to his forced separation from those he loved, or as a message of Christian solidarity.

In *Voulkos #1*, Gates honours the teachers he has only met through the objects they have left behind, and the global genealogy of the technologies and aesthetics that have shaped his practice. This work was made while Gates was Emeritus Fellow at the V&A researching 'The Question of Clay', 2020–22. Georgia Haseldine, Senior Curator

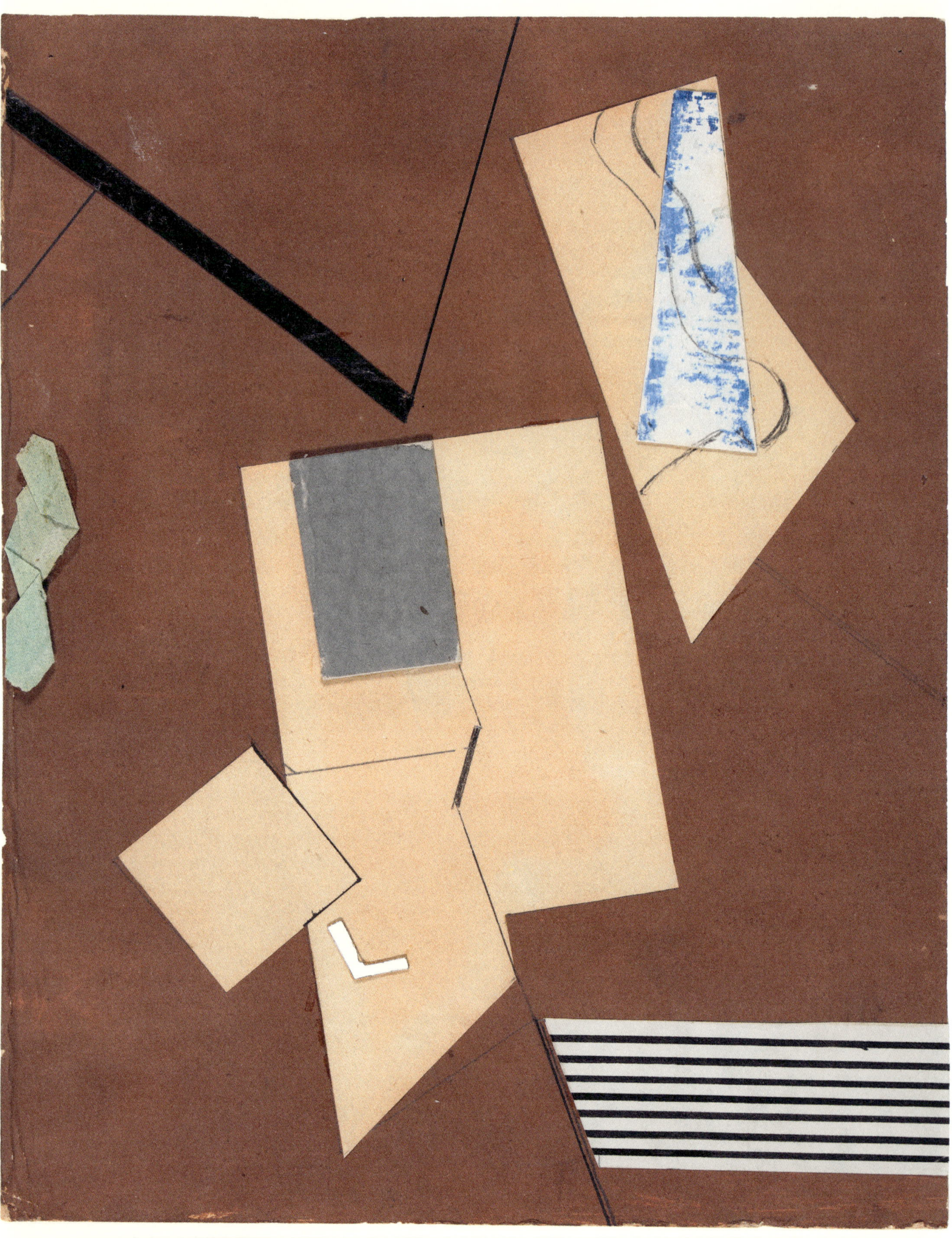

Bobadilla rug design, by Eileen Gray, about 1926–9, V&A

A bold arrangement of yellow, blue and grey geometric shapes animates the dark-brown background of Eileen Gray's design for the *Bobadilla* rug. Like many of her textile designs from the 1920s, the study is characterised by a tactile approach to developing a graphic concept – painterly elements of abstract lines and angular shapes come together with cut-outs and layered, folded papers. Gray typically developed rug patterns in gouache and collage, before details were transposed to graph paper as weaving instructions. The result in *Bobadilla* is a bold graphic statement that captures the energy of Gray's experimental design practice, which brought together craft and art. A trailblazer in her day, Gray challenged conventions of Modernist aesthetics and broke new ground as an independent woman practitioner in the early twentieth century. Rugs were a cornerstone of her practice and offer an important insight into her creative life.

Born in Enniscorthy, County Wexford, Ireland in 1878, Gray spent her childhood in London and attended the Slade School of Art (one of the first higher education establishments to accept women, from 1871), where she studied painting in 1898 before undergoing an apprenticeship in a London lacquer workshop. In 1902, she moved to Paris, taking up further training in drawing, lacquerware and cabinetry, while establishing herself on the contemporary avant-garde arts scene. She would remain in France for most of her life and develop a multi-disciplinary career spanning furniture, textile design, architecture and art. Fiercely motivated, Gray moved in circles of independent women and forged business ventures from her early years. In Paris, she developed affiliations with a network of women makers including the textile designer Evelyn Wyld, who specialised in handmade rugs and inspired Gray to move into the field from around 1907. The pair set up a carpet workshop in Saint Germain and collaborated for over 15 years, with Wyld looking after the production of Gray's designs. Together, they studied natural wool dying techniques from North Africa and developed a commitment to tapestry weave and hand-knotted processes, alongside locally sourced natural fibres, resisting contemporary trends for machine-produced rugs.

In 1922, Gray opened Galerie Jean Désert in 217 Rue du Faubourg Saint-Honoré as an independent commercial venture and outlet for her designs. The showroom operated under a fictious male name 'Jean Désert' (later changed to 'Jean Désert et E. Gray') and attracted an illustrious clientele of fellow artists and designers, as well as wealthy patrons. Contemporary critics of Gray's designs were often astounded by the bold originality of her work. An American journalist visiting the gallery in Paris in 1922 famously declared the experience, 'an adventure… a sojourn into the never-before-seen' – a description that Gray later adopted for sales invitations.[1]

The design for the *Bobadilla* rug is characteristic of Gray's interest in abstract patterns and the aesthetics of contemporary avant-garde art, from the layered collages of French Cubism to the bold geometries of Dutch De Stijl. Gray was interested in pushing the boundaries of contemporary Modernist design aesthetics that focussed on minimal, machine-inspired functional forms. Instead, she sought to combine mathematical rigour and geometry with playful, imaginative shapes, bold colour and sensual material choices, which she believed could bring delight to the user. Rugs became a signature element of her interior designs and circulated widely in the homes of her contemporaries.

While the commercial success of the gallery was not to last (Gray closed the venture in 1930), and Gray moved on to new projects in architecture and furniture, rugs and collaborations in craft would remain a design interest throughout her career. Zofia Trafas White, Senior Curator

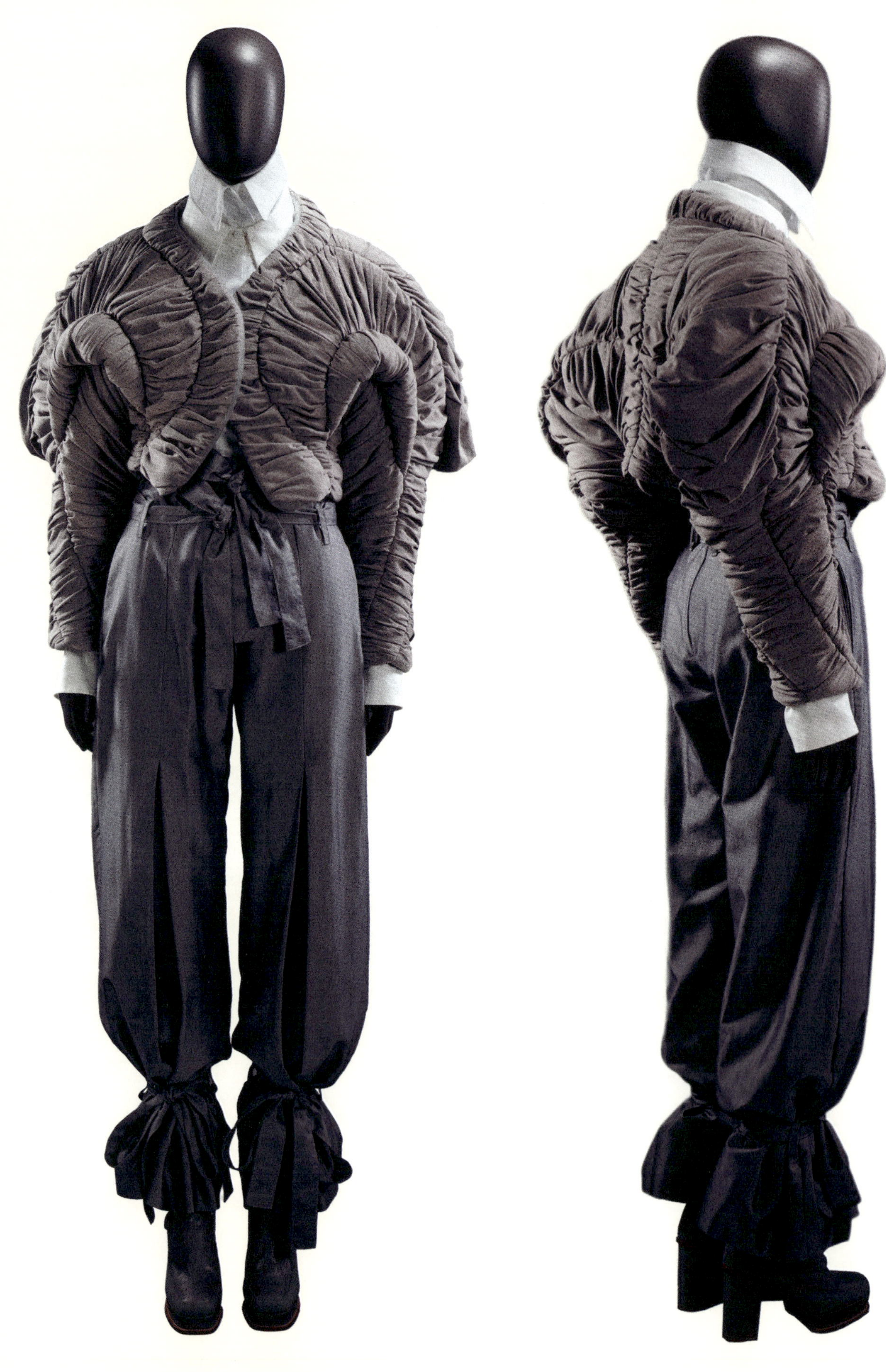

Ensemble, by Richard Malone, 2021, V&A

In the work of Richard Malone every thread counts as a statement, rethinking the fashion system. The 'curve' ruched jacket ensemble was the closing runway look of Malone's Autumn/Winter 2021 *25.03.21* London Fashion Week show. The grey jacket, with its detachable wool collar, is hand sewn and made from recycled PET polyester and deadstock jersey, gathered edge to edge, forming a sculpted, curved piece. Its internal structure is composed of wool and recycled wadding. The look is styled with a matching set of elements including high-waisted pleated trousers, a high-collar cotton shirt and heeled leather boots. Like every piece created in the Malone studio, the ensemble is part of a strict limited edition that is produced, numbered and quality checked in London. It encapsulates the vision behind Malone's eponymous label: visionary, sculptural garments that minimise the negative ecological footprint of fashion.

Based in east London, the Irish-born designer is deeply committed to responsible design and small-scale production. Malone trained on the fashion programme at London's Central Saint Martins, graduating in 2014 with scholarships and awards. Following early work in east-London creative incubators like Fashion East and the Centre for Fashion Enterprise in Hackney, he secured industry-wide recognition in 2020 for winning the International Woolmark Prize, marking the first time this prestigious fashion award focused on supply chain traceability. His ways of working openly challenge the lack of transparency in the corporate fashion system.

Malone's eponymous label is built on a business model that reflects a commitment to ethical making. Close collaborations with manufacturers are a pillar of his approach. His studio works exclusively with independent weavers or larger mills that have regenerative initiatives, using only organic, plant-derived and azo-free dyes, recycled polyesters and salvaged 'deadstock' fabrics. He is also an ardent advocate for slow production and ethical employment practices, building transparency and traceability into every piece of clothing he makes. From fashion show press notes disclosing maker wages to garment labels listing fabric sources, his clothes speak his design politics. He believes that 'Nothing should be considered luxurious or desirable that is harmful and exploitative'. Instead, he looks to make 'luxury limited-edition clothes from recycled and sustainably sourced fabric'.[1]

Beyond ecological credentials, the aesthetics of the 'curve' jacket look bring together many of Malone's transhistorical sources of inspiration – from symbolic circular, feminine forms to workwear aprons from his native Ireland, with echoes of historic doublet jackets and protective armour along the way. The collective effect is an outfit that envelopes and empowers the body, with padded, sculptural lines that can adapt to diverse wearers and body shapes. Malone is known to be a passionate supporter of inclusivity in the fashion sector, championing body positivity and gender-neutral clothing, often developing garments on his own body first, alongside collaborating with his clients. Notable wearers of his label include the academic and disability activist Sinéad Burke, singer and songwriter Björk and actor and singer Janelle Monae, among others. Each draw on Malone's signature sculptural looks, while aligning with his ethical fashion practice. Zofia Trafas White, Senior Curator

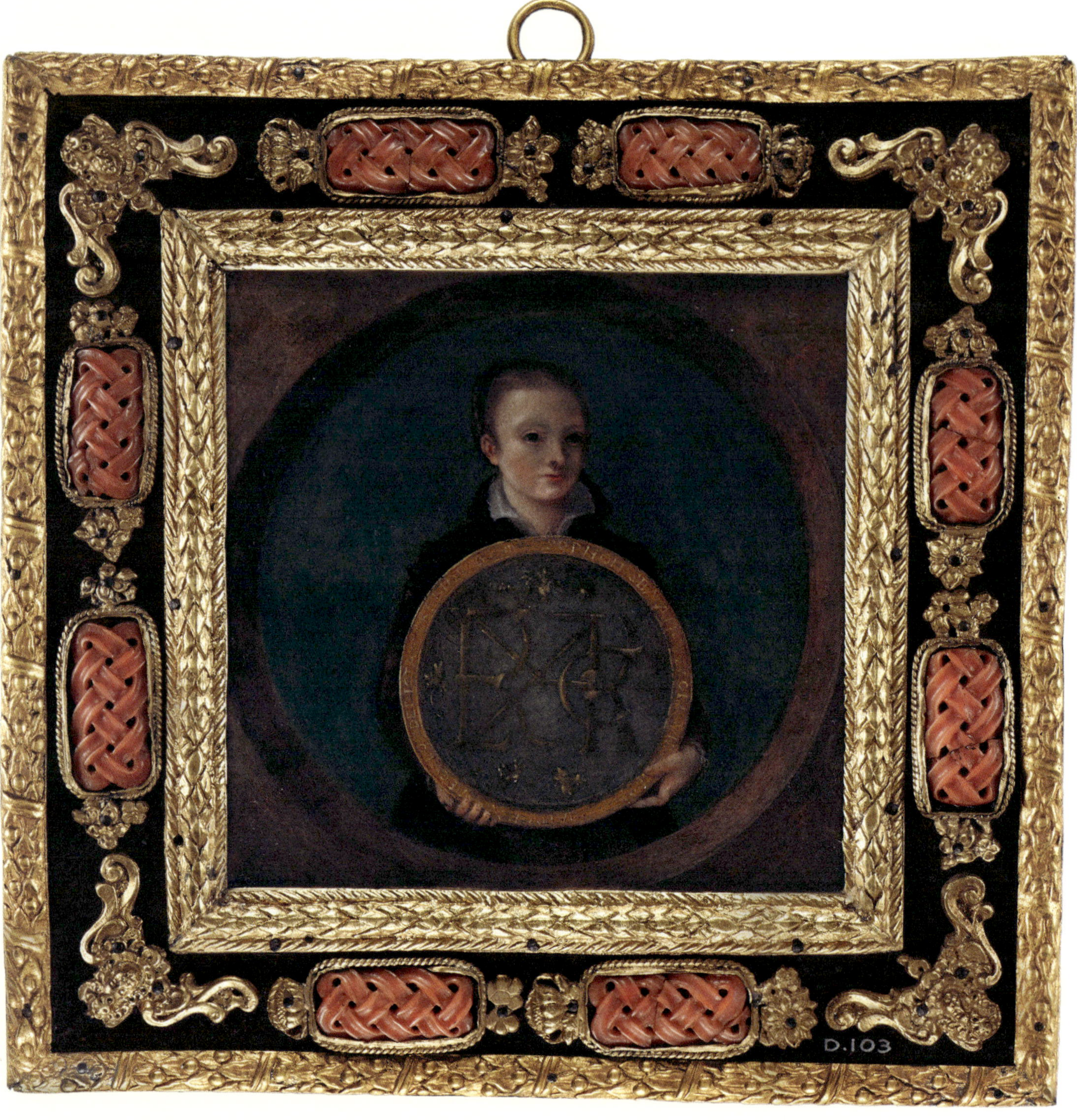
D.103

Portrait of Sofonisba Anguissola after a self-portrait, Circle of Sofonisba Anguissola, about 1530–1620, V&A

In this painting after a self-portrait, the celebrated Italian painter Sofonisba Anguissola portrays herself wearing a dark dress with a white lace collar, enclosed in an oculus in a three-quarter pose against a green background. As one of the few women working within a male-dominated discipline, careful crafting of her public image through self-portraiture was of the utmost importance to Anguissola and it was perhaps for this reason that she created more self-portraits than any of her contemporaries. In these paintings, each element speaks to her meticulous self-fashioning. Her style of dress, seen in many of her other self-portraits, presents Anguissola as both a painter and a noblewoman.

Anguissola looks out at the viewer as she holds in front of her a large medallion. The Latin inscription along the wooden frame reads: 'The maiden Sofonisba Anguissola, depicted by her own hand, from a mirror, at Cremona' – a necessary proclamation as a female artist in sixteenth-century Europe. In the centre of the roundel are the interwoven embroidered letters 'E R M A L C I', likely a monogram representing a Latin phrase touting the noble history of the Anguissola family and asserting Sofonisba's origins and aristocratic birth. Other European women artists include similar entanglements of monographic letters, a subtle but significant way to assert their identities.

This portrait still contains many unsolved mysteries. It is a copy on copper of a portrait miniature now in the collection of the Museum of Fine Arts Boston. The V&A's version was most likely made by a follower of Anguissola with access to the original during, or shortly after, her lifetime, or possibly by a later admirer. Although Anguissola's significant contributions to Italian and Spanish Renaissance painting have at times been omitted from the dominant histories of this period, her life was of great interest in Britain, and her work was highly coveted by art collectors. Anthony van Dyck, Flemish painter at the English court, met the elderly Anguissola shortly before she died, and said that he had 'received more beneficial knowledge of the true principles of his art from one blind woman than by studying all the works of the greatest masters of Italy'.[1] This account was relayed, alongside a print of the portrait, in an 1801 magazine article about Anguissola, indicative of her renown in Britain at this moment. The creation and survival of this copy is a vital and unique testament to the enduring legacy of Anguissola's fame, talent and influence.

Madeleine Haddon, Curator

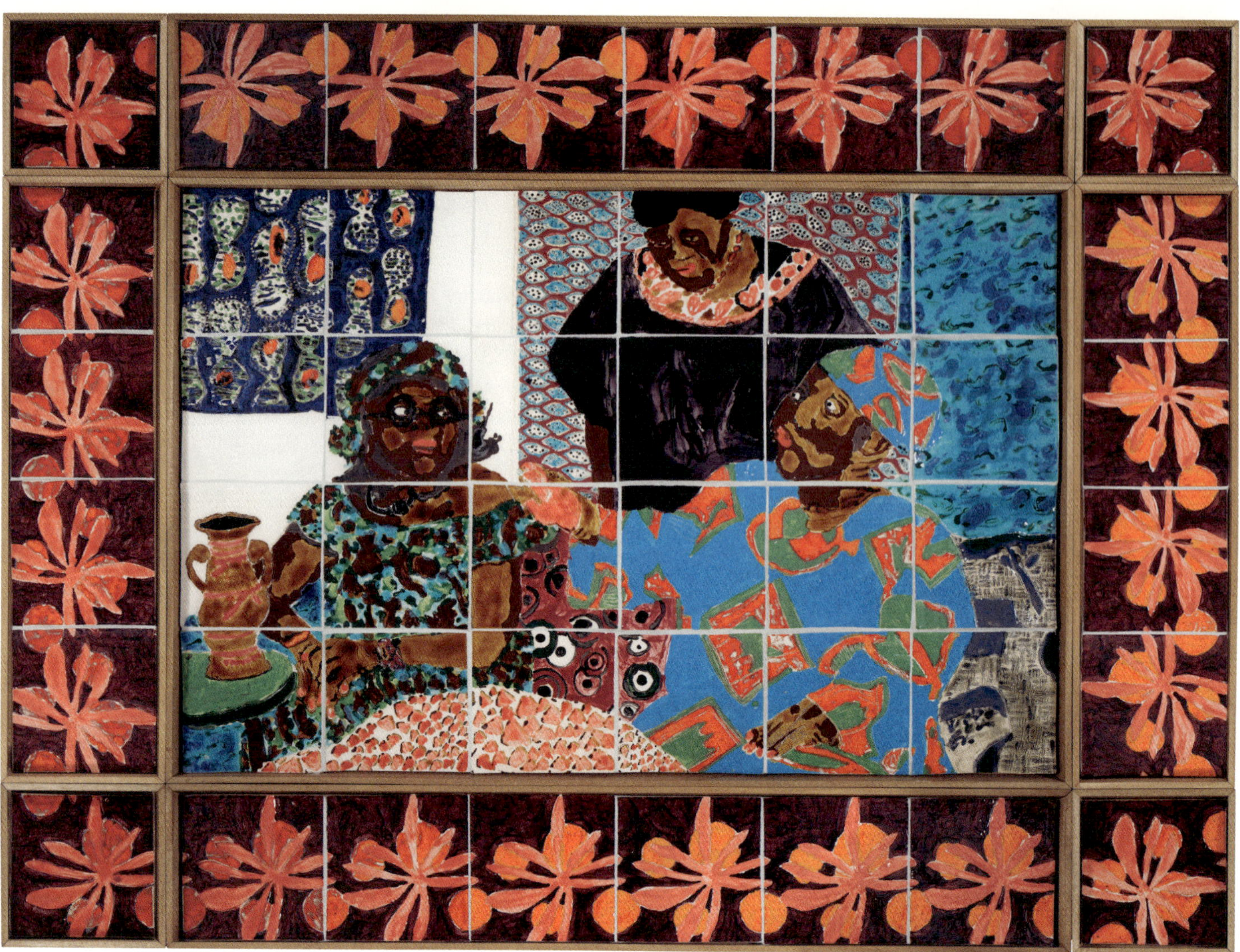

Aunty, Mum and Me Talking About My Fabric Collection, by Mawuena Kattah, 2016, V&A

Mawuena Kattah's ceramic frieze, *Aunty, Mum and Me Talking About My Fabric Collection*, invites us to gather round the table and share Kattah's passion for bold pattern. Vibrant textiles hang in the background, reminiscent of those sourced by the artist at Brixton market, conversation is in full flow and a tile border frames this moment as a dynamic group portrait.

Kattah's affinity for themes of belonging and friendship parallels the strong foundation of community in her creative background. Since 2007, she has been a member of design studio Intoart, an arts organisation based in Peckham, which supports artists with learning disabilities to expand their creative practice and develop enriching partnerships.

Kattah is a multidisciplinary artist whose practice spans drawing, painting, textiles, ceramics and screen printing. Her work is permeated by contrasting colours and playful patterns, repetition and tessellation of shapes. As the subject of the frieze suggests, her passion for pattern parallels her collecting of vibrant fabrics. Kattah draws particular inspiration from fabrics that resonate with her Ghanaian heritage and African wax textile traditions, often purchasing new examples from her local market in Brixton, south London.

In 2013, Kattah developed a series of works on paper whilst conducting research into colour and pattern across the V&A's collections. Building on this project, in 2016 she crafted *Aunty, Mum and Me Talking About My Fabric Collection* during a five-month placement with studio technicians at the V&A Ceramics Studio. In addition to textiles, family photographs are an important source for Kattah's work – both contemporary photos and archival images from Accra and Ho.

Kattah developed the frieze by adapting studio photographs of herself and her relatives. Transposing the composition onto a grid, she divided the design into numbered squares and planned how the surface of each tile would be worked: 'drawn', 'smooth' or a combination of the two. These prompts indicated whether she was going to incise the tile's surface to delineate shape ('drawn') or do so only by painting with glaze ('smooth'). The final frieze combines Kattah's abstract work with pattern and her interest in representing family, community and intimate feelings of belonging and home.

As architectural features, friezes define the stories regarded as being worthy of embellishing the fabric of our built environment. Historically, a frieze offered a prime space for a story to be committed to history, shaping narratives of identity and community. The threads of that legacy offer a fresh view on the significance of *Aunty, Mum and Me Talking About My Fabric Collection* as, by adapting the visual language of the historic ceramic frieze, Kattah's work frames friendship and community as the values we should be celebrating on the walls of our institutions.

Aunty, Mum and Me Talking About My Fabric Collection offers a joyful encounter with the artist's personal world, it is bold and memorable, enlivening its surroundings with a vibrant portrait of togetherness. Chloe Kellow, Assistant Curator

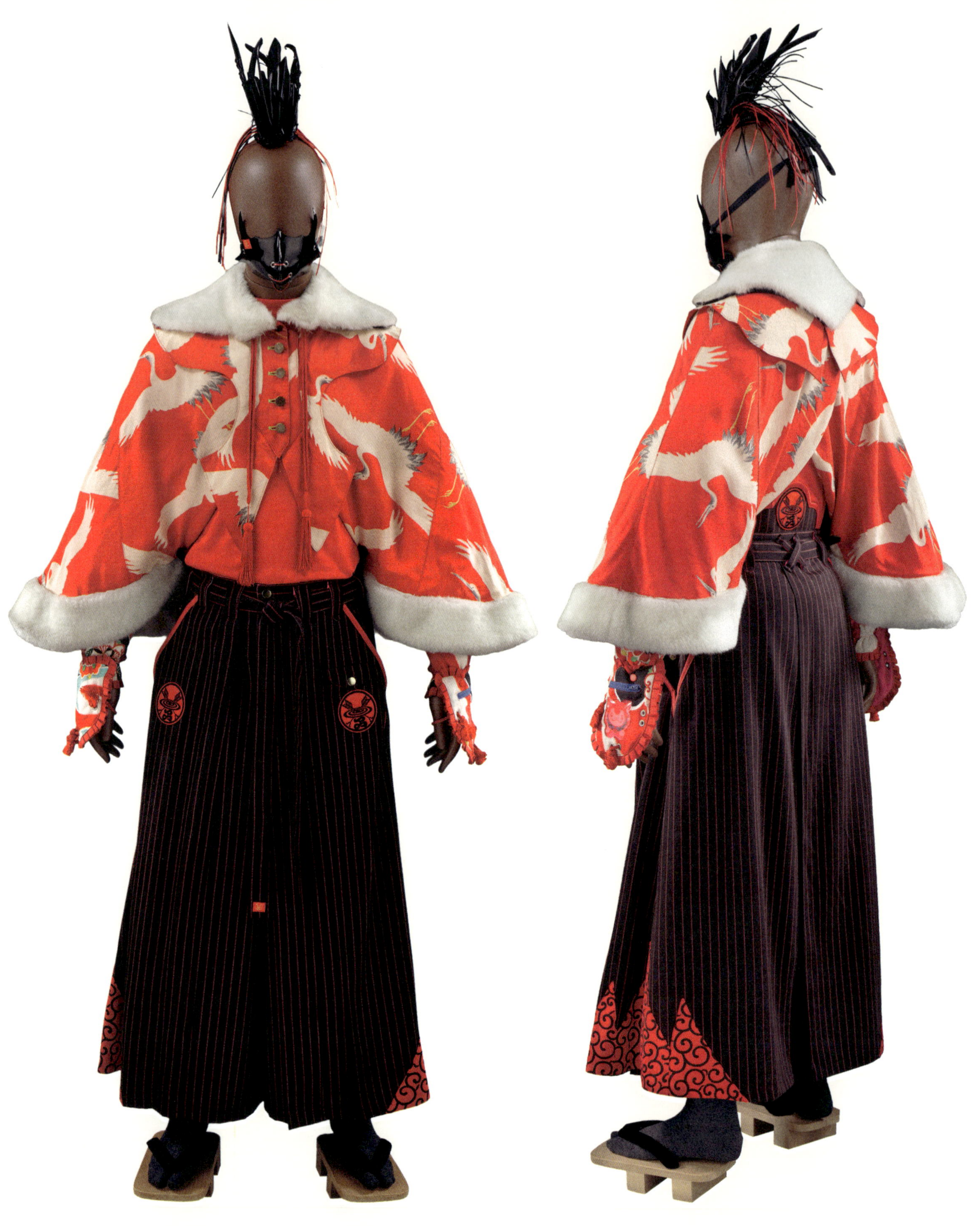

Ensemble, by Takuya Sawada for Takuya Angel, 1995–2011, V&A

Takuya Angel is a fashion brand that emerged in Japan in the 1990s as a radical form of street style. Founded by self-taught designer, DJ and musician Takuya Sawada, the label challenges the conventions of historic Japanese dress by mixing and matching them with various contemporary subcultures, drawing from a range of influences including aristocratic art from Japan's Heian period (794–1185), *kabuki*, Japanese anime and British suit design.

In this ensemble, Sawada reworked a vintage silk crêpe kimono into a cropped cape that references *horo*, a type of long, billowing, protective cloak worn by samurai warriors on the battlefield. The repurposed kimono fabric was trimmed and combined with modern synthetic textiles and decorations, including a faux-fur collar and sleeves, *mizuhiki* knot tassels, metal buttons and leather straps. Sawada's conceptual approach to design and fashion is rooted in his aspiration to revive and renew traditions of kimono wearing; many of his designs took their titles from historic clothing terms in an allusion to the enduring source of inspiration provided by these traditions. The designs, however, bear no clear relationship to the specific clothing item. In this instance, the connection to *horo* is also playfully obscure, gesturing towards cultural references without translating them directly.

Since the introduction of *yōfuku* (Western clothing) in the Meiji period (1868–1912), the everyday, sartorial experience of dressing in Japanese-style clothing has gradually been replaced by a growing preference for 'modern and progressive' *yōfuku*. Sawada sees his designs as a way of reintroducing aspects of Japanese cultural history while at the same time creating a new aesthetic and narrative around the nation's identity. Completing the look is a modern version of the *hakama*, a pleated lower garment, made with vintage kimono fabric and polyester twill suiting fabric. The precise way in which Sawada fused transhistorical elements to create new forms of clothing for a future Japan honours its sartorial history while allowing space for gender fluidity and individual expression. Characterised by its distinctive visual style and a clear conceptual message, Takuya Angel's bold, fantastical designs absorb elements from different cultures and seemingly operate without formal rules; the act of wearing these garments can become an identity performance, empowering wearers to subvert conventional societal roles.

Sawada styled this *horo* and *hakama* with funky accessories including a pair of mittens decorated with a cartoonish motif titled 'Angel Wings' – which Sawada has taken as a *kamon* (family crest) for his label – together with a sleek black fetish 'dragon mask' and a matching spiky cyberpunk head piece. The label's use of bright, contrasting colours and loud accessories injects an inclusive yet unique sensibility that frames the fabric of Tokyo's urban identity. The label's style rose in popularity in Japan in the late 1990s and early 2000s, marking an era of rebellious youth subculture that defined street style in Tokyo's iconic fashion district, Harajuku, at the time. This movement was captured in street fashion photography and cult magazines disseminated globally, such as *FRUiTS* magazine published by photographer Shōichi Aoki from 1997 to 2017. Through his creations for Takuya Angel, Sawada's work serves to reflect both the traditional and transcultural influences that have helped shape Japanese fashion today.

Noel Cheung, Assistant Curator

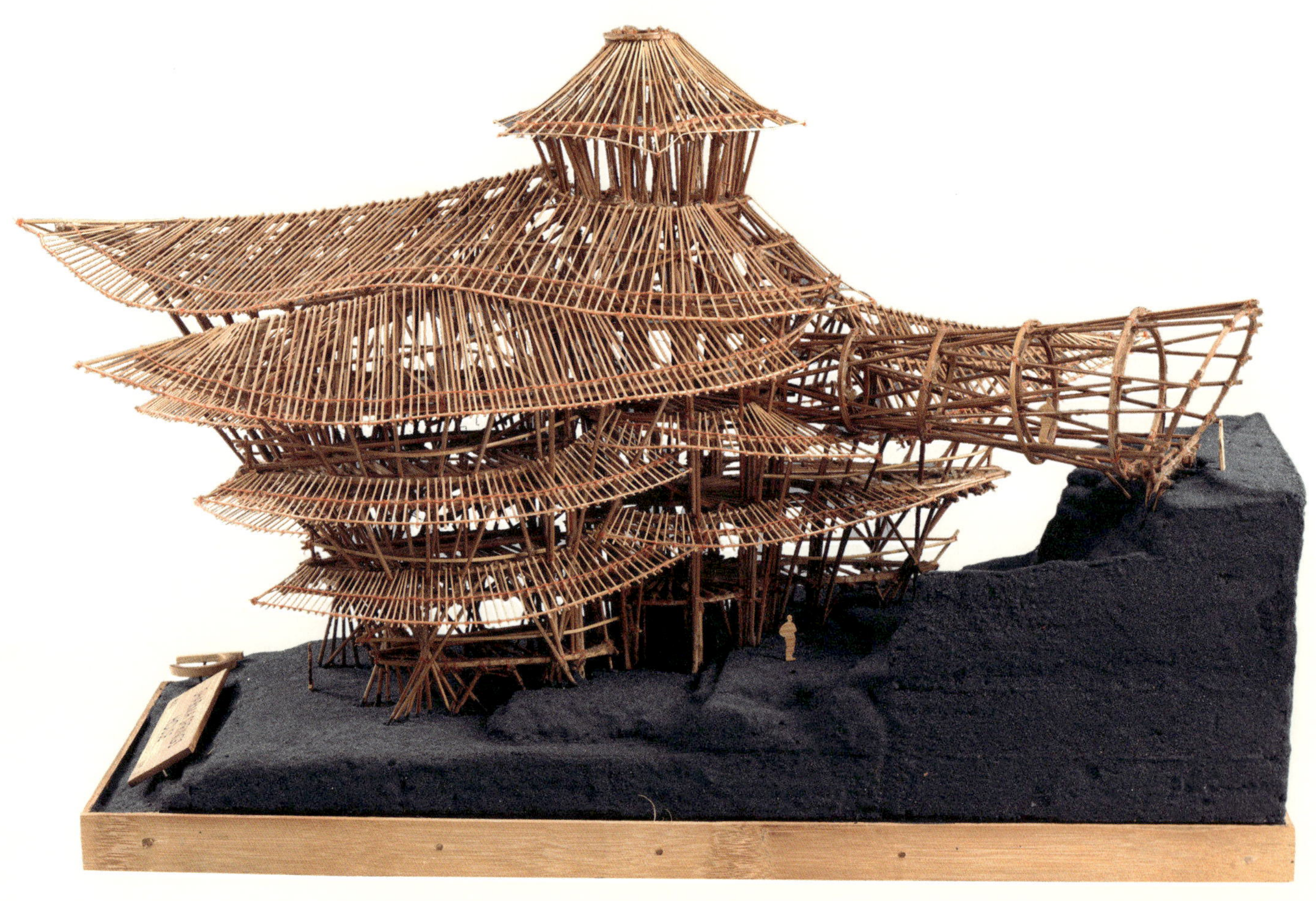

Architectural model for Sharma Springs residence, Bali, IBUKU Studio, 2011, V&A

When IBUKU's architects design a building, they don't start with conventional architectural drawings. Rather, they create sketches that are then translated into to-scale structural models made of hand-whittled bamboo sticks by local artisans.[1] This model is such a design structure. Created for the Sharma Springs residence, it illustrates the six-storey family home, which was designed to be built almost entirely from locally sourced bamboo. It is an almost fantastical structure, twisting and curving across various planes, not enclosed by exterior walls, but rather creating an open space that extends into its natural surroundings. But this building is more than just a beautiful, organic edifice. At the time of its completion in 2013, the Sharma Springs residence was the tallest bamboo structure in Bali. Its construction, using one of the world's most sustainable building materials, and one that also has a higher tensile strength than steel, serves as a clear testament to IBUKU's belief in bamboo as the 'green steel' of the future.

IBUKU believes its innovations in bamboo can change the way practitioners approach architecture – it addresses what it sees as the problems facing architecture today, taking a global view with regards to environmentally conscious construction. The name IBUKU, which means 'my mother earth' in Balinese, reflects the studio's design philosophy centred around sustainability and ecology. As one of the world's most sustainable building materials, bamboo is a type of evergreen grass that can grow rapidly in poor conditions without chemical fertilisers, and it releases 35 per cent more oxygen into the atmosphere than trees. IBUKU's experimentation with bamboo's materiality and performance is highly informed by locality; its unique bamboo dwellings reflect on the regional history of Indonesia and at the same time envisage a new way of connecting with and living in nature. IBUKU's founder Elora Hardy took inspiration from The Green School, set up by her father John Hardy in 2007, to create bamboo dwellings that blend with the environment. Despite its lightweight nature, bamboo is incredibly sturdy and can withstand heavy loads and strong winds. In addition to its versatility, its flexibility allows it to absorb vibrations, making bamboo an ideal and resilient choice as a construction material in earthquake-prone countries like Indonesia. The country has a long tradition of using bamboo as a construction material in small-scale, temporary structures. IBUKU takes the material further by inventing new ways of treating bamboo, enhancing its resistance to pests, and consequently, allowing for the construction of large-scale, permanent structures.

Beyond architecture and the environment, IBUKU is also engaged in social sustainability through working with local communities and providing training for artisans. For Sharma Springs, IBUKU's team of designers, architects and engineers collaborated with local bamboo artisans in the creative process. IBUKU's team created initial designs informed by the site – the foliage, rice paddies and natural contours of the land. The designs were then translated into detailed scale models made by local artisans. These architectural models were digitally replicated in 3D and studied to test structural integrity, during which process technical drawings were produced. On the construction site, experienced bamboo artisans would deduce from the architectural model and technical drawings the type of bamboo poles required for the build. With the use of traditional building techniques informed by local craftsmanship, IBUKU expressed a new layer of Balinese culture, one that is created by the people of Bali alongside those coming to live there, and which celebrates its local traditions and ecological knowledge.

Noel Cheung, Assistant Curator

Exterior rendering of V&A East Museum by O'Donnell + Tuomey/Ninety90 (CGI made 2018)

An Interview with V&A East Museum Architect John Tuomey

Claire McKeown

John Tuomey At the beginning, in 2015 when we won the competition, it was a fantastic feeling of embarking on an adventurous project. We took an approach that drove our team right from the start: of wanting to pull people into the space. The first idea we had for the V&A East Museum building was to try to turn a building inside out as a means of pulling people inside. Although the form evolved from that initial idea, the ambition remained. This building we have created is about sheltering the contents of the museum, while also standing the building on the ground in such a way that it looks like it's inviting people to pour in through the tent flaps – it's a circus kind of building I suppose.

As part of our design approach, we began by thinking, if this building was to take on an identity, then what jacket should it wear? It might have been curvilinear, it might have been angular, it might have been faceted, but I think the real drive was – because ours is a terraced scheme, from Sadler's Wells to the BBC, to the London College of Fashion, to the V&A – to make the V&A a pavilion and not an end of terrace. What we produced was a building in the round. If you just look at a section you would say that it's consistent with everything else on the project – scale-wise, level-wise, etc. But once it puts its jacket on, it stands free, it stands independent.

Claire McKeown I remember the conversations about the 'jacket'; it's a great metaphor that allows people into your way of thinking. I love how the surface of that precast concrete jacket plays with profiled peaks and troughs, responding to the geometry of the steel frame.

JT I had this prejudice in my head that the place to make buildings is on-site and that precast was repetitious and impersonal. But, when I visited the manufacturers, I thought 'Wow!', and I began to see that you could make something off-site which, when it's locked into place on-site, would be just as solid.

I think what our building is trying to say is that there's a refinement and a poetry in the realisation of prefabrication, which doesn't lose the craftsmanship, it just expresses it in a different way. It's a progressive representation for the V&A that seems to suit its mission.

CM The craftsmanship and the number of hours your team put in to develop each of those panels was phenomenal and it fits so well with the theme of making we have across our V&A sites – the idea of crafting the façade.

JT Just before I sat down here at home to talk to you, I realised I still have the very first model that we showed to you for the project. I'd made a sketch based on the sleeve of a Vermeer painting that's in the National Gallery of Ireland and I was trying to work with the folds. I passed the sketch over to one of my project architects and said, 'Can you make something like that?' That afternoon he gave me this. It's just thin cardboard but I keep it because it's the first iteration of the building. I don't know how many of them we've made since, but we've made a lot!

CM That iterative process is so interesting, because perhaps my favourite elements of the building are those circulation spaces: the space you've created between the elevation and the floorplates of each of the galleries and the range of volumes and views that you get as a result. It's amazing that, from that sketch of the folds of a dress and the idea of adding a jacket, you arrived at this building.

JT Yes, but that first thought was just a sheet. We didn't know how to make it. In fact, we didn't even know what it might be made of. It might have been metal; it might have been brick. But this is where the thought about the jacket comes from: there's a film that Wim Wenders made with Yohji Yamamoto back in the 1990s called *Notebooks on Cities and Clothes*. In it, Wim Wenders says

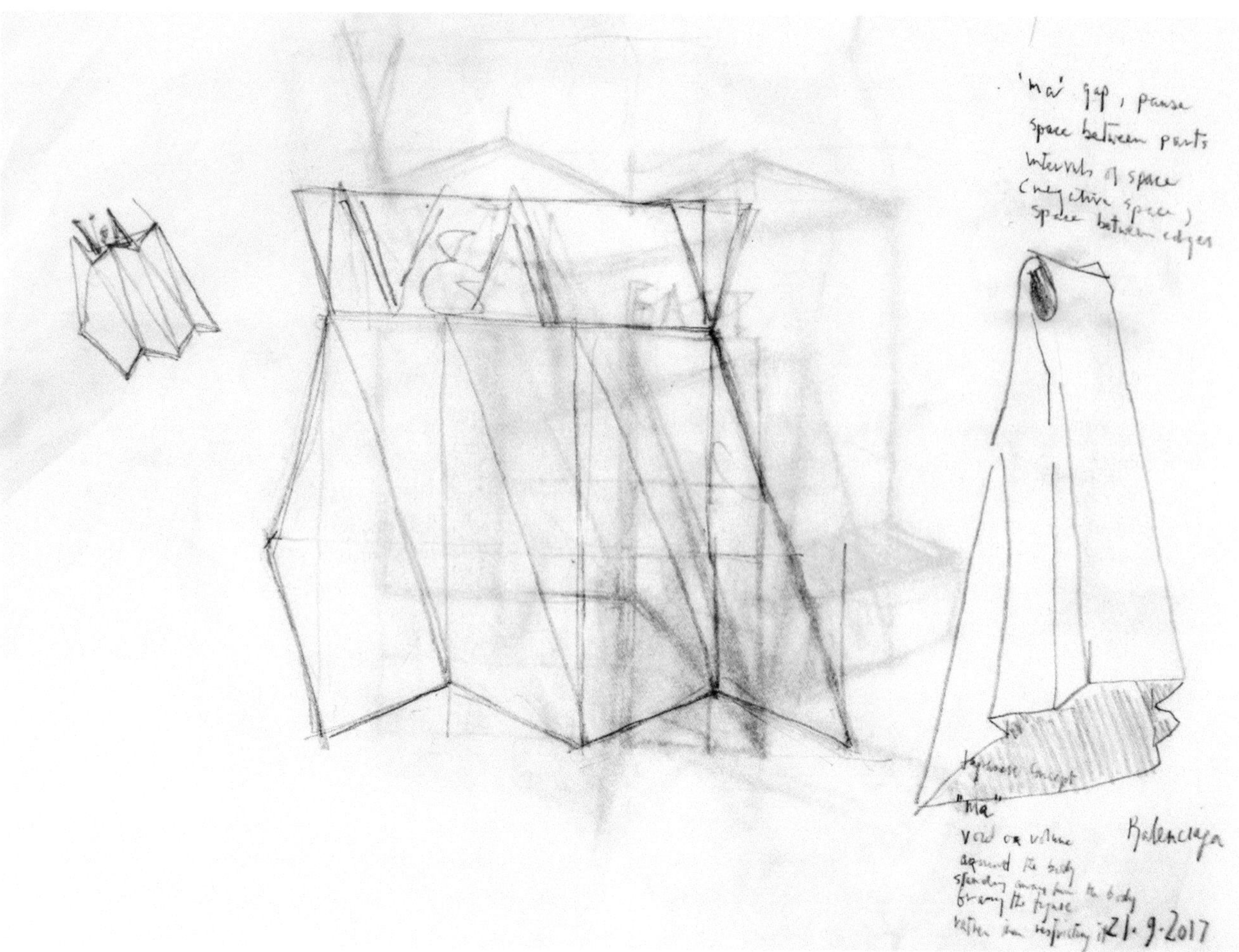

Concept sketch by O'Donnell + Tuomey, 2017

that when he put on his first Yohji Yamamoto jacket he felt like he was protected. I started thinking about that in relation to the space in between, which you also find in the Vermeer painting: there's the fabric that clothes you, there's the body that's sheltered, but there's also the space in between. So, I thought, why don't we put a thick crust on the V&A and then work into that crust? We can hollow spaces out of the thickness, so when the public sees the shape on the outside, they can feel that shape again on the inside before they enter the controlled space of the exhibitions.

We also had a lot of fun trying to make a visitor journey that would be full of surprises – that would be lively and sociable. You turn on a half landing and you meet someone coming down, or you find yourself overlooking where they were, and you feel, all the while, that you're in the in-between. You're on your way to see something, but the cascading journey is part of the preparation.

CM There was also the overlay of the Balenciaga dress, that was the same concept, right?

JT That's right. The V&A South Kensington had this beautiful exhibition about Balenciaga, and I didn't know about him until I saw that show. Balenciaga took priests' vestments and he hid the body inside these folded frocks. Nick Veasey was taking X-ray photographs, and he took one of the Balenciaga dress, and I suddenly saw that it's not only a folded surface on the outside, it's got structure on the inside and you can see its skeleton. I remember coming back to the office and saying to one of my project architects, 'Why don't we try to X-ray the building so that the structure, which has to be a steel frame, is not hidden by the skin, but is the skeleton behind the skin?'

We distributed that idea to our engineers, and we said that everything had to look like it made sense in an X-ray, like a digestive system or a skeletal system. I think everybody got that analogy and that is the discipline that controls the lift shafts, the pipe drops, the structural intersections – they're all part of this idea that came out of looking at this X-ray of this Balenciaga dress.

CM This is something we talk about a lot, how we can use our objects to inspire our visitors.

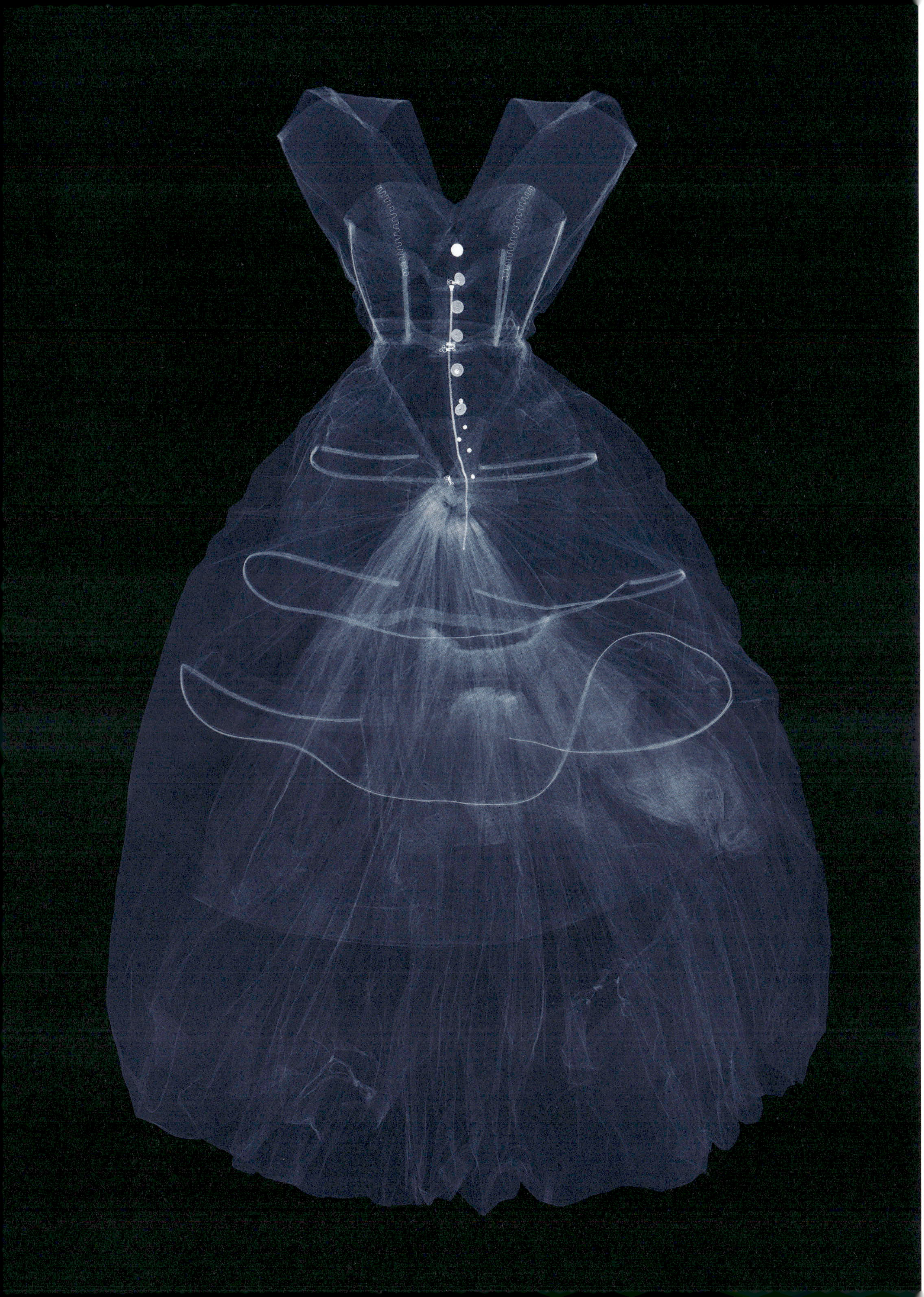

X-ray photograph of 1956 Balenciaga dress, by Nick Veasey, 2016

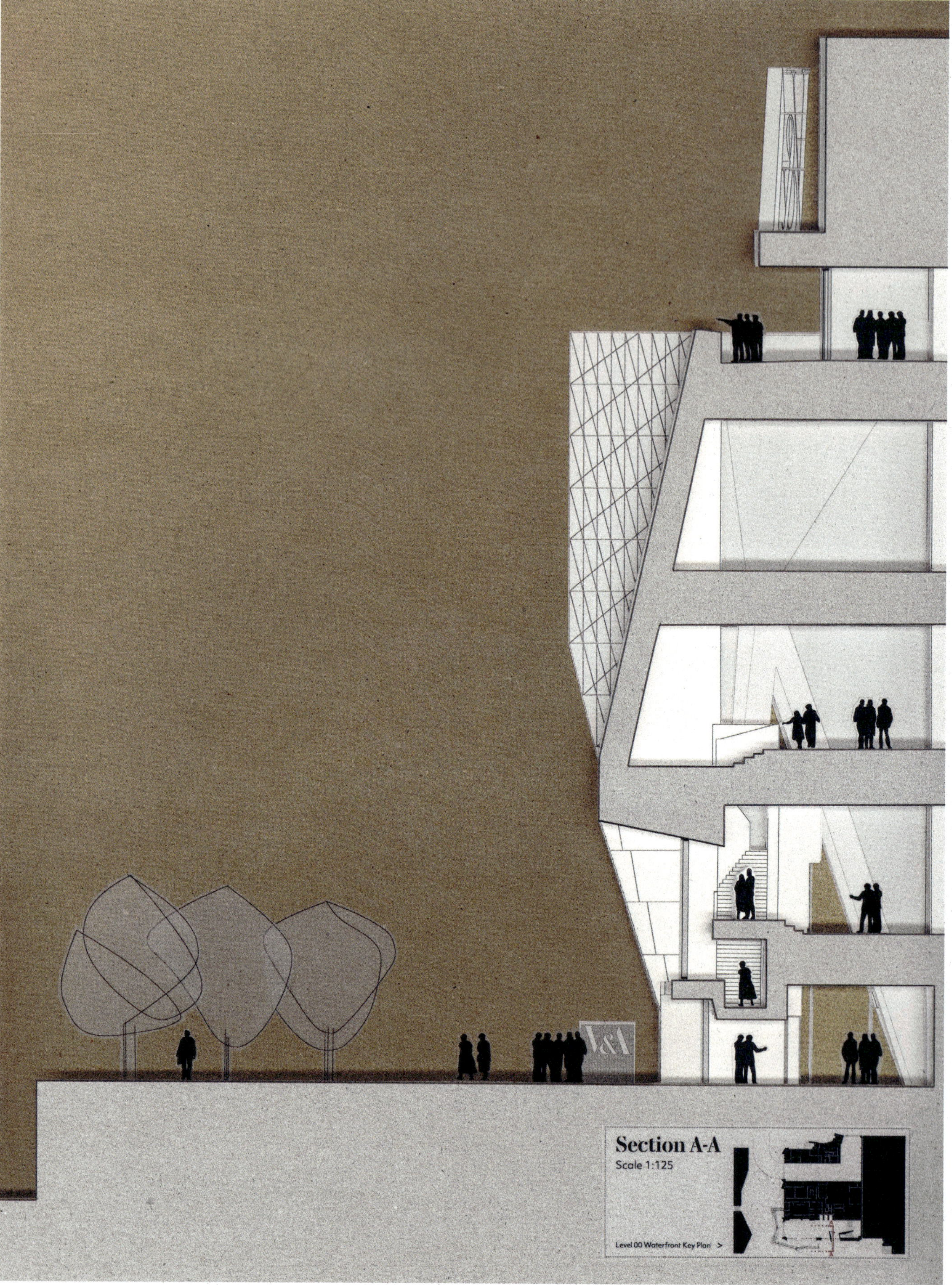

Section model photo by O'Donnell + Tuomey (made 2023 for Royal Hibernian Academy Annual Exhibition)

It's such a wonderful example that you went to an exhibition and now the V&A has a building that's informed by that exhibition, as well as by a Vermeer painting, and all these other ideas coming together.

JT If I have a purpose in my work, I think I'm trying to get across the idea that there is something poetic in architecture. I want to communicate my belief that buildings are alive with thoughts inside them; that they're not neutral. Buildings speak to each other, and they are also trying to speak to us, and they're there for us to work our imaginations around.

CM You've had an amazingly long career creating beautiful buildings, and here you've produced the buildings for the V&A and for Sadler's Wells, so a significant proportion of the East Bank. What was the thinking around putting those buildings together in a way that's creating a new bit of London in Stratford?

JT It's a privilege for us, but I feel that no matter what project we are working on, the real threshold moment is when the building gives something back to the world. Something happens between the inside and the outside that doesn't belong to either the inside or to the outside but that leaves you in the shelter of a building's generosity. The V&A stands up on its toes in order to make you feel that it's easy to come in and out. It's very invitational.

CM That idea of the building being invitational is so important to us. Our aim at V&A East is to engage with an audience that is perhaps underserved by the museum sector. To do that, we want to provide greater access to the collection and to inspire our visitors, but also to welcome them. We want to break down those barriers, the metaphorical ones and the physical ones, and those aims feel very aligned with yours.

In terms of how the building needs to both stand out, visually, in the terrace, but also not to be intimidating, that's a tough thing to get right.

JT I remember when I came to your boardroom with one of the in-progress models and I had put the V&A logo on the model. I remember your chairman asking would that not be a little vulgar to have such a big sign on the building. But for me, the logo itself is a beautiful and lasting piece of design; alright it's the sign for the V&A, but it's also a sign for perfect design somehow. In the end we put the V&A to one side of the building, so it would be over the entrance. When you see the composition of the façade it's not bang in the middle like an emblem, it's indicating how to arrive at the building. This little building was cooked up especially to be the V&A, and the more it echoes that the happier I am.

CM What was the biggest challenge for the practice when creating the V&A East Museum?

JT I think we learned a lot between the first and second design iterations. The first iteration was made in a competition environment, where you get very involved in the rather abstracted concept of how it could be. When I got to know the V&A better, through the tours and by meeting the curators, I realised that this is a house of many houses. That we needed to make something that would allow for, and make a home for, the diversity of content, but that doesn't simplify it. There is a degree of mystique about the V&A, so I tried to arrive at an architecture that had its own mystique. The building itself is very clear in its circulation and it's very logical in its structure, but it doesn't reveal itself completely all at once. You have to walk around it or think about it. I think that's a good preparation for this house of multitudes that is the V&A.

I'd say understanding the diversities in the culture of your organisation was the difference between this project and other projects. It's a highly complex ecosystem and I think we've relished that challenge.

CM We are a complex organisation, but we also have to think about the end users and their needs. You have to find an understanding of those relationships and dynamics, all the while producing incredible architecture.

JT Yes, but architecture, which is highly visible and highly physical, also exists when you look away from it. You remember the atmosphere or the aura of a place. And I think from the very beginning we wanted it to feel open-hearted somehow, as if it belongs to everybody. In 2015, the V&A had an exhibition called *All of This Belongs to You*, and this is an important message. Similarly, Alistair Spalding in Sadler's Wells wanted to put 'You are welcome' over the door. I think that culture goes right through all the thoughts about the East Bank, by all the architects; they want this feeling that you're in a place that puts you at ease.

When you get to the top floor of the V&A, in the event space, I like to imagine the people who have made the journey up looking down at the square, and that they might have in their minds a kind of double image of themselves, being on the terrace of the event space but also being down there in the square, as if they have mentally mapped their own journey. I want people to feel that even when they've reached the destination of their journey that they can still feel a thread of connection right back into the Olympic Park.

CM I can see that, not least as when you ascend the stairs your experience isn't the same throughout the floors; you have landmarks throughout that journey, which perhaps aid memory as you circulate.

JT You were asking about challenges: once I've thought of an idea like that – of wanting this continuous journey throughout the building – then the challenge is the complexity of all the security, structural and environmental considerations. It's getting the materiality of the building out of the way so that people feel as free to move about inside as they do on the street outside. If you're thinking about this concept of invitation, the first time you have to push a door is the time you think, 'Well, maybe I won't go in, maybe I'm not welcome here.' As soon as you're inside, you should feel like you have the whole building at your disposal – you really have that in South Kensington. People walk into the Japanese collection in South Kensington who might even just have been looking for a coffee because the whole building is laid out without borders. I love that, but in a modern building it's quite difficult to do because everybody wants compartmentalisation.

CM And on top of that we have a layer of challenges surrounding what the objects need, not just what the people need. I remember our long conversations about daylight in the various galleries and how we balance that with the conservation requirements for the objects, because without those wonderful windows the building would be incredibly uninviting. Balancing something like daylighting, or room temperature with the environmental needs of the objects created another layer of issues to navigate.

JT And the needs of the building as a physical structure created another layer again. We could have quite a long and technical conversation about the tolerances between the convergence steel structure and the concrete jacket – there's huge complexity in the tolerances between what's holding the building up and what's wrapping it.

CM Huge complexity, but also great beauty in that steel frame, though unfortunately you can't see it now.

JT It's amazing. Luckily, we have some X-ray images of it. Each component element had to be made perfectly because when the dry assembly concrete arrives on site it doesn't forgive any millimetre of variation. Those things are 14 metres long by 2 metres high and they fit together perfectly and then the lines that cross them have to meet exactly on the line.

CM I remember the anticipation when the first lorry came up with the precast panels. All the build team did a fantastic job, plus the engineers Buro Happold with the design; the preciseness that they managed to achieve in the making of those panels – the result is really beautiful. People often think it's made of stone. Do you remember all those conversations about pigment?

JT Concrete is stone in a way. It's made out of sand and gravel, so it has its origins in stone. But we wanted it to be pigmented so as not to be reminiscent of industrial grey concrete. We wanted it to feel like it was formed out of some stuff of the earth. The beauty of it is that it's a thoroughly modern, thoroughly economical, thoroughly carbon-aware project – there's no waste.

CM How do you feel towards the V&A East project as it draws to a close?

JT Now we are coming to the end of the project, I think that we all feel that together – your people and our people – we have made something very special. This has been a long project; actually, between the beginning and the end it will have been a 10-year project. But I've had the same architects working on it all of the time and I think all of us feel that we've been involved in something unique. I've always felt that it's nice that our architects have the chance to concentrate their minds on such an important subject, and when you look at the V&A and its collection and all the concentrated minds that are contained with the objects, it really is a perfect synergy.

Detail of the façade of V&A East Museum showing its precast panels, 2022

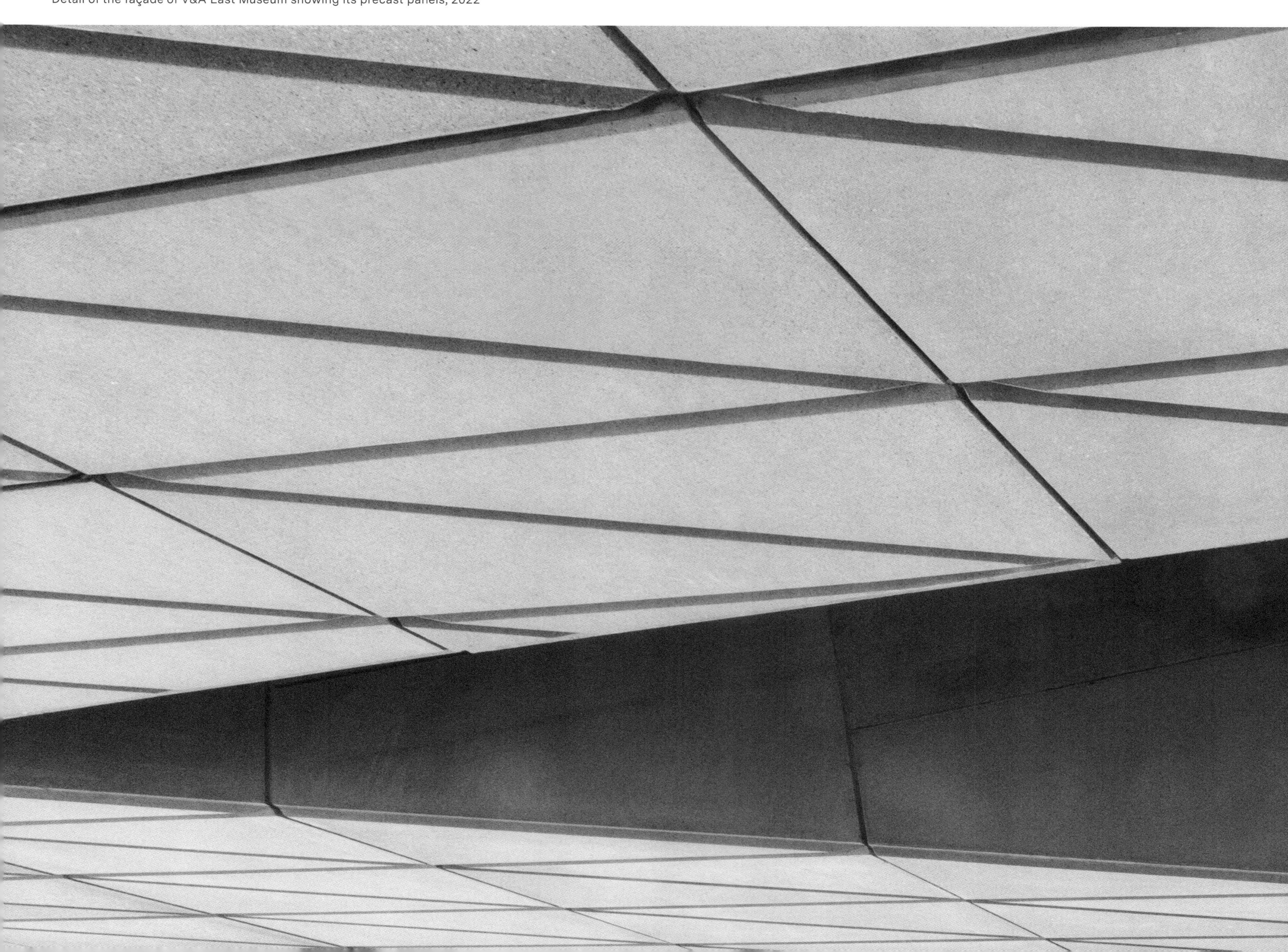

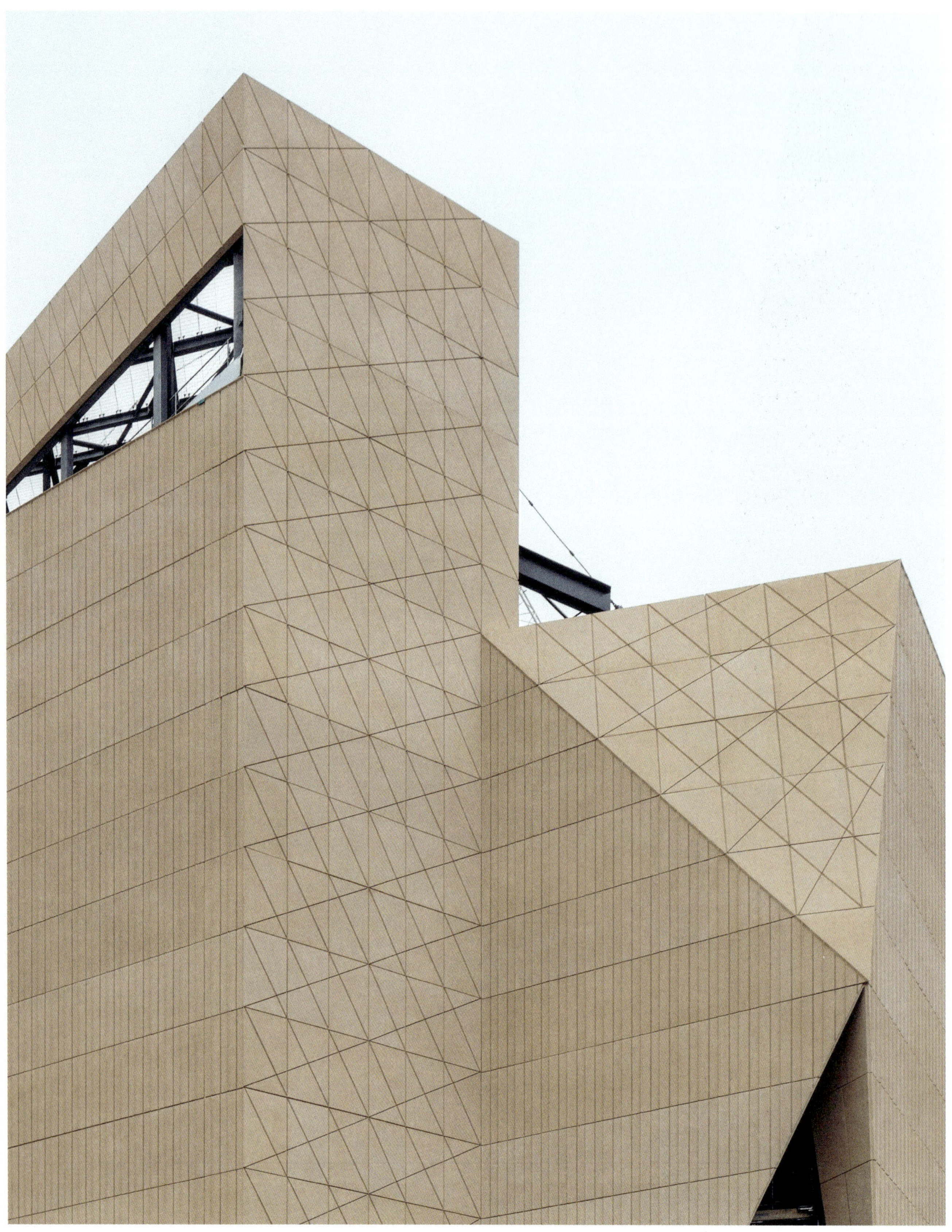

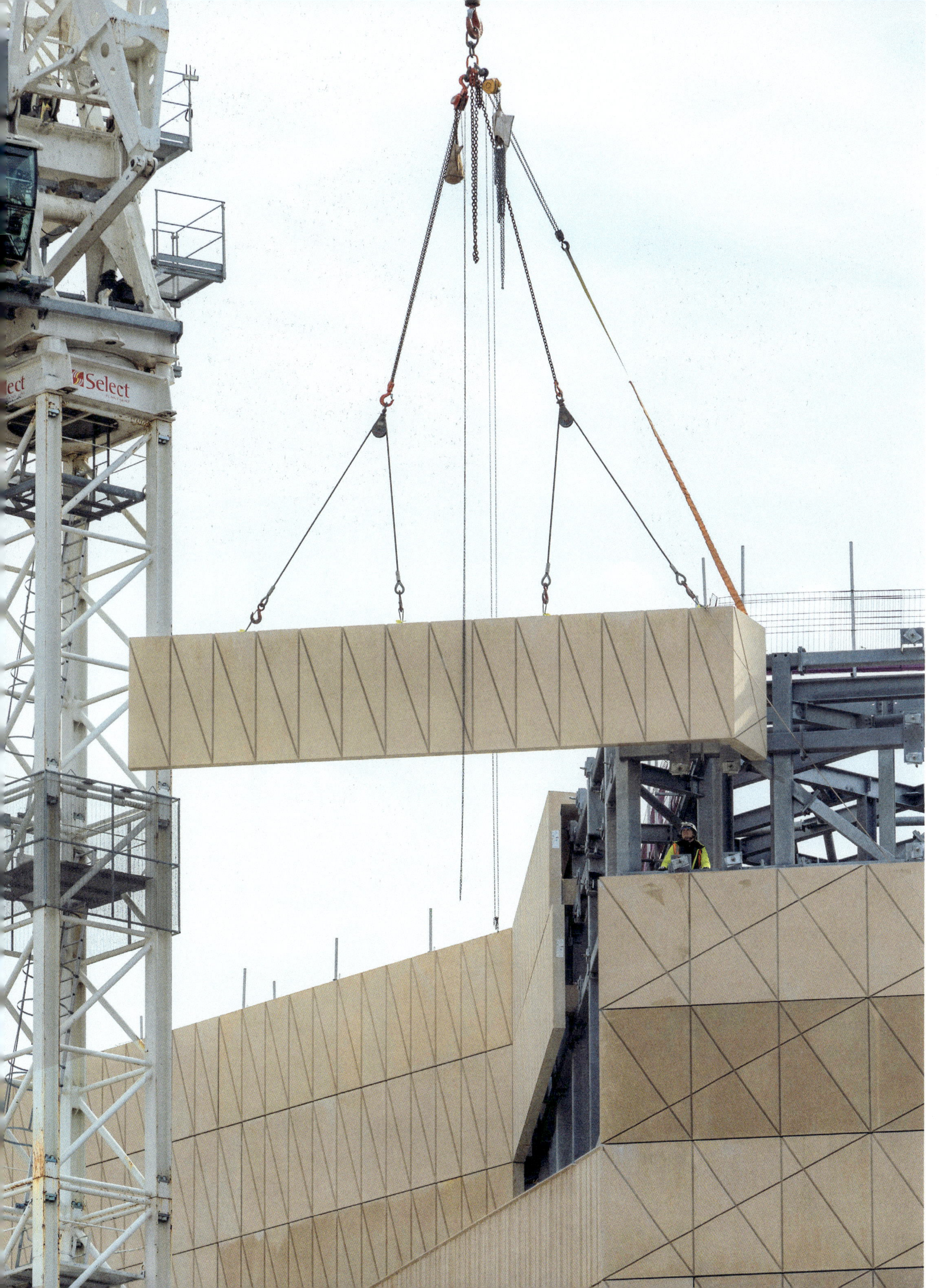
Select

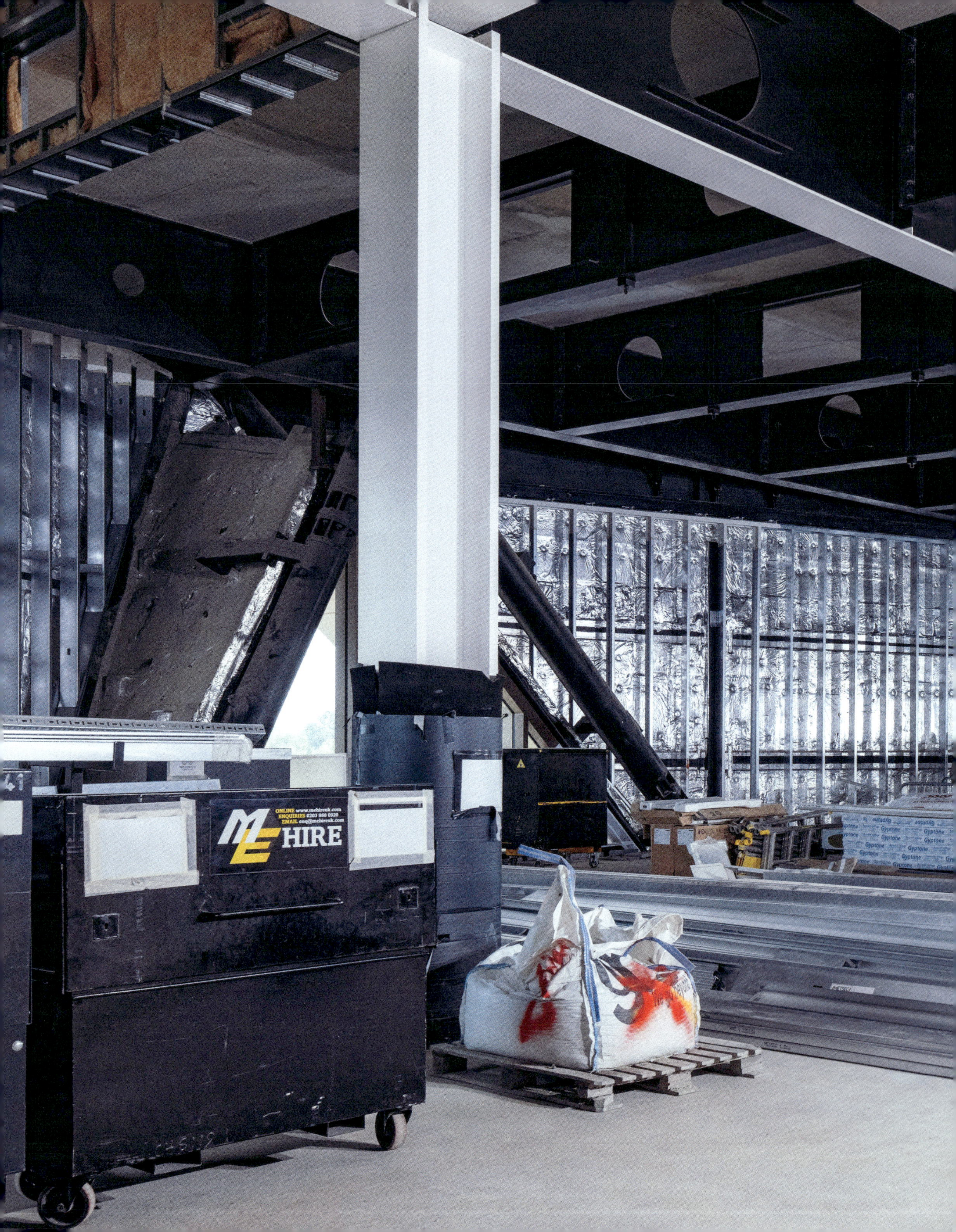
ONLINE www.mehireuk.com
ENQUIRIES 0203 968 0920
EMAIL enq@mehireuk.com
ME HIRE

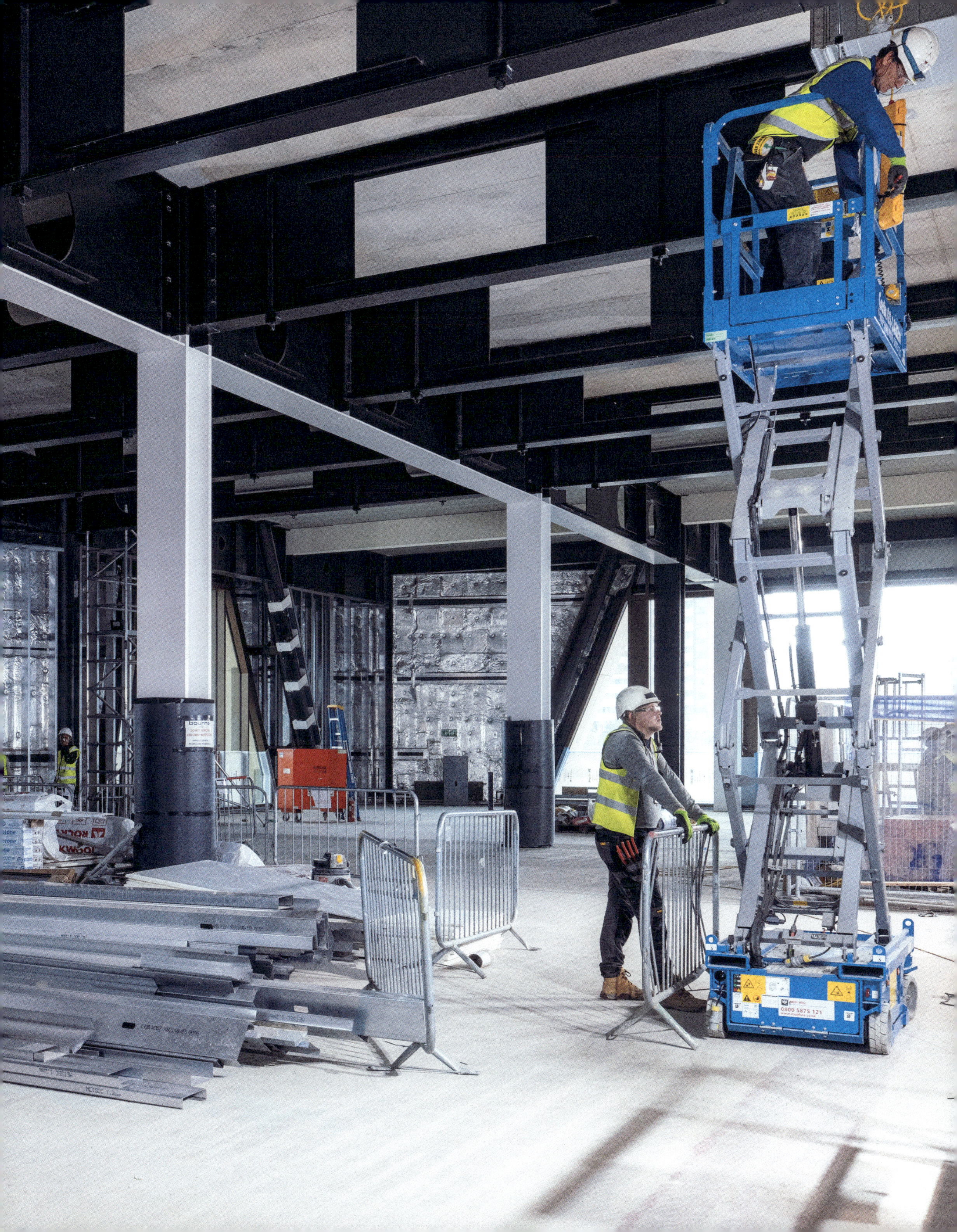
0800 5875 121

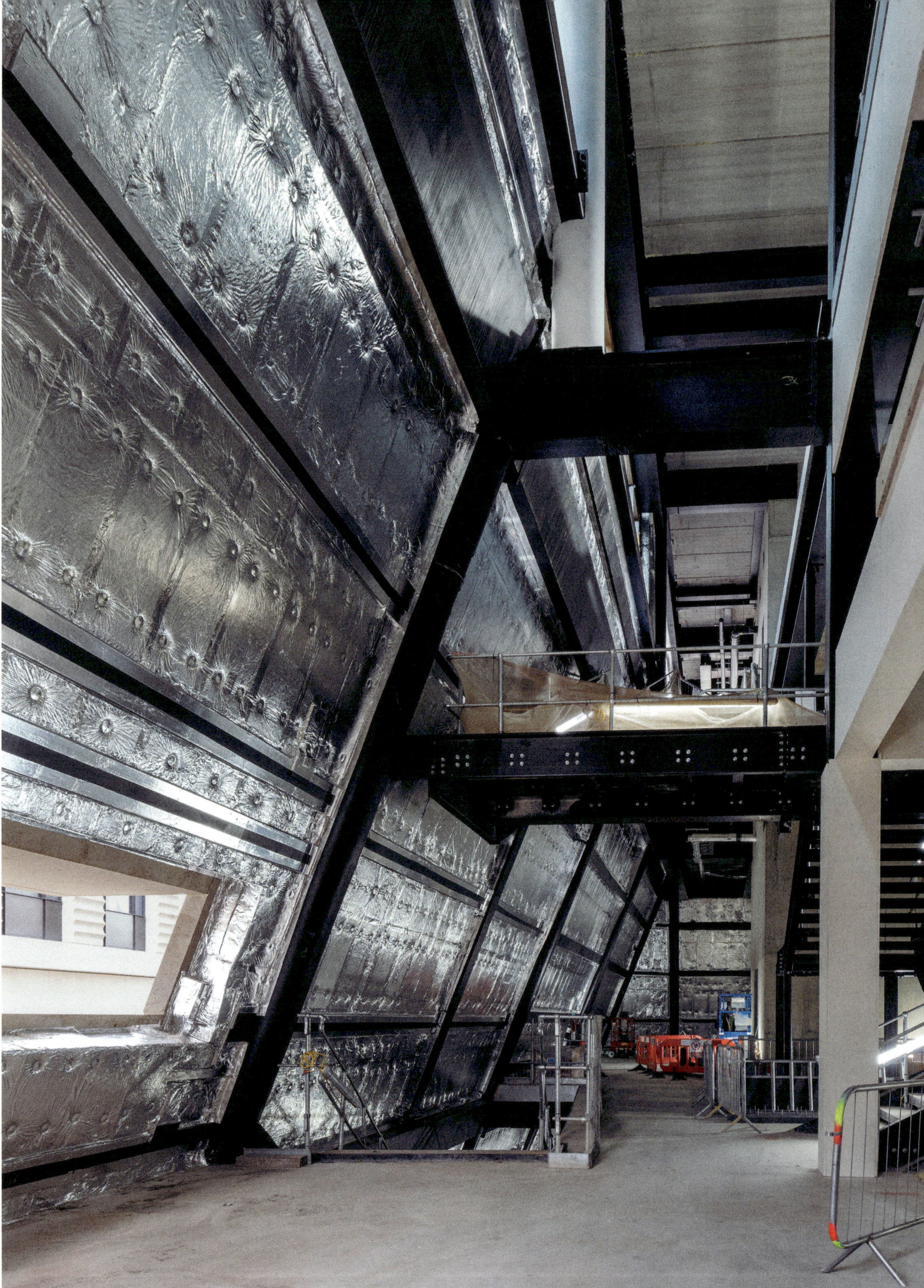

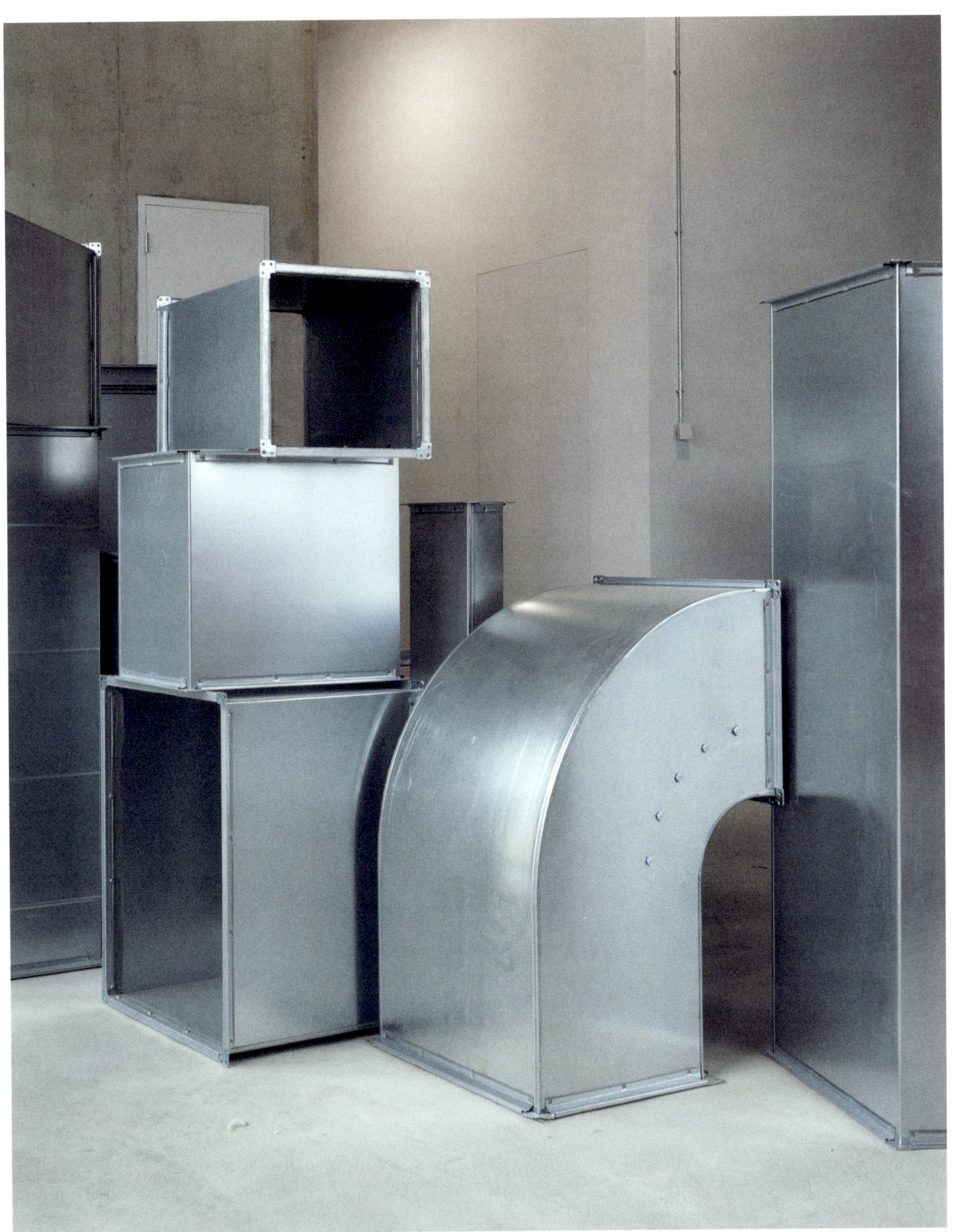

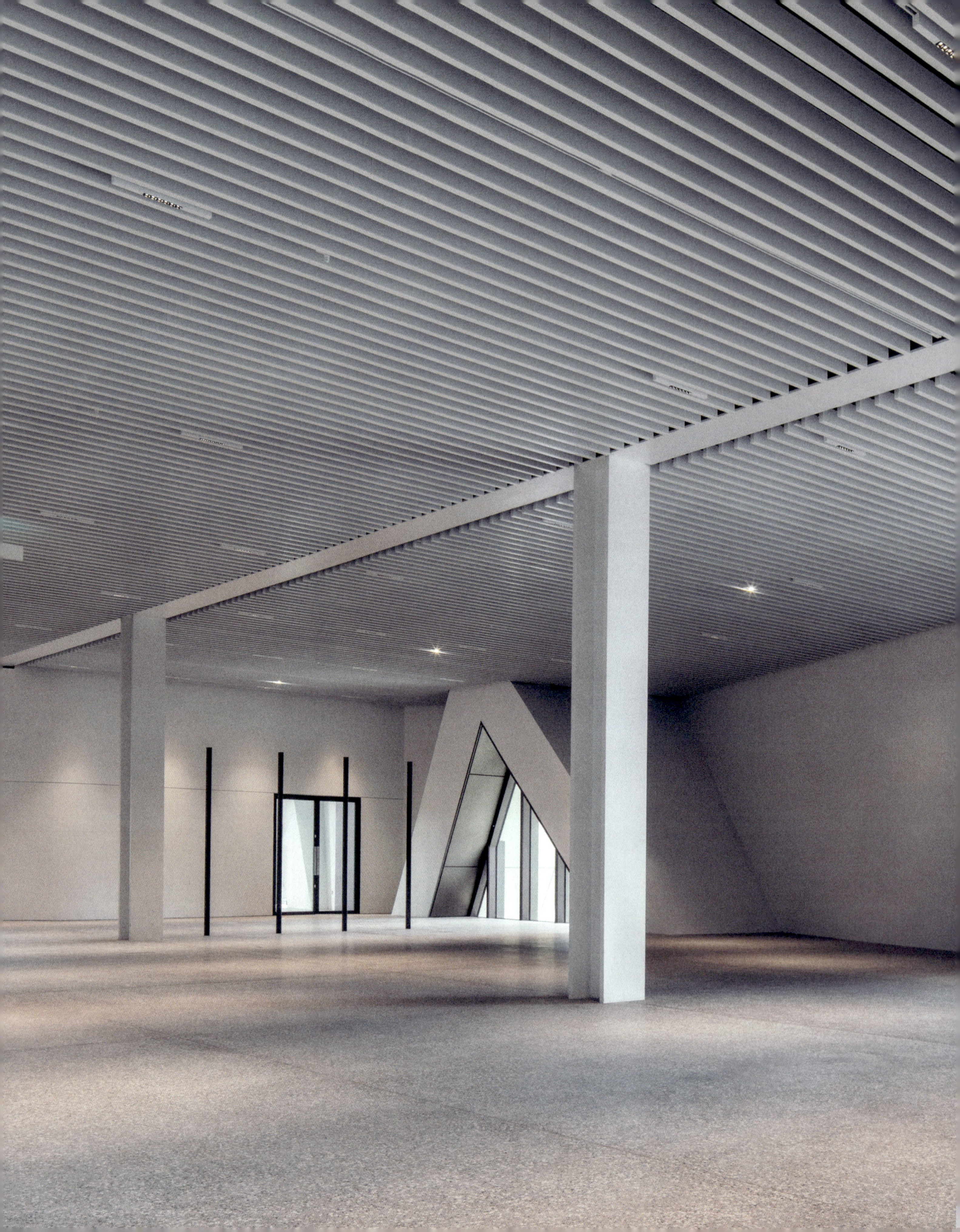

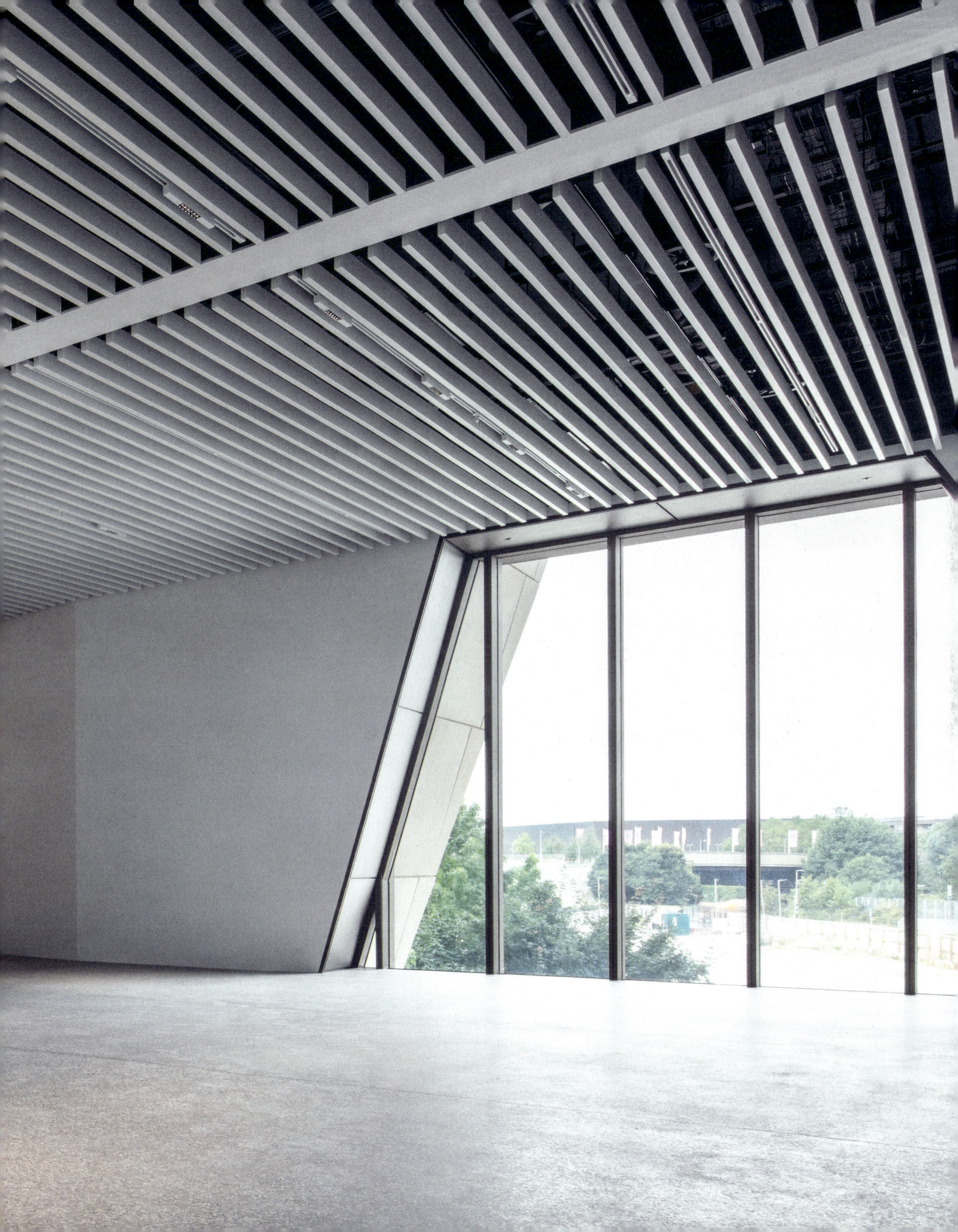

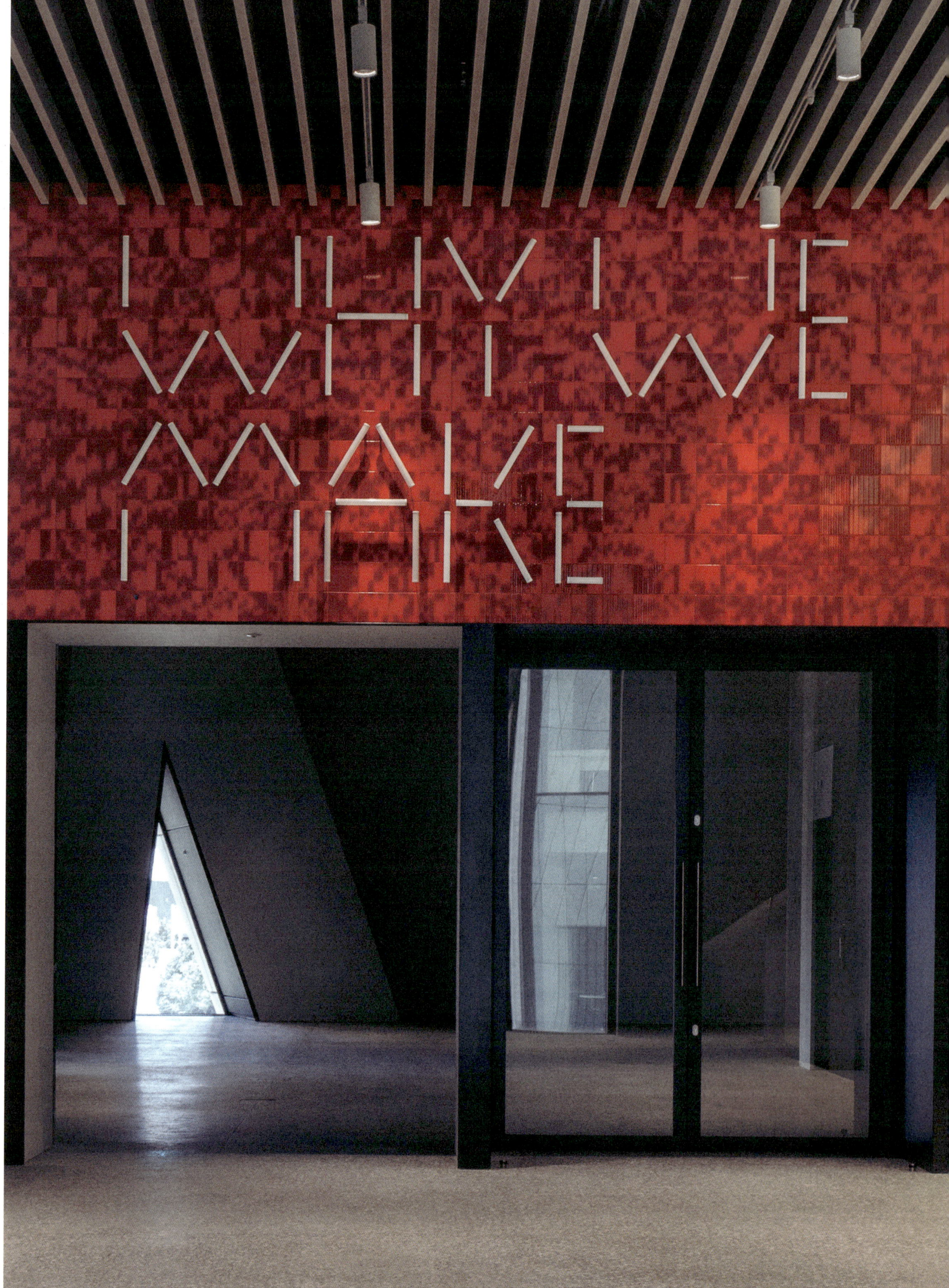

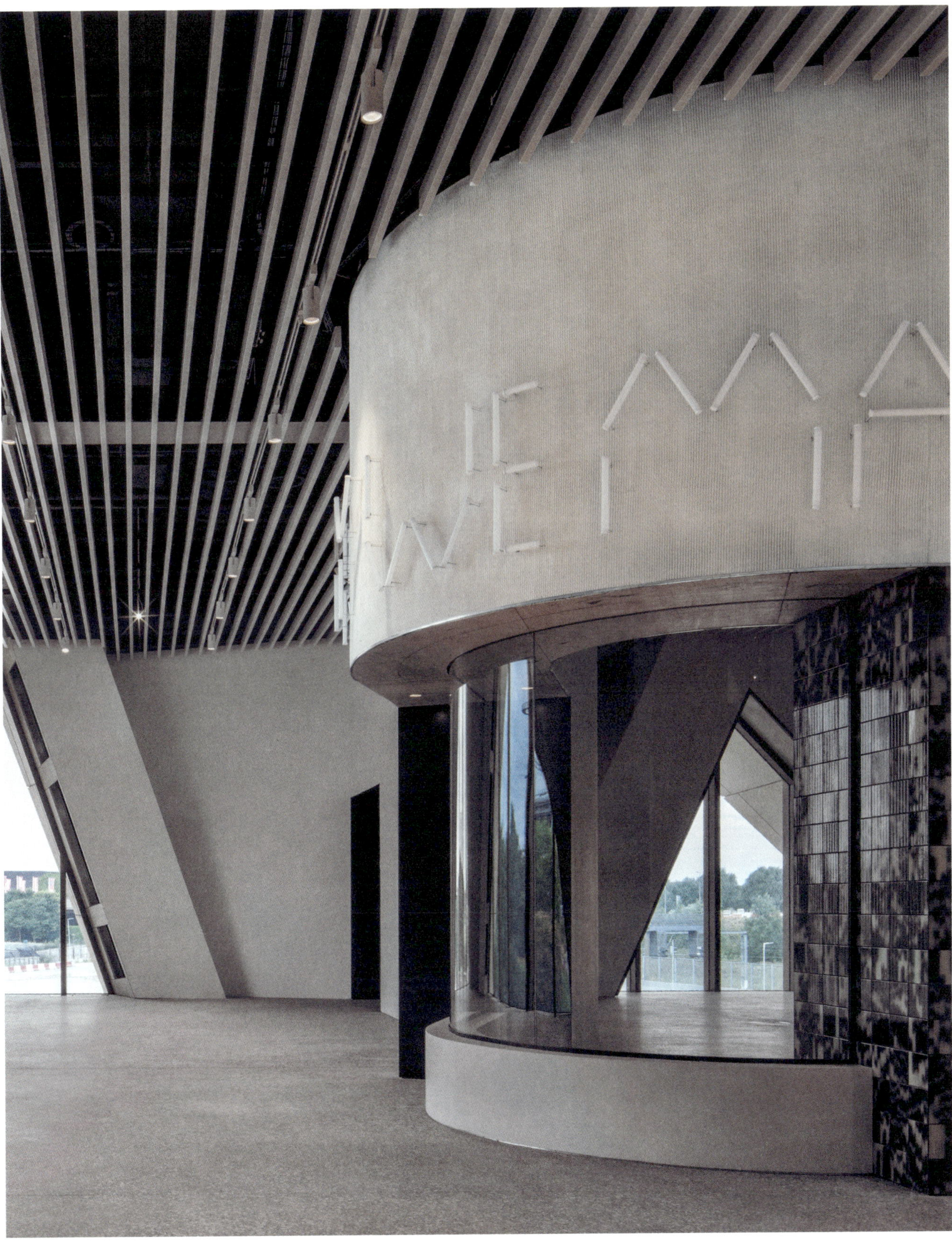

What

a Stor

Can

ehouse

Do

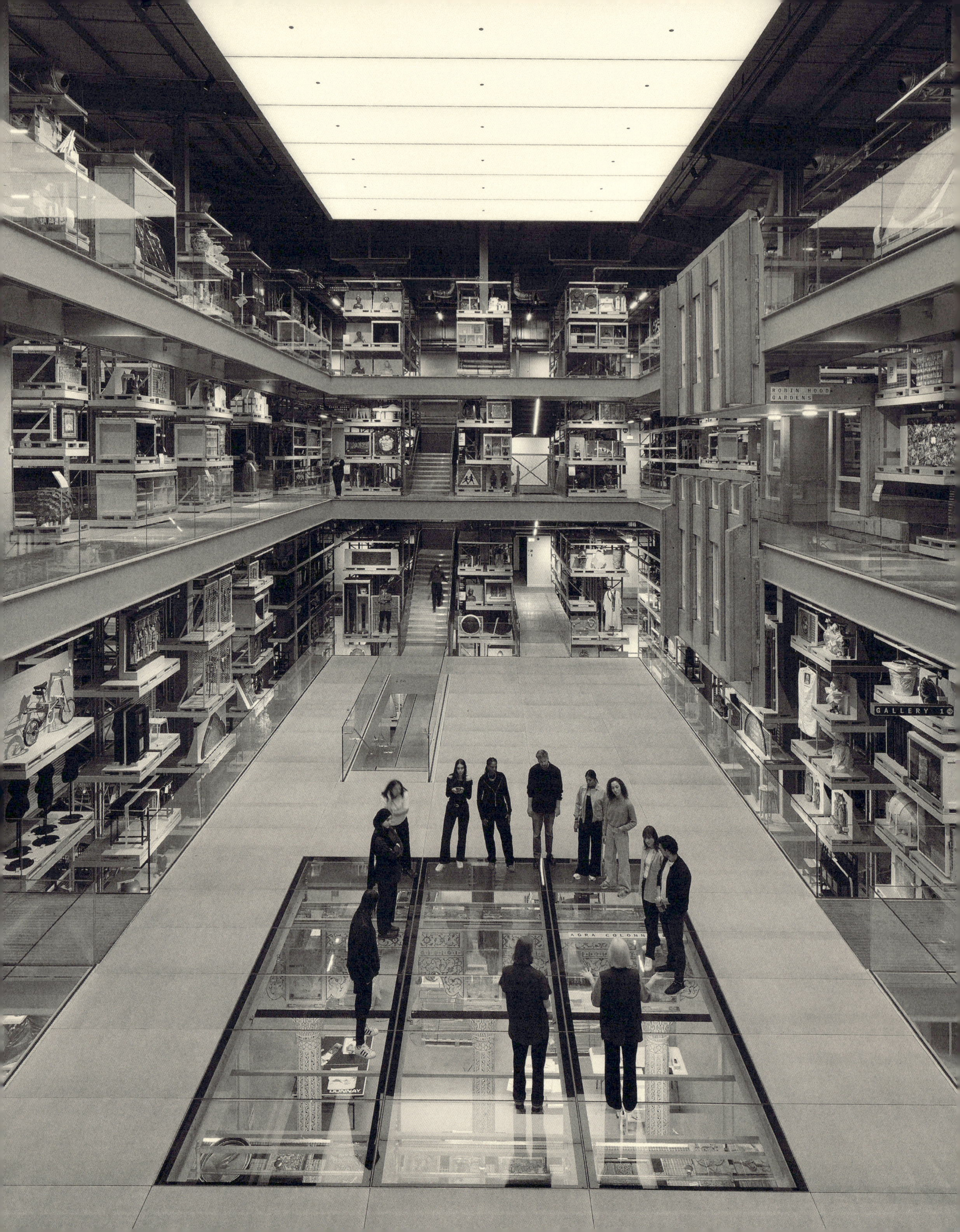
ROBIN HOOD
GARDENS
GALLERY 1

Weston Collections Hall, V&A East Storehouse, 2025

A storage facility is often thought of as a space of exclusion, intended only for those with privileged access. For national museum collections, this presents a problem: how can a nation really own a collection when the public can't access it? With V&A East Storehouse, the answer is to radically open up our storage by actively encouraging the public to come, visit and engage with the collection. It has involved a fundamental rethink in both the architecture and operational management of our storage space. Yet at the same time, it brings the opportunity of rendering transparent the care, labour and love that go into maintaining collections, while creating more meaningful, unexpected and serendipitous encounters with some 250,000 objects. This section explores the architectural, operational and curatorial challenges and opportunities that come with radically opening up museum collections.

Order an object appointment at V&A East Storehouse

A Working Storehouse
Georgia Haseldine

A storehouse is a place where things are held for future use, skilfully maintained and preserved for winter months or hard times. V&A East Storehouse, as the main storage facility for the V&A's multiple sites and collections, also holds provisions for future use, but in this case for creativity, design, inspiration and aspiration, tended to by staff specialised in skills from conservation and archive management to security. It is a place to scour for ideas about how to solve the most pressing issues of our day: what can fish-scale sequins on a bridal tiara tell us about the preciousness of waste materials in a world trying to wean itself off plastic? Or, how can the first fitted kitchen, designed to emancipate women from unpaid domestic labour – the Frankfurt Kitchen – potentially inform future designs for the sustainable homes our cities so desperately need? Underpinning the curatorial mission of Storehouse is the belief that the interests of the 'now' mixed with the knowledge preserved in objects from our shared past will provide us with direction to shape the future.

However, the current trend in the museum world for visible storage is not enough. Saying that you can see how objects are stored doesn't make objects in that store more useful. Visibility doesn't automatically empower the viewer, create oversight or institutional transparency.[1]

What is needed is a shared civic space based on exchange that is truly accessible to all. Pierre-Joseph Proudhon, the French anarchist, might have been more famous for saying that 'property is theft', but he also said, 'property is freedom'. He saw free access to resources that are held in common as the mechanism for a 'world of possessors', rather than one of the dispossessed.[2] In that sense, Storehouse is intended as a commons, a new place in our city where these resources truly are for and owned by the nation.

Working

The work of Storehouse is happening all around you. Objects tracked by barcodes are packed for loan, others are conserved, some are photographed while a selection are moved to a study space, ready for a community group to examine them. Every day new challenges arise. Where would you paint an accession number onto a sculpture made entirely from thin red wire? Can you photograph a mirror without accidentally making a self-portrait? What can keep a pair of trainers box-fresh when they are 30 years old?

Museum work is rooted in the perpetual question of how we should treat an object now, and consideration of the impact our decision will have on

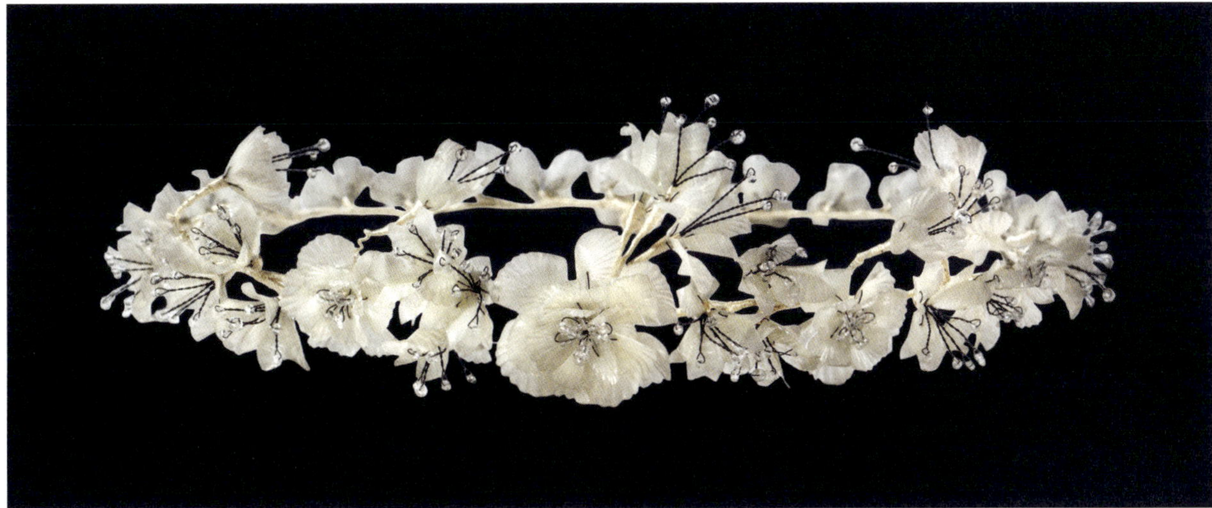

Circlet tiara with flowers made of translucent fish scales on wire, Unknown maker, 1870–74, V&A

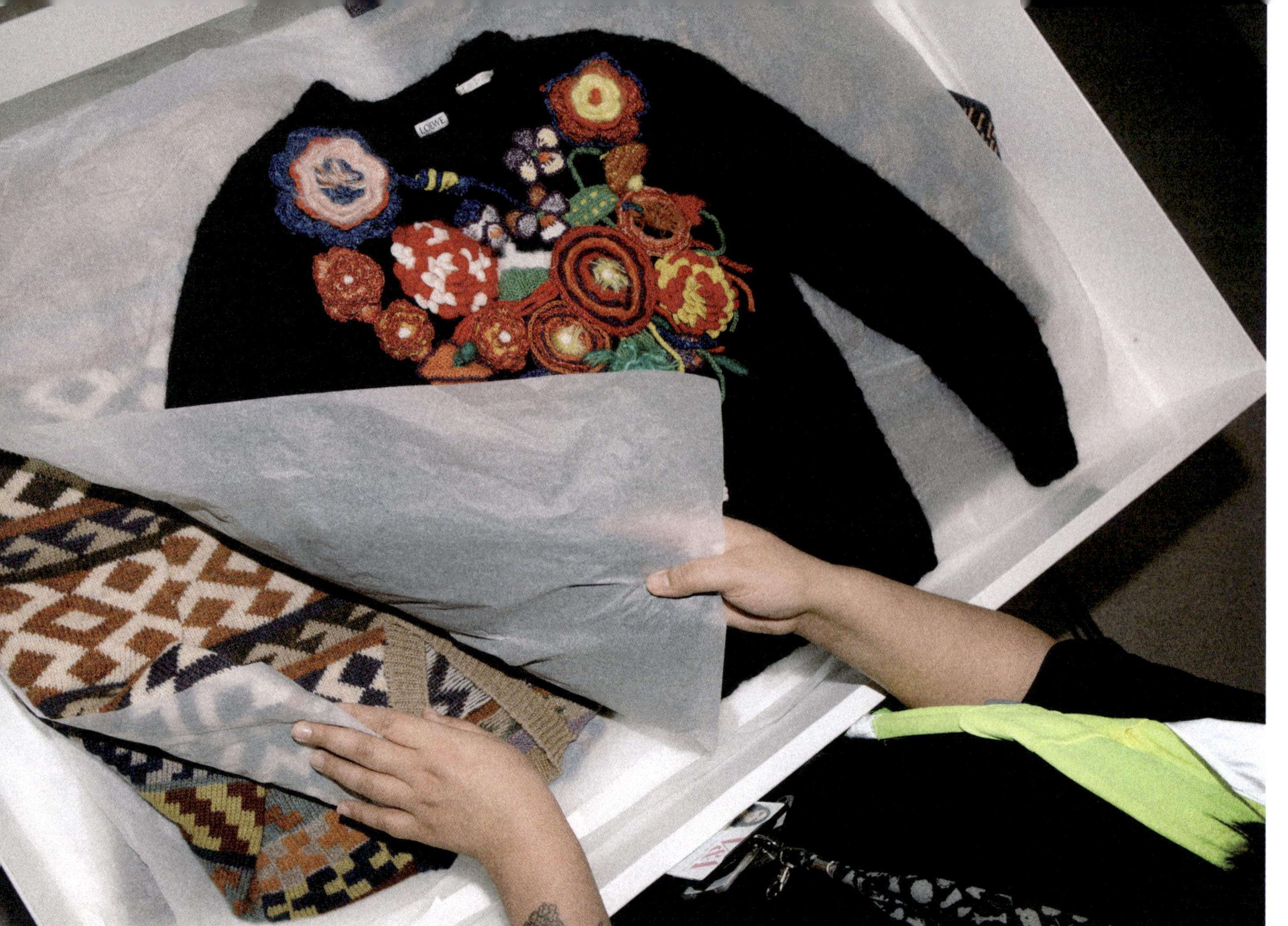
Unboxing textiles at V&A East Storehouse, including a 2018 Loewe jumper by Jonathan Anderson

its preservation over the next 10, 100 or 500 years. In museums, often we disguise the risks we take by exhibiting fragile objects for a short amount of time, supported by invisible mounts, behind glass, out of reach, inaccessible. Instead, in Storehouse objects are on pallets sitting on steel APR racking for easy retrieval using a cherry-picker. Sculptures are strapped into place with fabric strips and supported by wooden struts. Textiles are protected from light and dust with Tyvek. Archival documents are separated by acid-free tissue paper. Drawers of jewellery are housed in Plastazote cut-outs. It can come as a shock to stumble across a marble relief by Donatello mounted on metal mesh, and one might experience a brief rush of frustration to discover an object – a brocaded Guatemalan *huipil* for instance – entirely swathed in a protective wrapping, but, in reality, this is how most objects in museums across the world are best supported and stored. These storage mechanisms enable us to facilitate many visits a day to our object study rooms and to flip the priority of access: no longer do you need to first prove your professional or scholarly status in order to view an object; now the most compelling case for access is that you've never had access to it before.

Diller, Scofido + Renfro's architectural design, informed by community workshops and the technical expertise of V&A staff, has created a functional working museum store, which turns everyone who enters into a participant. The central core of Storehouse is what's called 'the public network', the areas through which visitors can direct their own explorations. Built into the fabric of Storehouse are large architectural fragments such as the fifteenth-century wooden Torrijos Ceiling from Spain, and Frank Lloyd Wright's cypress plywood office, designed for American businessman Edgar J. Kaufmann. It includes spaces to create and build alongside those in which to share and to remember, and it is in a state of flux, with continual small changes of objects coming and going alongside more obvious interventions in rapidly changing displays. As you walk around you will encounter responses to the installation of a fragment of the Poplar housing estate Robin Hood Gardens, a chair designed by local school children and a performance inspired by the Mughal-era colonnade of a bathhouse from the fort of Agra.

Storehouse is not a museum, and in the words of one local 19-year-old who has been shaping the project with us as part of our Youth Collective, it can therefore be 'much more interesting' as 'museums can't move fast enough'. The agility of the store needs to be deployed to open the collections to 'other peoples' interpretation' so that we can 'create a much more alive museum' to which everyone feels invited.[3] Making space for a polyphony of voices depends upon the technical expertise behind Storehouse's responsiveness and flexibility.

Collecting

A new object arrives at Storehouse. Papers are signed by security personnel before the object is unloaded from the van onto a trolley, coddled in blankets. Many steps and many hands have been necessary to arrive at this moment. Over a period of months, and sometimes years, the object has been assessed by curators, external experts and Trustees. It has been judged to have aesthetic significance, exemplify technical excellence, be historically important and document the society in which it was made. Now it is in the museum's care. A conservator will check its condition, technical experts will design its storage, researchers and curators will catalogue it, it will be photographed and uploaded onto the online collection so that anyone with an internet connection can access it. You can place an order to view it at Storehouse. Its life as a museum object has begun.

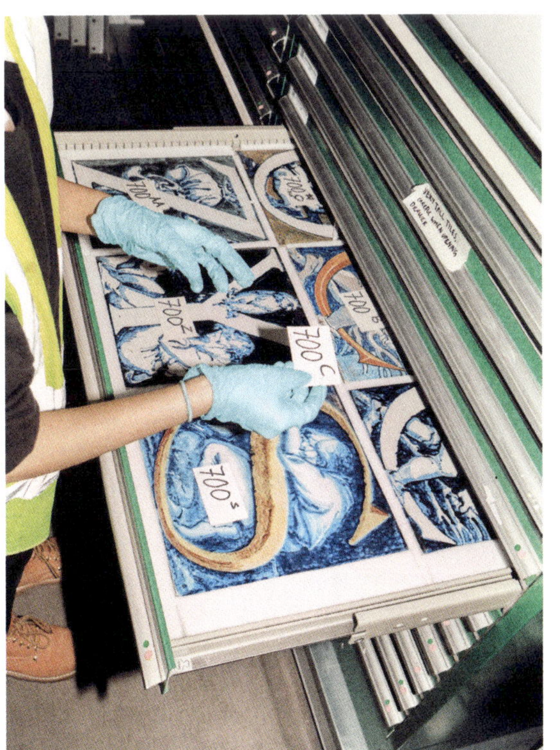

Earthenware decorated tiles at V&A East Storehouse

Each object in the V&A's collection bears the timestamp of the people and place that determined its value at the point of accession. Value will have been determined by various factors at the moment of acquisition: geo-political brinkmanship, colonial structures, the extractive logic of capitalism and various social routines and whimsies, which favoured or ignored certain makers as well as fashions, trends and material innovations. Perhaps most pervasive of all however, is the often racist and patriarchal mindset that dominated the culture of our predecessors, and which has largely determined the structure of our collections.

The V&A's collection is in fact a collection of collections, formed out of myriad donations of groups of objects collected by public institutions, trading companies and families. Understanding the history of each one is integral to our institutional self-knowledge as these assemblages of artefacts show how, over time, things and the people who made them have been systemised. Each collection follows its own logic, but the pervading influence is the Enlightenment era collecting practice of sorting by type. This style of collection aims to make subtle differences obvious through comparison. It stemmed from the Swedish botanist Carl Linnaeus's taxonomic categorisation system for plants, which he later applied to create racialised and racist categorisations of people.[4] Systems of categorisation inspired by Linnaeus are increasingly criticised as we come to appreciate that their claim to be objective not only has racist underpinnings, but has also erased other forms of knowledge and productive entanglements that tell more complex stories of global interconnection and creative exchange. The confusion between objectivity and representation is elucidated by Simone de Beauvoir in her feminist philosophical text *The Second Sex*: 'The representation of the world as the world itself is the work of men; they describe it from a point of view that is their own and that they confound with the absolute truth.'[5]

The process of collecting is always one of exclusion. Absences reveal who, what and where was devalued at particular points in history. Time and again you will see that we do not know the name of the person who made an object, these

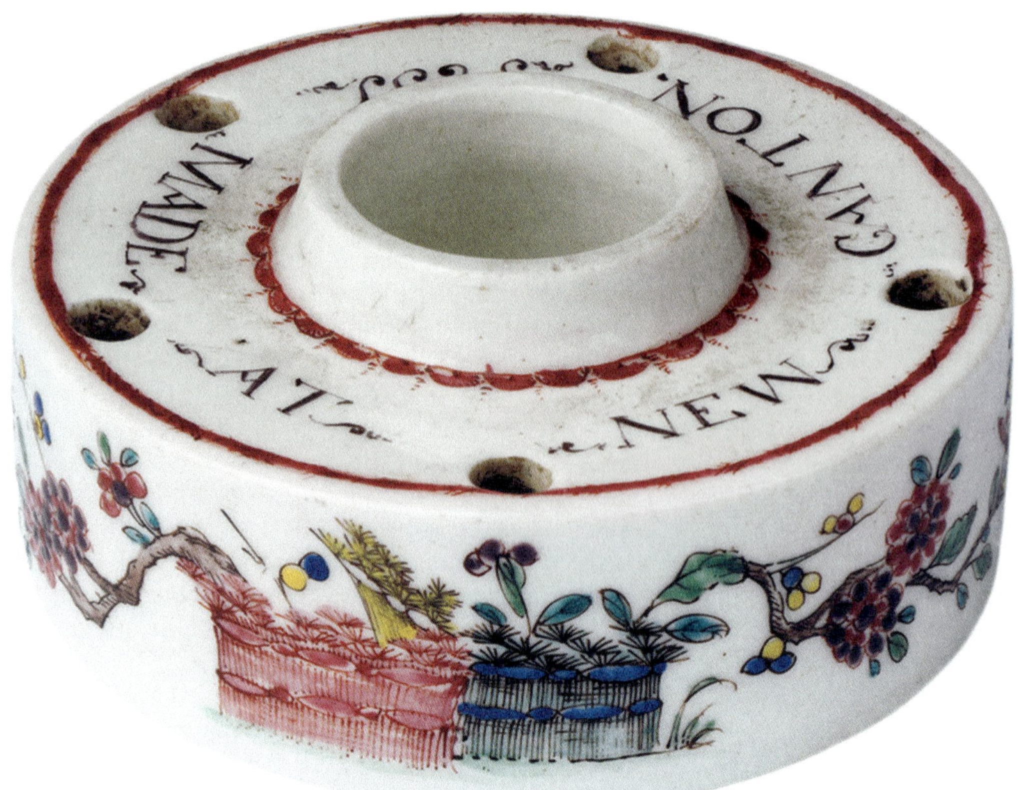

Soft-paste porcelain inkstand, by Bow Porcelain Factory, England, 1751, V&A

'once known' makers are lost to us because their identities were not seen as important and were therefore never recorded. Art, design and performance from whole continents has previously been excluded from the V&A's collection based on perceptions that their cultures were in some way 'inferior' or 'folkloric' compared to those of Europe and Asia. Sometimes these exclusions can begin to be carefully addressed by respectfully acquiring new objects that reflect contemporary global practice. A new project to collect the work of trans and non-binary artists highlights the previous silencing of their work. One example in Storehouse is a wallpaper created by Mx Justin Vivian Bond, which repeats a self-portrait blended with the face of make-up brand Estée Lauder, Karen Graham, interwoven with William Morris's 'Willow Bough' design.

The museum alone will not have all the answers and bringing voices of critics to the fore is essential. In one of the first displays at Storehouse is a work by the British sculptor Hew Locke, who shines a light on the extractive practices that have shaped the V&A's collection. In his collage *The Prize*, Locke weaves together strips of photographs, plastic flowers and prints adorned with beads into a trophy. This sculpture questions all the trophies given to the V&A to commemorate colonial violence. Locke captions it with the message 'get well soon', a satiric plea that points to the ongoing illness caused by colonial extraction worldwide. These are ideas explored by staff research groups, such as the Decolonising Reading and Listening Group, who have co-curated a display sharing many perspectives on a silver cup, which was awarded to the British Army's Commander-in-Chief Lord Napier to commemorate his violent raid on the Ethiopian Emperor Tewedros' fort at Maqdala in 1868. This process of understanding afresh requires a critical gaze. For theorist bell hooks, observation can be an act of opposition and lead to transformation: 'Not only will I stare. I want my look to change reality'.[6] Fostering this way of looking is a purposeful way to approach a museum store and one that can transform it into a place for 'fieldwork'.[7] Historically, fieldwork is the process of observing and collecting data out-of-doors or on-site about people, cultures and natural environments. By flipping this

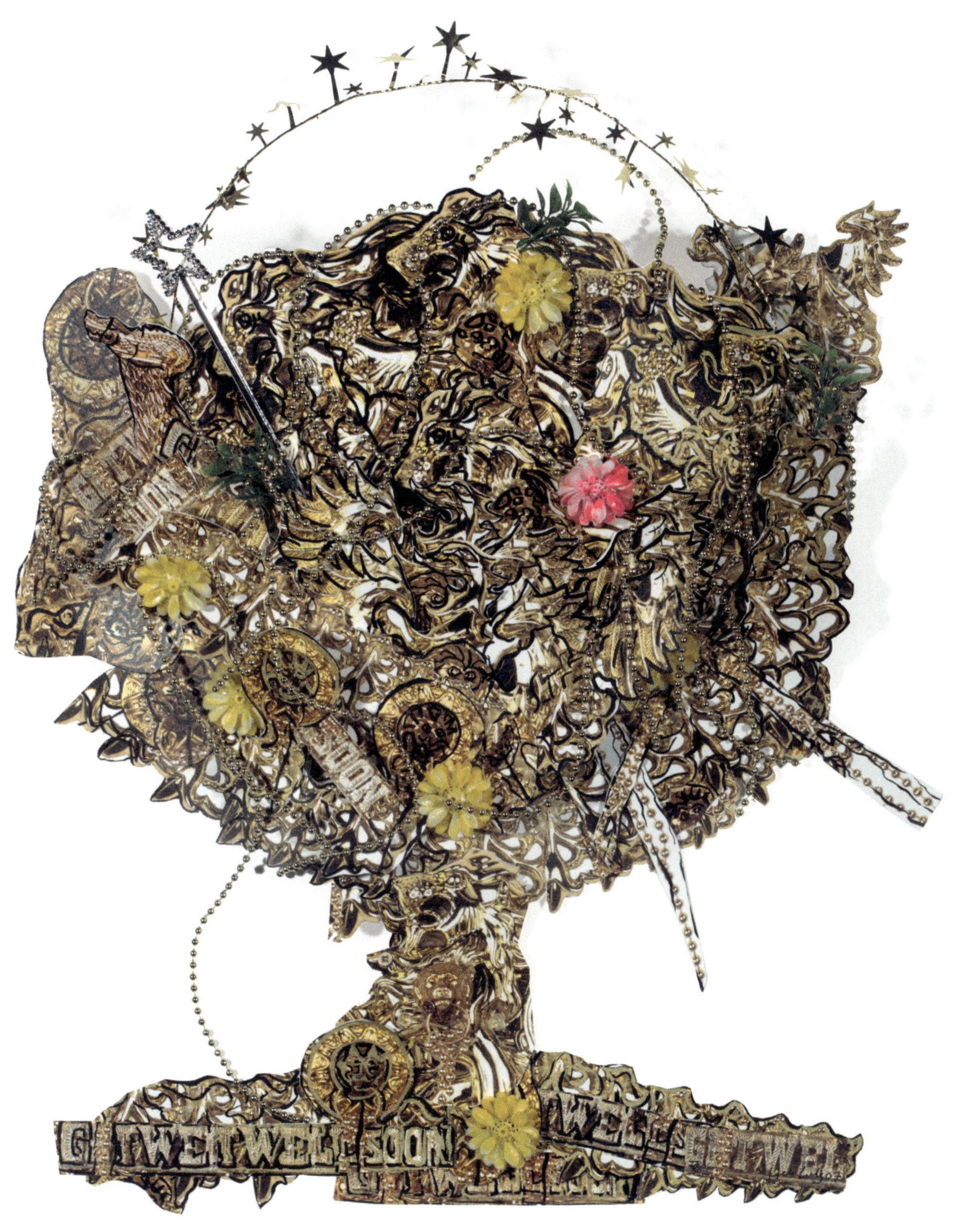

The Prize, by Hew Locke, 2006–7, V&A

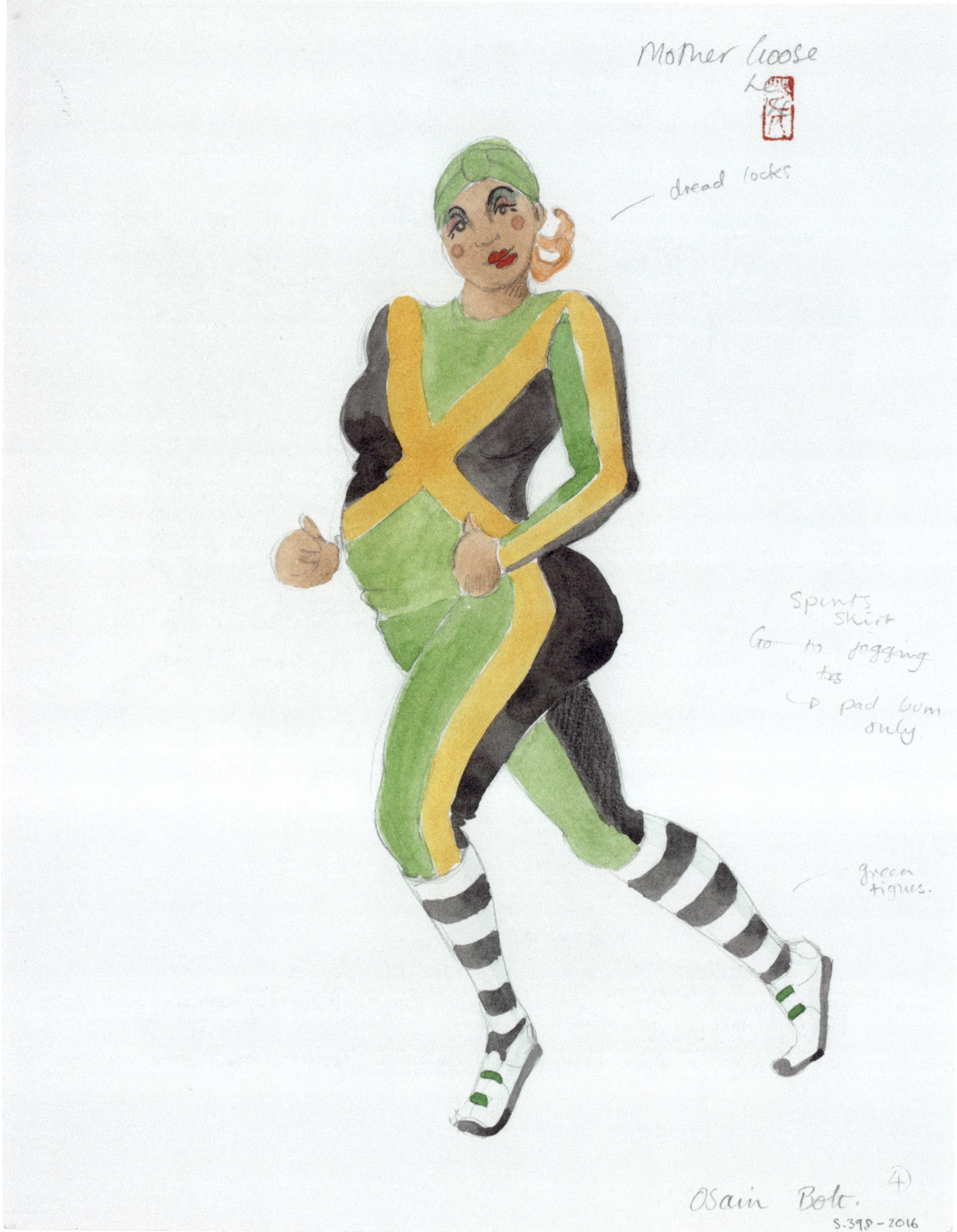

Costume design by Lotte Collett for the pantomime *Mother Goose* staged at the Hackney Empire, 2014, V&A

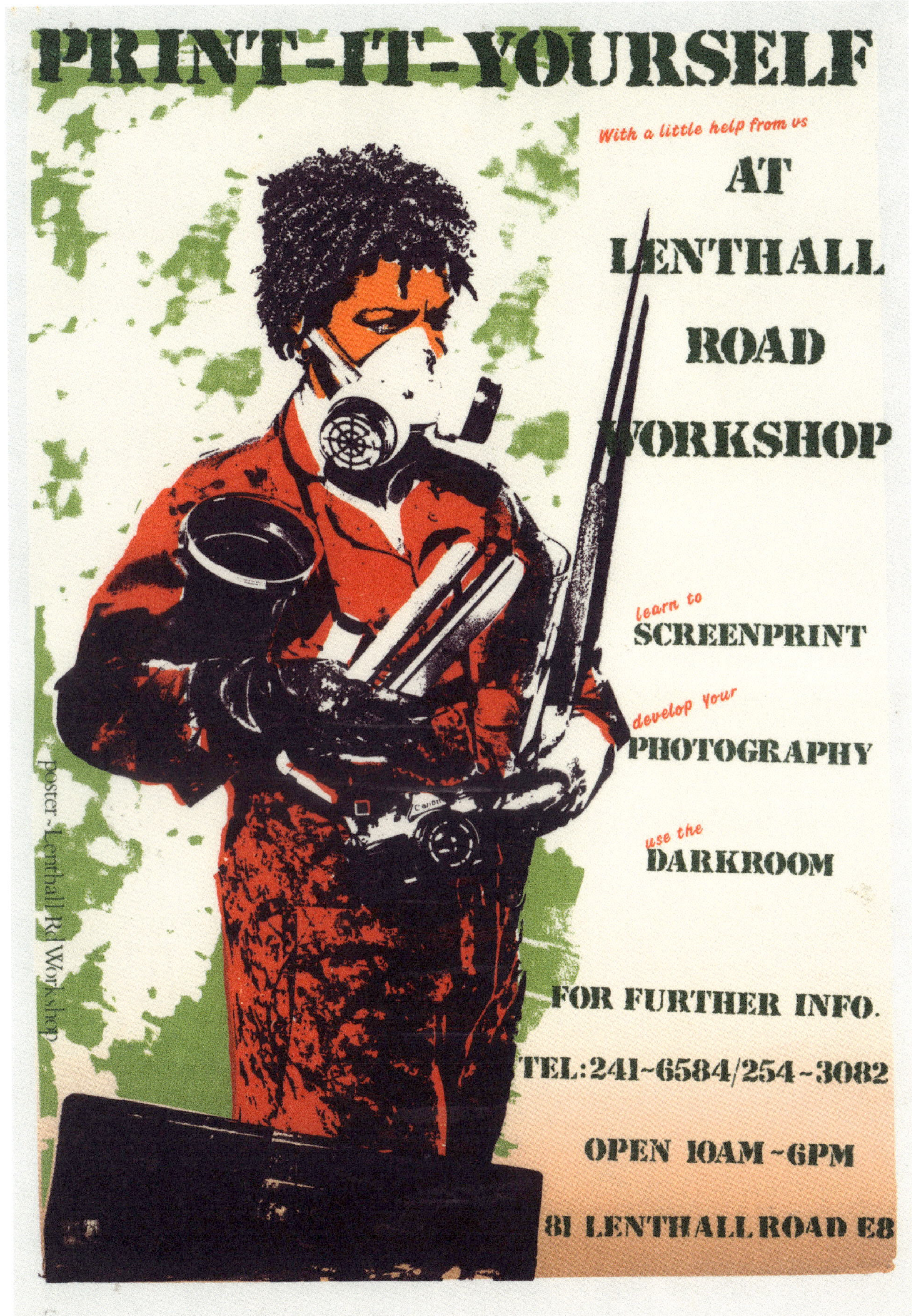

Print-it-Yourself, poster advertising the Lenthall Road Workshop in Hackney, London, about 1985, V&A

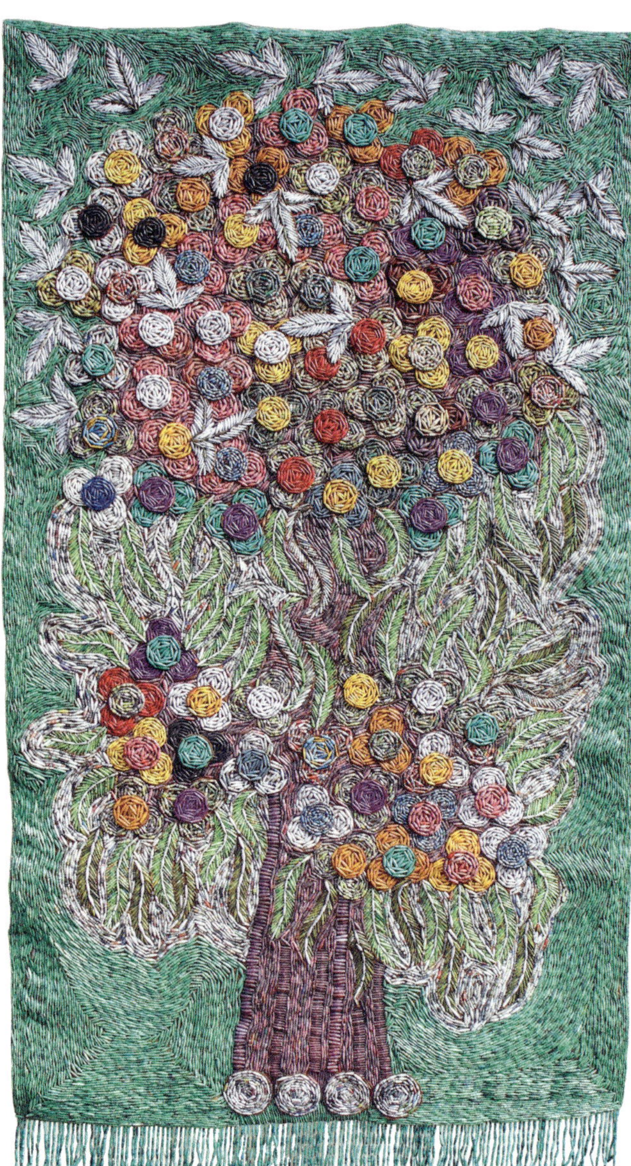

Ripe and Ready, by Sanaa Gateja, 2022, V&A

ethnographic technique back on the metropole, it brings to light the powerful stories of the history of the V&A's collection.

In the curated displays at Storehouse, we are interested in reading the silenced histories encoded in what the V&A has in its store. Here, objects are untethered from the collections they usually sit within and, in this process, open-up spaces for visitors to create new connections and meanings, rather than receiving fixed 'truths' of claimed universality. One display explores the role of extraction, asking how precious materials from underground bear witness to mining histories from around the world. Another looks at mahogany furniture, exploring the question of whether one can look past style and instead think of the people who were forced to labour in the Caribbean to grow the trees they were made from. Several other displays focus on making techniques, comparing the use of wooden printing blocks from different times and geographies, or looking at model-making as a practice that spans disciplines and is deployed by designers, architects, sculptors and factory workers. Here we explore how cross-cultural know-how creates a globally connected community of makers, of which Storehouse invites you to be a part.

Learning with our hands

A group of A-level chemistry and art students are crowded around a computer screen, reading the results of an X-ray fluorescence test on a small chip on an eighteenth-century porcelain inkstand, made in Bow in east London. The results slowly form a colourful graph on the screen: silica, lime, alum, lead and phosphorus are all present along with, intriguingly, some cobalt, perhaps added to counteract the reddish shades of iron, which can also be detected. Soon they are experimenting with this data, recreating recipes of the first English-made soft paste porcelains and testing them in plaster moulds. Remaking creates respect for the science, art and technology of manufacture, and these Newham students now want – in their own words – a 'Bow Porcelain Factory 2.0'.

Some discoveries can best be searched out by hand. At Storehouse the art and skill of learning with our hands is as important a stage of object study as the research of collecting provenance or historical sources. When you run your finger along a wooden groove or over the surface of a wax-resist decoration, our stored collections become a sourcebook from which to learn and make. This belief in makers' know-how is rooted in the history of the East End, which was known as 'the region of small makers', referring to a myriad of specialised craftspeople working out of workshops that often doubled as their homes.[8]

A seventeenth-century sampler by Hannah Downes at Shacklewell Quaker School in Hackney has embroidered upon it the poetic message that she practised her needlework so that she 'may learn both art and skill to get my living by my hands … and my own dame I then may be'. This cross-stitched message of craft skill and creativity being intertwined with independence still resonates today, for in the words of the founders of Hackney's community screen printing Lenthall Road Workshop, Chia Moan, Viv Mullett and Jenny Smith: 'Once you start seeing yourself as a person who can do things then you're in a position to take control of your life.'

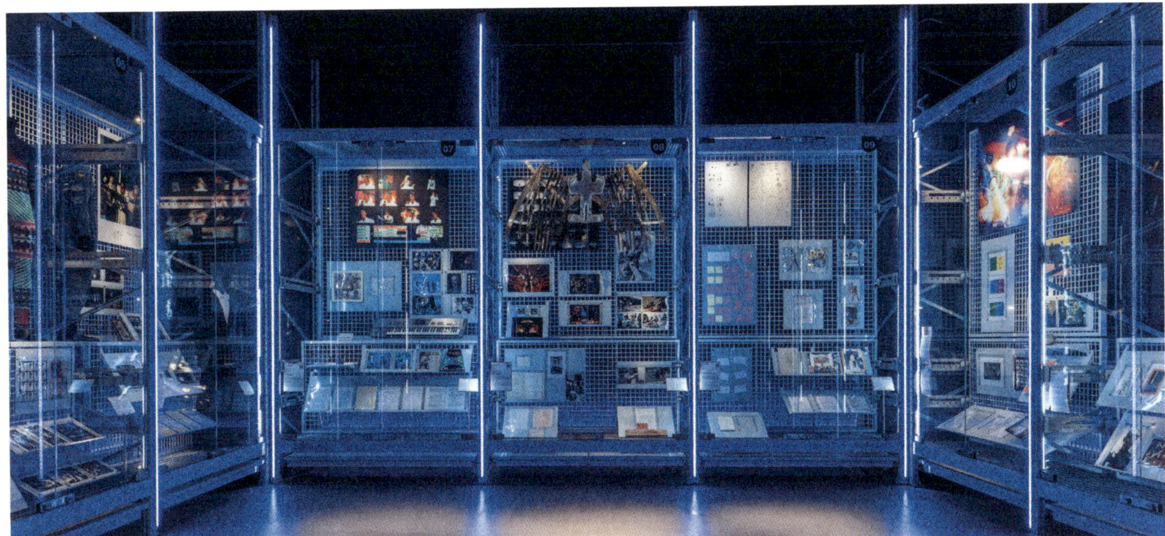

View inside the David Bowie Centre, 2025. Design by IDK. The David Bowie Centre is generously funded by Blavatnik Family Foundation and Warner Music Group. With thanks to the David Bowie Estate

The original purpose of the V&A was to share innovative manufacture and to inspire artisans to design for change. Practitioners today are eloquent about how their work contains a personal genealogy of traditions and influences that have come together in their practice. Sanaa Gateja's *Ripe and Ready* is made up of thousands of paper beads. These are inspired by the shapes of Egyptian beads, the history of African bead trade and the necklace of a beloved aunt that he remembers from when he was small enough to sit on her knee. The historical, political, personal and artisanal combine through technical skills, which Gateja has passed onto many women makers now employed in making beads at his arts enterprise centre Kwetu, meaning 'at home' in Swahili. Gateja reflects that 'art has given me peace of mind of how to relate to life'.[9]

With the opening within Storehouse of The David Bowie Centre, researchers and the newly curious are encouraged to become 'synthesisers' and 'magpies' in Bowie's image. Alongside the David Bowie archive, visitors are able to seek inspiration from the Theatre and Performance collection, which contains resources as varied as paintings by PJ Harvey, the 'flap-shoes' worn by Cockney music-hall stars, VHS recordings of rare performances and a bin from Glastonbury music festival. One archive we highlight is Talawa Theatre Company, a group formed by Yvonne Brewster to stage *The Black Jacobins*, based on C.L.R. James's influential history of the Haitian revolution. Brewster was determined to make the show as it was about the 'energy of a people trying to be born, as we as Caribbean citizens abroad appreciate only too well'.[10] Talawa's techniques, which can be discovered through annotated scripts and rehearsal plans, are a rich blueprint for performers to work from. As David Bowie said, art 'has always been for me a stable nourishment'; it is these provisions that Storehouse is laying down for you to feast on.[11]

Storehouse is a centre for museological innovation in the service of making the V&A's stored collections truly accessible and useful to local communities. The objects, archives and books it contains are a sourcebook for new thinking rooted in our shared past. Its creative studios, performance spaces and work-in-progress displays are places for new making that speak to the urgent needs of our time. Activist adrienne maree brown states that 'it is so important that we fight for the future, get into the game, get dirty, get experimental'.[12] Storehouse is a space to do this. Georgia Haseldine, Senior Curator

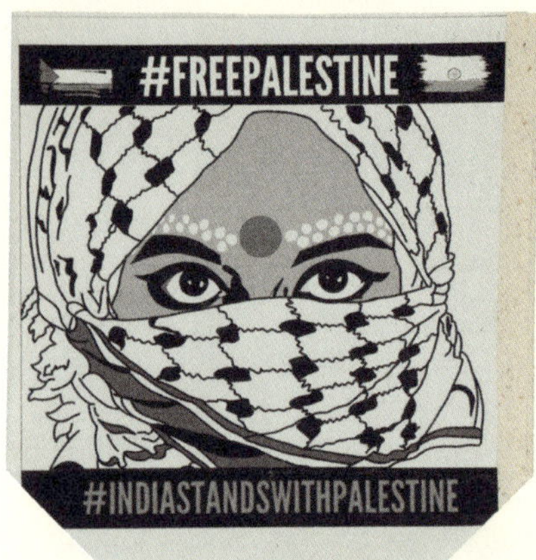

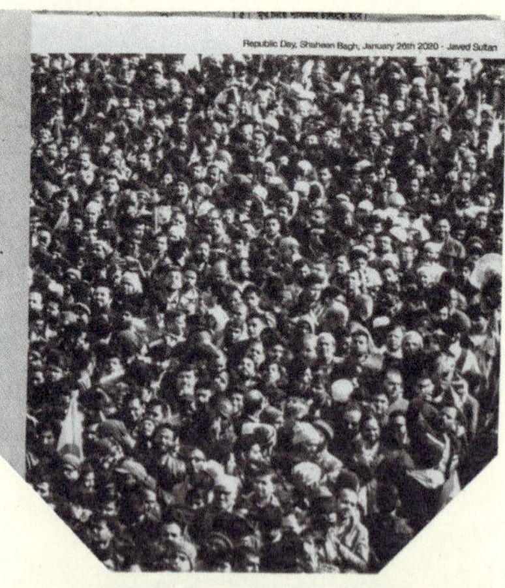

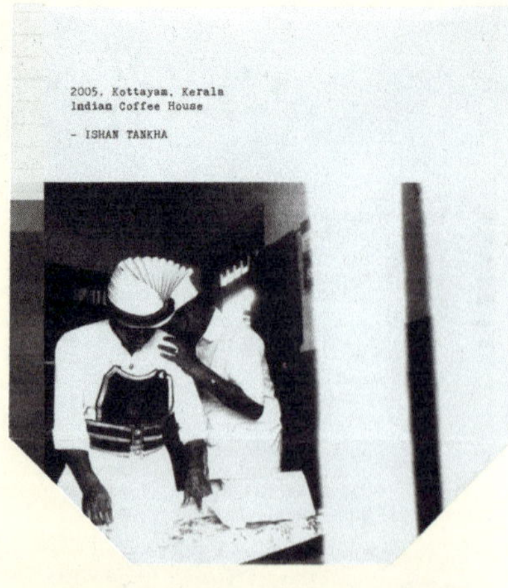

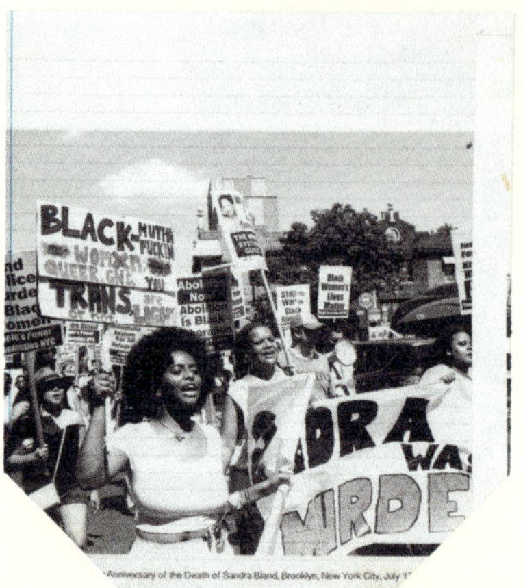

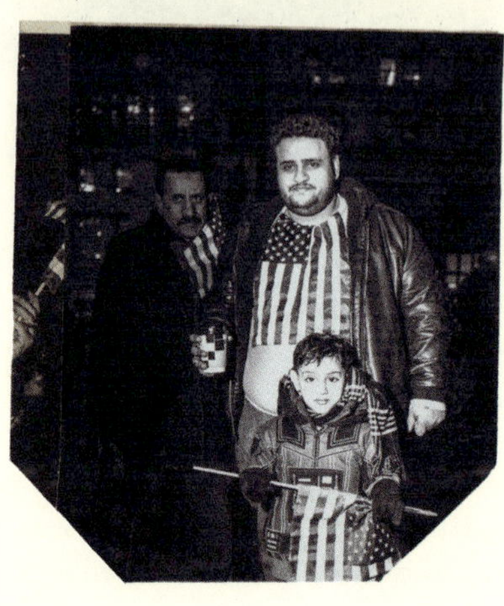

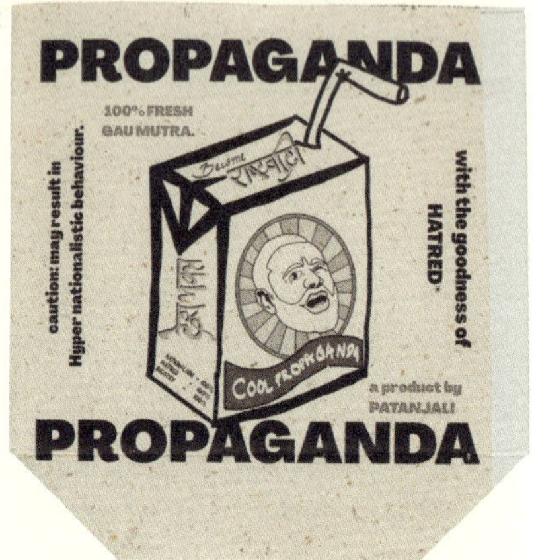

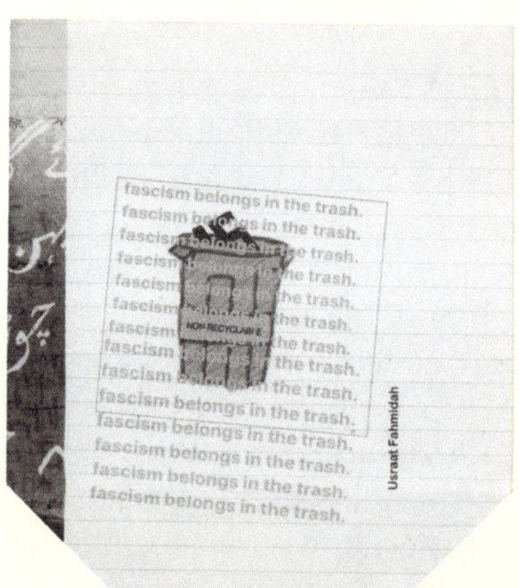

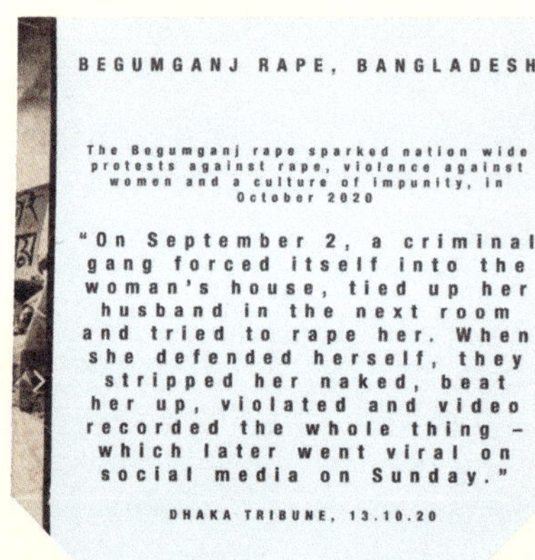
BEGUMGANJ RAPE, BANGLADESH

The Begumganj rape sparked nation wide protests against rape, violence against women and a culture of impunity, in October 2020

"On September 2, a criminal gang forced itself into the woman's house, tied up her husband in the next room and tried to rape her. When she defended herself, they stripped her naked, beat her up, violated and video recorded the whole thing – which later went viral on social media on Sunday."

DHAKA TRIBUNE, 13.10.20

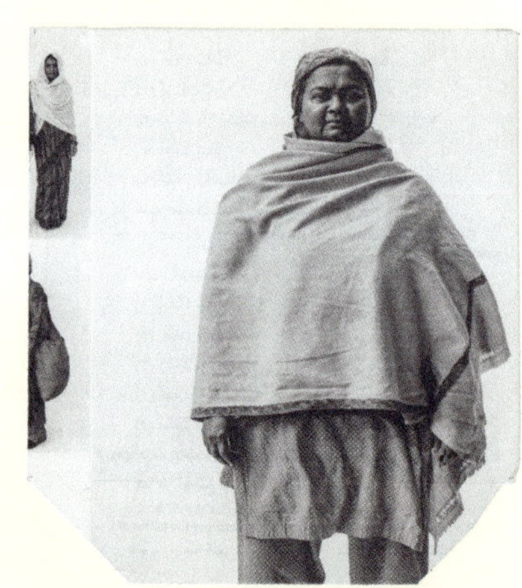

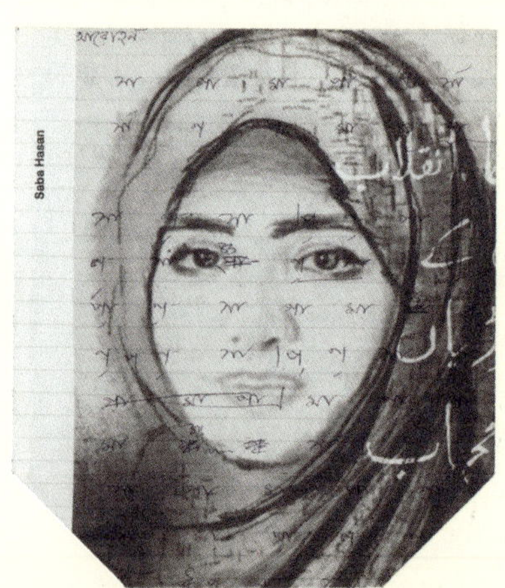

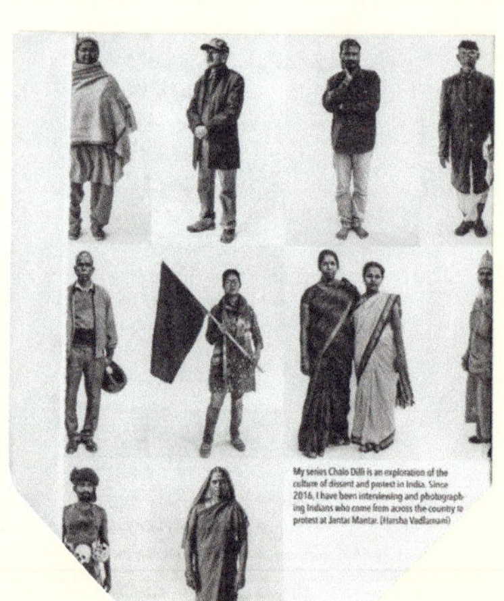
My series Chalo Dilli is an exploration of the culture of dissent and protest in India. Since 2016, I have been interviewing and photographing Indians who come from across the country to protest at Jantar Mantar. (Harsha Vadlamani)

"Don't give me religion, give me food" is written on the chest of Kat Jr from a protest rally in College Street in Calcutta.

Turbine Bagh *Samosa Packets*, by Sofia Karim, 2020–21, V&A

The samosa packet – made of scrap paper and commonly seen on the streets of India and Bangladesh – has been transformed by Sofia Karim into a vehicle for telling stories of resistance and sharing the creative expressions of artists worldwide. Karim's project began during her time in Dhaka when she purchased various packets of samosas and discovered that the recycled paper bags they came in were made from court papers – 'endless lists of court cases including cases of individuals against the government' – offering an inadvertent portrait of Bangladesh's broken justice system.[1] This finding inspired her to collect more packets from the streets, where she found similarly disturbing messages including nationalist poems and propaganda news clippings.

In Delhi, in 2019, the Shaheen Bagh protest emerged in opposition to the Indian government's Citizenship Amendment Act, which discriminated against Muslims. As a British Bangladeshi activist, architect and artist who passionately advocates for human rights in Bangladesh and India, Karim saw an opportunity to use these packets as a medium to depict the current state of Bangladesh.

Karim incorporated *Samosa Packets* into her ongoing project and eponymous exhibition, *Turbine Bagh,* aimed at securing the release of imprisoned artists and political activists. In 2020, she called for contributions on Instagram, inviting artists, writers, poets and thinkers to design samosa packets engaging with the political situation in India and Bangladesh. The diverse response included photographs of activists protesting against authority, thought-provoking drawings, powerful statements and even musical scores, all of which Karim printed onto used paper to create the samosa packets.

Karim's dedication to capturing unheard stories that demand global attention serves as a means to disseminate political issues and prevent the isolation of activists fighting for justice. She witnessed the transformative power of art and activism through the exhibition *Turbine Bagh* at Tate Modern, featuring the banned series titled 'Crossfire' (2010) by her uncle Shahidul Alam, a political dissident and photojournalist who was imprisoned by the government of Bangladesh. The series focused on documenting extrajudicial killings conducted by Bangladesh's Rapid Action Battalion. The popular reception of his work in the exhibition gave Alam immense support during his time in jail. This experience deeply resonated with Karim, motivating her to actively support political prisoners and reinforcing her belief in the influential role that public exhibitions can play in effecting meaningful political change while expressing genuine concern for the prisoners.

By documenting and celebrating the courage of those who speak out and strive for change, Karim aims to communicate globally. *Turbine Bagh* now resonates with people worldwide, encouraging active participation in their local social and political discussions. The project has expanded to encompass a wide range of topics, including Palestine, Black Lives Matter, Rohingya refugees, illegal imprisonment and censorship. Through the medium of the samosa packet, Karim extends her message beyond museum walls and into the streets, spreading awareness and inspiring action. Miri Ahn, Assistant Curator

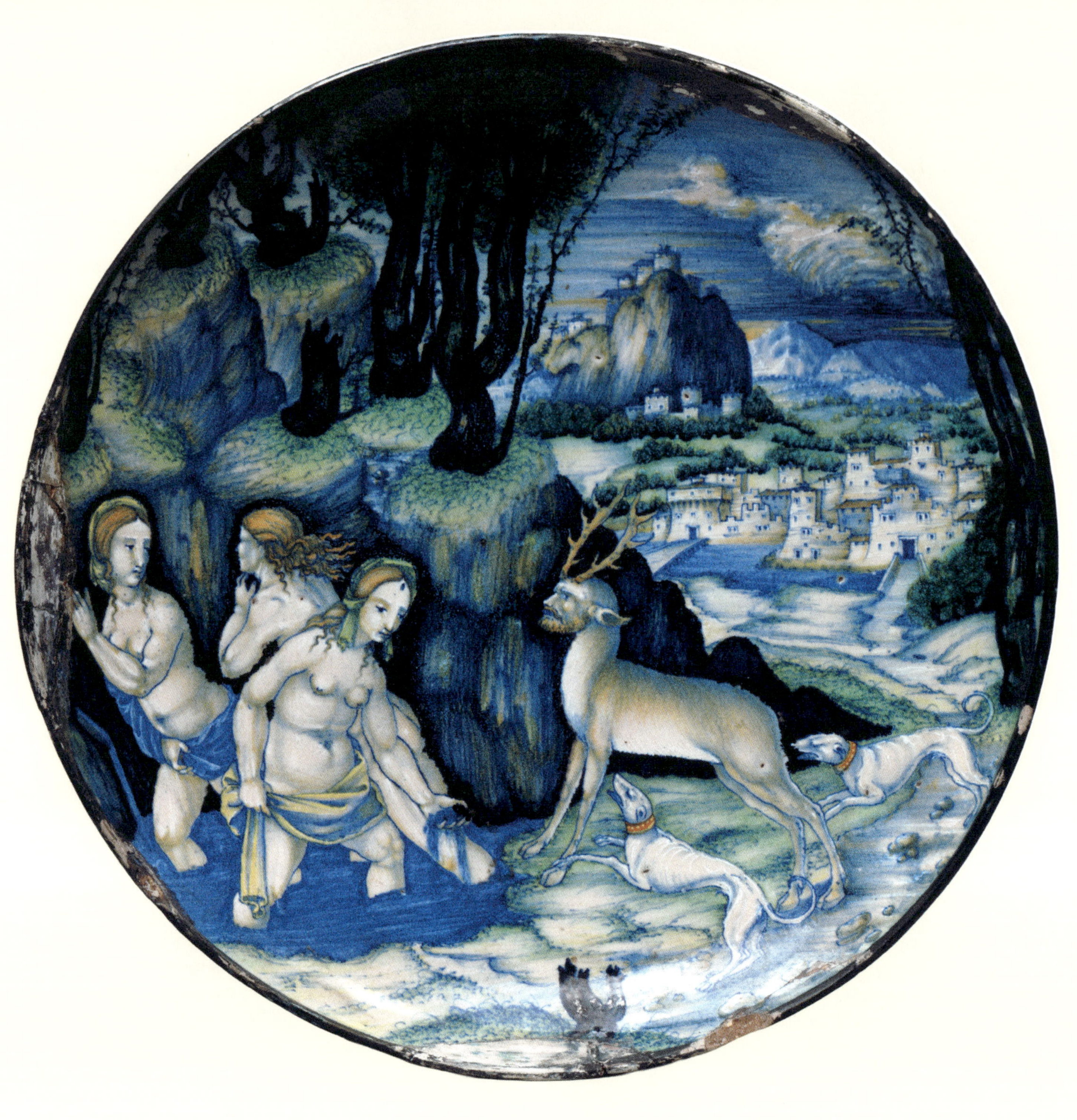

Tin-glazed dish, Unknown maker, about 1540, V&A

In this sixteenth-century tin-glazed dish we see a scene from Ovid's *Metamorphoses*. The goddess Diana transforms prince Actaeon into a stag as punishment for him having seen her while she was bathing. The prince's own dogs turn on him as he transforms, his human face looking out from a stag's body. Yet beyond this mythical scene, we also see in this object much broader narratives about trade, market forces and the circulation of production techniques across vast territories. Though this dish was produced in Casteldurante in central Italy in around 1540, and while we often consider painted *maiolica* to be a great achievement of the Italian Renaissance, the techniques used have origins that predate this by several centuries, drawn from the ceramic traditions of the Middle East and Northern Africa. Moreover, the dissemination of ideas that helped the tin-glazing technique to develop and evolve into a pictorial form is often understated. The story behind the production of this Italian *maiolica* dish could only unfold thanks to the movement of objects, people and techniques, combining ideas from different sources to develop the craft in new and innovative ways.

The practice of covering clay objects with a tin glaze had been used since about 800 in territories that are currently part of Iraq. Islamic makers in these territories developed a new recipe that would produce a white glaze using tin oxide, possibly motivated by a desire to compete with imported Chinese white stoneware (a precursor of porcelain). Ceramic objects coated with this white, powdery glaze could then be painted with coloured pigments before firing. This technique spread through the Islamic world, first across North Africa and then southern Spain.

Italian craftspeople first encountered tin-glazed ceramics in the thirteenth century when these ceramics were imported from Malaga in Spain.[1] As with Chinese white stoneware in the Middle East several centuries earlier, imported objects stimulated the local market to produce a new, competing product. In response to this, Italian potters started to produce their own tin-glazed pottery, now known more generally as *maiolica*, and began to use the pictorial potential of this medium more extensively than had been seen before.[2] In the fifteenth and sixteenth centuries, ceramics decorated with biblical or mythological stories taken from antiquity were produced in large numbers by workshops in central Italy, and were often praised for being an innovative genre combining technical and artistic skill.

Italian painted *maiolica* was exported to Central Europe, North Africa and Spain, even reaching as far as the Spanish territories in Central America. Italian makers themselves emigrated to other parts of Europe taking their skills with them.[3] As it spread around the globe, this technique became known under different names: *faience* in France, *delftware* in the Netherlands and *talavera* in Spain and Mexico. In Britain, it was revived in the early twentieth century and known as *majolica*. Even now, reproductions of Renaissance tin-glazed dishes are still produced in Central Italy to satisfy the tourist market, and so the tin-glazing technique continues its journey to this day. Serenella Sessini, Assistant Curator

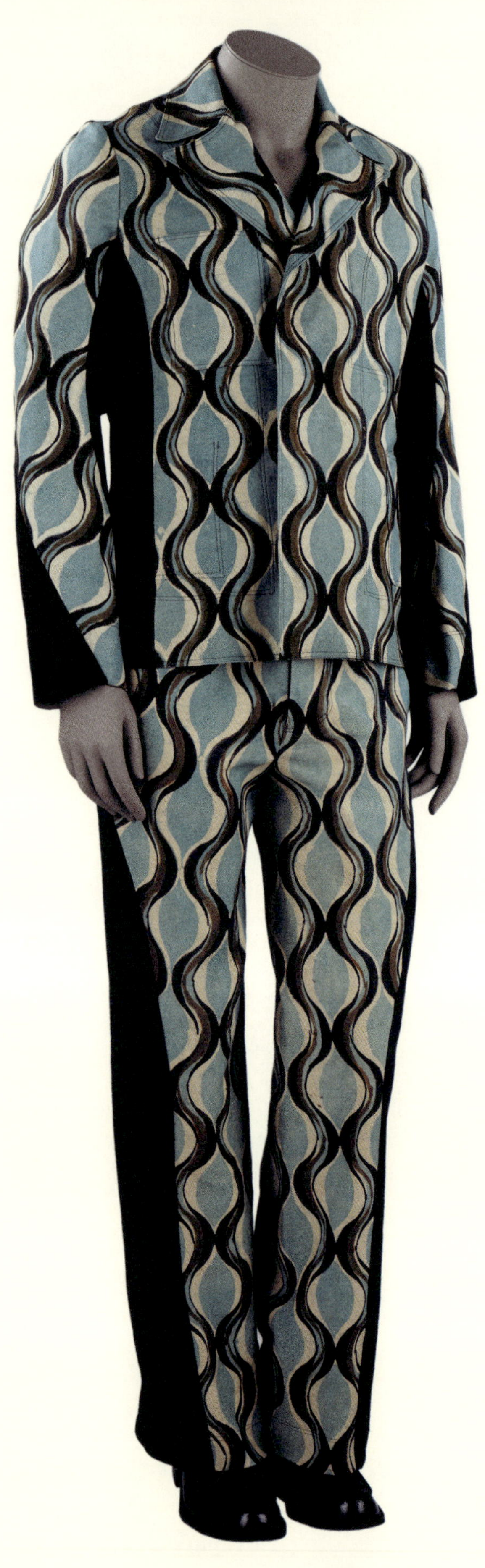

Suit, by Rahemur Rahman and Aranya, 2012, V&A

The bright block-printed denim ensemble pictured here is the result of a collaboration between east-London designer Rahemur Rahman and Aranya, an eco-sustainable, fair-trade company based in Dhaka, Bangladesh. It is composed of two parts, a jacket and a pair of trousers, and is decorated with a wave pattern. Rahman's inspiration for this piece came from looking at colourful layered West Bengal and Bangladeshi textiles in the V&A collections. Through this collaboration, and by foregrounding traditional techniques, natural dyes and sustainable working practices, Rahman and Aranya are redefining the meaning of garments labelled as 'made in Bangladesh'.

At Aranya's site in Dhaka, Rahman and Aranya's artisans met to look through the company's archive of block-printed patterns, some of which date back to the 1970s, using sketchbooks to capture their responses. Rahman describes their relationship as an exchange of skills, with Aranya helping him learn artisanal techniques, while he helped them with creative design. As Rahman himself says: 'This hierarchy of having a star designer at the top doesn't fit with what I am trying to do, and I quite like the idea that everyone sees who I collaborate with.'[1]

The suit is produced using a traditional wax and resist block print technique, which involves applying layers of wax to a fabric with a hand-carved block print, before dipping it into a dye. This process is repeated multiple times to achieve a striking pattern. The wax is then removed by washing the textile in hot water, and then coloured with a natural dye paste to make it even brighter. Rahman and Aranya's artisans combined their skills to push the boundaries of this technique, which would usually be used to decorate garments with simpler one- or two-colour patterns to be sold to local Bangladeshi customers. After extensive testing and trials using different fabrics including jersey, silk and hemp, they eventually settled on denim as the best material to achieve a high-quality four-colour pattern.

Traditional craft becomes modern practice in this particular ensemble, made to be worn by all genders. The designer grew up in east London where he witnessed his parents' hard work in the textile industry. His 'Children of the Rag Trade' collection, which includes this suit, was created as a response to Bengali (as well as Polish and Somali) workers' labour in this industry. As a 'child of the rag trade' himself, Rahman intended this dedication as a token of gratitude for the legacy that rag trade workers are leaving behind and the inspiration that their children have taken from it.

Working only with natural dyes, Rahman and Aranya were able to produce a piece that speaks to sustainability, heritage and the importance of traditional crafts. By helping to showcase the talent and expertise of Bangladeshi craftspeople, while foregrounding traditional techniques and prioritising human and environmental sustainability, they really are shifting perceptions of what it means to be made in Bangladesh.[2]

Serenella Sessini, Assistant Curator

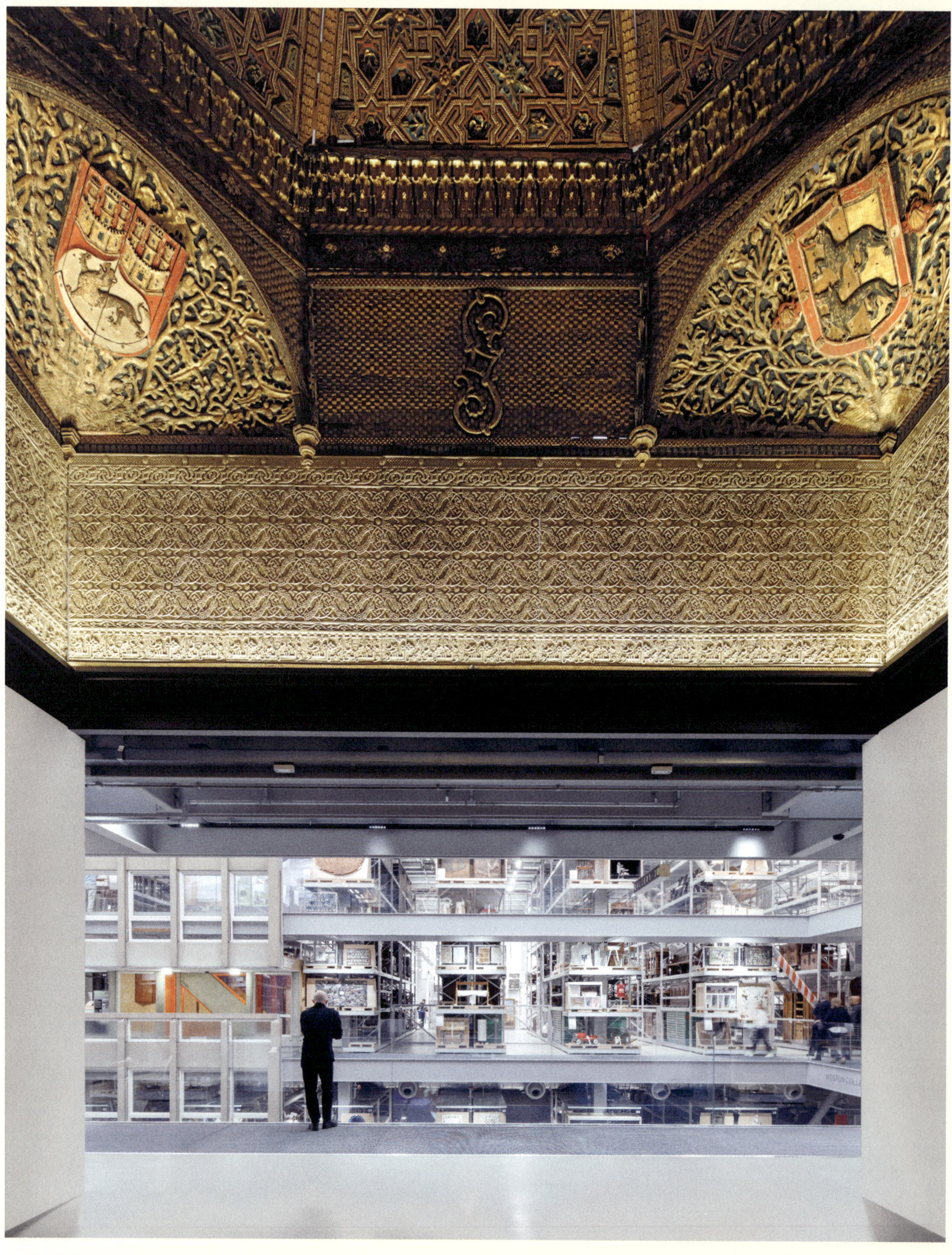

Torrijos ceiling, installed at V&A East Storehouse, 2024

What can a wooden ceiling tell us about the diversity of Spain's medieval past? This object encapsulates a period when the Christian elite in Spain were engaged in conquering Muslim territories, while also adopting Islamic artistic styles and techniques to decorate their homes and the furnishings of their daily lives. It shows how, in the complexity of past societies, there lies a fascinating story of cultural interconnections.

This ceiling comes from the palace in Torrijos, near Toledo in central Spain. It was once one of four spectacular domed ceilings crowning the building's four corner towers. The palace was built in the 1490s by a noble couple, Gutierre de Cárdenas and Teresa Enríquez. Their coats of arms can be seen at the four lower corners – two wolves for Gutierre and a lion beneath two castles for Teresa.

The couple was part of the royal circle of the Catholic monarchs Isabel of Castile and Ferdinand II of Aragon. In fact, Gutierre had introduced the royal couple to each other by saying '*esse*', 'that one' as he pointed out Ferdinand to Isabel across a room. For this, he earned the privilege of adding a floriated 's' as one of his heraldic devices. This can be seen around the base of the ceiling, between the coats of arms.

The Torrijos palace represented Gutierre at the height of his power and wealth. Yet the main aesthetic of this ceiling is the Islamic style of its eight-pointed stars and the use of panels and a central boss in gilded muqarnas – a distinctively Islamic design element that resembles clusters of stalactites. The plaster frieze, which runs around the wall below the ceiling (a replica of the original), includes an Arabic phrase referring to the pleasure of drinking. These Islamic elements are combined with Gothic style ornament including spikey leaves, perhaps representing thistles or *cardos* in Spanish, a pun on the name Cárdenas. This combination of Islamic and northern-European styles was very common in Spanish architecture at this period.

The Torrijos ceilings were made using a technique known in Spanish as *carpintería de lo blanco*, or 'white carpentry', because of the pale colour of the pine from which they were constructed. This was a well-established technique in Spain by the thirteenth century, though it probably originated in North Africa where existing examples can be dated to the mid-twelfth century. Workshops of specialist craftsmen, who may have been of different faiths, prefabricated such ceilings to decorate palaces for both Muslim and Christian patrons, as well as for churches and synagogues. The surface decoration of gilding and coloured pigments made these expensive productions. The high point of this technique was in the fifteenth century, when the Torrijos ceilings were made.

By the late nineteenth century, the Torrijos palace was in a bad state of repair and its owners dismantled and sold off its luxurious furnishings. By 1917, the palace had been demolished. Today, this ceiling offers us the chance to collaborate with specialists in 'white carpentry' and its historical context, both in Spain and further afield. It also opens up opportunities to engage in conversations with the museum's audiences about the complexities and connectedness of cultural history, artistic production and taste.

Mariam Rosser-Owen, Curator

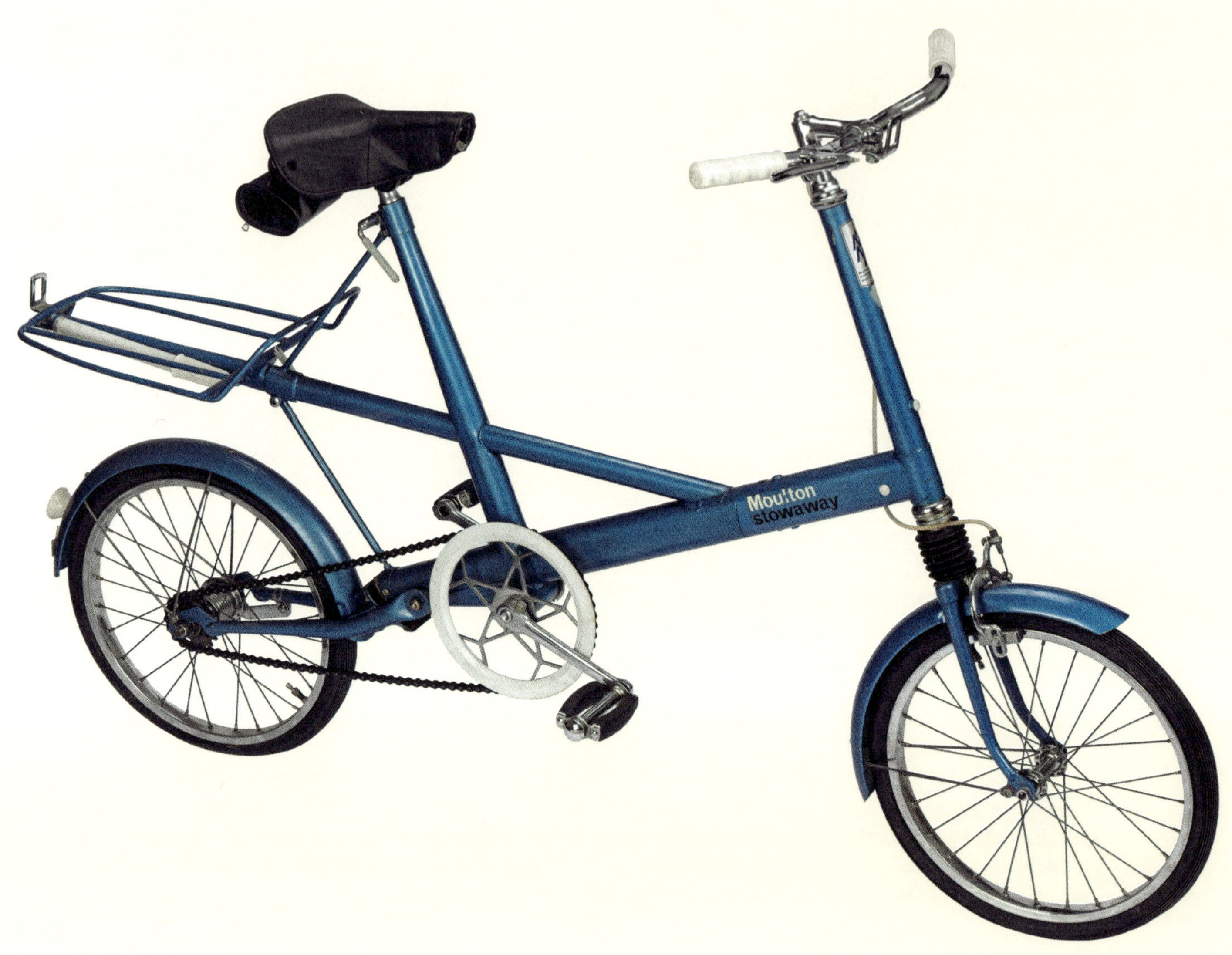
Moulton
stowaway

Bicycle, designed by Alex Moulton, 1962, V&A

The 1962 Moulton bicycle looks quite unlike most street bikes today. With 14-inch wheels, compared to the standard 26-inch, riders could cycle faster on smaller, more pressurised wheels, with less effort and rolling resistance. A capital F frame moves the crossbar much lower down, creating a unisex bike enabling any rider to easily step over the frame. A suspension system between the frame and wheels, inspired by Alex Moulton's previous work engineering Mini cars, absorbs bumps encountered on uneven roads. It can also be separated into two halves, promoted as a storage solution for car boots, enabling commuters to park outside cities and cycle the last few miles to avoid traffic-clogged streets.[1] At the height of their success, 400 Moultons were being produced a week from a factory in Bradford.

The Moulton bicycle is one of over 600 objects in the V&A's collections conferred an award by the Council of Industrial Design (CoID, later the Design Council) in the UK's post-rationing consumer boom. Presented between 1957 and 1988, these CoID awards were established to encourage industry to recognise the commercial potential of good design, and to educate the consumer in identifying examples of well-designed products. Featured in the CoID's Design Index, a catalogue for consumers and trade buyers to consult at one of the national design centres across the country, they represent a snapshot of UK design and manufacturing for everyday life. Many of these were collected by the museum's Circulation Department, adding such seemingly mundane items to the museum collections as a fire extinguisher, a chemical toilet and a street bollard.

Dedicated to disseminating contemporary design across the UK, the V&A's Circulation Department was established in the 1850s as one of the earliest examples of an institution touring artwork through regional museums and public libraries, art schools and education colleges. It gathered both historical and contemporary material into its domain, but by 1959 the soon-to-be Keeper of the department, Hugh Wakefield, noted it was the 'growth point of the Museum ... as the national collections of the present and of the past one hundred years'.[2]

In light of its role as a treasury of contemporary design, Director of the CoID, Gordon Russell, hoped that the Circulation Department would display the winners of the CoID awards and acquire them for the permanent collection. In 1957, he approached the then Keeper, Peter Floud, who proposed to collect only those designs related to the living room, as 'the average person would not expect to find washing machines in the same building as, for example, Renaissance sculpture'.[3] However, when Hugh Wakefield became Keeper in 1960, he revived the proposal, managing to collect all the previous award winners. Over the course of the next 17 years, the V&A collected and toured nearly two-thirds of the winning designs. Sadly, following governmental budget cuts, the department was dissolved in 1977, with the collections distributed into the care of the closest materials departments. Their radical approach to contemporary collecting gifted the museum with many hallmarks of British design from its mid-twentieth century heyday. Kristian Volsing

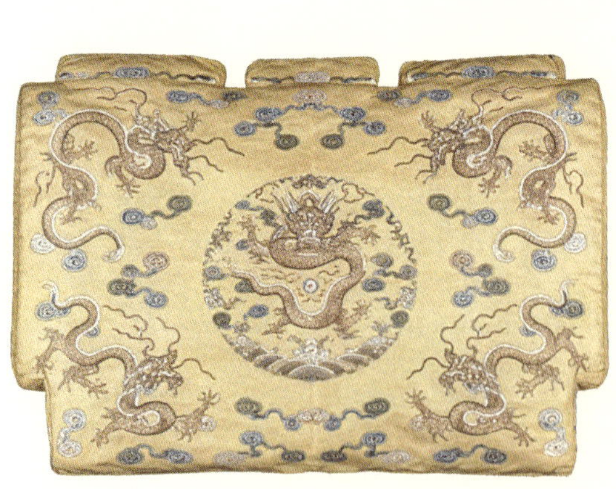

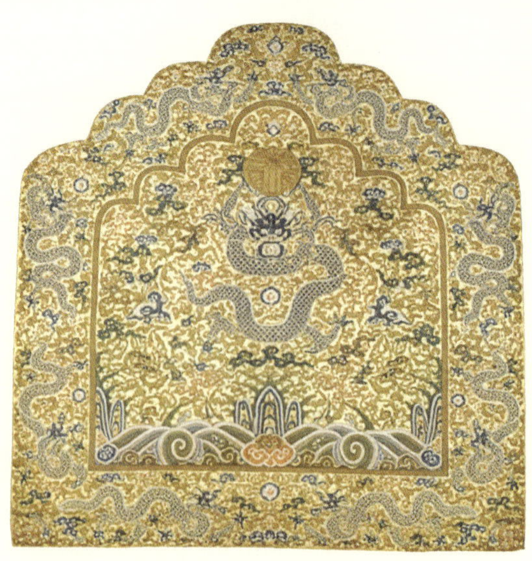

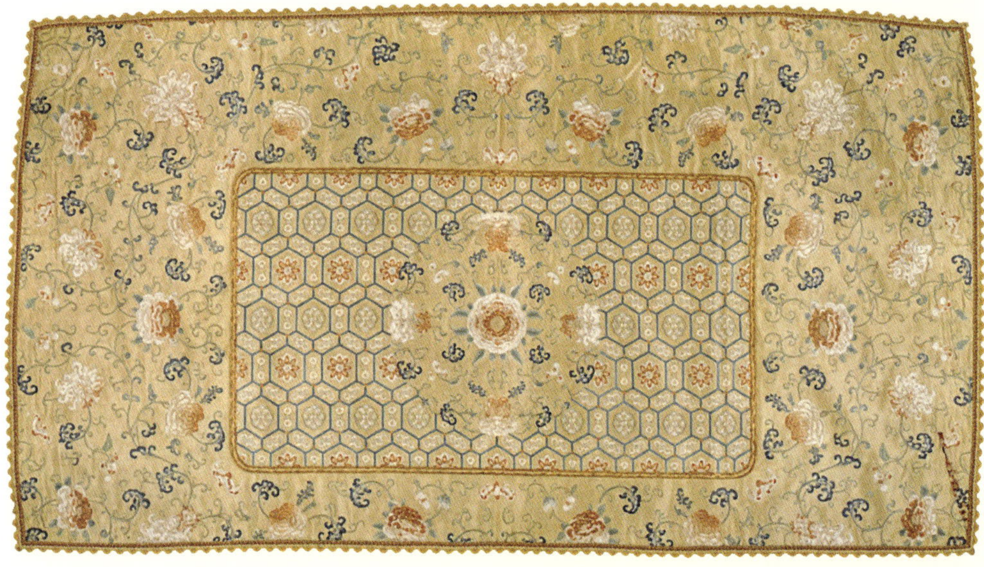

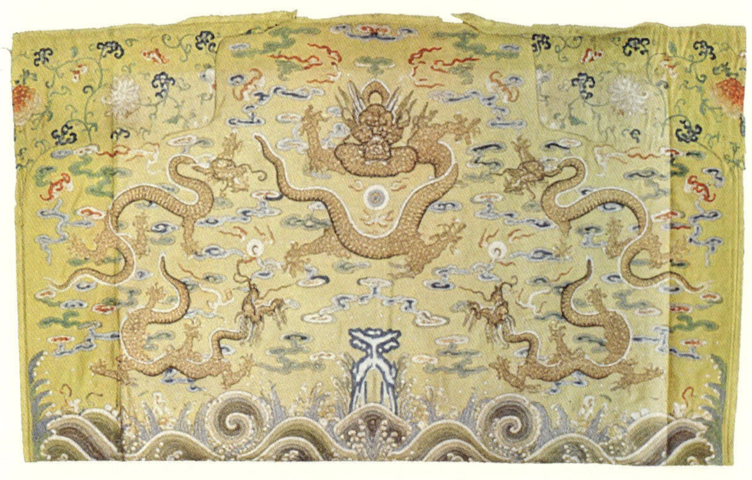

Looted textile fragments, Unknown makers, China, eighteenth to mid-nineteenth century, V&A

A question often asked today about museum collections in the UK is, 'How much of this was stolen?' The answer is that a small portion is indeed loot. Plundered by the British military as part of its empire-building campaigns, objects were often subsequently gifted or sold on to museums. This is how the cushion covers and fragments here came into the V&A's collection.

The textiles originally furnished the living quarters of the Qing dynasty emperors in the Yuanmingyuan, a vast complex of gardens, scenic sites and over 3,000 architectural structures ranging from temples to silkworm farms.[1] Dyed with buds from the pagoda tree, the rich yellow silk ground is the colour that, for nearly two millennia, had been reserved for the use of the emperor and his family.[2] They are embroidered with symbols of wisdom, prosperity, longevity and the celestial realm represented by dragons chasing pearls, peonies, bats, clouds and the character shòu 壽.

An estimated 1.5 million objects were looted by British, French and Indian soldiers at the end of the Second Opium War (1856–60) from the Yuanmingyuan, including these textiles taken by Field Marshal Garnet Wolseley. In his *Narrative of the War with China* in 1860, Wolseley recounts, with the interest of a connoisseur, his explorations of the Yuanmingyuan during the three days of looting. When he reaches the private apartments of the emperor, he describes the textiles he would acquire for himself: 'The cushions upon the chairs and sofas were covered with the finest yellow satin embroidered over with figures of dragons and flowers.'[3] Wolseley participated in and, as he ascended the ranks of the British army, led several notorious military campaigns where loot was brought back to Britain. In addition to the Second Opium War, this included the suppression of the Indian Rebellion (1857), the Third Anglo-Ashanti War (1863–4), the Anglo-Zulu war (1879) and the Nile Expedition (1884–5).

These textiles entered the V&A's collection as an afterthought. In 1917, Louisa, Dowager Viscountess Wolseley, sent them back to the museum with a curator who had been visiting her at home in Hampton Court Palace to arrange a loan of her significant collection of Old Sheffield Plate. They were accompanied by a note from her: '10 Pieces of embroidery from the Summer Palace a gift to the V&A museum.'[4] On receiving the textiles, the V&A sent a note of thanks to the Dowager Viscountess saying that, 'they will be of great value and interest to students here who are now giving particular attention to works of Chinese art'.[5]

What are the current possibilities for restituting objects like these? UK national museums can legally only restitute objects that were Nazi loot, as decreed by The Holocaust (Return of Cultural Objects) Act, 2009. Despite this restriction, museums can and should continue to conduct detailed research into the histories of contested objects in their collection; work transparently and creatively with communities to interpret them; develop global partnerships such as long-term loan agreements; and ultimately advocate for political change so that museums have greater legal freedom in decision-making behind restitution. Georgia Haseldine, Senior Curator

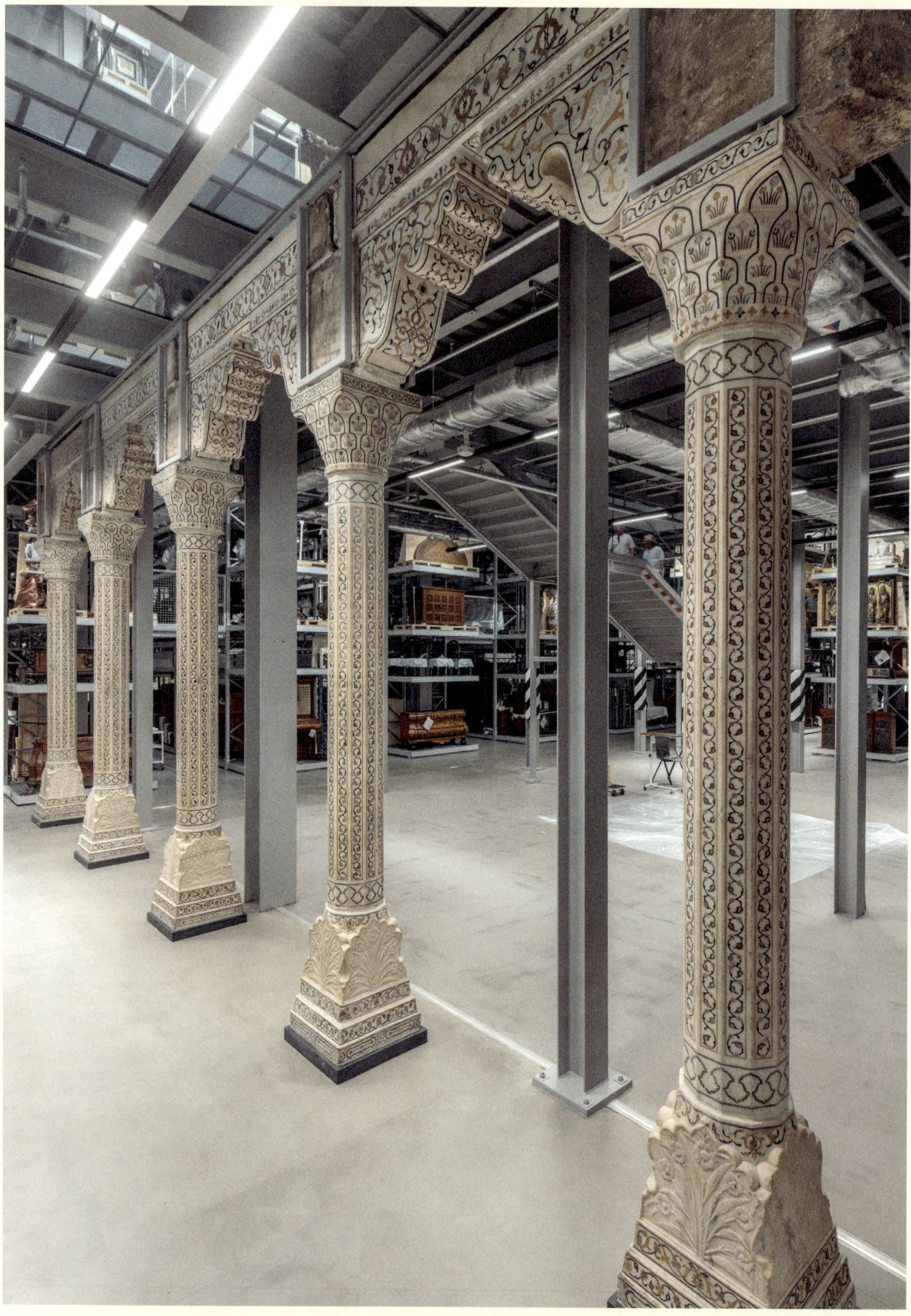

Agra colonnade, about 1637, installed at V&A East Storehouse, 2024

Separated from its original context by space and time, it is easy to overlook this colonnade as a piece of functional architecture. Dating from the 1630s, its columns were once loadbearing and supported the roof of a veranda outside the hammam of the Mughal emperor Shah Jahan in Agra Fort.[1] Five columns, five plinths, five capitals, eight brackets and four lintels comprise the present structure, which is self-supporting, grounding its weight through the constituent components to the floor.[2]

Like most buildings constructed for the emperor, the colonnade is made of white marble whose surface has been richly decorated with floral designs in colourful stone inlay and relief carving. The post and lintel construction and overall surface decorations are the two most prominent features of the structure and beg the question: why does the colonnade look the way that it does?

One straightforward answer is that climatic and environmental conditions played a part in determining the form of Mughal palace architecture.[3] Agra summers are long, with both hot-dry and hot-humid weather conditions. The palaces in the fort were developed in dialogue with the weather whereby climate-adapted design elements such as courtyards, verandas, water features, deep overhangs, large rooms, terraces and suitable materials created cool microclimates.[4]

The veranda offered a transition zone between the hammam and the terrace. Being open on three sides the area was ventilated and breezy, reducing temperature and humidity. There may have been provision for covering the openings with screens of woven vetiver grass, which were kept moist and released their sweet scent through evaporation. The white colour of the marble, its smooth and shiny surface, reflected the sun's rays, while its thermal mass made for comfortable interiors.[5]

The intertwining plant forms and floral designs on the colonnade traversed palaces and monuments inside and outside the fort, binding them visually and thematically.[6] If one envisages the decorations as blankets of flowers scattered across the grounds it becomes easy to comprehend their unifying tendencies. The florilegia in these buildings are in fact metaphors for real and paradisical gardens.[7]

Gardens were perhaps the earliest sites where the Mughals created microclimates in Agra, once a picturesque city with an abundance of gardens lining both banks of the Yamuna River.[8] The first gardens were laid by the founder of the empire, Babur, and his courtiers as antidotes to 'the heat, biting wind, and dust'.[9] The inspiration for these sanctuaries was the Persian *chahar bagh* – a geometrically organised garden, which doubles as an Islamic symbol of paradise.[10] Mughal gardens were veritable oases, with pavilions, running water, blossoming fruit trees and sweet-smelling flowers. The concentration of vegetation and water imparted a distinct microclimate to these grounds.

Contemplating the colonnade in a climatic and environmental context reveals how the forms of Mughal palaces followed function. The construction of palaces, like the laying of gardens, was partly motivated by the desire for pleasant living and working environments. This can be thought of as the substantial function. Overlaid on this was the metaphorical function, communicated visually by the floral designs. And yet it wasn't just the visuality of flowers that connected both sites and reinforced their paradisical associations. Underlying the apparent primacy of vision was an embodied need for comfort fulfilled by the microclimates that must have made the sites feel paradisical. Is it not then plausible to consider that paradise is a microclimate? Revati Mann, Assistant Curator

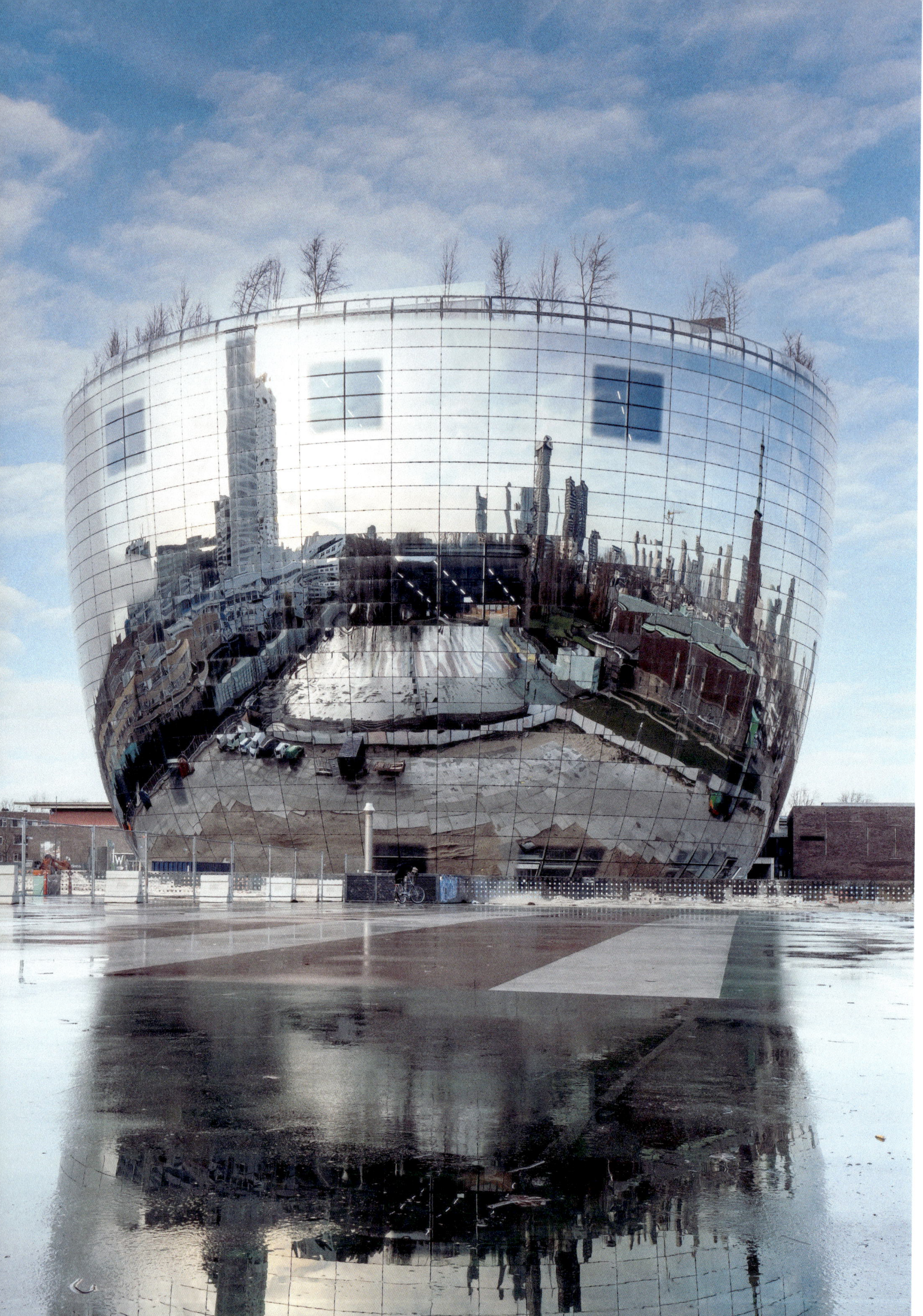

Depot Boijmans Van Beuningen, 2021

Depot Boijmans Van Beuningen
Sjarel Ex

King Willem-Alexander, Prince of Orange-Nassau, opened the new Depot Boijmans Van Beuningen on 5 November 2021. It was a prestigious event attended by school children, dignitaries, museum supporters and sponsors of the panes of mirror glass that form the building's exterior. For the event, that exterior was adorned with five firmly cabled acrobats, dancing against the backdrop of an expansive Dutch sky, which was reflected in the façade. The Depot was complete, fully furnished and ready for use. Worldwide, hundreds of journalists covered the spectacle on newspaper front pages, social media, radio and television. 'This is the future, just get used to it.' So ran the headline in the *Financial Times*.

The team at Museum Boijmans Van Beuningen spent 16 years of concerted effort on this project: a concept for a new museum typology within an architectural development in the city centre, where hidden collections could be made visible.

It all began with the simple wish to build a new depot. That idea grew and, as work progressed, we gained greater clarity of the form and function of the building. Moreover, the Depot is set to evolve further still when the neighbouring Museum Boijmans Van Beuningen reopens, and the two buildings are able to work in mutual support of each other.

The design brief, which was completed in 2010, encompassed everything that a museum might wish for in relation to collection management. The design outlined an ideal new neighbour to the Museum Boijmans Van Beuningen: a new facility dedicated to the maintenance and study of the collection.

The focus at the Depot is on explaining the process of conservation by putting it on view. It contains restoration rooms, a quarantine area for pest control, a photographic studio, booths where films can be screened for visitors and exhibition space for artists' installations drawn from the collection. This is complemented by the print room and reading room where readers can pore over the book collection. An educational programme is also on offer and includes customised tours, extending to the collection compartments; restoration projects are explained as they happen; individuals can be granted the opportunity to study particular works of art; and a smartphone app is available for works of art that feature prominently at the Depot. It is also from the Depot that items head out into the world on loan.

Originally (if we rewind to 2004 for a moment), I envisaged the ideal depot in the form of a human brain: a brain in the sense of a fully automatic, associating storage system; a memory based on knowledge, recollection, context, association and intuition. As I pictured it, a depot would be a fanciful, interrelating system, just like Kurt Schwitters' *Merzbau*. At Schwitters' studio he fashioned an ever-growing installation in which art and life were integral components. He stashed every manner of thing inside it: colleagues' artworks, memories of a lost son, hidden experiences in objects, relics. Everything fitted into a plasticity that grew rampant – including into the garden of his house in Hannover – in multiple layers with grottoes and caverns connected by viewing holes and sightlines. A three-dimensional diary made of objects.

The architect John Soane created a different type of instrument in his London home, and one intended for public use: a collection of architectural and artistic objects gathered for the instruction of his students. Each object had a particular position, and Soane was one of the first collectors to create efficient storage systems, such as the triple wall cabinet for the collection of paintings by William Hogarth, also intended to protect his collection from sunlight and keep it in a stable good condition.

There were other sources of inspiration when drawing up the new Depot Boijmans Van Beuningen, a space that not only makes accessible the museum's expertise in relation to its objects, but also offers access to advanced equipment for the purpose of gaining and sharing new scientific insights. It is more than simply a back office for physical management. The Depot

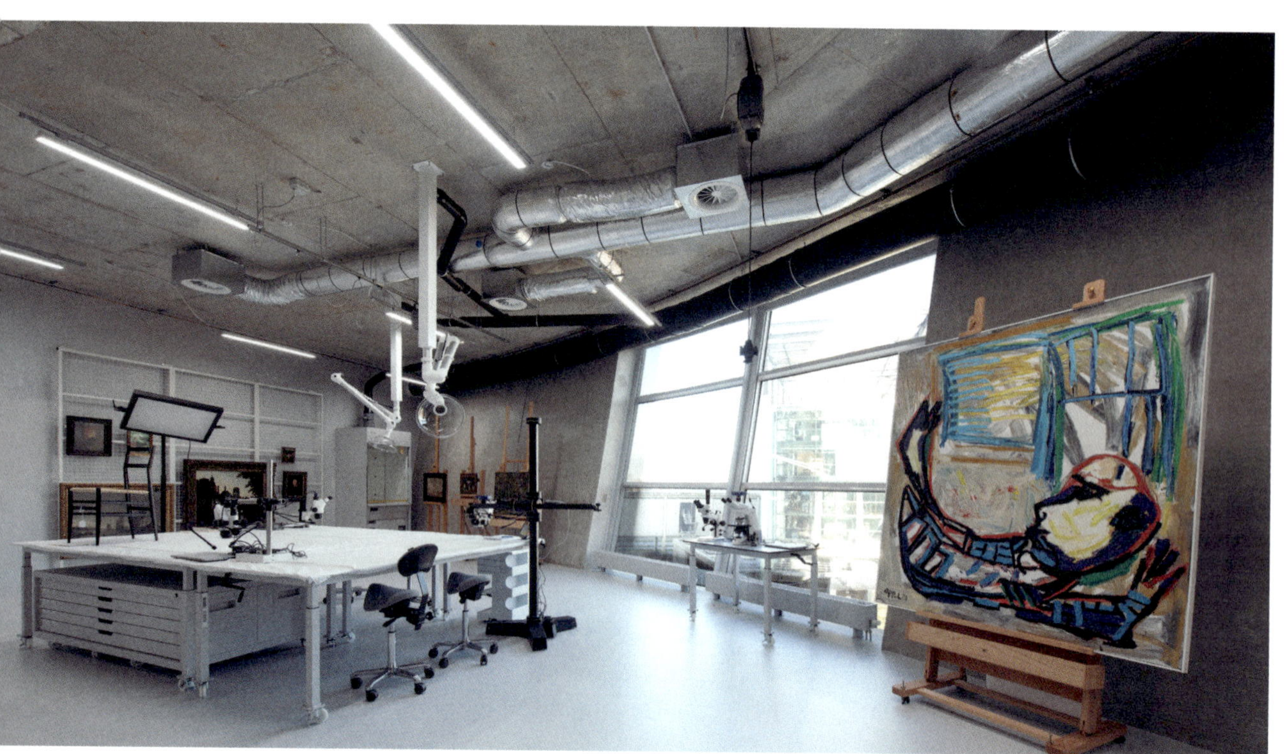

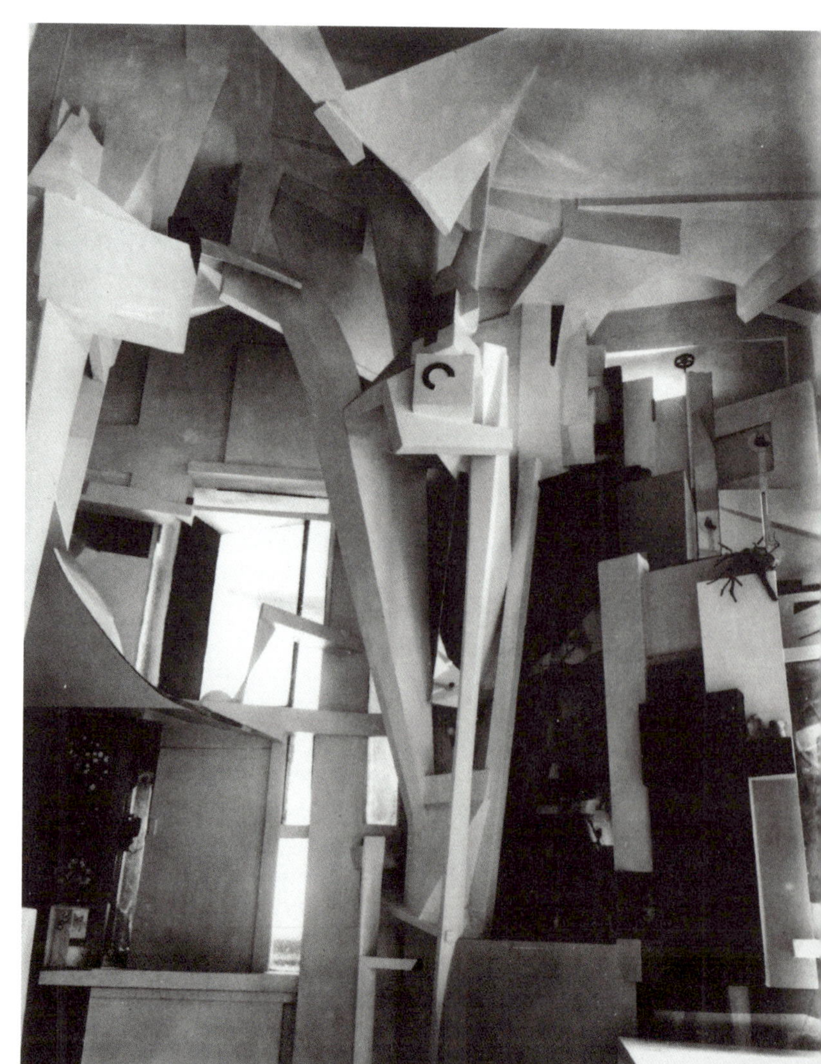

above Restoration rooms at the Depot, 2021
below *Merzbau*, by Kurt Schwitters, 1933

is an instrument where, amid functions normally kept concealed, the dynamism and character of the collection becomes visible.

I am keen to draw a comparison with a library. Libraries provoke us to browse. It is in a library that we see the convergence of stories, ideas, points of view and ways of thinking. You might visit just to find one book and come out with another three besides. Metaphorically speaking, should that not also be possible at a depot as well? The cloud, replete with all possible knowledge and information, is a splendid invention, but how do you know what you are looking for? Databases are not so ideal when trying to seek out, understand and unlock unfamiliar objects and artworks; for that you need to be able to use your senses and directly observe colour, size, smell and weight.

The Netherlands is a country obsessed with museums, having the greatest museum density in Europe and a plentiful assortment of collections. However, a few decades ago it was clear that the professionalisation of heritage conservation was leaving the nation lagging behind. In around 1990, the Minister of Culture, Hedy d'Ancona, decided to address this in the form of the Delta Plan for the Preservation of Cultural Heritage in the Netherlands. Funds were made available for both passive and active conservation. Utrecht, where I was working at the time as Director of the Centraal Museum, built a new depot to help relieve the museum, and it was there that I noticed for the first time the amount of enthusiasm and curiosity generated by tours of that new depot. Being amid so many artefacts seemed to allow people momentarily to disengage, without feeling at all imposed upon, and learn to appreciate conservation itself, in all its facets. It seemed that the physical confrontation with a selection of objects defiant in the face of their perishability was the trigger for something that generated curiosity and astonishment. It is perhaps equivalent to taking a peek behind the scenes at a theatre. You become witness to creation and see how ingenuity works. In this I could see the value in the creation of a programme concerning each artwork at all stages of its existence, including the prosaic, where the process of management, conservation and restoration is made transparent.

One of the premises of the open depot is that the management of objects and artworks can be of interest to the public. But just how interesting is it really to see how others work on something? The museum initiated experiments

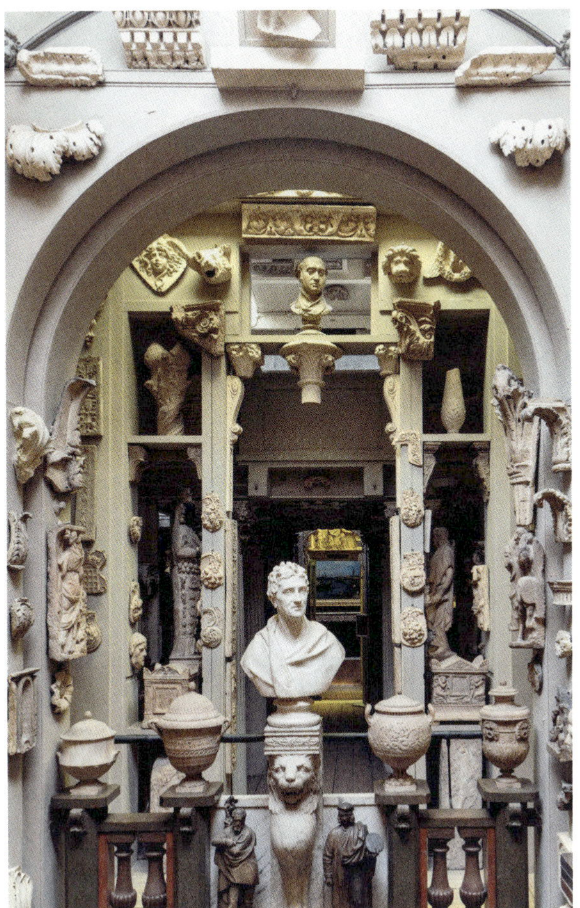

Interior of Sir John Soane's Museum, London, 2021

in that vein. At an open day we included an 'oddly interesting' programme about art shipping cases and crates. Just how does one make a shipping crate for art; what are the criteria and best practices? The technical support service demonstrated what kind of custom work is involved with a crate: factors relating to handling, strength, weight, internal climate, flight direction, vibrations and, in terms of typical causes of damage, red flags such as forgotten screws. This practical seminar was the best attended and remains a success to this day.

Another more substantive experiment was also an unexpected success. The collection contains a large stock of antique textiles: some 5,000 items deriving principally from nineteenth- and twentieth-century legacies. They were relatively unfamiliar and had been neglected for years. A specialist team was organised to inventory, describe, photograph and store the items in dust- and acid-free conditions. Activity of this kind takes many months and, normally speaking, is carried out in a secluded space at an anonymous depot; but we took a different approach. The workspace was simply a large room in the museum circuit open to the public;

staff members and their jobs were put in the spotlight. There was a display case on hand to exhibit important items, and we also had a helpdesk where passers-by could ask questions. Moreover, two qualified experts attended at set times of day as guest curators, sharing their knowledge of each item. The surprising element was the knowledge of the subject among collectors and enthusiasts alike and the rich exchange of knowledge within that group. The experiment also brought countless regular visitors to a halt; their interest piqued by the activities.

The idea of the Depot provided the oxygen for another premise: the relationship between Museum Boijmans Van Beuningen and collectors. Would the Depot be able to reflect and facilitate that relationship? In addition to the two very great donors highlighted in the museum's name, a good 1,750 private individuals have jointly donated some 50,000 objects to the collection. This represents a third of the total collection. There have been ties with collectors since 1849, and they are still commonplace to this day. The Depot's response is to manage and look after museum collections together with artwork belonging to private individuals, where the 'looking after' is done in compartments for hire with the professional support of museum staff: an artworks hotel where the owner is welcome. Collectors meet one another and discuss areas of interest and share knowledge and advice; it engenders a social dynamic among the collectors and a buzz about the collections being put on public display. Moreover, a private individual participating at the Depot has only to open their compartment door for visitors to come streaming inside.

Some 1,500 square metres is available to third parties as depot space. There appeared to be demand for this facility and it was more varied than anticipated. The Depot now contains large, cumbersome items for which collectors lacked the space at home, nascent collections under construction, legacies from studios not yet collated and corporate collections – a category that we initially overlooked. The latter are usually large contemporary collections to which considerable investment is attached. Given that they attract a much greater public than they would if solely on corporate premises, a company can justify freeing up resources and people for this.

Even the remarkable Verhalenhuis Belvédère (Belvédère House of Stories) came on board, storing and exhibiting objects at the Depot and using it as another site for telling the stories of maritime and migration history shared by this organisation. It is a collaboration that, although unanticipated, fits well with what might be expected of a transparent heritage institution in a city whose residents are drawn from 150 nationalities.

As plans for the Depot progressed, it became apparent that there was widespread interest in participation in this new museum typology. This prompted us to re-examine our capacity projections and for the concept to undergo a few major shifts. The percentage of space accessible to the public was increased from a cautious 20 per cent to 50 per cent, and later to 99 per cent of the total area. We had previously assumed 90,000 paying visitors a year, however we now began to wonder what the maximum figure could actually be; how many people could we handle?

Work at the Depot goes on at all hours of the day; one has only to consider the many hundreds of works on loan and the conservation treatments per annum. The introduction of the public into the space could not be allowed to pose a hindrance to this work. A flow study undertaken by the Erasmus University produced valuable information. In the space of 52 six-day weeks, the building would be able to handle some 275,000 to 300,000 visitors: a modest thousand a day. And how many tours could we then give? Answer: we could take along a maximum of 60,000 people in groups of 13 into the depths of the building.

As it turned out we were indeed busy, in part because of the long run-up to opening. The museum publicised the idea of a depot accessible to the public and did so far and wide. This included lectures and symposia that fuelled professional curiosity and later innumerable interviews and two global publicity campaigns to ignite wider public interest. The first of these campaigns was during the silver opening in 2020, at the height of Covid-19, when the main contractor had just completed; the second was on the occasion of the royal opening in November 2021. Both campaigns reached some 3.5 billion people worldwide.

The function of 'treasure house' sparked enormous curiosity but the iconic design by MVRDV Architects gave wings to the building itself. The design in its present form landed on the table of the panel that awarded it first place out of entries from 47 international architectural

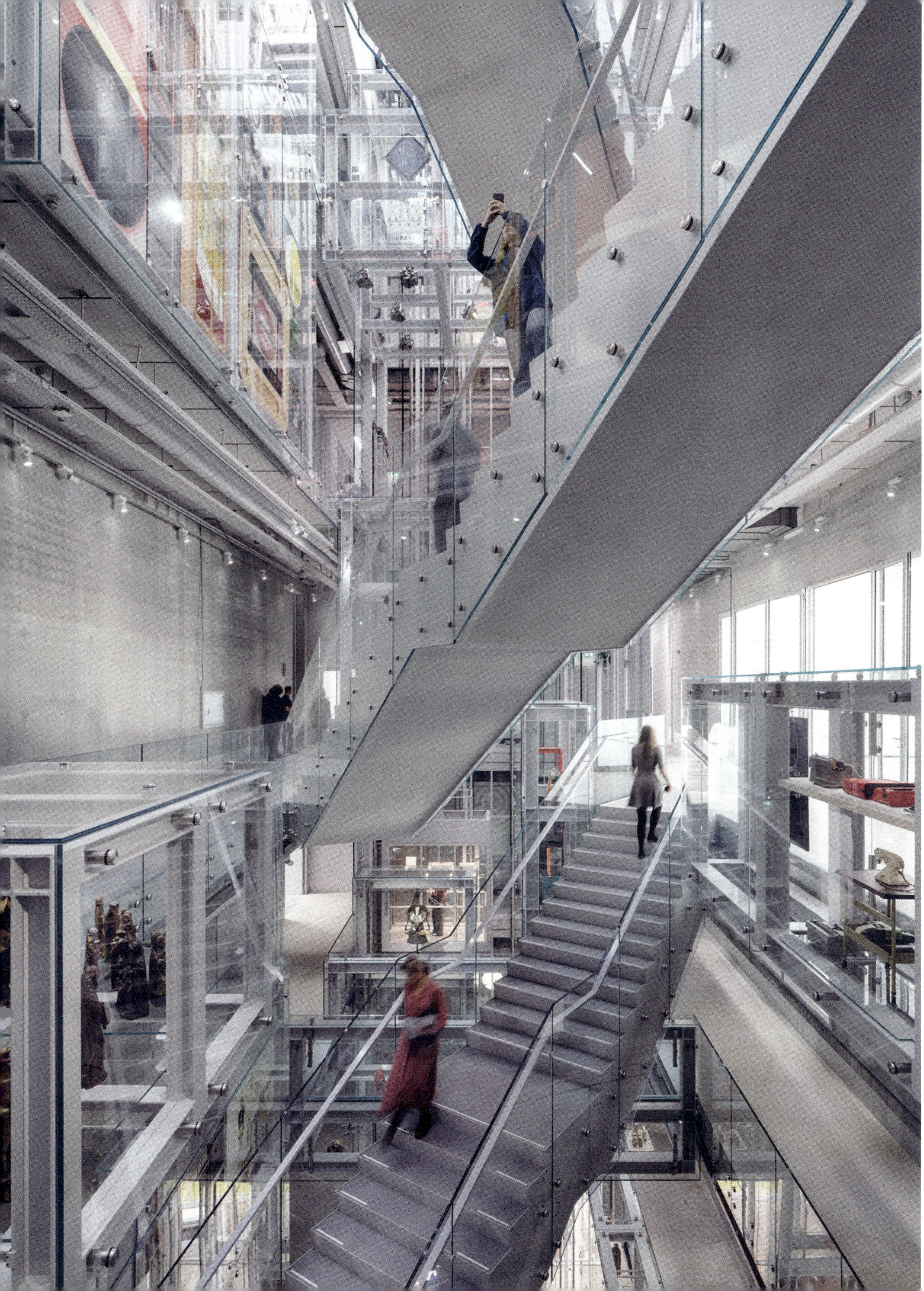

Atrium and stairways of Depot Boijmans Van Beuningen, 2021

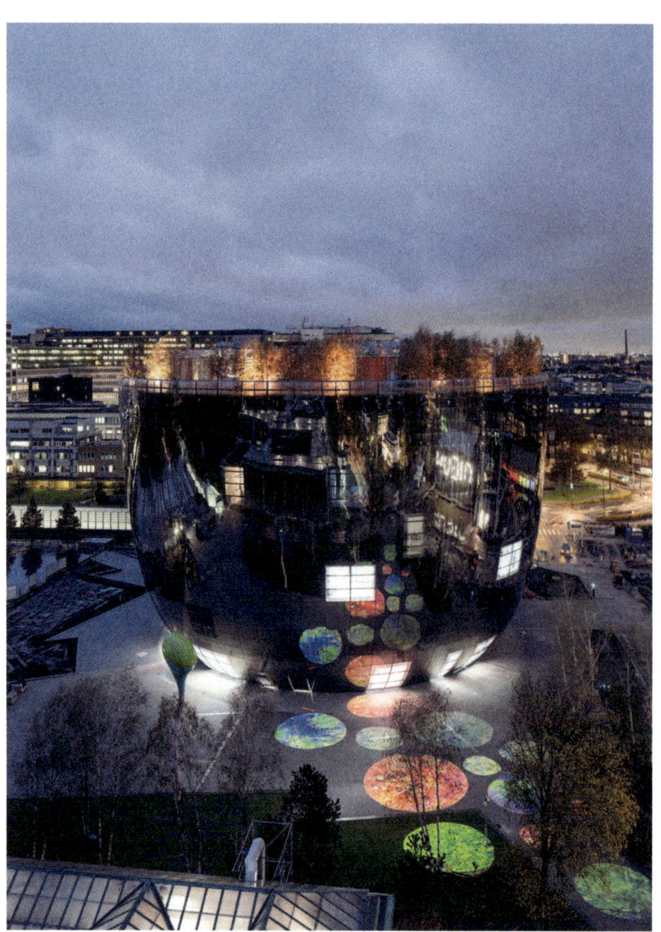

Depot Boijmans Van Beuningen showing the rooftop garden and light art by Pipilotti Rist, 2021

firms. The founder/architect of MVRDV, Winy Maas, was solidly behind his concept, even if there were moments of tension concerning whether it would indeed be possible to deliver convex mirrors of this type. Maas also played an instrumental role in convincing the city to accept the building, a process that took approximately five years. Discussions and even multiple judicial procedures on the desirability of building a depot next to the museum, the sightlines around the building on the construction plot and the disturbance to birdlife and patients at the neighbouring hospital were brilliantly resolved. The present perception of the architectural result, with its mirroring skin, is getting metaphorical; Dutch novelist Allard Schröder recently observed that the Depot does not stand in the city, but the city in the Depot.

The interior is based in its entirety on the museum's design brief and was realised by the architect in collaboration with several artists and designers. Each material in a compartment of its own – 14 of them in total – jointly amounting to more than 5,500 square metres. We maintain five temperature zones and several humidity levels alongside a generic percentage of humidity and warmth in the building. In addition, each collection space has its own specifications as required. Compartments with metallic objects are drier than average. Spaces allotted to black-and-white and colour photography are kept, respectively, cold and colder still. The building is sustainable. Its thick concrete walls have a stabilising effect on the changing seasons. There are solar panels on the roof. Rainwater is used to flush the toilets. The building has its own ground-coupled heat exchanger in the depths far below ground level. And even the use of materials is in line with sustainability rules.

Decisive choices were made during construction: in particular, concerning the interior. We plumped for an atrium model with a stairwell five storeys in height in the centre and expansive galleries around it. The art compartments, technical rooms and exhibition rooms give out on to this. When Winy Maas installed the Piranesi-style stairs, the museum asked artist/designer Marieke van Diemen whether she could add something else by way of contrast, perhaps in the style of suspended display cases. Her design, amounting to a total volume of 400 cubic metres, was executed in the same materials as used for the lifts and handrails and can accommodate small exhibitions and ensembles drawn from the collection.

It was at around this time that my flights of fancy concerning Schwitters began to fade away and I started to envision the Depot as a machine set in motion by human hands that might belong morphologically somewhere between Fritz Lang's *Metropolis* and Charlie Chaplin's *Modern Times*, but with *Thunderbirds* and James Bond never far from sight either.

With greater visitor numbers now projected we needed to enlarge the entrance area. Artist/architect John Körmeling designed a free-floating vacant space in the hall for lockers and furnishings with additional capacity for 400 visitors. The restaurant in the building's roof garden was contributed by Concrete Architectural Associates. Outside, the colourful work of light art by Swiss artist Pipilotti Rist radiates across the pavement and mirror glass every evening, taking the building and its public space to a higher realm in yet another way. Finally, a contribution not to be underestimated concerning perceptions of the building came from film director Sonia Herman Dolz through her lyrical documentary *Depot – Reflecting Boijmans*, which premiered in 2023 at festivals and in Dutch cinemas. She drew a parallel with the construction process of our first building in the Museum Park in 1935, focusing effortlessly on the creation and reception of the new building.

Even now, there are still opportunities to be exploited for this new typology. The Depot offers a spectacular and detailed insight into the collection. In the future, alongside the visitors, increasing numbers of users and participants will be making use of the Depot as a tool for research, art conservation and collecting. It is also a good medium through which to impart the ABC of heritage management to private individuals: a source of knowledge and a storage-cum-distribution centre for the whole professional heritage sector. Worldwide, professionals are adopting whatever they find useful from the Rotterdam model. To date, some 125 museums, cities, provinces and international delegations have visited.

Early visitors during the preparations in Rotterdam were the V&A. Over the years, this led to a friendly and interesting exchange of insights. Now both the Depot Boijmans Van Beuningen and V&A Storehouse are finished, comparison reveals distinct differences in choices, execution and perception. From a visitor's perspective, the Storehouse offers a wandering experience through a monumental three-dimensional grid. The walk itself is spectacular, with numerous close encounters with stored pieces that make the experience unforgettable. On the other hand, the Depot resembles a beehive, providing a free-flowing slalom over five floors.

The unique nature of the Storehouse experience lies in its focus on practicing crafts in separate studios under the supervision of specialists. Rotterdam stands out for its attention to collectors and collecting as well as its emphasis on the practice of conservation. The Storehouse includes period rooms and interiors, such as an office designed by Frank Lloyd Wright. The Depot features compartments and spaces for changing exhibitions and installation artworks.

For both the Boijmans Van Beuningen and V&A, it is the first time in the history of our organisations that our collections, tangibly and organisationally, are all around us. Having previously needed to search for collection items in remote storage sites, we now have greater oversight of and insight into those collections and their development. At the Depot, this is proven time and again when putting together exhibitions, when drawing up collection and deaccessioning plans, and when publicising the collection; no doubt the same will be the case for the Storehouse. Both institutions have enriched the museum field with new premises that will serve as examples for the future of many more museums.

Sjarel Ex, Former Director, Boijmans Museum

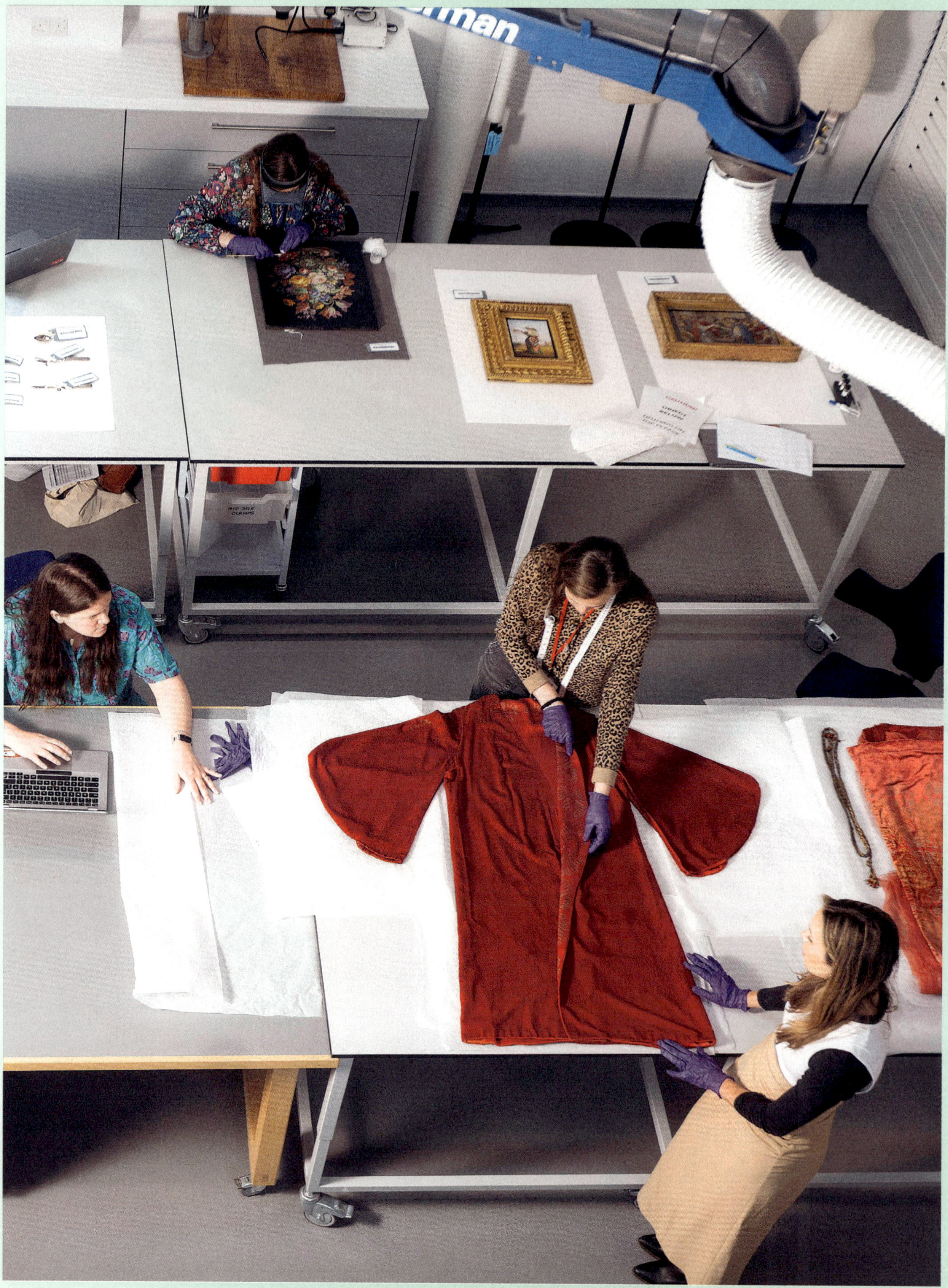

Multi-purpose conservation studio, visible from the Conservation Overlook, 2025

A Day in the Life

For the first time, V&A East Storehouse is putting the labour of museum work on show. Visitors are watching photographers documenting our collection, studying how technicians prepare objects for loans out to exhibitions around the world, as well as watching conservators clean and restore objects.

By bringing these processes and people to the fore, we reveal the many hands needed to care for our objects to make them radically accessible. We hope that showing how we work inspires the next generation of museum professionals. From devising workshops for school groups to the technical virtuosity of a costume mounter, there are many (often hidden) roles to uncover. In this spirit, several colleagues who have been instrumental to the creation of V&A East share a day in their working life.

Kate Parsons
Director of Collections Care and Access

When I started out in my career, I had no idea that my job existed. Now I know it's the job that helps to make the magic happen; to enable the whole museum to work. The core function of the Collections Care and Access division is to facilitate the care and sharing of our collections. That role goes from preserving, treating, moving and documenting individual objects to installing exhibitions, as well as supporting international loans and dealing with the legal, logistical and practical aspects of managing a collection. We sometimes have to be secret keepers too, so we can safeguard the collection. For example, we don't talk about when or how an object will be moved. You might want to know how all the objects got to Storehouse, but all we can say, for their safety, is that they got there by road transport.

What you see at Storehouse is the operating system for the whole of the V&A. Our teams are welcoming visitors into our working facility, to witness the varied work that takes place behind the scenes to care for our collections and enable them to be shared and shown. At its core it is all about enabling access, either through providing more information about our collections, or by caring for them so they can be moved and shown. I don't see enabling access to our collections and care of them as being in opposition to each other, which is, historically, how this dynamic has been presented. These two elements are not in conflict, in fact, without one the other doesn't exist, because if we don't share our objects then people won't see museums as relevant or as part of their future, and that poses a huge risk to the longevity of a museum's collection as well. Every part of every object at Storehouse will be available for the public to access, up close, on demand. To make this possible, we have considered access with every decision we have taken, with every object that has moved here. For example, our expert teams have devised new packing and storage methodologies to minimise object handling.

As custodians for the future, we have to balance risk, assessing what is actual and what is perceived risk. My job is to enable us to make evidence-based judgements around decisions surrounding objects, and to develop policy and procedures based on risk assessments. Often, such decisions are not easy or straightforward. To help our audiences engage with this element of our work, at Storehouse we are asking various questions to see how our audiences judge and think about risk. An example of this is the question surrounding the risk of light exposure. We are asking, if you were presented with five prints all from the same edition, would you sacrifice one to constant light exposure and preserve the others out of the light, or would you limit exposure across all five prints so they all they all degrade a little, but equally so? I am excited that Storehouse will be a space where the public can meaningfully inform how we manage and safeguard the collections for them, and for future generations.

Philippa Mackenzie
Former Head of Collections Move Programme

My role was to head up the Collections Move Programme for the Blythe House Decant Collections Project Team. All museums have collections that are not currently on display but need to be carefully managed in storage. They are used for exhibition programmes and displays, for research and as loans to other institutions.

Blythe House is the Grade II listed former headquarters of the Post Office Savings Bank near Olympia. Owned by the Government, it has been used for museum collections storage for the last 40 years. The V&A collections at Blythe House numbered 260,000 objects – including furniture and sculpture, fashion and textiles, poison arrows, ceramics and paintings – 915 archive collections and 350,000 library books. The Government's decision to sell the building in 2015 set in motion the project to remove (or 'decant') all the collections from the building to a new home at V&A East.

I led a project team who, from 2017, were responsible for preparing the collections for the move. This involved painstaking documentation, condition and hazard checking, photography, specialist packing and barcoding of everything in the collection. This work was critical to identify, manage and track all our items at every stage of the process.

Our day-to-day work evolved throughout the life of the project, with the focus shifting as preparation workstreams were completed and transport began. I would split my time between Blythe House and the Storehouse, having regular meetings with the contractors responsible for transport, installation planning, health and safety, team management, programming and administration. I also met with teams across the V&A to anticipate issues and remove barriers to progress. Given our legal responsibilities for both the staff and the fragile and historic collections, a significant proportion of time was spent on progress reports and demonstrating accountability for the safety and security of the objects.

What was new about this project was the significant and admirable shift in focus to increased and broader public access. This challenged the teams to find ways to balance enhanced public access and greater visibility of the collections with collections care and management. Another exciting challenge was the inclusion of display elements and the involvement of architects in the internal arrangements of racking, working to realise their vision whilst still providing viable storage solutions.

The project threw up daily challenges, and there was a great deal of satisfaction to be derived from working with the team to solve them. Any frustrations tended to stem from delays and obstructions that were not within our gift to rectify – such as the pandemic. Being involved in the care of an historical or iconic object, even if just for a short time, is very satisfying. A beautifully documented and packed object is balm to the soul! Leaving things in a better shape than I found them was my motivation.

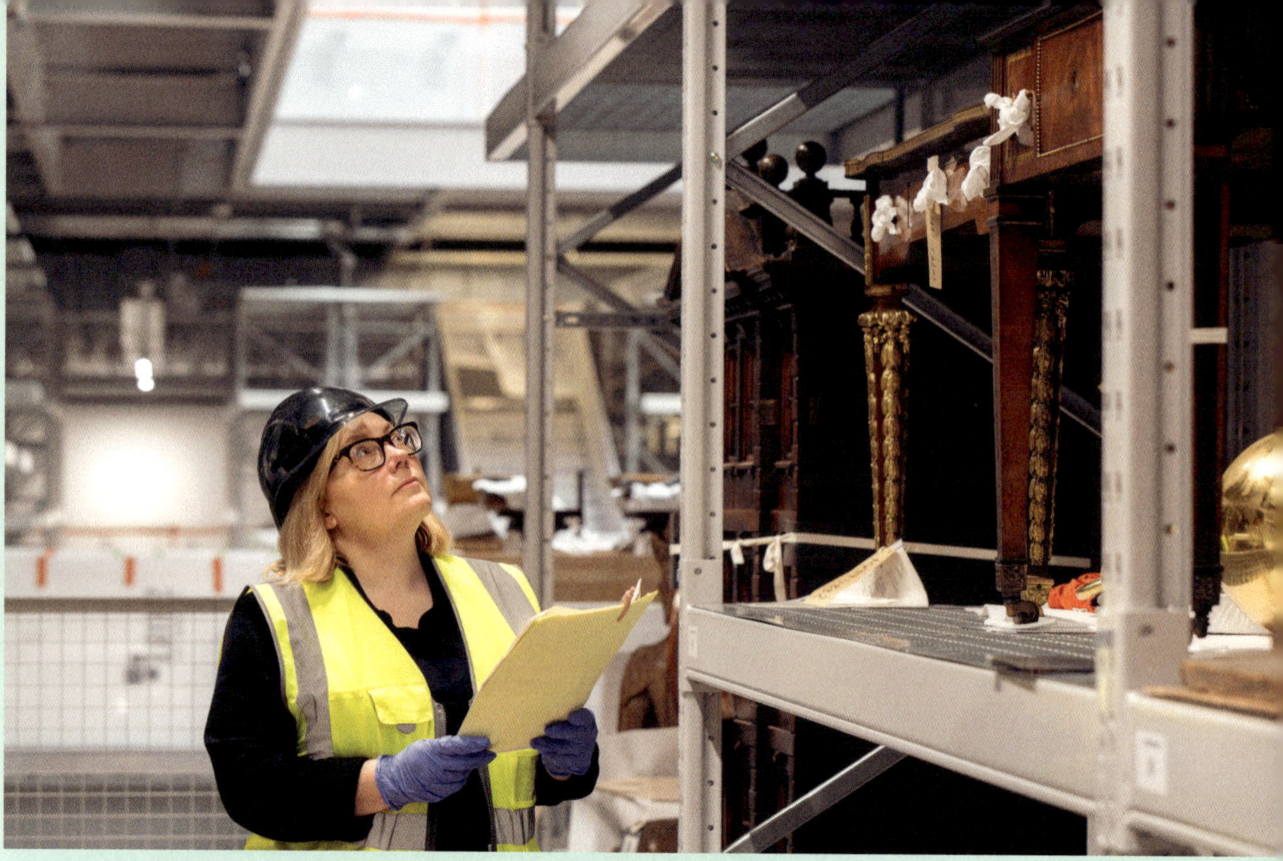

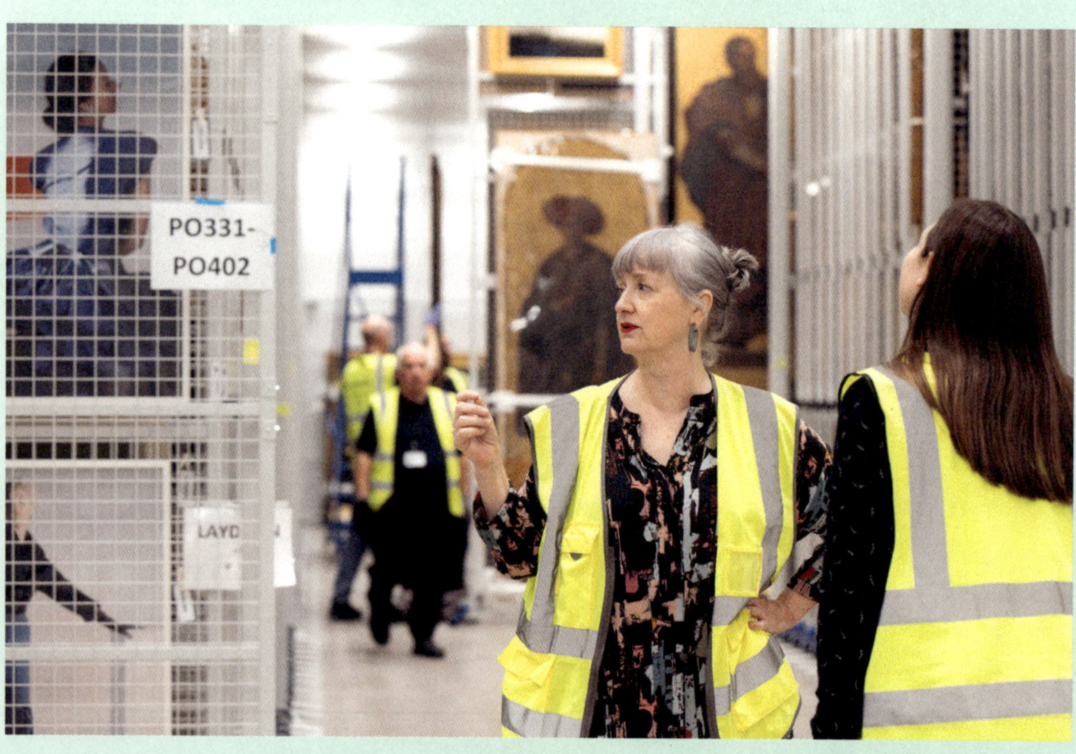
PO331-
PO402

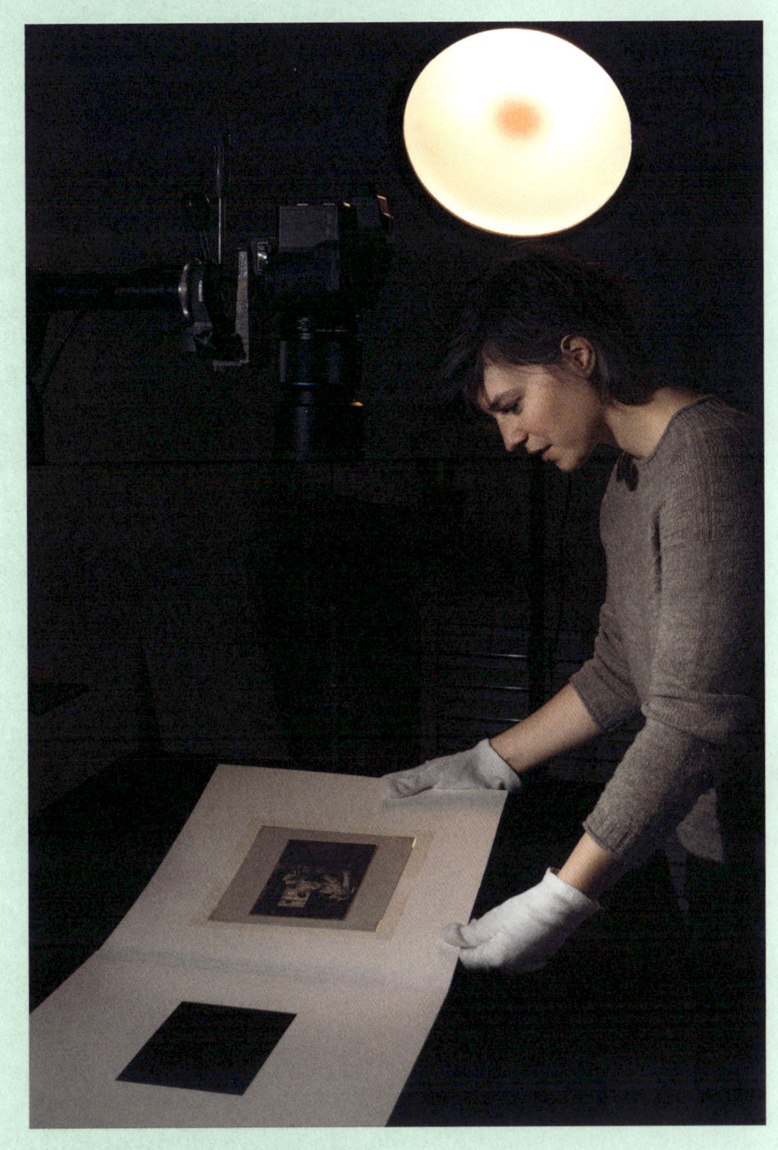

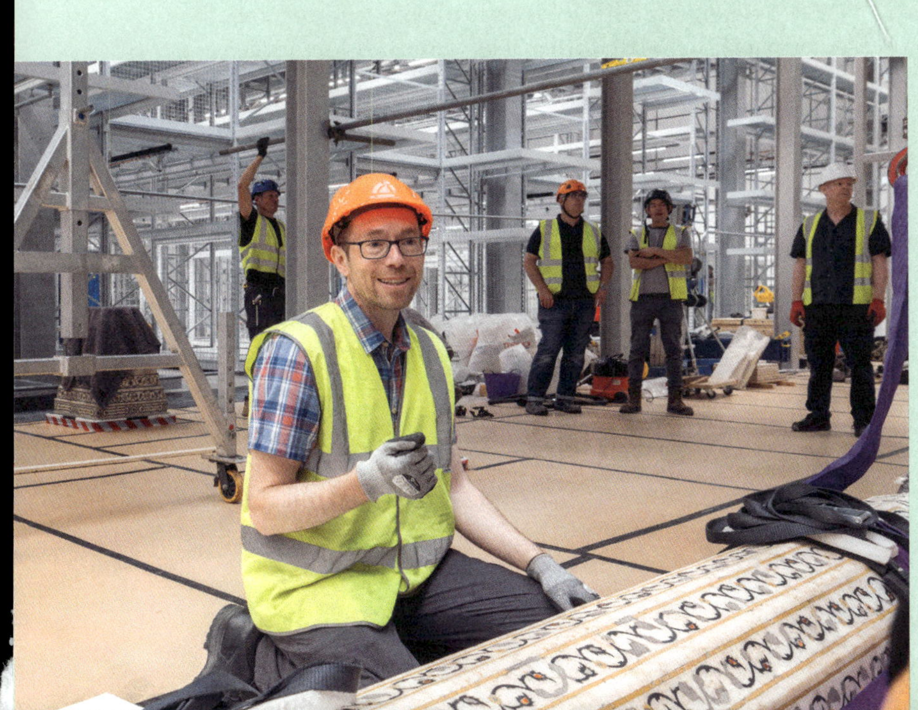

clockwise from top left

Kate Parsons, Director of Collections Care and Access, location checking objects in the Adjustable Pallet Racking, 2024; Kira Zumkley, Head of Photography and Digitisation, in the dark room, 2023; Matthew Clarke, Technical Manager in Technical Services, unwrapping the Agra Colonnade, 2023; Philippa Mackenzie, Former Head of Collections Move Programme, helping the team populate the racks with paintings and photography, 2024

Matthew Clarke
Technical Manager in Technical Services

In my role as Technical Manager in Technical Services, I am responsible for the management and organisation of the work of a team of technicians and apprentices. My team works on projects at different stages of delivery, undertaking object handling, mounting, installation, packing, storage and transport across the V&A.

Our role is key in realising the visions of curators, architects and designers, leading on the safe and secure installation of museum objects. In the case of Storehouse, this has included designing large structural mounts for architectural objects such as the section of the Robin Hood Gardens and the Torrijos ceiling as well as creating delicate solutions for showcasing fragile jewellery or mixed media collages.

Frustrations can emerge from being at the end of the critical path of project delivery, right between build completion and opening. This can often lead to squeezed object installation periods, due to other delays, and requires us to react to resolve those issues in order to deliver on time. That said, I do think that overcoming these frustrations leads to an increased sense of achievement and satisfaction when a project is delivered successfully.

My day will usually start with a morning briefing and check in with my team to talk through the upcoming work. This will be followed by meetings and site visits to attend. Each day will typically include a review and update of the team's work schedule and processing of new and upcoming work requests. My work extends across multiple V&A sites as well as to various conservation studios and storage locations.

One of the biggest challenges I face in my role is reduced funding. This, combined with ever greater expectations surrounding the quality and scale of the end result, means that a great deal of creativity is required for my job. Longevity and reuse of object supports is a key part of the solution to this challenge. Technological solutions are also valuable. Storehouse, in particular, has increased my use of 3D visualisations and modelling to convey complex design information to the project team.

I love being able to apply my engineering background in the museum environment. Working collaboratively with external designers, architects, artists, build contractors and engineers is always a lot of fun. I am excited that visitors to Storehouse can now see our work, which so often is invisible to them in traditional museums.

Kira Zumkley
Head of Photography and Digitisation

As the Head of Photography and Digitisation I am responsible for the strategic direction of my department and the day-to-day management of a team of around 10 imaging professionals across the V&A family of sites.

My team's focus is on digitising the V&A collection, but that can be done in many ways. Usually, we photograph objects in the studio, but we can also photograph them in the gallery, or even before they make their way into the museum, for example in an artist's studio. Most of this is done using traditional photographic techniques, but occasionally we also use advanced imaging techniques such as 3D imaging or X-rays, which have enabled us to understand everything from the construction of a couture dress to the detailing of delicate relief sculptures.

I often work onsite at the studio in the V&A South Kensington. My days involve digitising objects from the V&A collection – used in books, on the website and for press purposes – as well as meetings with teams from across the organisation. Occasionally I also give tours or training to external colleagues who are interested in what our department is doing and want to learn from us. The V&A East project is very exciting as it not only adds two fantastic sites to the V&A museum group but also provides my team with three new and bespoke spaces to carry out high-end photography and digitisation. With more sites than ever to display the V&A collection it will be challenging to manage requests across all museums, but I am looking forward to working in our new studios, as well as making the most of the opportunities they offer for how we digitise objects at the V&A.

A big challenge for my profession is and always has been budget. The equipment we use is very expensive and everyone in my team needs specialist knowledge that is not taught in standard photography degrees. We do our best to share our expertise with colleagues across the globe and learn from other museum professionals.

Not only does my team work to contribute to the V&A's vision of making the collection more accessible to the public and preserving it for future generations, but we also want to make sure that our work and images spark creativity and add value to what our colleagues and the V&A do.

Bhavesh Shah
Preventative Conservation and Data Scientist, Collections Care and Access

I am responsible for preventative conservation and data analysis for the V&A. I oversee the management of the environmental monitoring system, which provides crucial insights into the impact of temperature, humidity and light on the museum's collection. I also conduct research around the mechanisms of object damage, such as fading, and assess the potential impact of climate change on the museum's long-term preservation efforts.

A significant portion of my time is dedicated to analysing environmental monitoring data using various data science tools and methodologies. I also ensure the smooth functioning of the environmental system by maintaining sensors and preparing them for upcoming projects and exhibitions. Collaborative meetings with estate managers, project co-ordinators and exhibition managers are also an essential part of my routine. My role includes the effective communication of complex technical details to other members of V&A staff in a manner that is easily comprehensible, ensuring smooth collaboration and understanding across teams.

One of the significant challenges I encounter in my role is the complicated task of understanding the impact of environment on the objects within the museum's collection. This involves developing my understanding of how environmental conditions can lead to damage or deterioration over time. This is a common theme of researchers in the field of preventive conservation. Recently, I've been using data science to model future climate change scenarios inside the museum building. We are always striving to safeguard the collection and preserve the museum as a resilient and sustainable institution for future generations to appreciate and enjoy.

V&A East is an ambitious project that will be opening storage to the public. This has posed its own challenges for the conservation and estate team to address, balancing the safety of the collection against the desire to allow people to see more of it. As part of this project, I am responsible for offering advice and support to ensure that the environmental conditions do not pose a risk to the objects. This involves assessing and addressing any potential issues that may arise, while also proactively identifying and mitigating risks that could impact the objects' preservation. I am always learning new things related to data science, science, software applications, coding languages and, most importantly, the objects themselves.

Hannah Auerbach George
Former Research Fellow, Material Resources

My job is to find out interesting and little-known things about objects in the museum's textile collection. I take this information and use it to inspire new ways of thinking about sustainability going forward. For example, last year I was looking into Ardil, a regenerated protein yarn made, in the mid-twentieth century, from peanuts. This fibre was discontinued in 1957 as it was thought to be a poor substitute for wool. However, in the context of the environmental harm caused by the textile industry, regenerated protein fibres are being re-evaluated as they can be made from waste and are potentially compostable.

The V&A East project is an exciting development for me as its aims and values reflect the kind of research I have been doing. It highlights how a museum collection can be hugely relevant to contemporary challenges, such as climate change and overconsumption. Opening up the collections and making museum practices more transparent is only going to benefit the way we relate to and use collections in the future.

I work in the V&A offices, from home and I also spend time in archives and the British Library. This mix works well with the three main aspects of my role: if I'm at home, I'm usually writing; if I'm at an archive, I am collecting research; and if I'm in the V&A, I'm often having meetings, attending lectures or disseminating my own findings as talks or presentations. A bonus of working from the V&A is that you can always go see something inspiring if you get a mental block.

I get the most satisfaction in my job when I follow a hunch and it comes through. For example, when I track down a piece of information that I need for my research in an obscure magazine or journal. Most frustrating is hitting a dead end. Sometimes you can spend an entire day in the library reading and find very little of use!

The challenge for roles like mine is always finding funding. I am funded by an external research grant from the Business of Fashion Textiles and Technology at the London College of Fashion, which, in turn, is funded by UK Research and Innovation. The V&A Research Institute, where I am based, is always hosting interesting fixed-term research roles from different specialisms funded by a variety of sources. At time of writing, my role is coming to an end, so for me the challenge is how to capture and use what I have achieved before I leave so that my work has a legacy. Often, these types of roles generate lots of interesting findings that can be lost once the research contract ends. To ensure my work has longevity, I have been writing for the V&A blog, updating the archival records with my findings and publishing papers on my research, which are freely available to access.

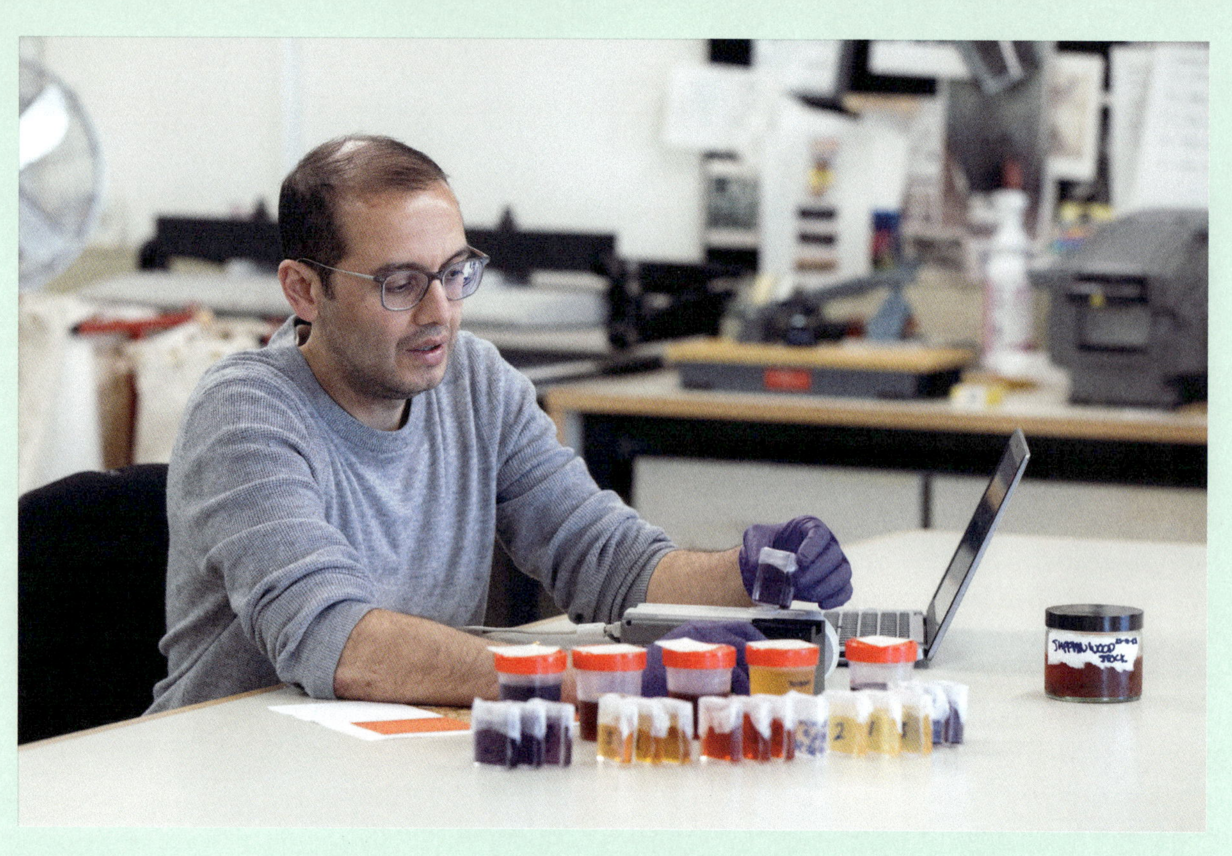

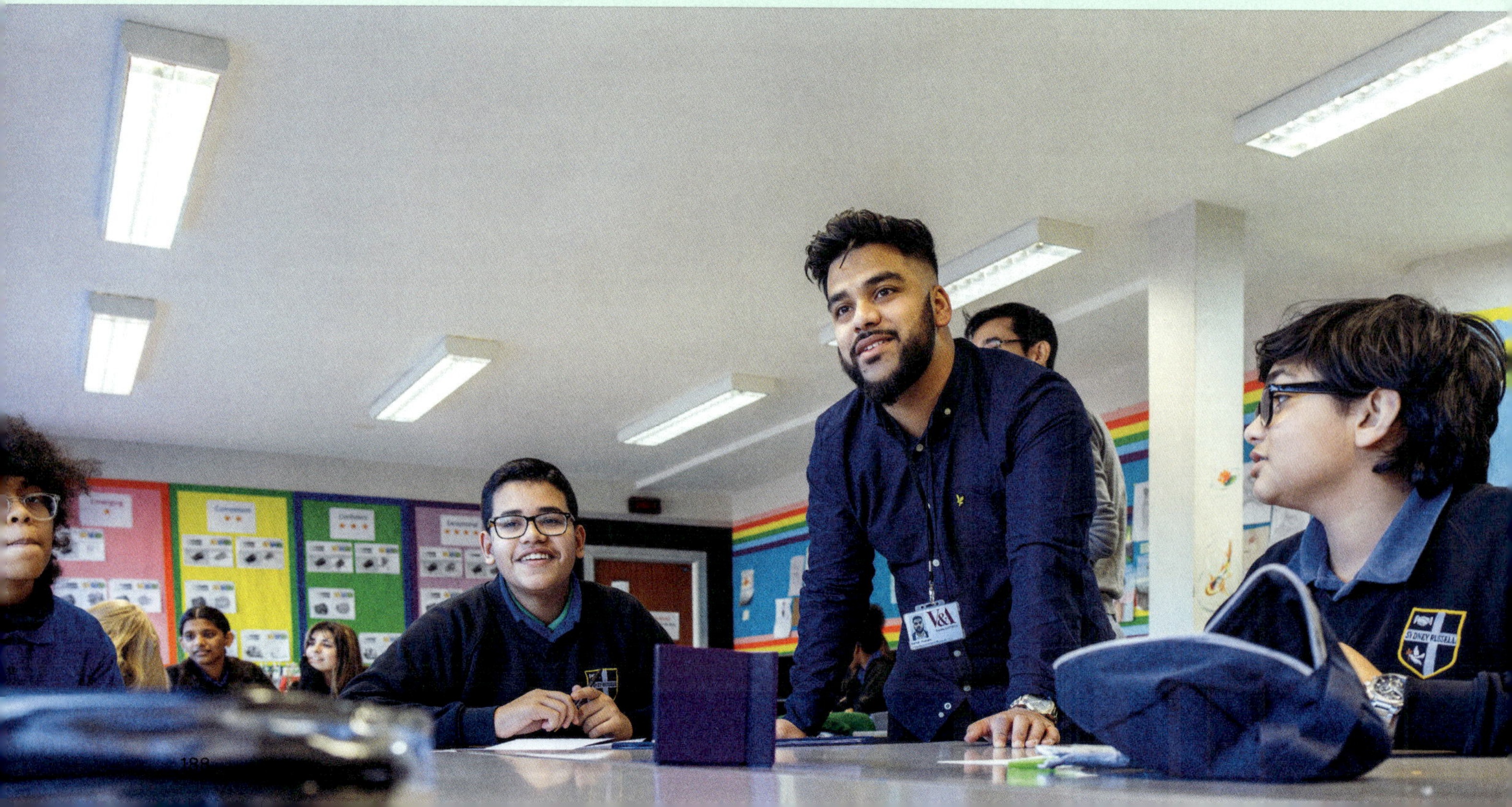

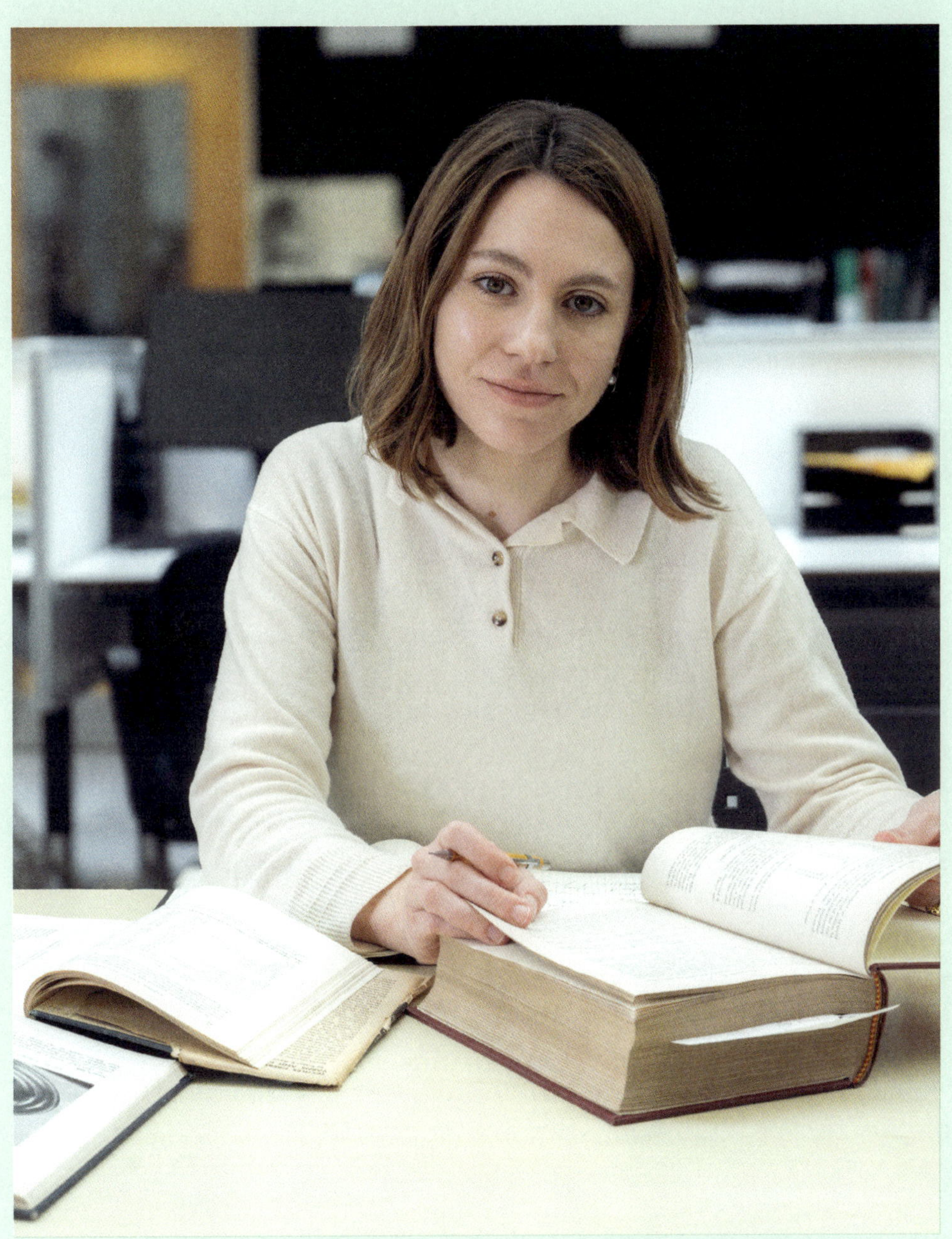

clockwise from top left
Bhavesh Shah, Preventive Conservation and Data Scientist, Collections Care and Access, experimenting with microfading techniques, 2023; Hannah Auerbach George, Research Fellow, Material Resources, with research materials, 2025; Kamal Hussain, Community Engagement Coordinator, V&A East, delivering a V&A workshop at Dagenham Park School, 2023

Kamal Hussain
Community Engagement Coordinator, V&A East

My role is to ensure the successful running of the various programmes created by the V&A's Engagement team, helping to involve audiences with the museum and its collection. Programmes include the V&A Youth Collective – a group of young individuals who help shape V&A's events and content – and our weekend retreat, Nourishing Ourselves, designed for young creatives.

I also managed the Your Collection programme, which involved taking objects from the V&A into schools in east London. Programmes such as this guarantee that young people are given the opportunity to see and learn more about these objects. Our visits also mean that students are provided with an insight into some of the roles available in the museum sector. I feel that it's so important for external professionals to visit schools and talk about the opportunities that are available in different fields as this empowers young people to envision their future.

For me, no two days are ever the same. The Monday before a school visit is always busy as I need to check everything is in order for the visit to take place. There will be DBS checks and teams within the V&A, including security, will need to be informed of any objects due to be leaving the museum. On the day of the visit two people must courier the objects to and from the school. The logistical aspect of this programme is quite lengthy, so there are a lot of issues that can come up at any time. The car journeys are probably the biggest cause of frustration; on average we are in transit for around four hours on the day of a school visit, couriering the objects. That said, the feeling of contributing to something great makes it all worthwhile.

V&A East was always intended to be different to more traditional museums, and that really comes across in the holistic way we work with, and are guided by, our audiences. I'm proud to have such a key role in presenting opportunities and access to our audiences in east London. My greatest sense of satisfaction is seeing the excitement in young people when they see the objects we bring into schools. We had our first visit to a school for young people with special educational needs and disability in early 2023, and the young people in that space were so captivated by the objects it has left a lasting impression on me. I hope that this is the same lasting impression that this programme has on young people.

Robyn Kasozi
Former Senior Brand and Campaigns Manager, V&A East

I was formerly Brand and Campaigns Manager for V&A East, a role that sits within the Marketing Department of the V&A. There is a widely held belief that marketing is all about selling, however that is only one element of the role. With V&A East, we are trying to reach new audiences, not served by our other sites. As such, my focus was on building audience engagement, creating that feeling of connection to V&A East as a brand.

I worked with teams across the V&A to ensure that the vision of V&A East as a champion of creativity for change, and a platform for diverse artists and designers, was reflected in our creative outputs, as well as in our collaborative partners. This approach was built into a set of guidelines that everyone working for and with V&A East can see and follow.

It is important with V&A East that we don't just land in east London and go into broadcast mode, so co-creation and listening is key. I spent a lot of time talking to people and building relationships with the Youth Collective, creatives, ambassadors, agencies and potential partners. I've enjoyed partnering with members of different communities in east London to brainstorm audience-building activities. I think process is as important as output, as we want to bring people on the journey with us.

Generally, in a day, I would hop around a lot of different tasks, including working on creative briefs for campaign films, researching what other institutions in the sector were doing, putting together mood boards and reviewing budgets. I really enjoyed how much dialogue I had with the Curatorial team. I think this is quite unique in large cultural institutions and it was one of my favourite parts of the role as I felt that we were all equally committed to creating two radically accessible spaces.

I think there is a wider recognition in the cultural sector now that previously the sector was quite elitist. There was a misconception that curatorial excellence and broad appeal were mutually exclusive. My greatest frustration stems from this in that there's still so much 'othering' on racialised or classist grounds. There are a lot of misconceptions about east London and about the people and communities here. Some individuals and organisations in the sector will tell me that 'young people don't care about collecting', or act as though east London has 'recently become creative'. Neither are true, and it's a disservice to our audiences. It's also an excuse not to try. Although there's no risk of that with our team.

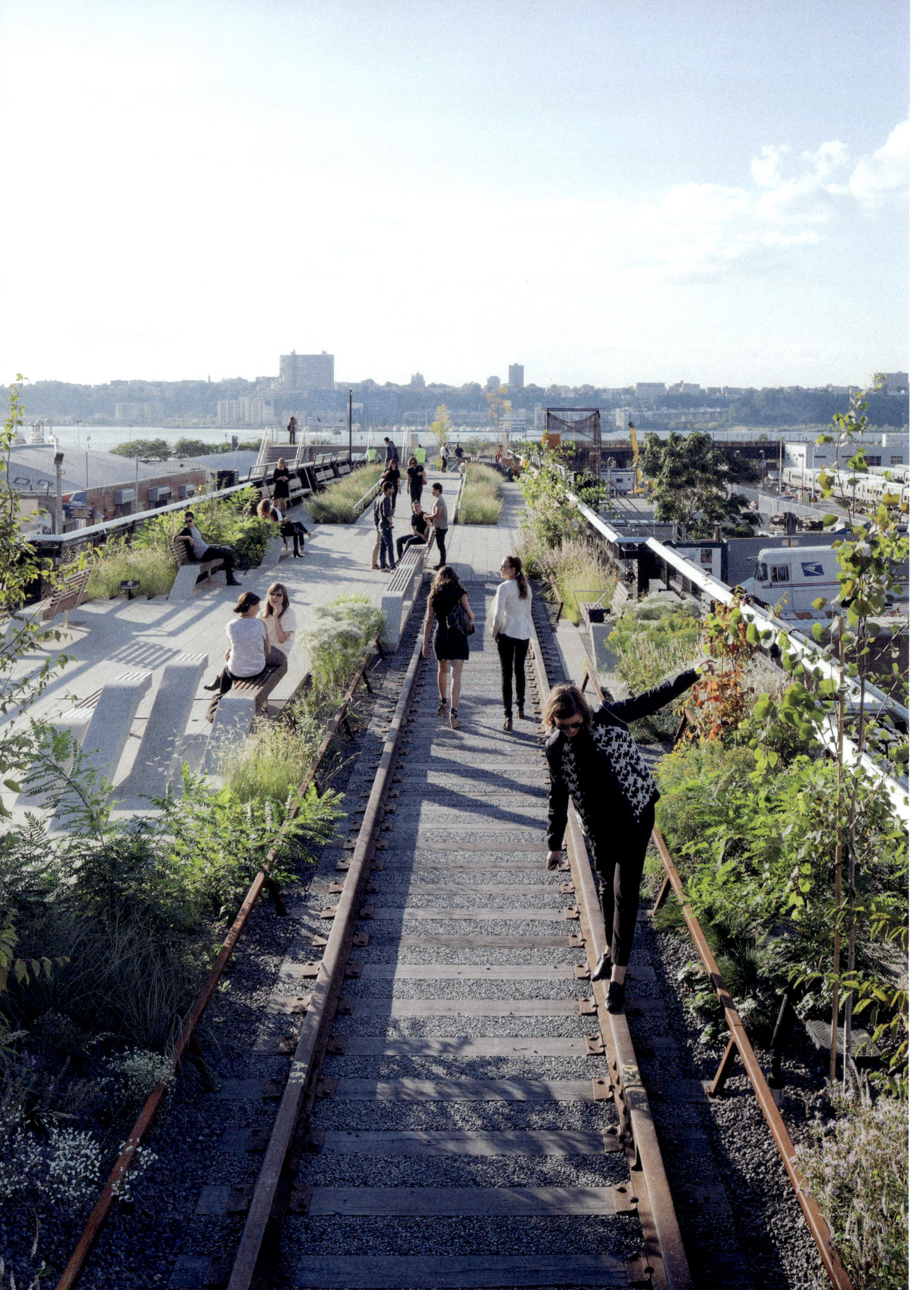

The High Line, designed by Diller Scofidio + Renfro in collaboration with James Corner Field Operations and Piet Oudolf, 2000–19. Photograph by Iwan Baan

An Interview with V&A Storehouse Architect Elizabeth Diller

Tim Reeve

Tim Reeve It is great to be talking to you about our partnership in east London. I thought it would be interesting to start our conversation by going back to the beginning of your work, which spans so many different forms – architecture, urban design, installation, multimedia performance – but always with a particular focus on cultural and civic projects and approached with a curatorial mindset. Is there is a narrative arc that takes you from your early work to the project at the V&A East?

Elizabeth Diller There's no direct arc, just a great desire to make art and to question authority. I spent half of my high school years cutting class and hanging out at the Museum of Modern Art (MoMA), wandering the collection and sketching in the Sculpture Garden. As a student studying photography and film at Cooper Union, I was drawn to space-making after taking an introductory course at the architecture school. I eventually graduated with a professional degree in architecture, but I never intended to be an architect. I wanted to look at the world through both the lens of an artist and that of an architect. I was a dissident of sorts, and questioned the institutions of art and architecture, wanting to find an alternative path. That was in the early 1980s, a time of great distrust of institutions and what they represented.

When Ric and I started our practice, we did guerilla projects on borrowed sites. We later accepted invitations to create public works in urban spaces, but stopped short of showing in galleries and museums.

TR What do you bring from those early days to what you now do at iconic world institutions, such as MoMA?

ED MoMA keeps popping up in my life. In 1989, we were invited to create an installation for MoMA's 'The Projects Series'. It was an installation that took a critical stance against the conventions of the museum. That project changed my perspective. That was when I realised we no longer had to throw grenades at the institution to try and break down its walls; we could just walk through the front door and critique it from within. Our installation, *Parasite*, was all about the guest/host relationship. Accepting the invitation was a way to broaden our audience while maintaining our voice.

Twenty years later we were invited back to be the architects tasked with expanding the museum. We never lost that critical spirit. In our interview we were very vocal in our critique of MoMA's lack of interface with its urban context, its generic galleries and the half mile walk from the front door to the first gallery. MoMA welcomed these comments. With an influx of new curators and the prospect of expansion, this was the opportunity for the museum to rethink its hard subdivision between disciplines, its relationship to the public realm and its own collections legacy. The new MoMA wanted to be more inclusive of geographies and histories missing, or deliberately omitted, from their collection. This was a time of reflection and space mattered. It turned out to be a great collaborative process. As architects, we were at the table, not only fulfilling the brief but also expanding MoMA's appetite for change.

TR It reminds me of the journey that the V&A has been on at the South Kensington site over the last 20 years, bringing in established or emerging architects to help us make sense of a 170-year-old building that has just been added to and reshaped over the decades.

ED Contrary to the geo-fixed and stable nature of museum buildings, what fills them inside must reflect the changing needs, values and technologies of the times. Reviving existing buildings requires the curiosity of an archaeologist and the skills of a surgeon. You have to decode the logic of the architects that came before you. You learn quickly that if you touch something here, it affects 10 things over there. It takes so much unwinding

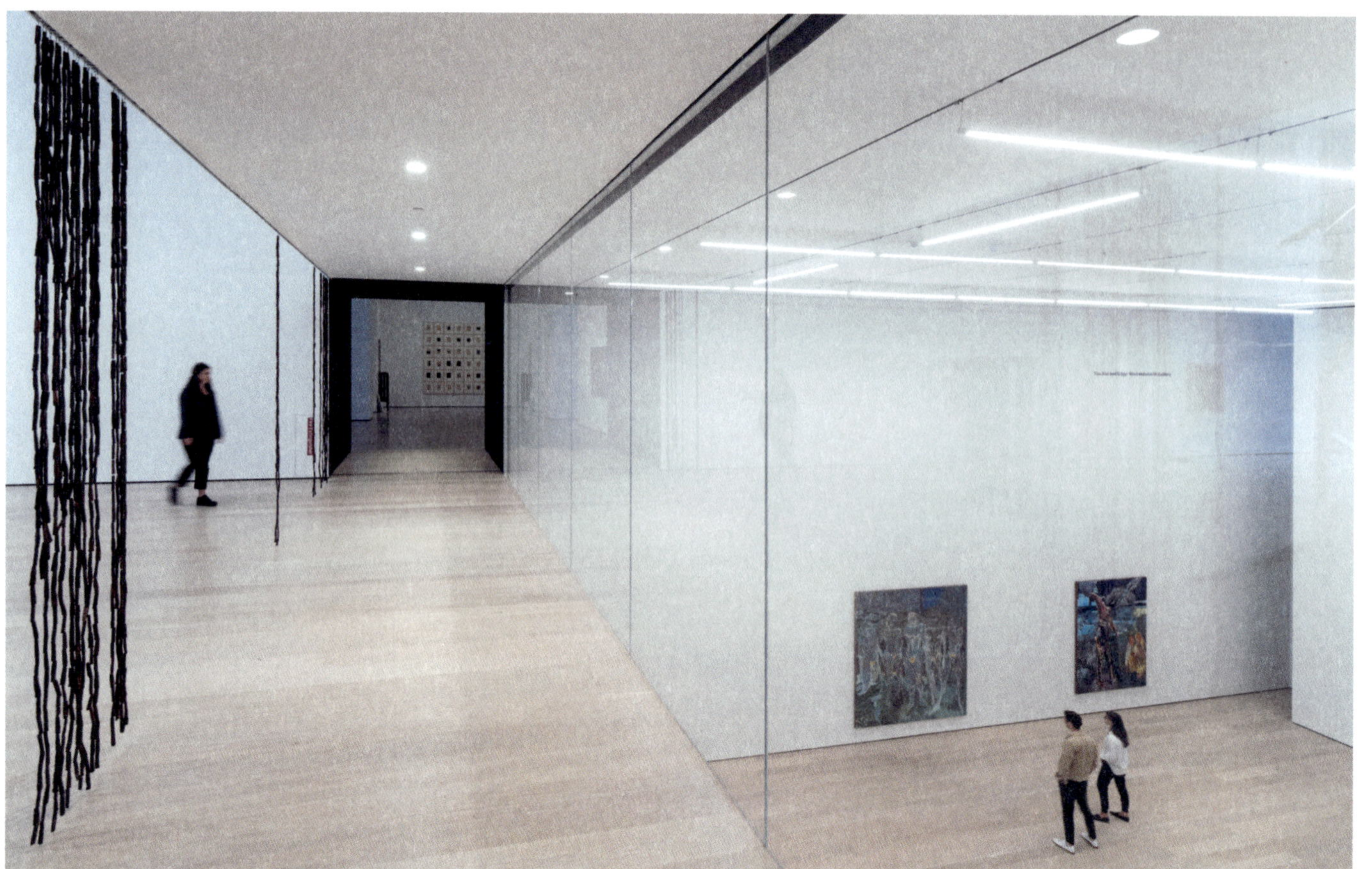

Galleries for MoMA, New York, designed by Diller Scofidio + Renfro, 2019

just to make a simple change. Renovation of historical buildings is not for the faint of heart.

TR I was just looking at the letter you sent to me five or six years ago with a copy of your book about the High Line. That is one of your most famous projects with an amazing approach to adaptive reuse, which is the way I think of the use of the broadcast centre at Here East, where the Storehouse is located. I remember the High Line being described as 'a master class in urban regeneration' and it was the first of its kind with its transformation into a public space that can be used for lots of different things and that people can take over in a variety of ways.

ED In 1999, the outgoing Mayor of New York signed a court order to have the 1929 structure demolished. It took a vision, citizen activism and a good incoming administration in City Hall to reverse the court order and give the adaptive reuse of the High Line a shot. No one could have imagined its success in New York, or the viral effect it would have globally. The High Line evolved at the same time as the redevelopment of the Lincoln Center, which was a half century old and needed a total reboot. The studio matured with those two parallel projects, and I became fond of breathing life into twentieth-century structures that had little advocacy to protect them. The broadcast centre was much younger and ideal for repurposing.

TR I think I'm right in saying that when we first met you admitted that you'd always had a crush on the V&A, and also that this particular project at V&A East represents the natural evolution of your practice and thinking. It's a historic space, but also an emerging new public space in terms of the Olympic Park, post-Olympics. It's a new building, but it's adaptive reuse in that it's replacing a data centre and creating a very untypical museum building – a new paradigm for collections access.

ED I already had a great interest in the V&A, not only because it had all these fabulous eclectic collections, but because it was brave enough to stage a David Bowie retrospective, a show on extreme footwear and one on equipment for protest. For me, the V&A represents an institution that is not only a custodian of historical objects, but also of the breadth of design culture, collapsing high and pop. The V&A's openness to new thinking resonated with that of my studio. Yet, bringing the collections into a featureless and generic media building was a challenge: the building's shortcomings had to be turned into its assets.

Attracting the public into a hybrid storage-facility-cum-museum was the bigger and juicier challenge. We all share a curiosity about what is behind the curtain, what we are not meant to see. A storehouse is almost the opposite of a museum, for in the latter everything is pre-processed by curators ready for display. They decide the stories they want to tell; they select objects from the collection; they configure them in a gallery; and they provide a script that defines the narrative. A storehouse, on the other hand, is unfiltered and only organised by classifications. There could be infinite stories told by the recombination of items therein.

We saw the V&A's collections as an assortment of species – furniture, fashion, metalwork, architectural fragments – an array of artifacts at different scales, made from a range of materials, by many hands, at various times, for a variety of purposes. The opportunity for visitors to construct their own stories, without being led, was appealing. We wanted the public to see unfiltered, pre-curated works. That is something that goes back to my anti-institutional starting point.

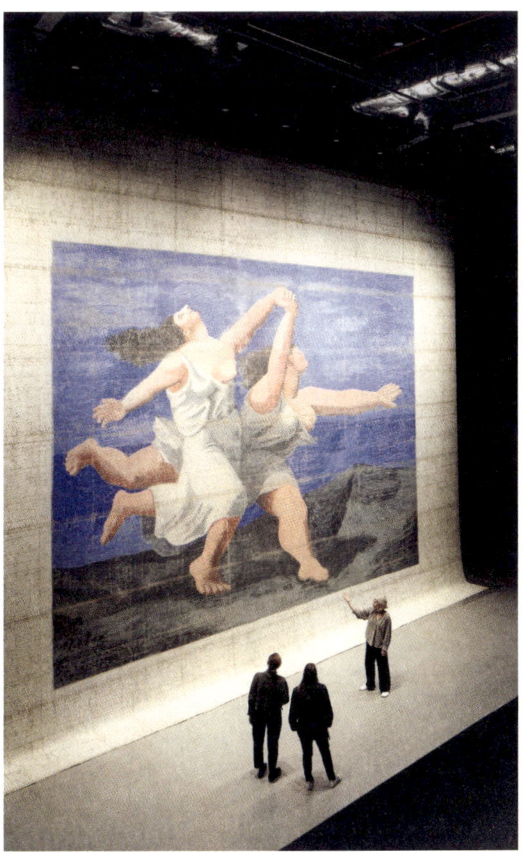

V&A East Storehouse, Gallery 2, The David and Molly Lowell Borthwick Gallery, showing *Le Train Bleu*, 1924, frontcloth by Pablo Picasso and Alexander Schervashidze

TR I remember at the competition stage the six organisational principles you set out: unassuming, optimised, excavated, inverted, sublime and 4D. Key was that architectural move to create a completely unique public space that brings people right to its centre, allowing them to immerse themselves in the collection. In your design, you start in the middle with the key public spaces, you then go into a semi-public realm, and then to the most secure, private areas around the outside. Once you had decided on that first architectural move, of placing the public spaces at the centre of the building, how much did it take you by surprise that the concept really worked?

ED It seemed inevitable from the start. We wanted to make an immersive cabinet of curiosities to highlight the diversity of the collection, and rather than having the public passively look at the collection in a cabinet pushed up against a wall, we wanted visitors to find themselves embedded within it.

Conceptually, we densely filled the entire volume of the space with objects and then 'cored' out the centre to make a void that could bring in light. The public would enter this void with objects receding into infinite space in all directions. This would produce a sort of hallucinatory effect – a sublime moment of sensing the immensity of the collection.

TR The craft that goes into how objects are housed and transported is exposed in the new display typology that you've created around the ubiquitous museum crate, achieving that back-of-house experience in a way that can be carried off with real authenticity.

ED We achieved a good balance. When we visited the V&A, it was fascinating to see objects in an 'in-between' state, before they're put on display, still covered with plastic or bound by protective material inside crates to protect them in shipment. There's a beauty in seeing an object stabilised by prosthetics in a just-opened crate, or one about to be closed. It expresses the vulnerability of the objects. That's when we decided that the transport vehicle and display case would be one and the same.

TR When you were designing the Storehouse, we were also navigating the tension that exists in museums between access and our need to safeguard the collection for future generations.

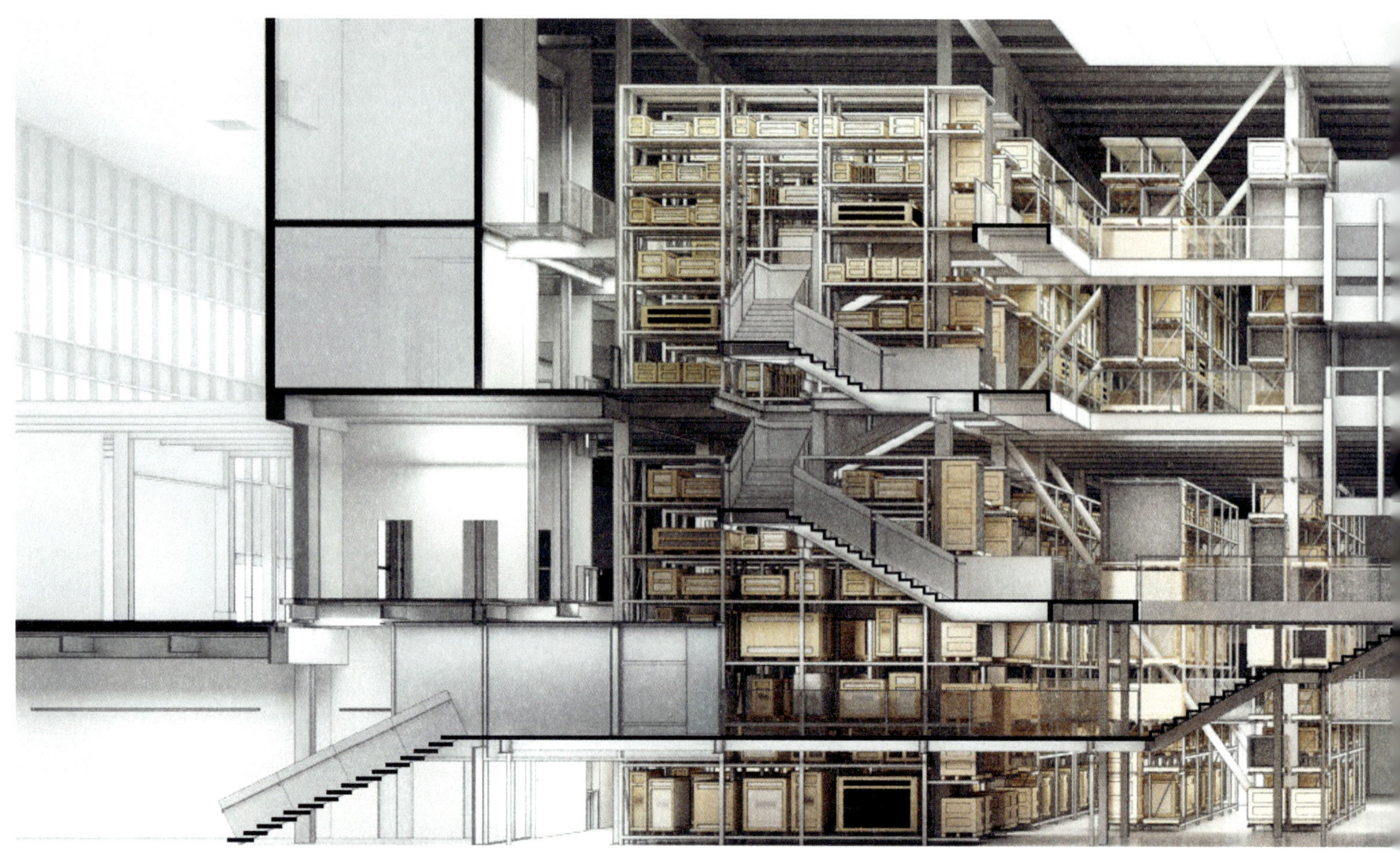

Because your job is to push the boundaries and push us as a client to be a bit more radical, how do you feel we balanced those two elements in the Storehouse design?

ED I think we achieved a good balance. The V&A allowed us to experiment with this hybrid model, neither museum nor storehouse. By opening up storage, it would empower the public to see more of the collection in a new way. It would make the viewers less passive. Rather than receiving information, they would find themselves in the act of discovery. But, institutionally, this model not only challenges conventions of display and storage space but also highlights the conflicting objectives of curators and conservators.

With the V&A's curators, there was this fabulous opportunity to bring out more of the collection, but it created tension with the conservators, whose role it is to protect and restore collection items. The challenge was how to spatialise a publicly accessible storage facility in which curators and conservators would also be active. Of course, it would be impossible to make all of the storage accessible, so how do you control access? That's where the concentric model came from. An obvious logic for a deep footprint building is to put the most accessible materials closest to the front door with easy access. Our approach was the opposite. We organised the building in concentric layers from the centre to the periphery. The most accessible artifacts are in the centre – the area we cored out of the warehouse to allow light in. The least accessible artifacts are closest to the periphery, which was perfectly suited to an opaque building originally built for media. The beauty of this concentric model is that what might be off limits to the public can still be part of the *mise en scène* of this infinite collection.

TR The other dimension that you've had to take into consideration is scale, both of the space that we have at the Storehouse and the varying scales of what you call the 'species of objects'. The collection includes everything from a piece of ancient Syrian pottery right up to a three-storey fragment of Robin Hood Gardens. Trying to reconcile these things in the face of such volume is part of the beauty, but also part of the challenge, because some things will get lost and some things that would not normally be prominent will take centre stage.

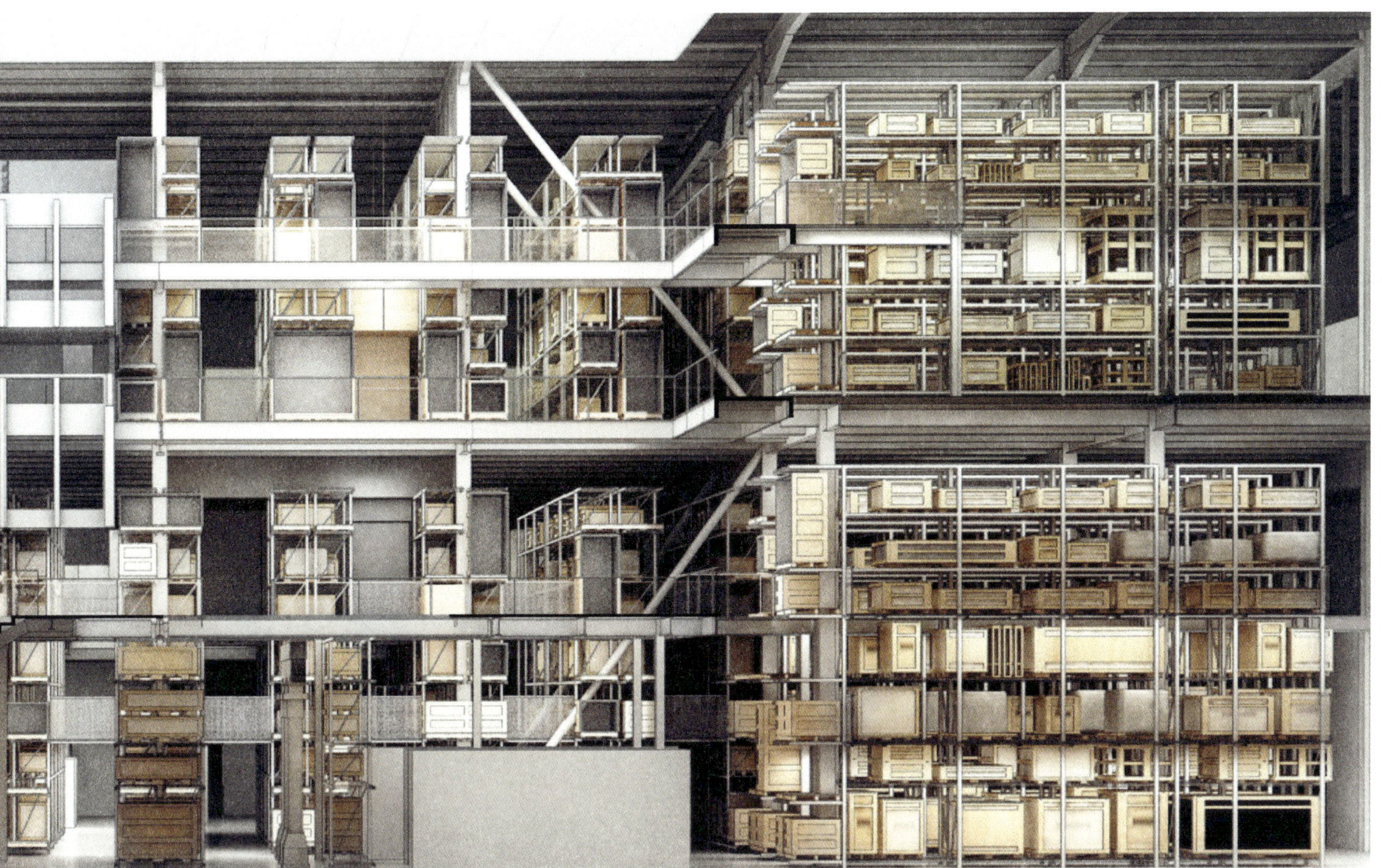

Render of Storehouse by Diller Scofidio + Renfro, 2018

ED What is visible to the public is the heterogeneous sampling of collections, a delirious mix of taxonomies.

TR Talking specifically about the large objects, they are difficult for us to display and they're often in storage. But in a space of this scale, they shouldn't be hidden away, they should be brought to the fore. You have come up with this amazing idea of deploying those large objects to create a kind of a spine for the visitor experience. Let's talk a bit about how you saw the large objects as a gift rather than a challenge.

ED The storage system is ultimately pretty flexible. There is the pallet, the crate and a racking system. We hacked the ends off the racking system so that you can see the cross-section of the shelving. It makes the objects more available. In the Weston collections hall you can find yourself next to a bust or inside the Frankfurt kitchen. What is offered is super-juxtaposition of architecture and artifacts, free of traditional classifications. The neutrality of the racking and shelving is key to the power of this idea – it's neutral to content; it only cares about size and weight.

TR Working with what is just a humble warehouse building in east London creates quite a unique overall atmosphere and I imagine that the atmosphere in the Storehouse, when it opens, will be something special and unprecedented.

ED If we're successful, it will feel like you're getting a sneak peek behind the scenes. The informality is part of the invitation to the public to go where they are not usually invited. Of course, we had to calibrate how much you can see and touch, but wherever you are you will be aware of breathing the same air that these objects live in.

Seeing an object in the distance draped with a protective shroud will trigger the imagination: What's under there? What's that shape? The Storehouse won't feel like a warehouse, or an archive, or a museum. It will feel like a place of the in-between.

TR I think there is going to be a real theatricality to the building. The shrouding and bracing of objects, those views through to the conservation studios or to the shop floor, with objects moving about, I think it will have a unique theatricality.

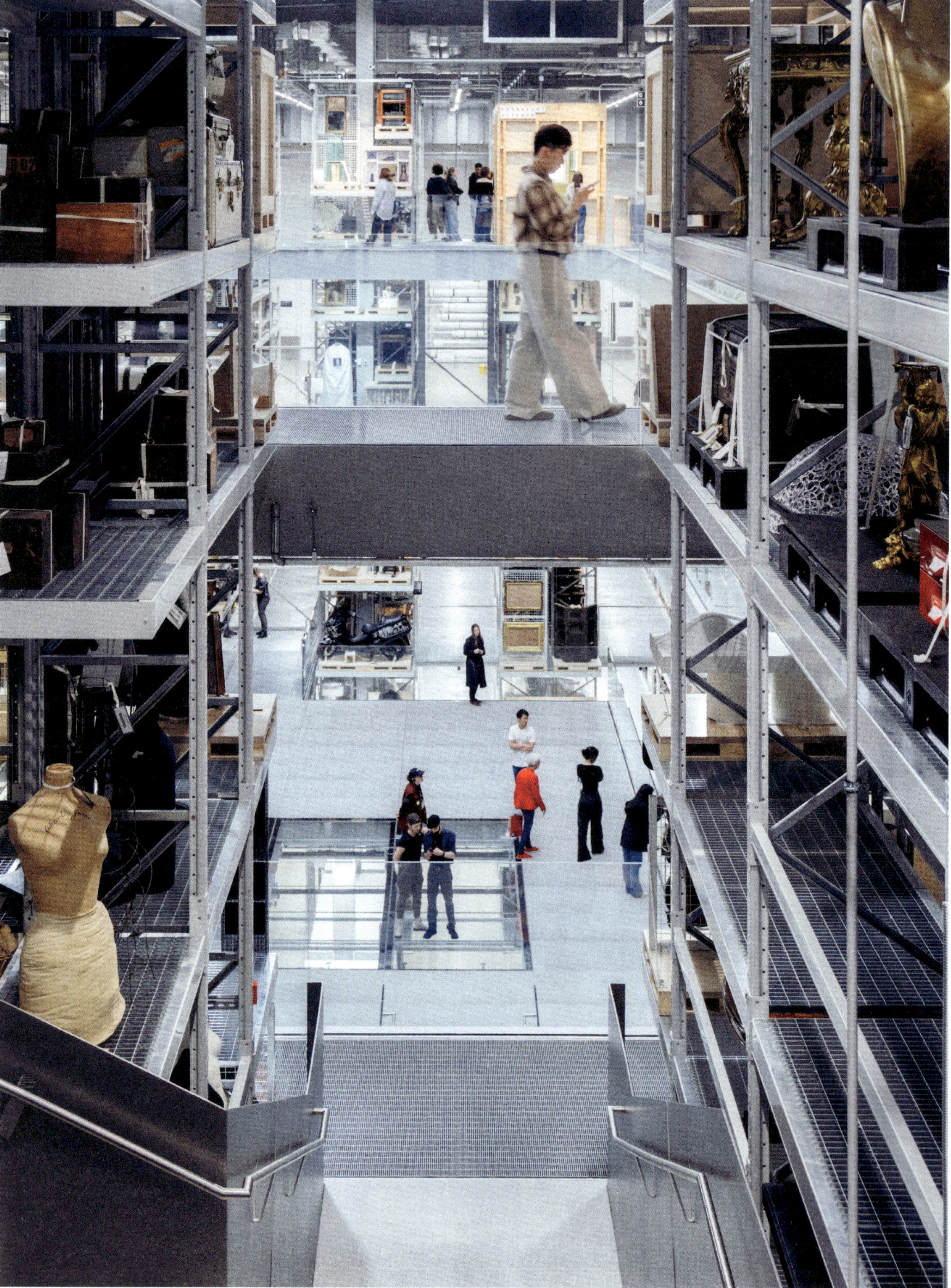

V&A East Storehouse, 2024

ED Part of that theatricality is the thrill of having the agency to make your own course, to see things at your own pace and to not have them explained to you. It's one thing to be in the audience and watch a play on stage, it's another to go backstage and see a performer practising their lines, or to watch a stagehand rig the lighting. The thrilling moments in the theatre are not the final 'ta-das', they are the messy moments in the preparations, the not-quite-yet-consumables.

TR Let's finish by talking about how we want this building to be taken over, occupied and used. It's for a specific audience in east London that, over the decades, has not been well served by major national institutions, or by large-scale public investment in culture. It's also happening at a particular moment in global terms; the world has changed very rapidly since we began this project. What are your hopes for the Storehouse going forward and what do you think it will mean to the people of east London? Beyond that, what mark might this building leave in museological architectural terms?

ED I hope it will draw a younger crowd; I imagine an informal vibe that instils a sense of curiosity in people. When you enter, it shouldn't feel like you're walking through the doors of an institution, with everything slick and finished. It should feel perpetually unfinished. We are used to going to museums where entire period rooms, extracted from any historical context, are seamlessly present. In the Storehouse you will see all the seams.

In terms of the broader impact, museums can only display so much of their collections and as time passes collections will grow. It makes sense to change the paradigm and blur the division between what's on display and what lives behind closed doors. The Storehouse will be a good testing ground for this. We'll learn from it, and it could serve as a model for other institutions. I also hope that it will have repercussions for the V&A site in South Kensington. This is an opportunity for conversations to be had between the museum and Storehouse that bridge sites, content and populations.

TR That is exactly what I hope and believe will happen. We are learning as an institution about where we are, where we are strong and where we could do more. I think that already the work we are doing on the Storehouse is starting to reverberate back and ask us to question how we do things, why we do things and who we're doing things for. A big part of the legacy is that this will encourage others to go further and to be a bit more confident, a bit more ambitious.

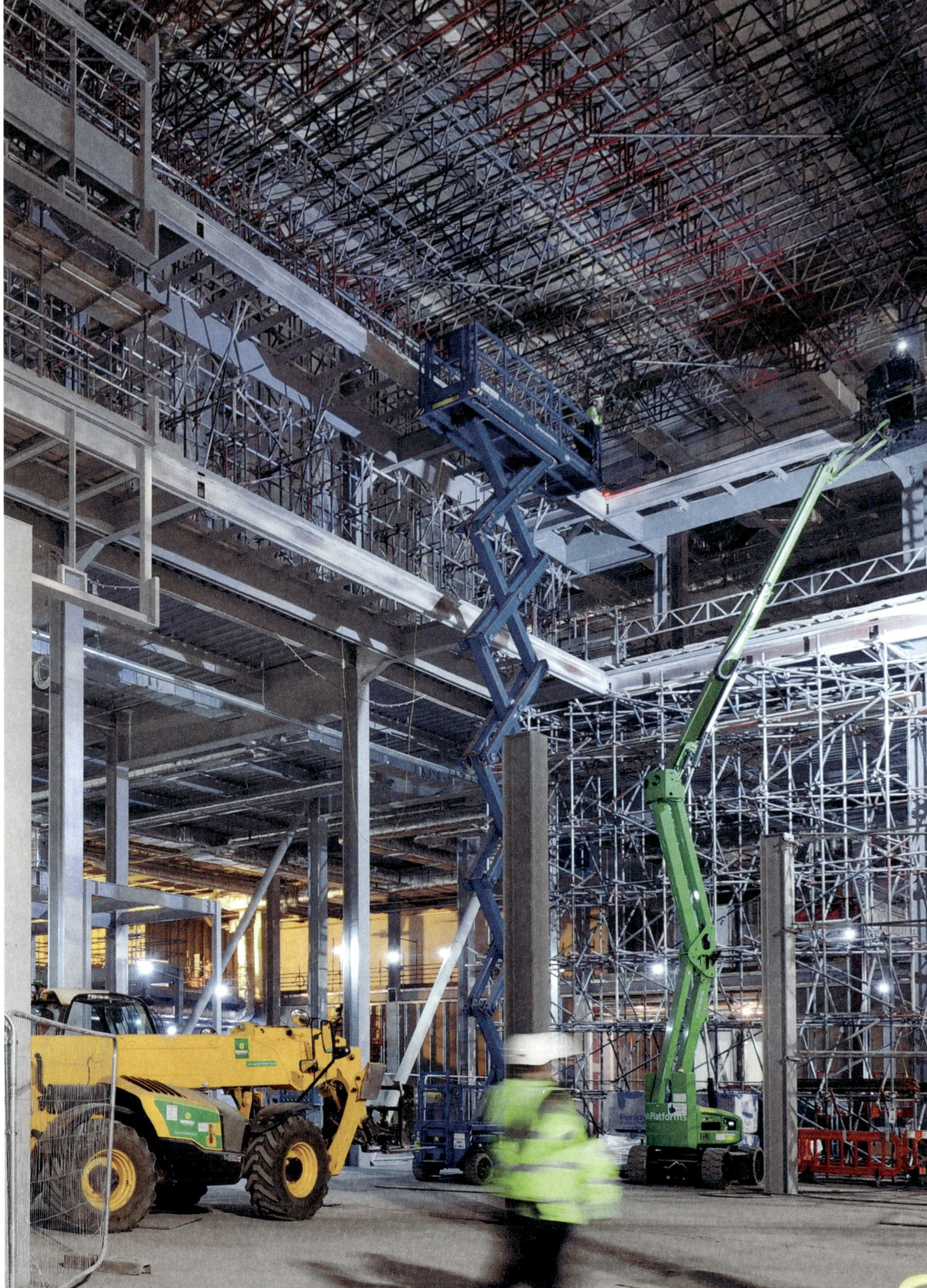

opposite The transforming of V&A East Storehouse captured in 2017 and 2022

this page and overleaf V&A East Storehouse in later stages, 2024

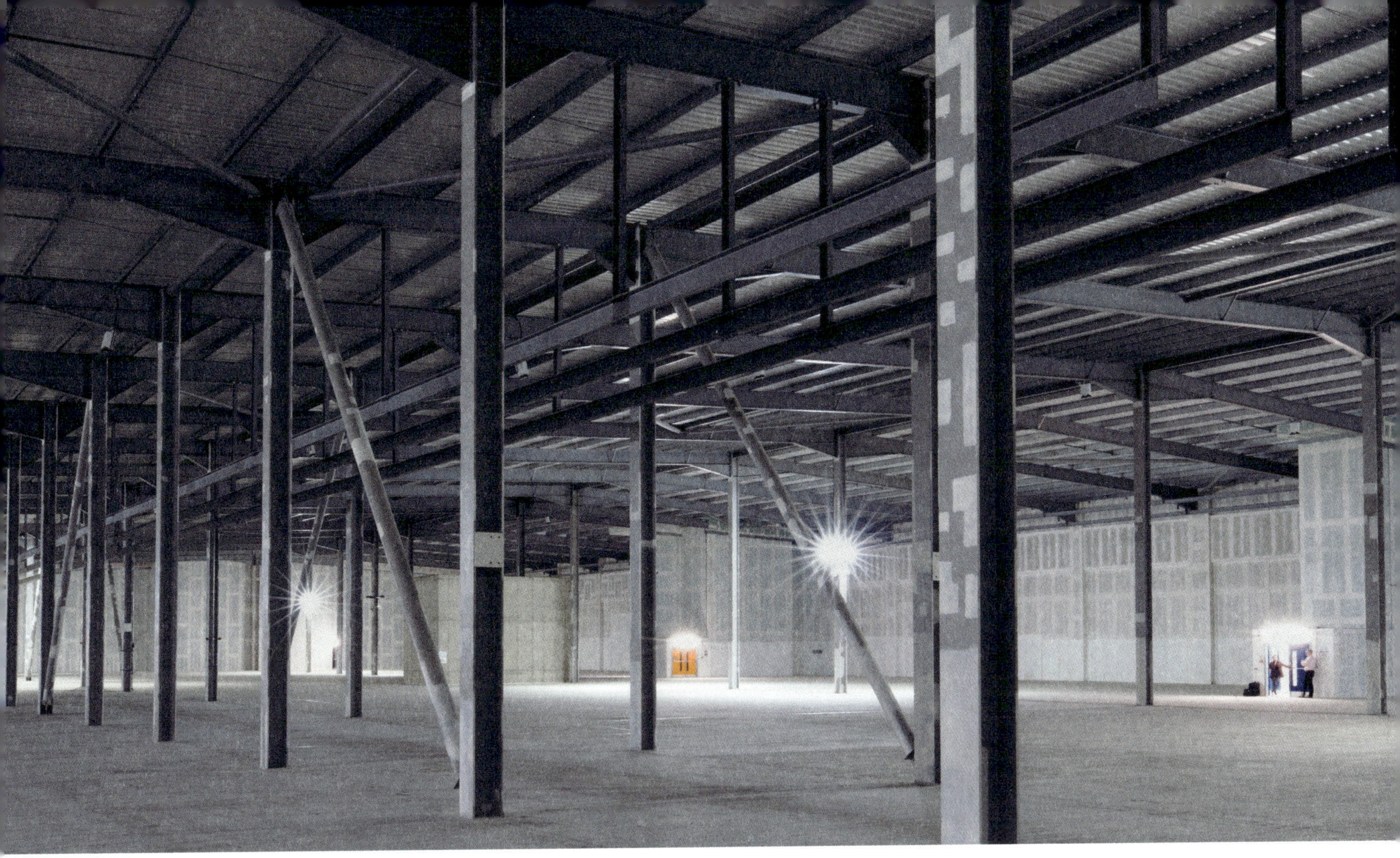

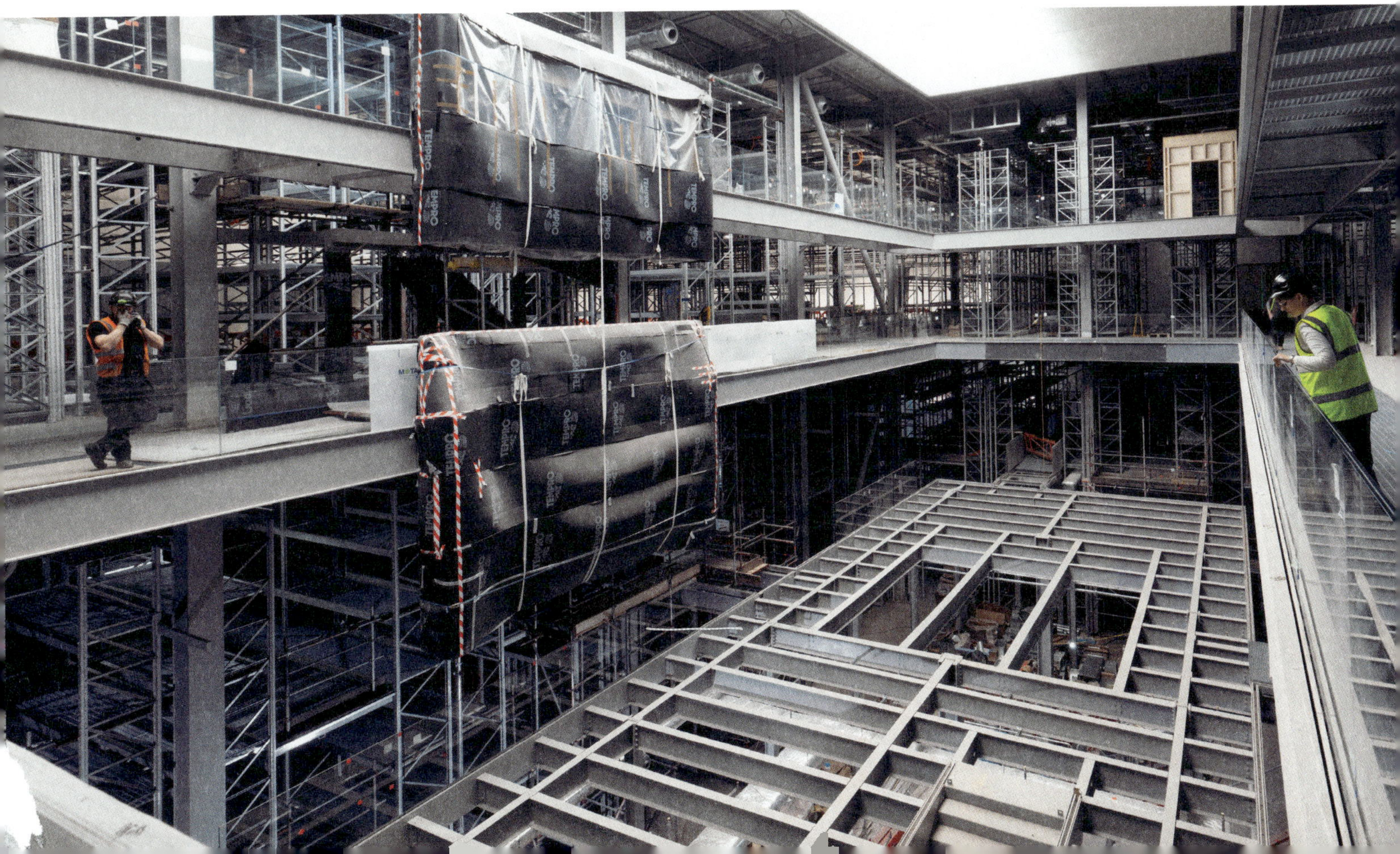

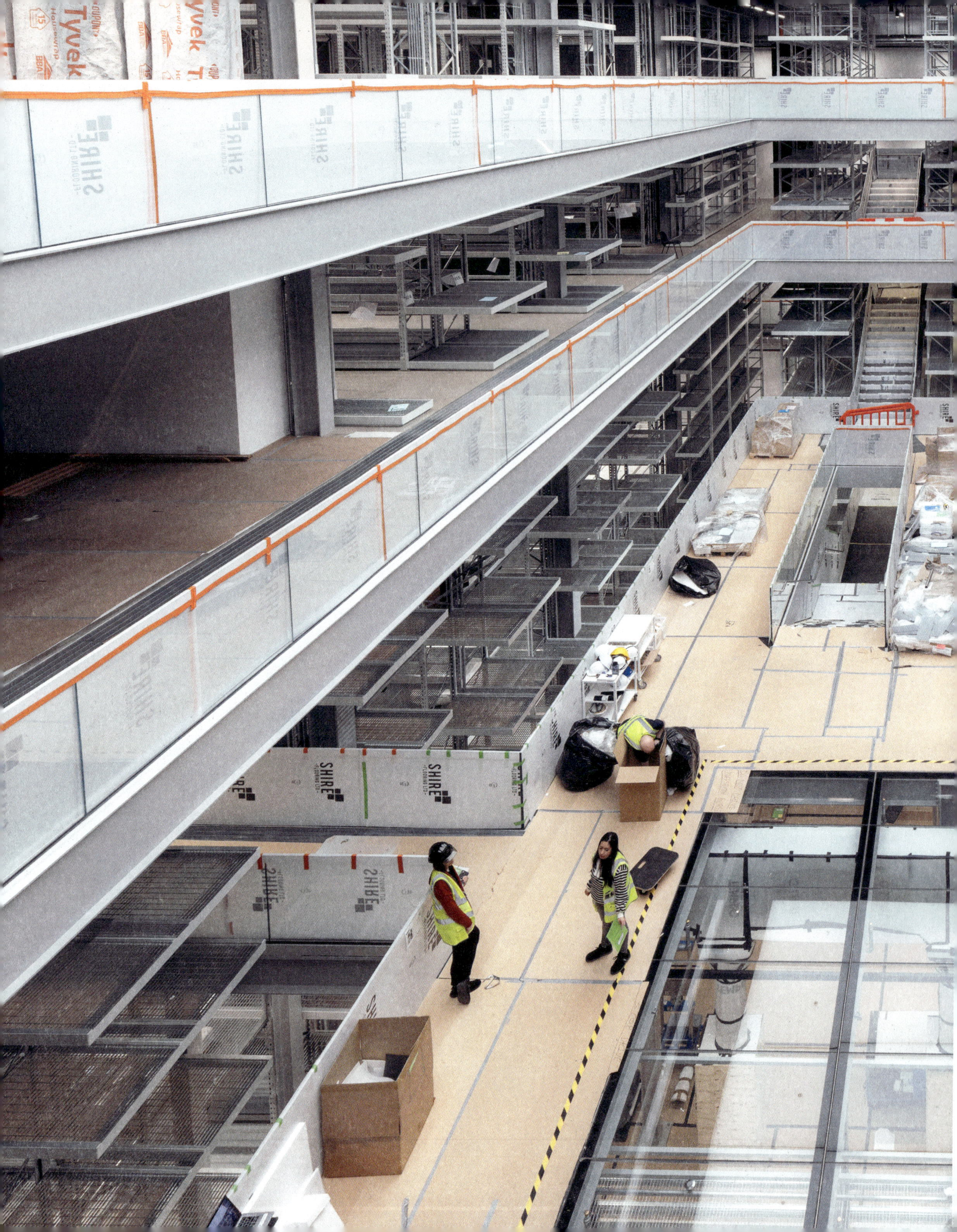
Tyvek
SHIRE

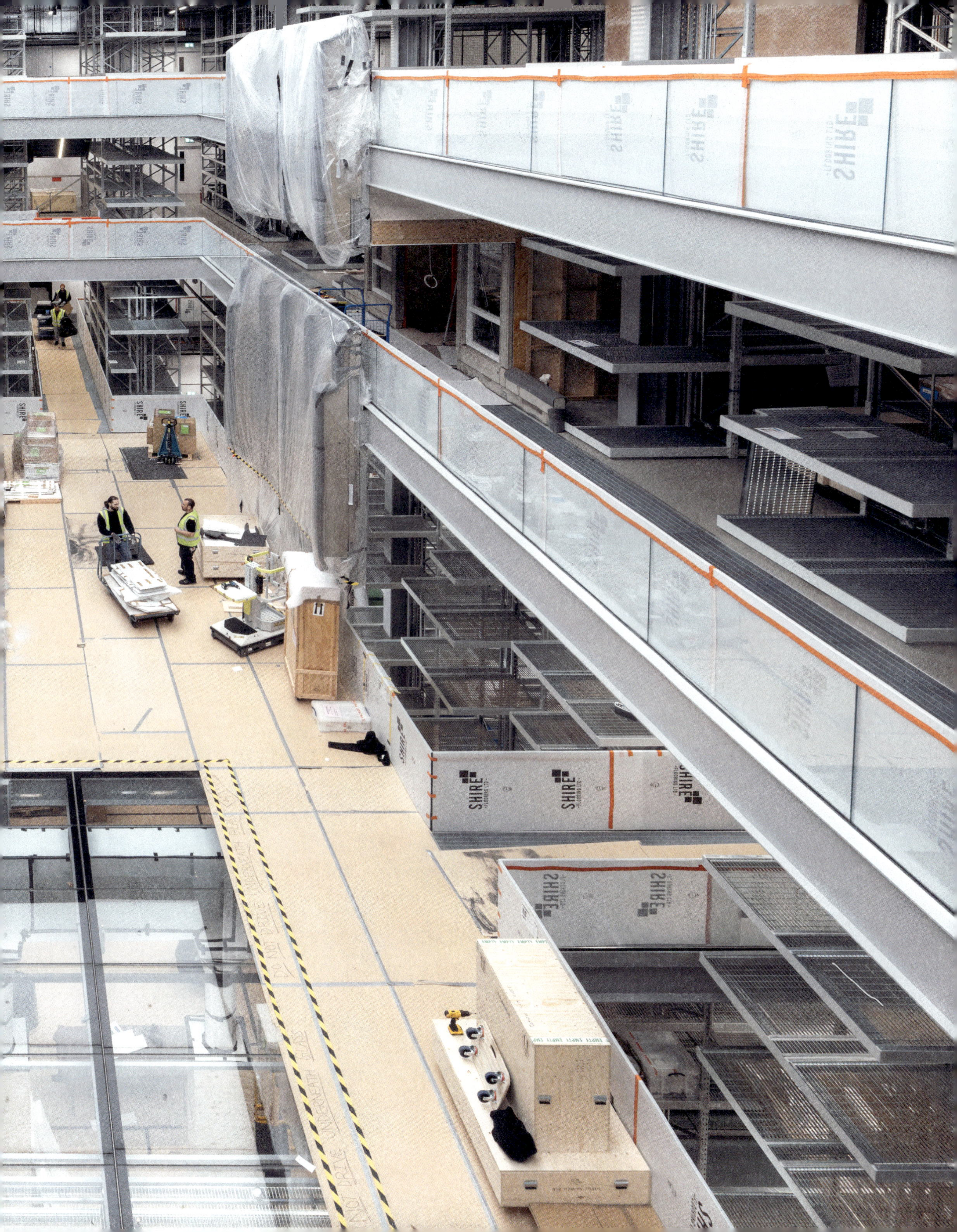
SHIRE

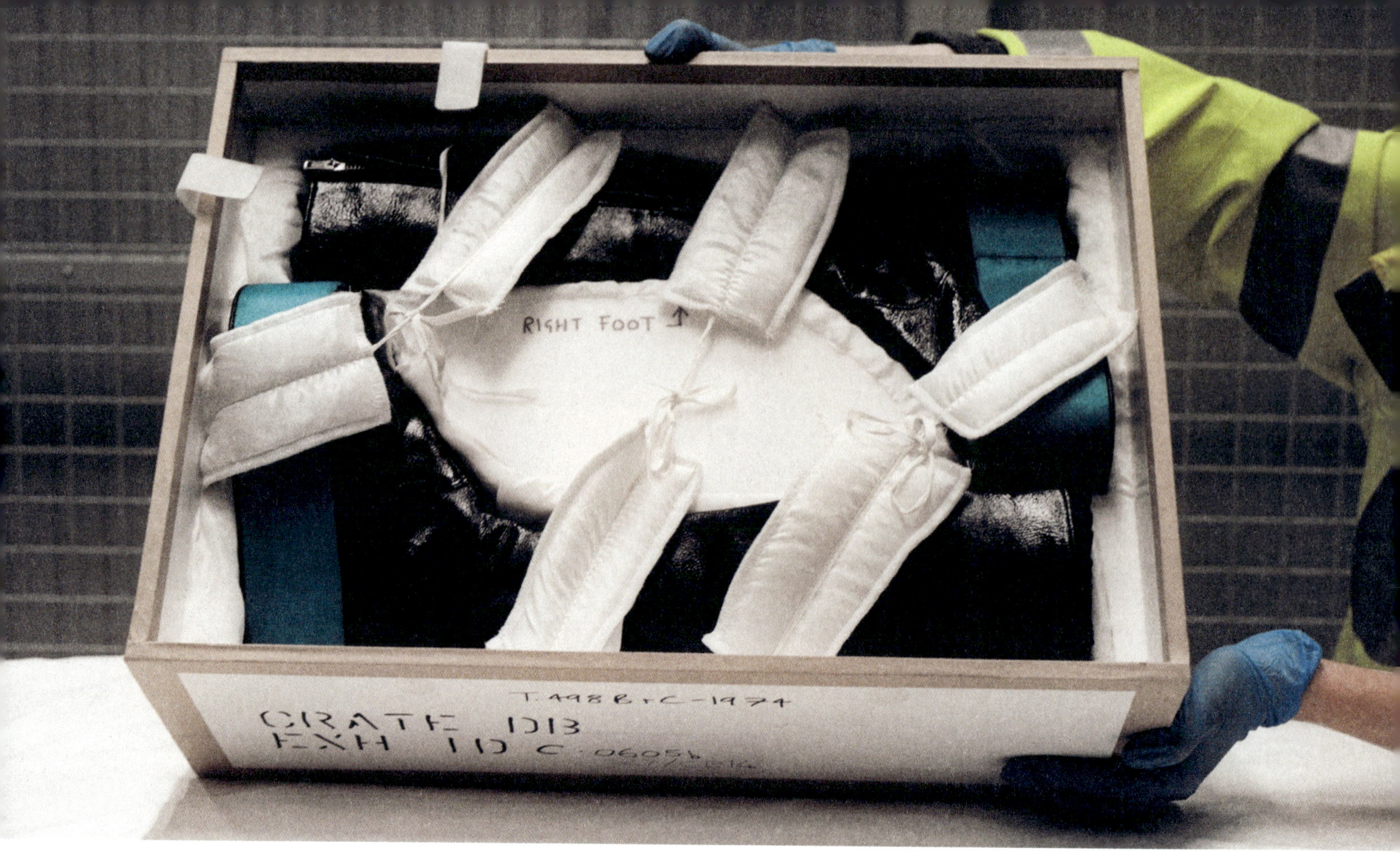

RIGHT FOOT
T.498 B+C-1974
CRATE DB
EXH ID C.0605b

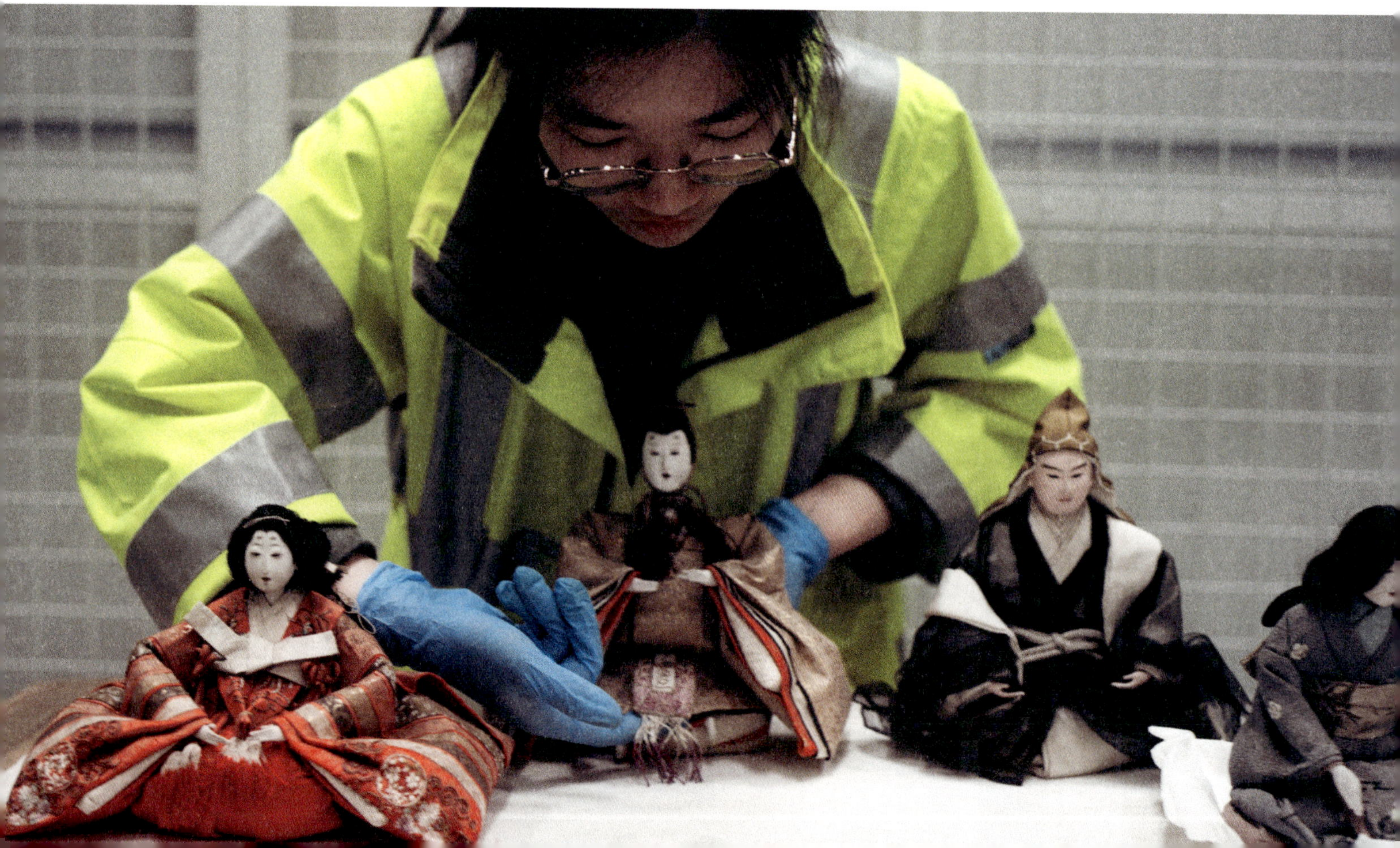

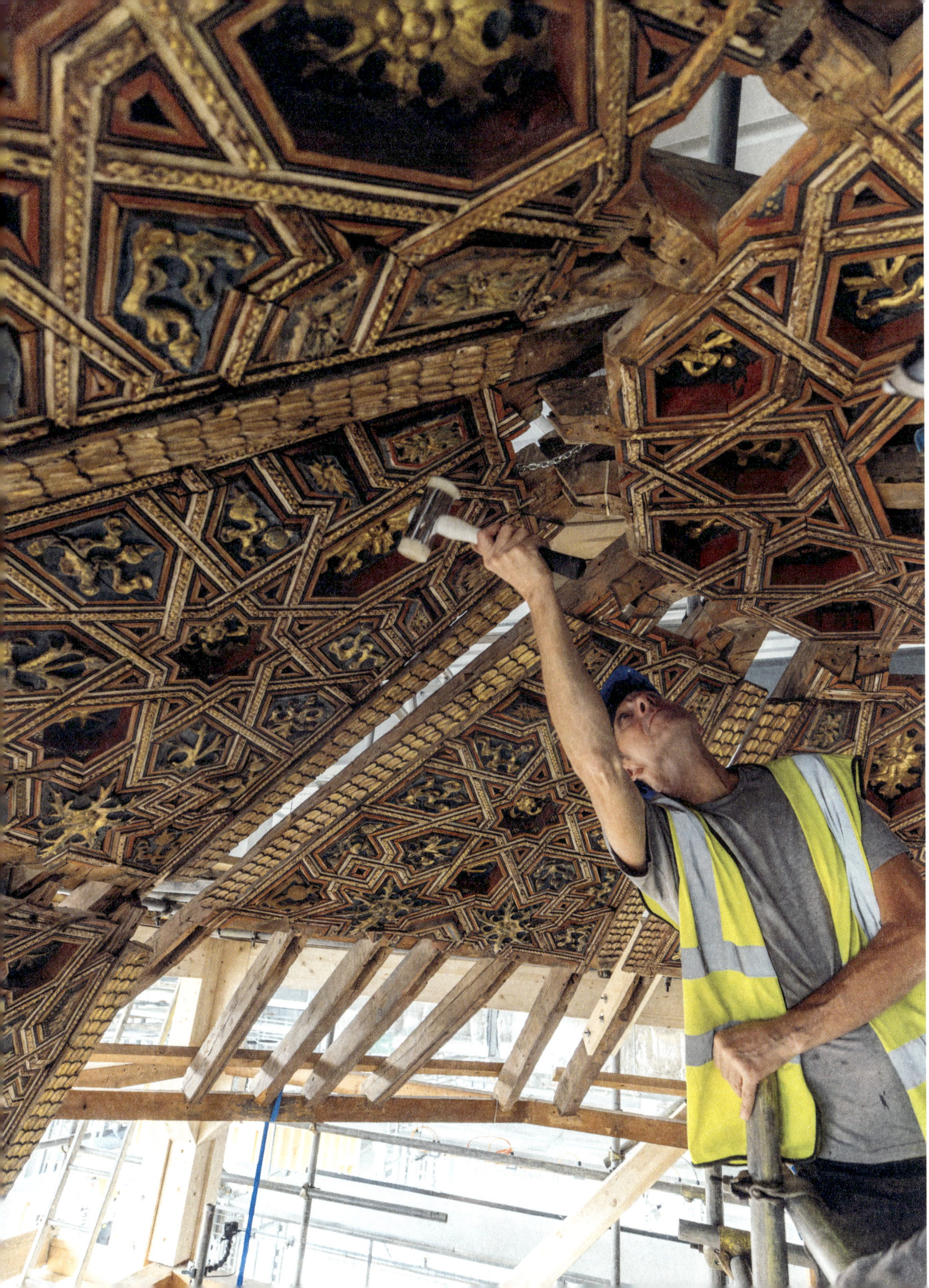

Installing small and large objects at V&A East Storehouse, 2023–4

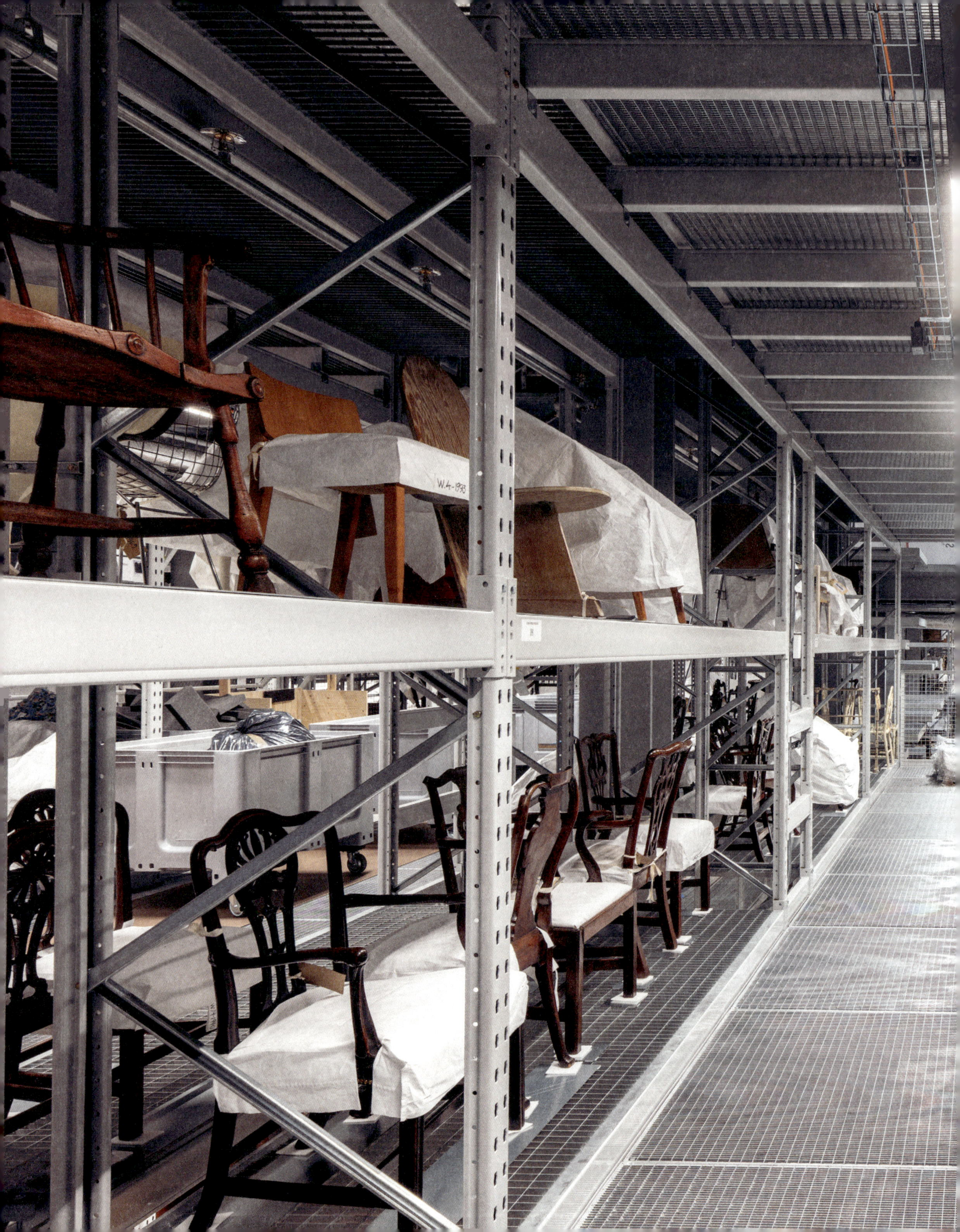
W.4-1993

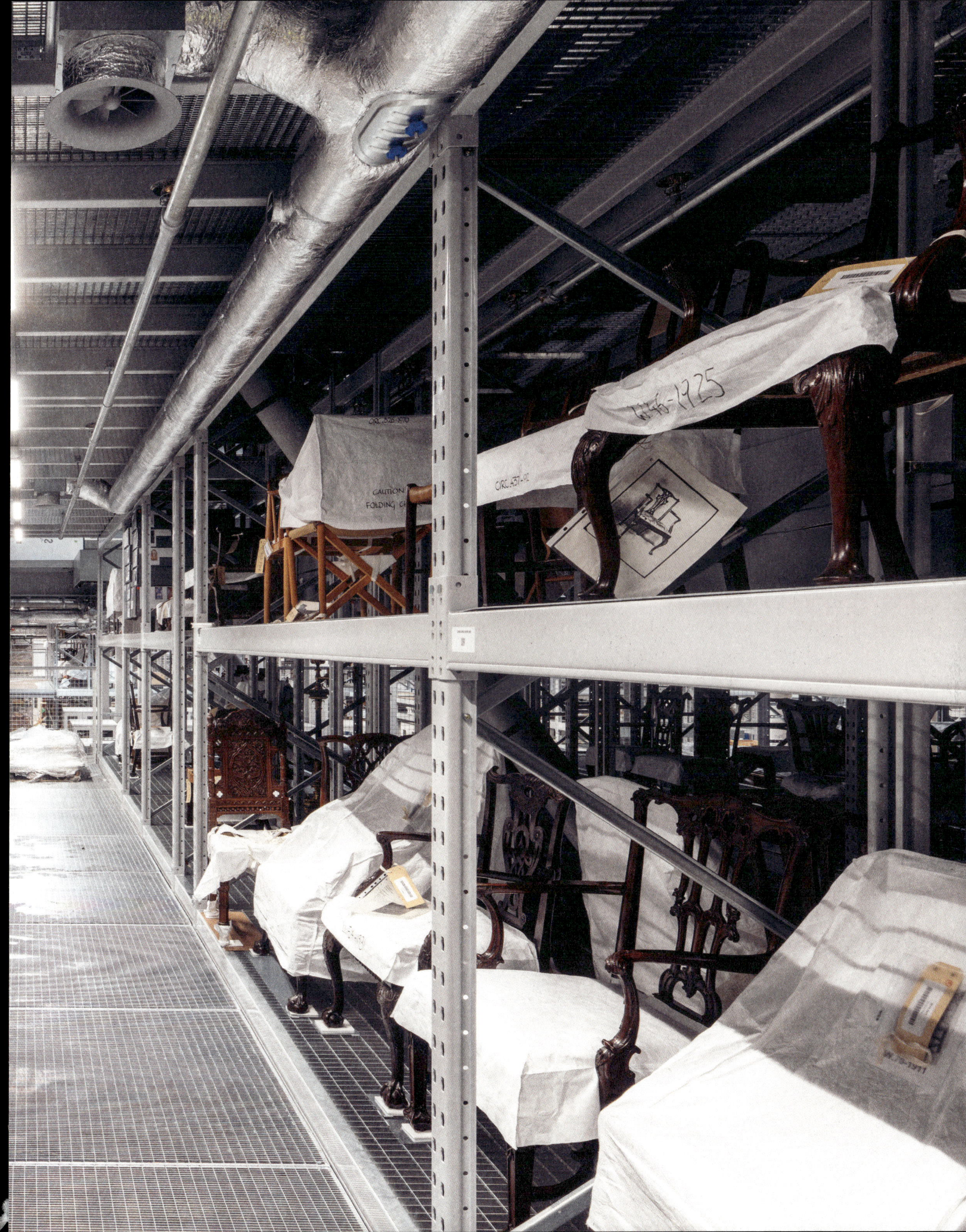

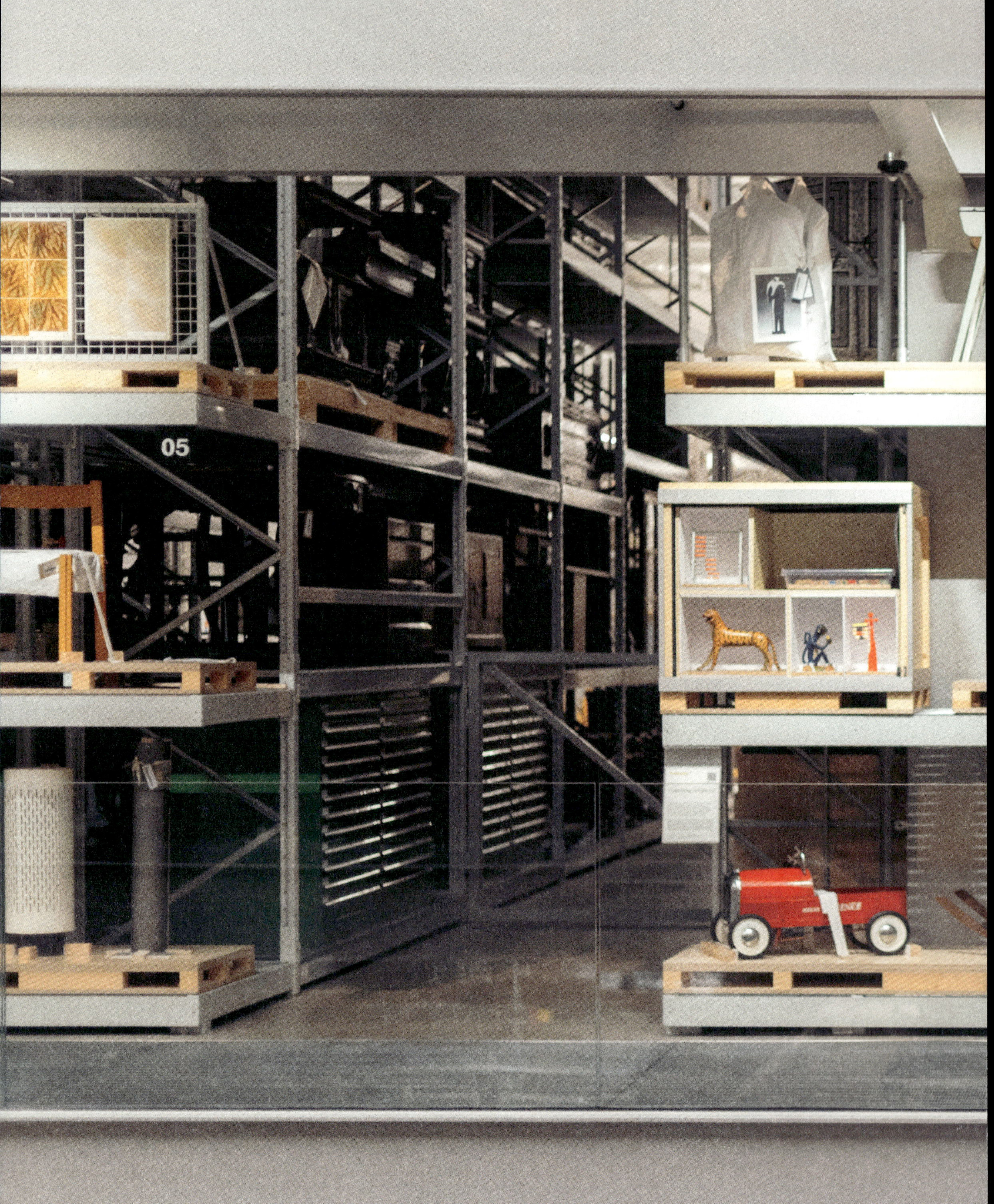
05

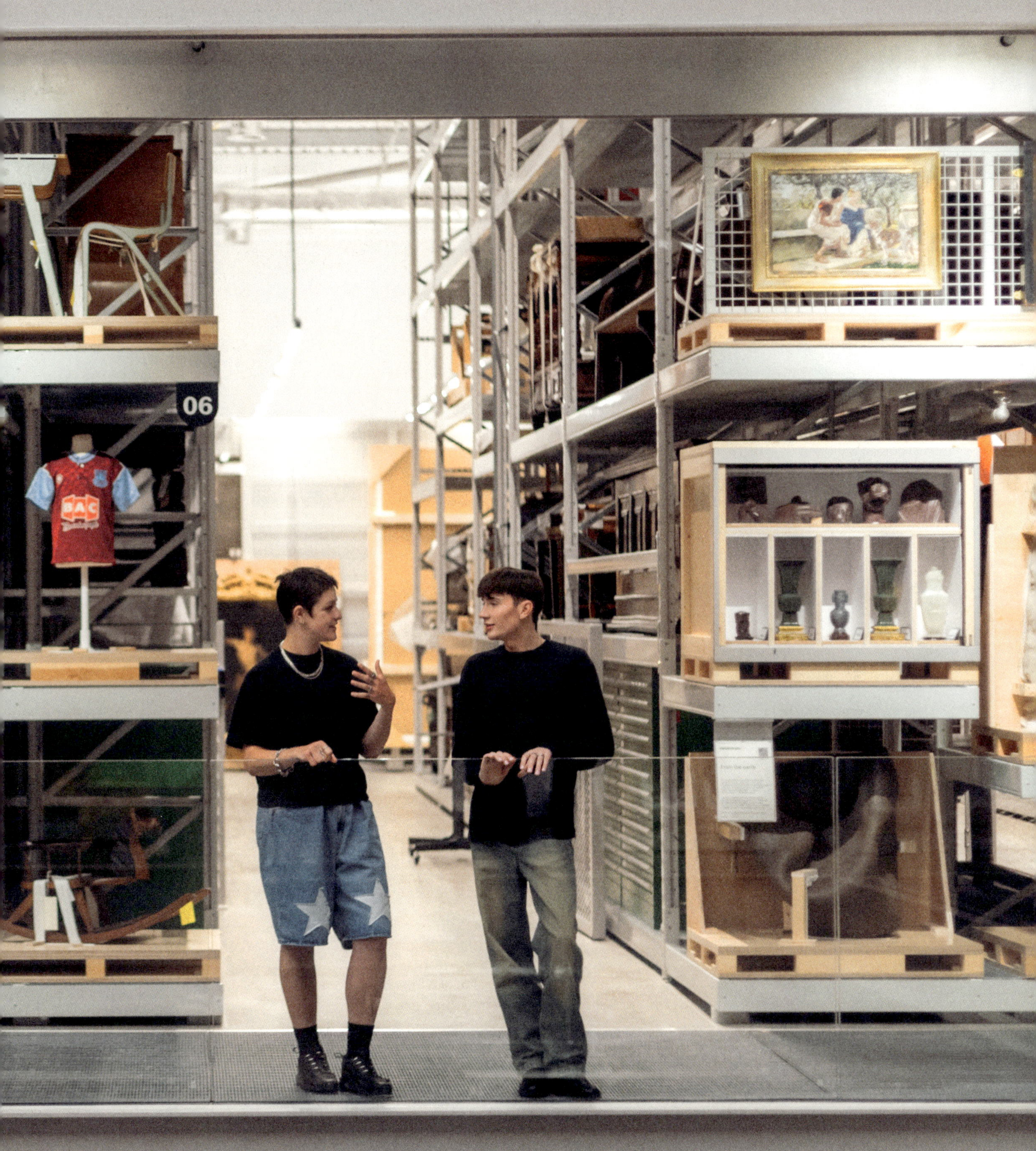
06
BAC

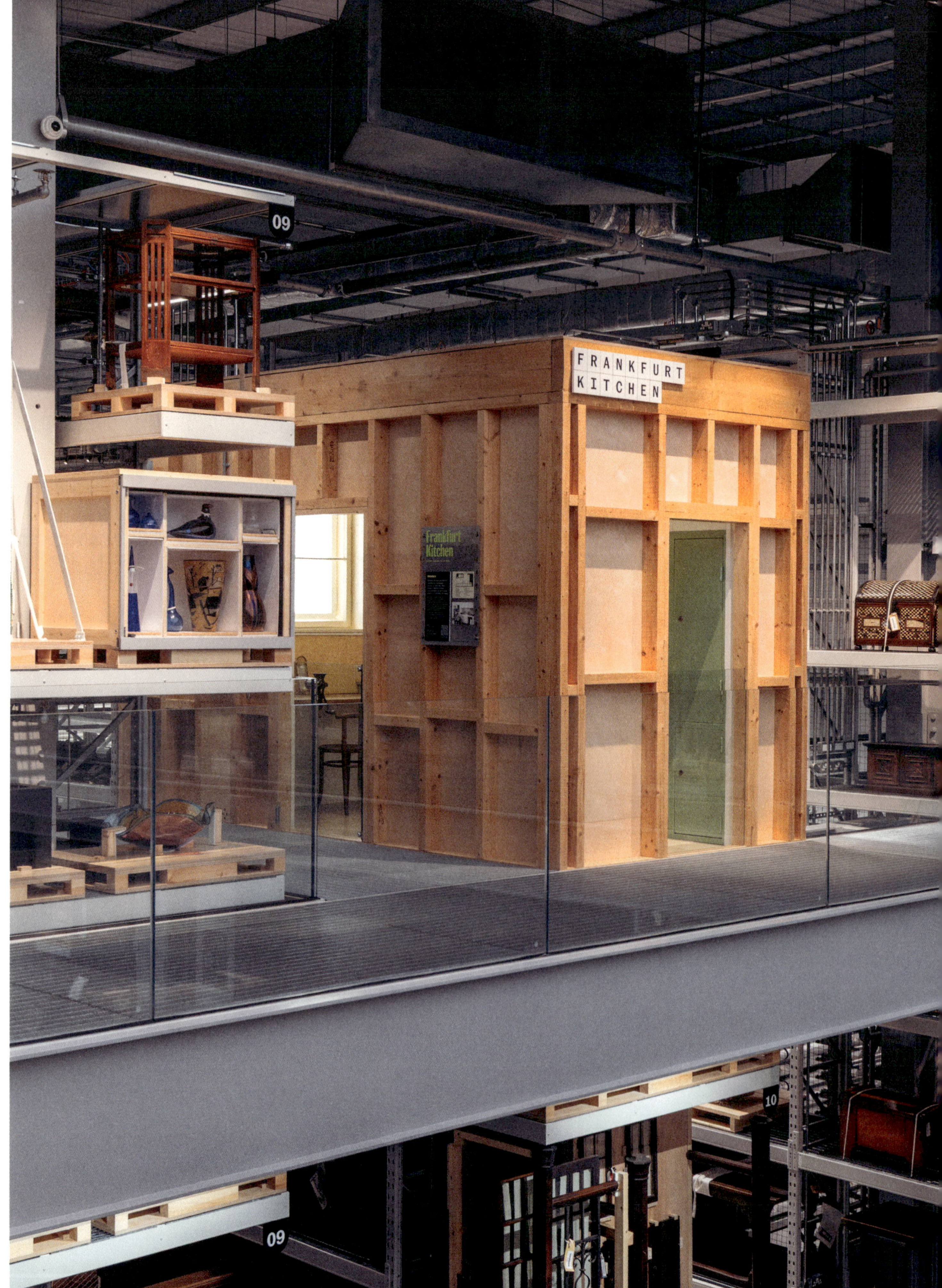

pp. 207–8 Views of Storehouse with objects wrapped, 2024

previous spread, this spread and overleaf Views of Storehouse with objects unwrapped, 2025

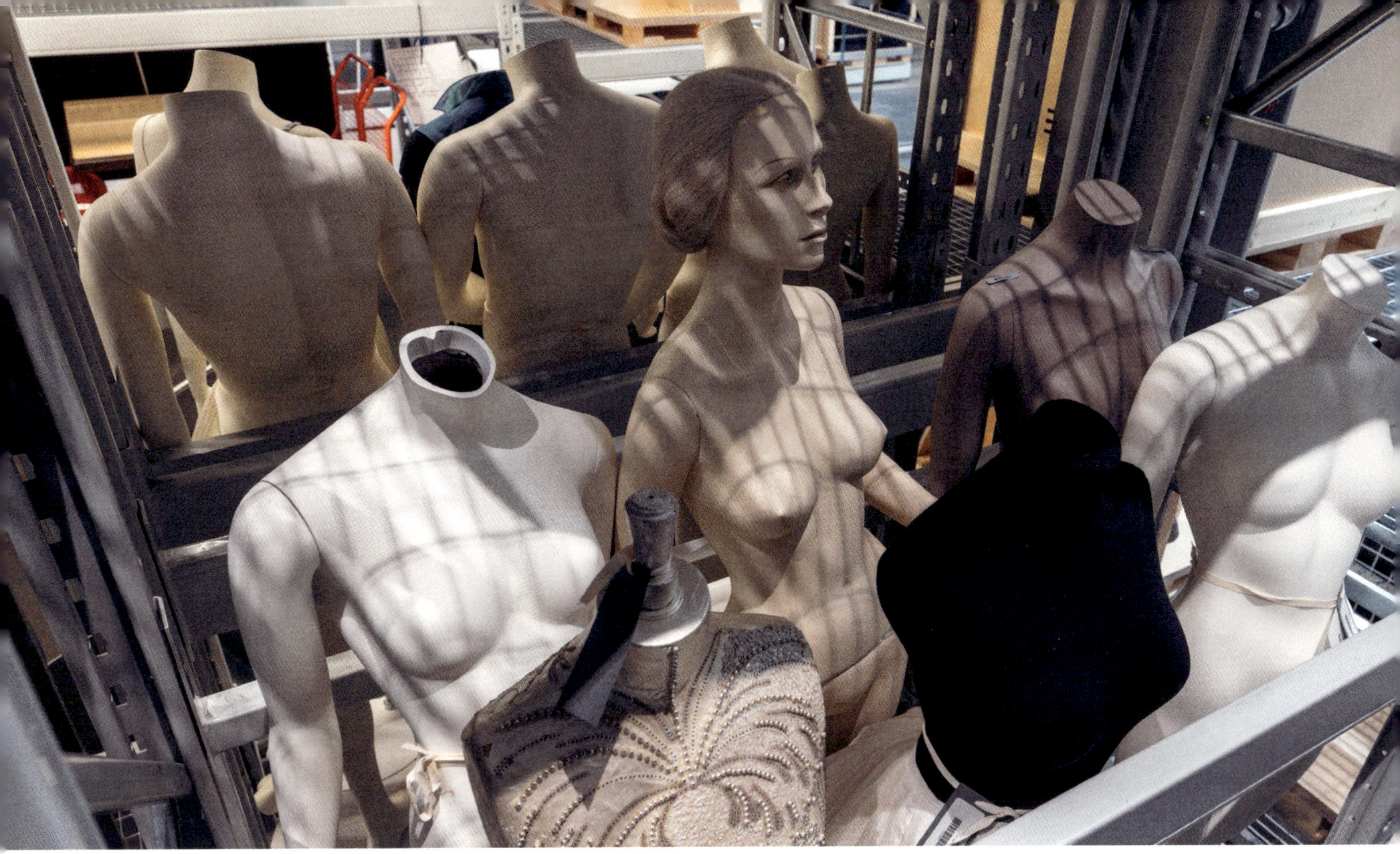

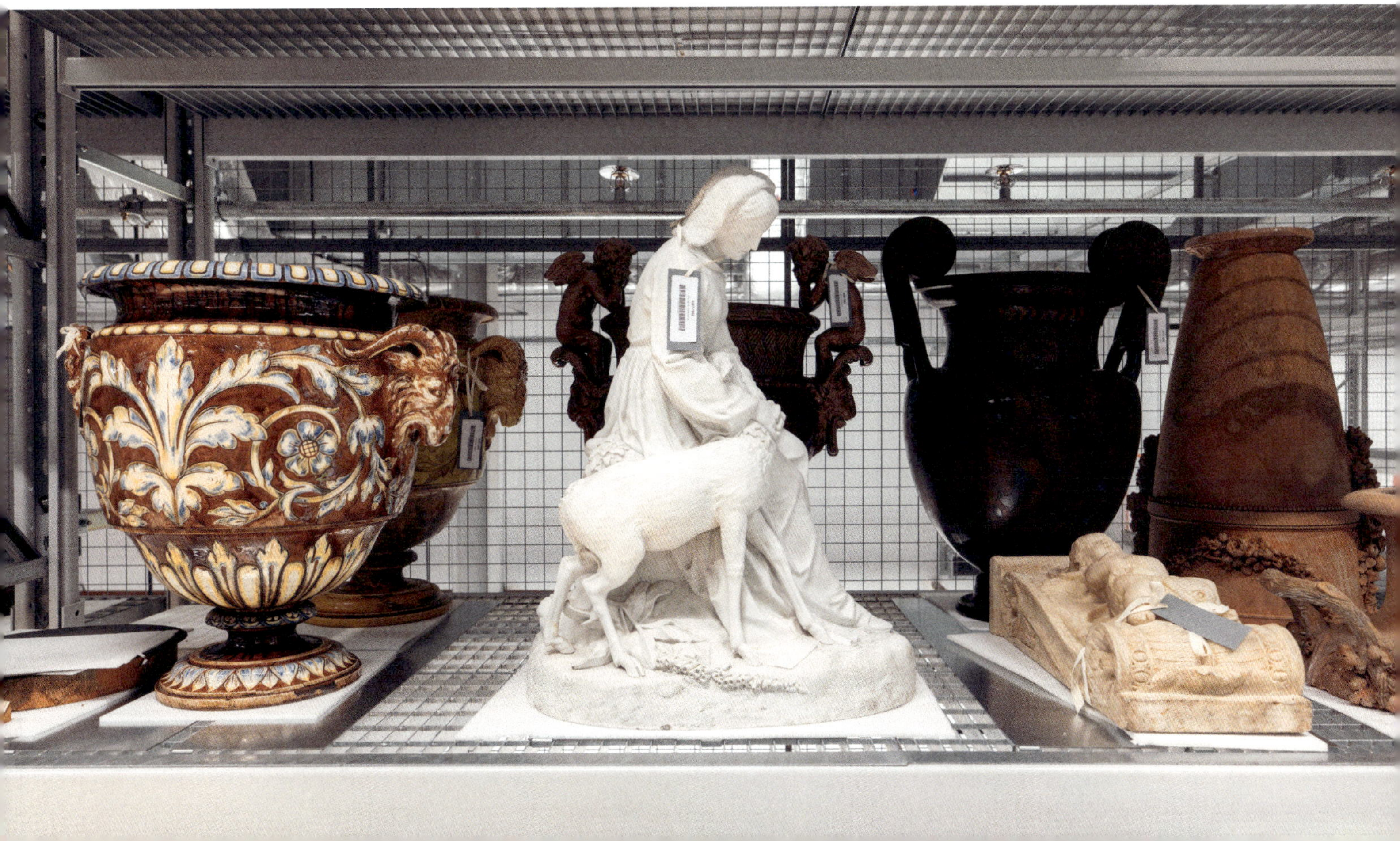

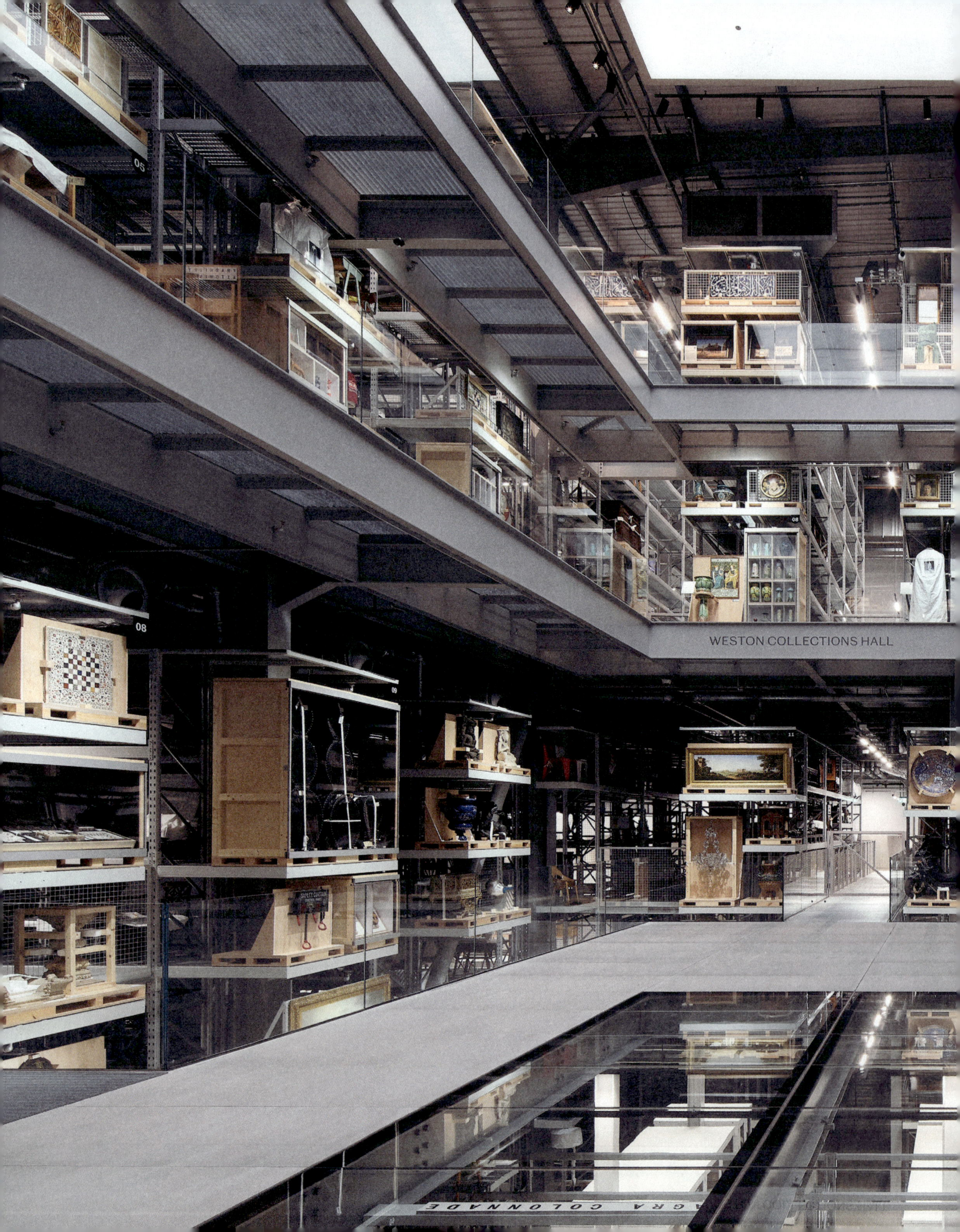
WESTON COLLECTIONS HALL

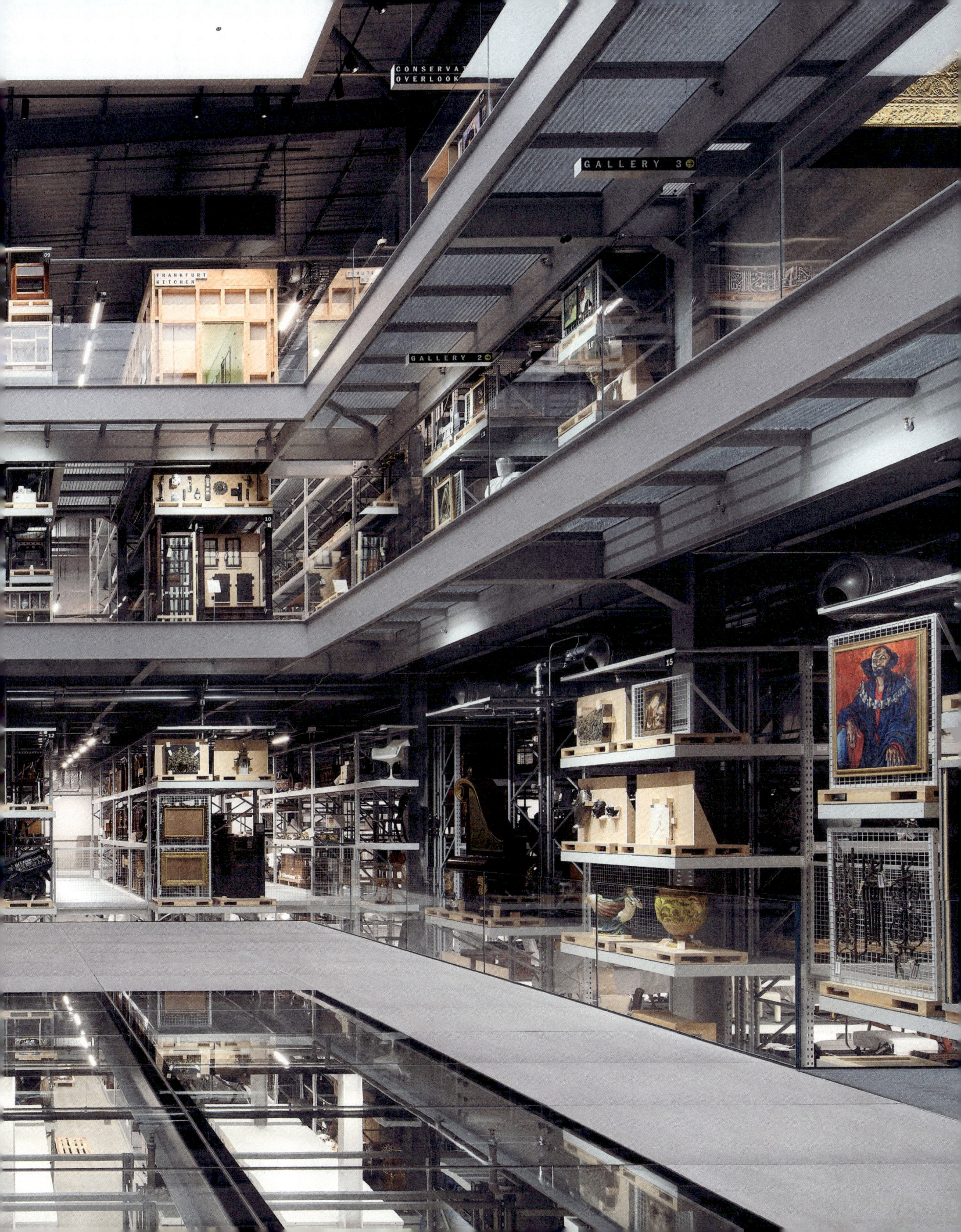
OVERLOOK
GALLERY 3
FRANKFURT KITCHEN
GALLERY 2

Global

Nar

ratives

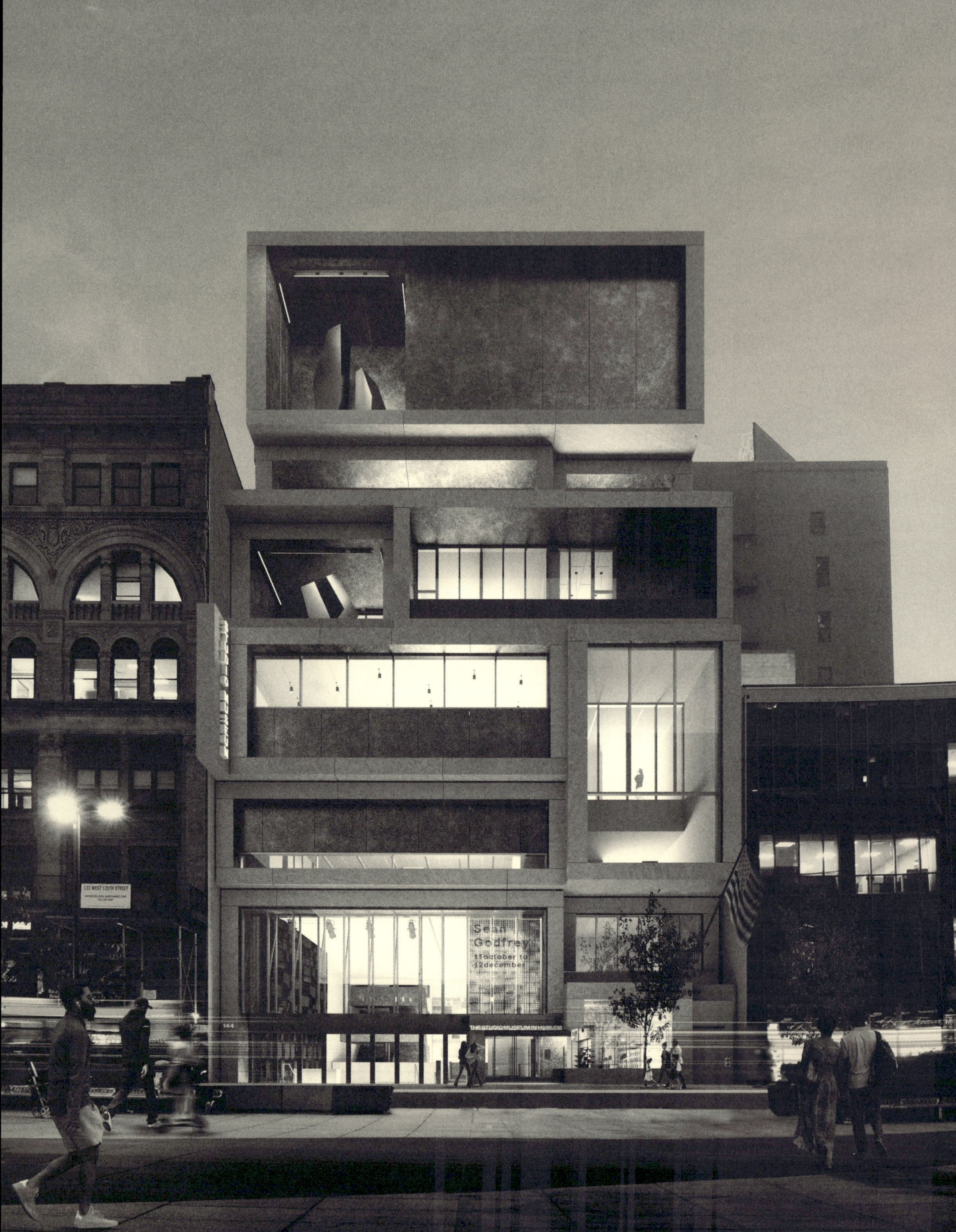
132 WEST 125TH STREET
Sean
Godfrey
11october to
12december
144
THE STUDIO MUSEUM IN HARLEM

Render of Studio Museum in Harlem, USA, by Adjaye Associates, 2024

Museums today are wrestling with their place in the world. After facing decades of critique for their perceived (and often real) elitism, racism and sexism, many museums have explicitly shifted to a more progressive agenda about who they serve and what they do. Polyphony, diversity and care have moved to the top of the agenda, while at the same time the commitment to maintaining and preserving collections persists. Indeed, one of the key challenges for many museums has been a dramatic expansion in their role. Museums are no longer just a repositories for objects, they also act as community service providers, platforms for debate and catalysts for political activism and social change. This section looks to institutions around the world that are pushing forward new cultural models from which we can learn and seek inspiration.

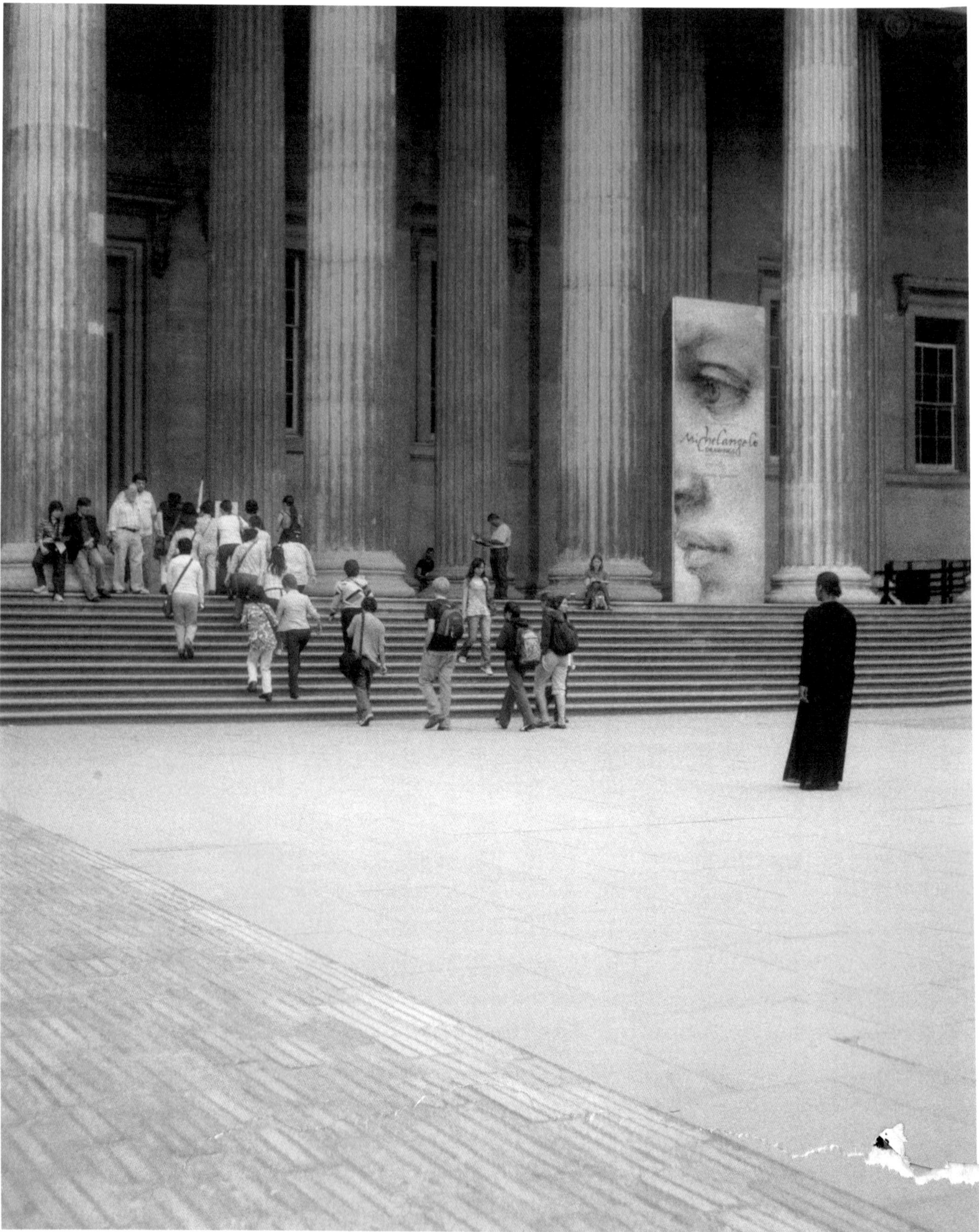

When and Where I Enter, The British Museum, 2007, from the 'Rivington Place' portfolio, print by Carrie Mae Weems, 2006–7, V&A

The Future Museum: Purpose, People, Possibility

Madeleine Haddon

Museums around the world are increasingly offering a wide range of resources and experiences that have become fundamental to our societal well-being – resources and experiences that are increasingly rare to find through other encounters. Museums aim to create experiences of sacred transcendence, wonder and inspiration. But, in recent years, the responsibilities of museums have expanded to include encouraging intercultural dialogue and connection, providing programmes to spark innovation, self-expression and equality, and serving as essential public spaces of care. With decreased public social infrastructure and the increased secularisation of society, many museums have courageously and acrobatically assumed roles previously filled by governments and religious institutions. Simultaneously, public attention towards and international attendance of museums have never been greater. Based on the number of new museum projects breaking ground across the globe, museums have more of a stake in our future than ever before.

But what is a 'museum' today? Given the many forms museums have taken, it can often feel as if we have lost our collective understanding of what a museum is, and this lack of consensus has led to the word itself becoming hollow. Perhaps such a consensus is no longer necessary, but rather, being nimble and adaptable is vital to the survival of museums, allowing them to remain relevant and, most importantly, serve diverse audiences. As Lesley Lokko OBE, founder of the African Futures Institute in Accra, argues, maybe museums should be looking to the collective memory of the diaspora for a deeper understanding of a way of being that exists beyond traditional structures and provides a vital means of addressing questions about belonging, home, equity, race, and social and environmental justice.

As museums place greater focus on polyvocal rather than monolithic narratives, speaking to and connecting with the personal stories of individuals, perhaps it is time to embrace a more fluid and evolving definition of the word 'museum'. If museums are to ever fully represent global diversity, what it means to be a museum should not be constrained by a single definition. Rather, the concept of the museum must be plural, constantly expanding and even, at times, contradictory. The creation of V&A East has been an opportunity to assess the transformation of the definition of 'museum' and to consider the role we want to play within this shift. In parallel with our project, there are many other institutions who have taken up this call to arms, in each instance defining, fashioning and adapting themselves to the specific needs of their respective locations and audiences.

This section features eight interviews with leading cultural figures who are shaping the future of museums. Speaking to these individuals has made it clear that, while the idea of the 'museum' originated from the desire to preserve, display and study the past, museums of today are focused as much, if not more, on informing our present and future. For Thelma Golden and the Studio Museum in Harlem, for example, art is not just exhibited for, but also created in dialogue with its Harlem community and Black creativity, a constant exchange that deepens artistic creative practice. Similarly, in Sydney at the Powerhouse Museum, Lisa Havilah has spearheaded a process that brings together curators, makers and leaders from the communities whose stories are being told, allowing them to collectively design programming and installations so that their perspectives are always deeply embedded in all aspects of Powerhouse's telling of their stories.

The museum leaders featured here each bring a unique perspective and contribution to this subject. Each one shares similar aspirations to V&A East for their institutions: a commitment to serving local audiences, cultivating intersections between local and global dialogues, fostering transhistorical and cross-cultural

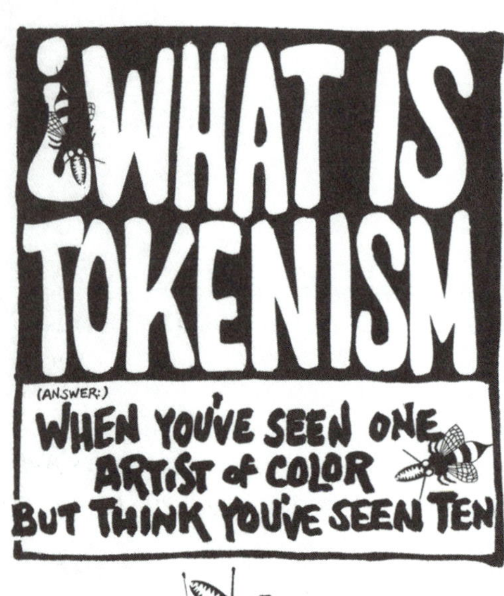

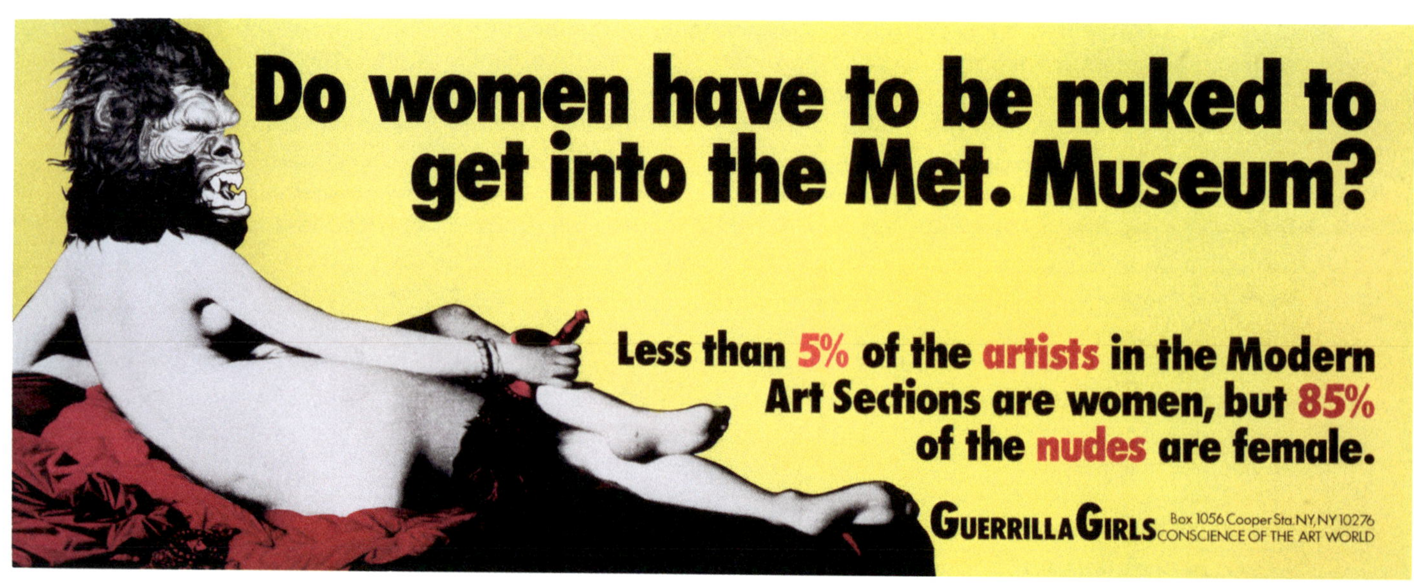

above Flyer by PESTS, 1980s, V&A below *Do women have to be naked to get into the Met. Museum?*, poster by Guerrilla Girls, 1989, V&A

We, the undersigned, deplore and oppose the Government's intention to introduce admission charges to national museums and galleries

and Crosby/Fletcher/Forbes
—and Lund Humphries

Write in protest to your MP
and send for the petition forms to
Campaign Against Museum Admission Charges
221 Camden High Street
London NW1 7BU

We, the undersigned ..., poster by Theo Crosby, 1970, V&A

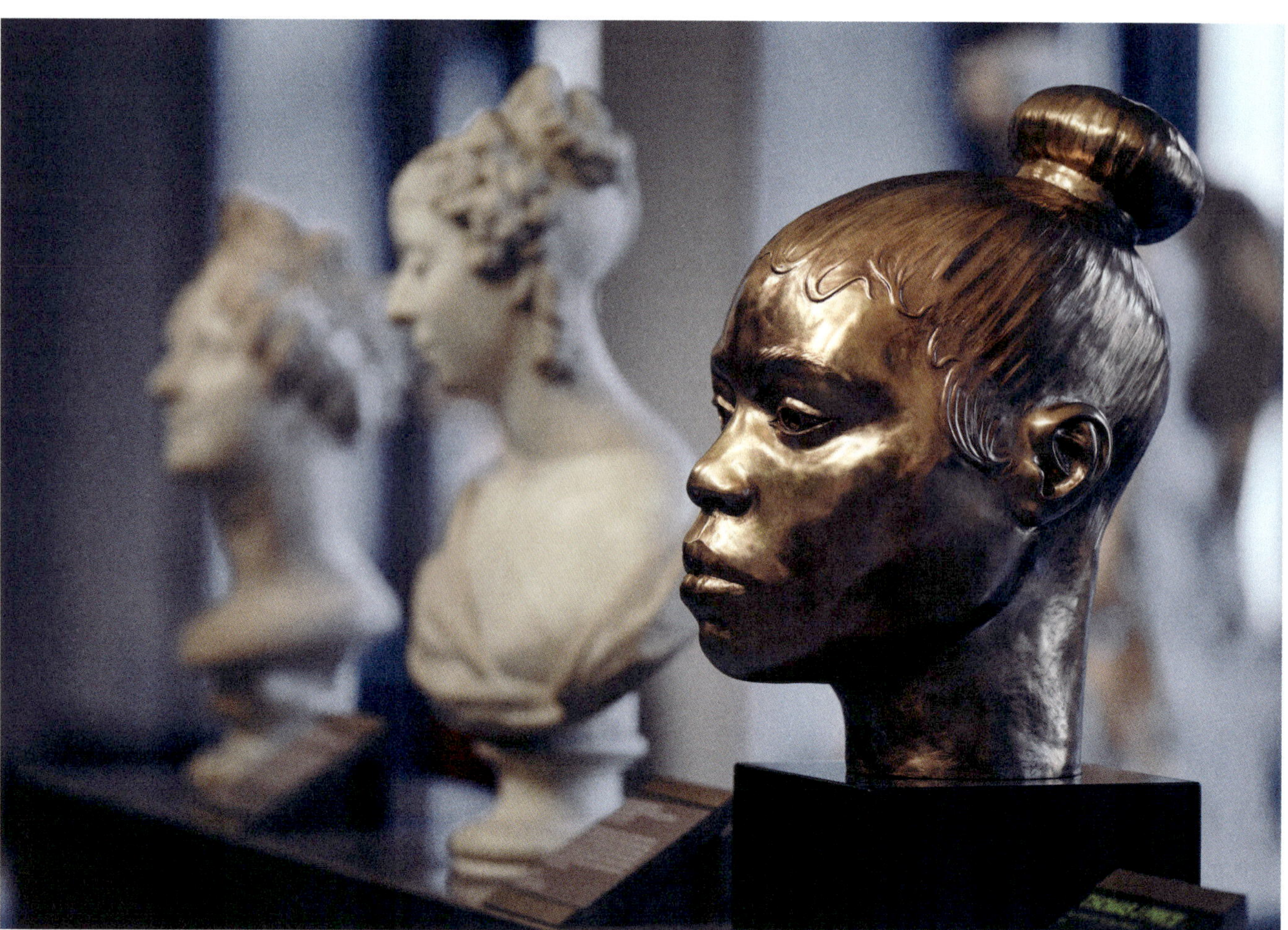

Installation view: *Thomas J Price at the V&A*, 22 July 2023 – 27 May 2024, featuring *Lay It Down (On The Edge Of Beauty)* (2018)

conversations, being a platform and resource for the next generation of creatives, giving more diverse audiences ownership over museums and inspiring the next generation of cultural leaders.

Alongside our own exploration of what a museum can be, a broader rethinking and debate around the definition of the museum has been taking place. Between 2016 and 2022 the International Council of Museums (ICOM) debated their definition of 'museum', reconsidering a definition that had previously been in place since 2007. The ensuing disagreements between ICOM's representatives from 142 countries in search of a common language for how to define 'museum' gets us closer to what it means to be a museum today. Museums do not mean the same things in different countries, cities or even neighbourhoods. Moreover, who, if anyone, should have the authority to decide what it means to be a museum and what the role of a museum should be? Given the original purpose of museums, many representatives took issue with the lack of focus on the preservation and care of collections within the new definitions proposed. Ultimately, in August 2022, 92 per cent of ICOM's membership approved the new definition of a museum as: 'A not-for-profit, permanent institution in the service of society that researches, collects, conserves, interprets and exhibits tangible and intangible heritage. Open to the public, accessible and inclusive, museums foster diversity and sustainability. They operate and communicate ethically, professionally and with the participation of communities, offering varied experiences for education, enjoyment, reflection and knowledge sharing.' In sharp contrast, the Oxford English Dictionary, the resource to which a person visiting a museum is most likely to turn, defines a museum as: 'A building or institution in which objects of historical, scientific, artistic or cultural interest are preserved and exhibited.' This definition provides minimal insight into the complex reality of what the museum's role in society has become in the twenty-first century and highlights the challenges that many institutions, such as V&A East, face in reshaping public perceptions of and encounters with museums. The only shared words between these attempts to define a museum are 'institution', 'exhibit' and 'collect'.

When the question of 'what is a museum?' was posed to the leaders building the museums of the future, the focus of their responses was not on institutions, exhibitions or collecting. For Aditi Anand at the Migration Museum in London, her answer centred on the value of storytelling, which preserves individual identities and allows the museum to create personal connections with its visitors such that they see the museum as a place to better understand themselves. Meanwhile, for Isabelle Reijelle at the Museo de Arte de São Paulo, its location at a critical site of political gathering for the city has meant that, since it was first designed by architect Lina Bo Bardi, it has remained dedicated to creating spaces where Brazilians of all backgrounds feel welcome to gather. For Sandra Jackson-Dumont at the Lucas Museum of Narrative Art in Los Angeles, museums are about care, whether of histories, objects or each other.

The responses of these eight cultural leaders collectively encompass the breadth of what a museum can be today, and what we aspire to achieve with V&A East. It is a place to communicate history and memory beyond the limitations of a physical edifice, but also where stories about art and culture can still be encountered as both intimate and collective experiences. This was something particularly important for the architect Alejandro Aravena in designing the Art Mill Museum in Doha. With this space he hopes to create a museum that is fully integrated into the city's daily life, to achieve a porousness and a continuous dialogue between the museum and its location, while also providing opportunities for intimate encounters with the art works within. It is a place of gathering to unlearn structures that have been imposed on us; a place for diverse communities to see themselves reflected and feel ownership over their historical and contemporary narratives. This was key to Michael Armitage, who founded the Nairobi Contemporary Art Institute to support the growth and preservation of art from East Africa, championing that local and global cultural narratives should always be seen as in dialogue with one another. It is also a place for differing opinions, critique, questioning and making mistakes, through which a more just society can evolve.

From these perspectives, the museum of today is first and foremost dedicated to the people it serves, not the objects that populate it. This is a shift in the focus of museums from their original intention of collecting and presenting objects to that of empowering people. Most importantly, what remains is that the purposes for which museums serve their public today know no boundaries. This makes their existence more necessary and urgent than ever before.

We also asked these cultural leaders for their advice ahead of the long-anticipated opening of V&A East. We were reminded to listen to our communities and to ensure that they feel long-lasting ownership over our spaces. It is crucial to be patient and develop solid foundations, and infrastructure that embodies our values and reflects our goals, as this will dictate each future step. The difficult conversations must happen now, and fear of getting it wrong on the first try should not impede creativity with our approaches. As Jackson-Dumont observed, 'to do this work, you need to be able to stand within the difficulties'. Underpinning all of this is the very reason the V&A was founded: to welcome new audiences and bring national collections closer to the public to whom they belong.

The definition of a 'museum' should be constantly challenged, discussed, reconsidered and reinvented. Recognition of this is why V&A East is just one among a family of V&A sites designed to serve different purposes and audiences in response to the needs of their communities. What may feel like a moment of crisis for museums has the potential to lead to invention and innovation. Museums offer new possibilities in multitudes – be it for placemaking, community-building, pleasure, education, preservation or political debate. It is a tall order, and they are destined to fail at times, but it is worth the challenge. Museums are far from archaic and irrelevant institutions. Rather, they have far more potential than ever before. So, what is a museum today? It is an opportunity.

Madeleine Haddon, Curator

Aditi Anand
Artistic Director, Migration Museum, UK

What does the word 'museum' mean to me? This is something we grapple with all the time at the Migration Museum because we're not a museum with a traditional collection. How I define a museum is as a place of stories. What's exciting about having a physical form to that is that it allows for stories to be told and interpreted in so many unique ways. They can be told through the lens of the people who lived them, through an artist's lens, through objects, art and media, and through participatory practice. A museum is also a sort of town square. It's a place where people can gather who might not necessarily come into contact with one another at any other point in their daily lives.

A museum is also a place that helps us to understand our current moment, answering questions such as, 'How did we get here?' and 'Where are we going in the future?' I think a lot of museum definitions of the past have been about preserving history, but for me, a museum is as much about our present moment and our future as it is about the past. It's about providing that historical context to help us have better conversations about the present and future.

In the time that I've been with the Migration Museum, we've developed the idea of what a museum can be. We've talked a lot about what kind of collection we could have. There are so many interesting museum collections already, so one idea was to think about how we work with other institutions, and with people who have interesting things locked away in their attics and who have interesting stories to tell, to develop a more dispersed collection that lives across different institutions and different individuals. It might be that it is made available digitally, or loaned, or else presented in the museum space in a more fluid way.

So much of it starts with people. Whenever we're building exhibitions or trying to think about what stories we want to tell there's a huge element of going out and collecting the stories, working with personal archives and collections, and with other museums. It's always incredibly participatory. Even at a very basic level, I want texts to be in the first person and for people to write their own captions, so the information is not being presented through my lens as a curator. It's a museum that is trying to shed light on the way migration both to and from these shores has really shaped who we are as individuals and as a society. It involves challenging histories around colonisation and enslavement and how we all got to be here. It's about helping people find that personal connection and ultimately the mission is to help people understand each other better.

Alejandro Aravena
Architect, Art Mill Museum, Qatar

I will start by slightly changing the question from 'What is a museum?' to '*Why* a museum?'

The 'why' of a museum is because we, as architects, have to create the space where the relationship between people and art can take place. Where personal and intimate encounters with artworks can occur, when the art speaks to your inner self, and where also collective, epic narrative encounters can happen, fuelling that sense of purpose that art is able to build.

What we architects do is to give form to the places where people live, in this case, to the place where art can be enjoyed, both as an individual and as a shared experience. You could have art at home, and it could speak to you, but that dimension of the collective would be missing. The risk in an institution is that you create that sense of collectiveness, yet it doesn't speak to you personally. So how do you create an experience that balances these two elements? This is part of my task as an architect, and these two dimensions – the personal and the collective – offer one way of answering the question 'What is a museum?'

I also have to keep in my mind the question of why a school kid might be interested in going to a museum, or why a family might choose to visit a museum rather than going to the park. I have to identify the forces in play and translate them into a design.

We have to think about the museum building not only as an institution but also as part of a place. There is the risk that the structure could become generic, a space where there's no connection, no relationship to the public or the collection. A museum should have the capacity to be adaptable, but at the same time it should reflect the place where it is located, where it is rooted. There is also the risk of a museum becoming a 'blind box' that has a very closed perimeter and no relationship with the city around it. One of the things about which we were very careful with the Art Mill Museum was trying to ensure that all the facilities in the museum – the shop, cafe, theatre and restaurant – could work both for the inside and for the outside, so when the museum is closed they can keep on serving the city.

We have to understand the different dynamics in play: carefully creating the right conditions for the works of art to be exhibited so that intimate and collective relationships can take place, while also asking if and how the museum can enter into a recurrent relationship with the local population, trying to ensure a porous relationship in terms of life and the museum. The question becomes not only 'Why go to the museum?' but also 'Why come back to the museum?' Art then is not just a product; it becomes part of the process.

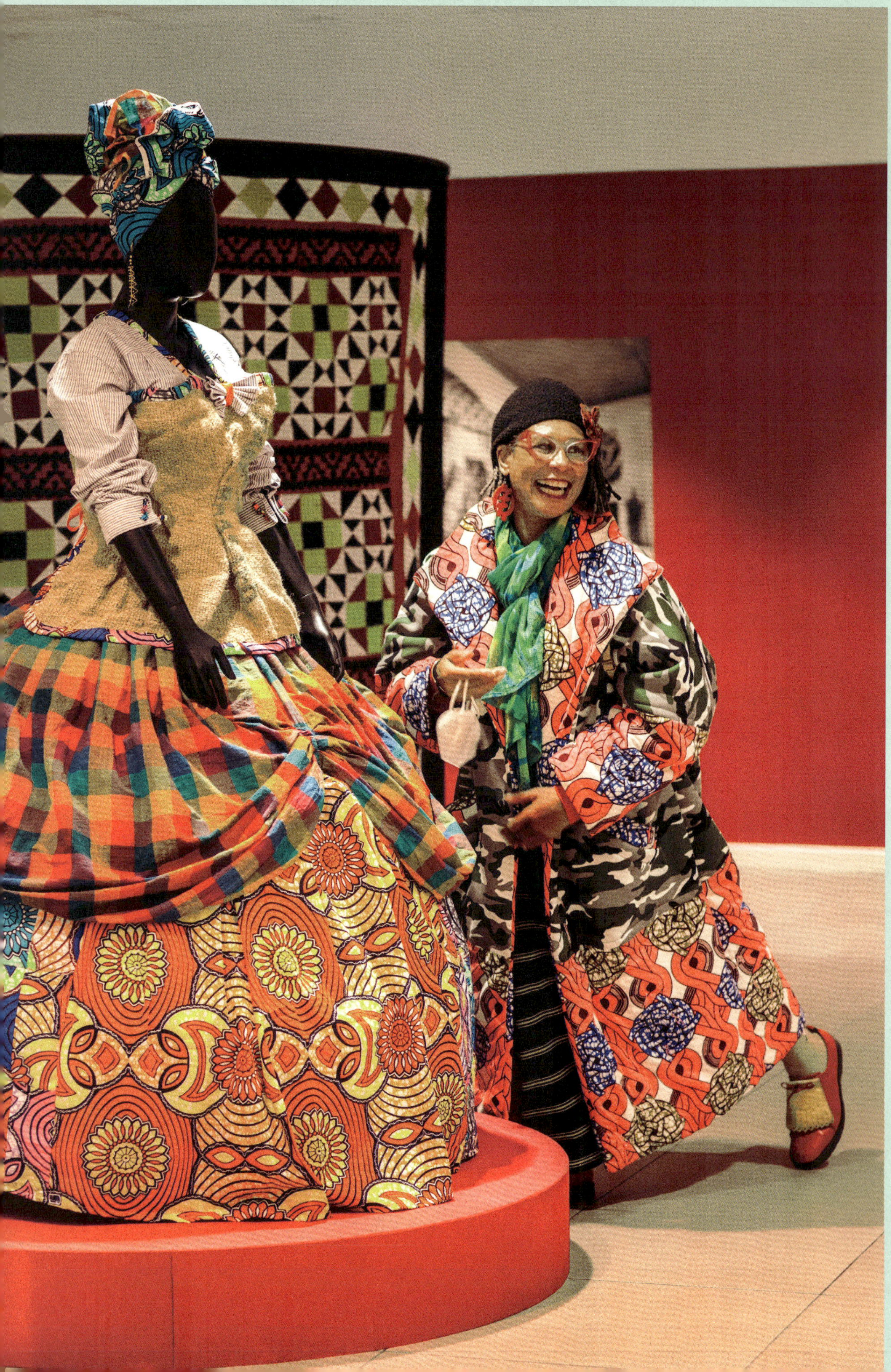

clockwise from left

Karen Arthur with her dress *Queen Joyce* at the launch of *Taking Care of Business* at the Migration Museum, 2022; Concept images by ELEMENTAL of the Art Mill Museum, Doha; 'Mwili, Akili na Roho', Installation view, Nairobi Contemporary Art Institute (NCAI), 2022

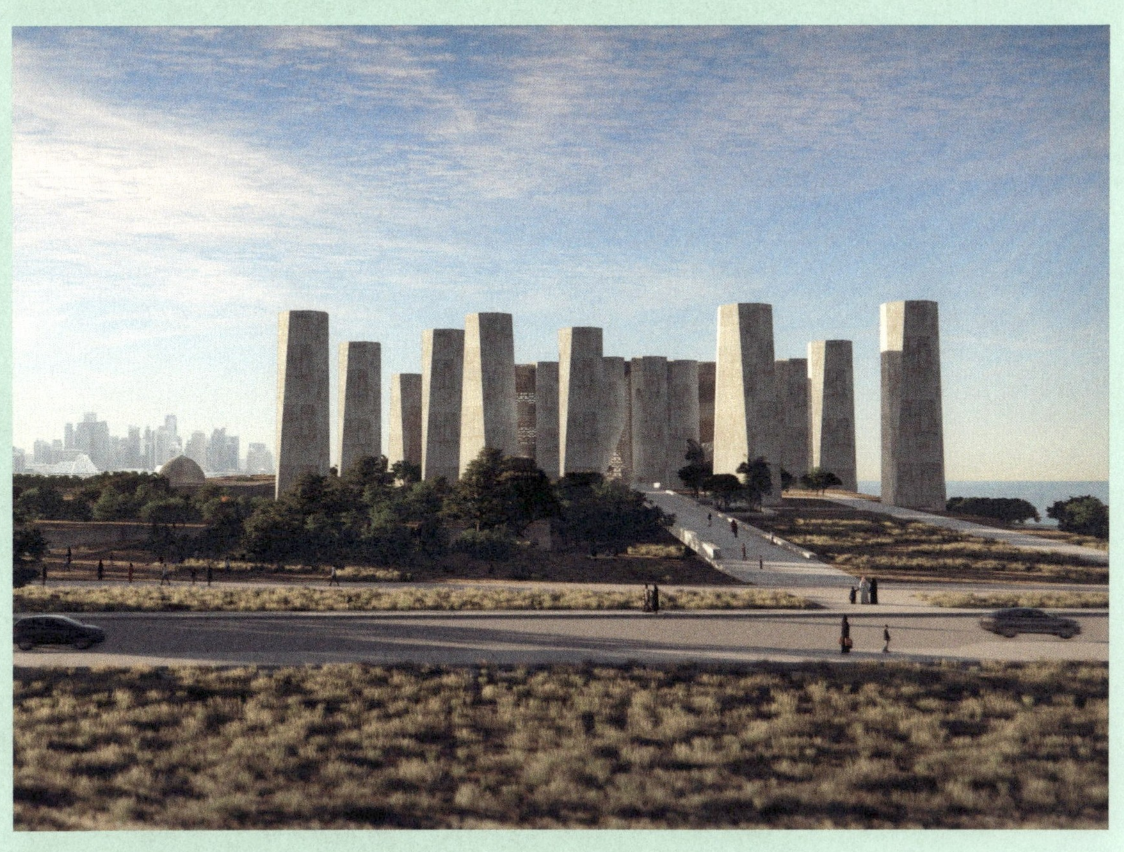

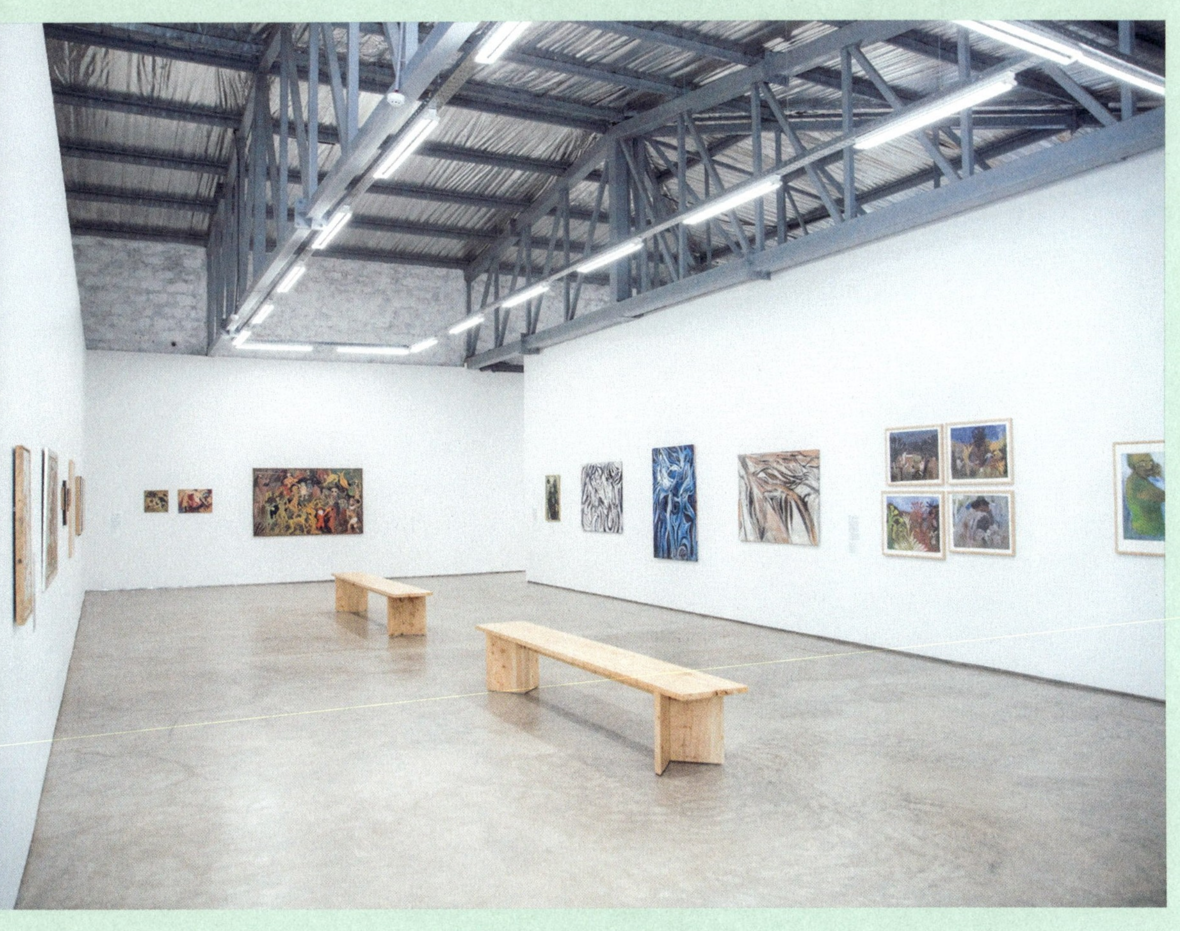

Michael Armitage
Founder, Nairobi Contemporary Art Institute, Kenya

A museum is a space that's relevant to culture, both past and present. Beyond that I find it quite difficult to define because I think what museums are is largely down to what they define themselves to be. They offer some sort of relatively permanent repository of culture where people can come and learn about the past. I'd almost prefer to think in terms of 'institutions' rather than 'museums'. Part of the issue with museums, for me, is that they try to claim too much ground. Historically they've tried to be the authority – whether socio-politically or forming a cultural dogma. With institutions you're saying that there is a way that you want to think about things, but which has the potential to be opposed, whereas with museological thinking there is a hierarchy and an exclusivity. That's why, with the Nairobi Contemporary Art Institute (NCAI), I found it more useful to think about starting an institution, as opposed to starting a museum.

At NCAI we are standing on the shoulders of many other museums and different types of art institutions and cultural spaces. We also reflect the cultural context in Kenya, where education has historically been a very highly regarded part of society. The idea with the NCAI was to create a space where you could go and learn about art and give art history space and context.

The thing I like about institutions is you can also have counter-institutions. You can have two institutions with different philosophies and attitudes, and they can live side by side. In terms of the word institution, when it came to naming NCAI it was about creating a pressure on what we do; to make sure that we can provide certain types of learning and create space to be critiqued. For me, it was also about leaving space for someone else to create something with the same 'weight', perhaps with a different approach, and for that to live alongside NCAI.

In terms of the role of NCAI's collection, it's important to create an accessible collection that an artist or audience in Kenya can visit to see the work of artists who have come before. In my mind, there is also the necessity of a collection to contextualise what is being made now.

When I was setting out the conceptual cornerstones of my practice, I wanted my work to have a direct relationship to an East African audience, which I considered to be my first audience. This meant it was important to me to make figurative paintings of people from the region, so that if somebody walked into an exhibition of my work, and they had no art background, there was something immediately familiar in what they were seeing. There is a similarity in this to my approach to NCAI. It's fundamentally about local audiences and thinking about what's necessary in order to connect and form relationships with them.

Thelma Golden
Director and Chief Curator, Studio Museum in Harlem, USA

The essence of what a museum should be is a challenging notion caught in a state of constant negotiation. Yes, museums exhibit great works of art, but there have been many examples that push past the museum as a site for simply viewing by encouraging critical thinking and alternative perspectives. While museums are spaces that commit themselves to the presentation and interpretation of objects, what makes them so significant is that they do so on behalf of the public, both present and future. For me, the building is just the container, the museum itself is activated through a commitment to community and the cultural identities that shape community, because although it is true that museums are a space to encounter art, really, they are a space to encounter each other. The definition of the museum is evolving, powered not only by programming but also by the many ways in which the public responds to a museum's presence. In 1968, the Studio Museum in Harlem began as an artist residency, a place for Black artists to create and contest the dominant narratives circulating in the greater art world. Since then, we've relocated and adapted. More than anything, we remain open to new possibilities as the first museum dedicated to artists of African descent. Our new building, which integrates Harlem's architectural history and stands tall on 125th Street, the neighbourhood's 'main street', will also function as a cultural community sanctuary, a place for reflection and self-expression.

On the one hand, museums have raised me. I grew up going to the Met in New York and took internships both there and at the Studio Museum, where I eventually returned. Through the museum's urge to connect people to artists, who in turn connect ideas to material form, I have created a life that connects me to a deep lineage that works to document, study and preserve Black artistic production.

On the other hand, I grew up in the wake of a political and cultural movement that challenged the authority of the traditional art museum. The 1960s and 1970s in the United States were a time of renewed self-assertion among marginalised communities – a time when there were calls for independence rather than assimilation. One result was the establishing of a group of culturally specific arts institutions. In New York City, these included Alvin Ailey American Dance Theatre, Dance Theatre of Harlem, the National Black Theatre, El Museo del Barrio, Ballet Hispánico and the Studio Museum. These years were crucial to me because I came to understand museums as institutions that could explicitly take positions of advocacy – as contrasted with traditional art museums, which maintained certain positions implicitly while appearing to stand above the fray.

So, for me, a museum is a place where art can be used to raise issues, engage communities and assert pride and social solidarity. At the same time, museums can be a place where people gain new perspectives on culture, history and society.

Lisa Havilah
Chief Executive, Powerhouse Parramatta, Australia

Powerhouse Parramatta, one of the world's most significant new museum projects, is being built on the lands of the Burramattagal people of the Dharug nation, in one of the most diverse and fastest growing parts of Sydney. We are very honoured to build our museum on unceded First Nations land. The Powerhouse acknowledges First Nations ownership every time we speak about the museum, and it is central to how we are redefining the Powerhouse.

I feel that there is an image of 'the museum' in people's minds that we are fighting against: objects in cabinets, star architecture, a location in the middle of a city, labelling, explaining and siloing. Powerhouse Parramatta will be a new institution that will redefine what a museum is: a place that is in service to the community. This is a major shift in hierarchy, putting the community at the top as the owner of knowledge and as the owner of stories. The Powerhouse is working in service of those stories.

We have established a First Nations directorate who are working right across the institution to change everything from our HR practices to how we collect. Now, with First Nations collections, we have become caretakers of material instead of acquiring it. This has significantly shifted the relationship between the institution and the community. I believe that it is important for communities to see themselves reflected in the institution and to feel connection to the stories told. We are always looking at how we can establish collaborative structures that embed our communities in longitudinal ways.

We are trying to de-institutionalise the Powerhouse; it's almost like cracking it open, to give it more air and space, so it's more relevant and has more meaning. I think that cultural infrastructure is a great gift in terms of establishing and embedding new models and ways of thinking within an institution. When you start out, what you do initially lays the foundations of that institution for the next 100 years, so the first step you take is so important. That first step is critical for defining the next 5,000 steps.

Lesley Lokko
Founder and Director, African Futures Institute, Ghana

To answer the question of what a museum means to me I have to answer in two ways. One is as somebody who is half British, with an understanding of the power of museums in the Global North and a reflection on what museums have meant to me over the last 50 years. The other is as an African with a very different attitude towards institutional memory.

As an architect, so much of my training has been invested in the physical infrastructure of a museum, so I know that if I think of the word 'museum' generally the image of building typology comes to mind. As an African architect it's much more ambiguous because there isn't that legacy of a particular kind of edifice where you might go to find the past. The short answer is that I'm quite conflicted about it. The long answer is that I think architects have some responsibility to try to resolve that.

I think one of the most profound conversations I've had about museums and architecture occurred about 25 years ago. I'd taken a group of students from Cape Town to see the Red Location Museum, built by the architect Jo Noero in Port Elizabeth, South Africa. I noticed that the signage in the museum was in three languages – English, Afrikaans and Xhosa – which are three of the 11 official languages in South Africa. I could see the word 'museum' repeated many times, for example 'museum bookshop', 'museum restaurant', etc., and I could work out what it was in Afrikaans but in Xhosa the words didn't seem to be repeated in the same way. Eventually I asked a security guard if he could translate the Xhosa signs for me. 'A place that you eat', 'a door that goes to the outside', etc. 'But what's the word for "museum" in Xhosa?' I asked. He looked puzzled for a moment, then replied, 'We don't have a word for that.' I asked, 'So, what do you call a building like this?' He thought about it for a few minutes and said, 'Well, it's a building for white people.' And so, I said, 'Well, what do you call a building where you go to remember things?' And he just looked at me and said, 'Madam, you don't need a building to do that.' And while it was a throw-away comment it really got me thinking about the relationship between an edifice and memory, and 25 years later I'm no closer to understanding what that is. It remains a compelling question and one that we're not paying enough attention to.

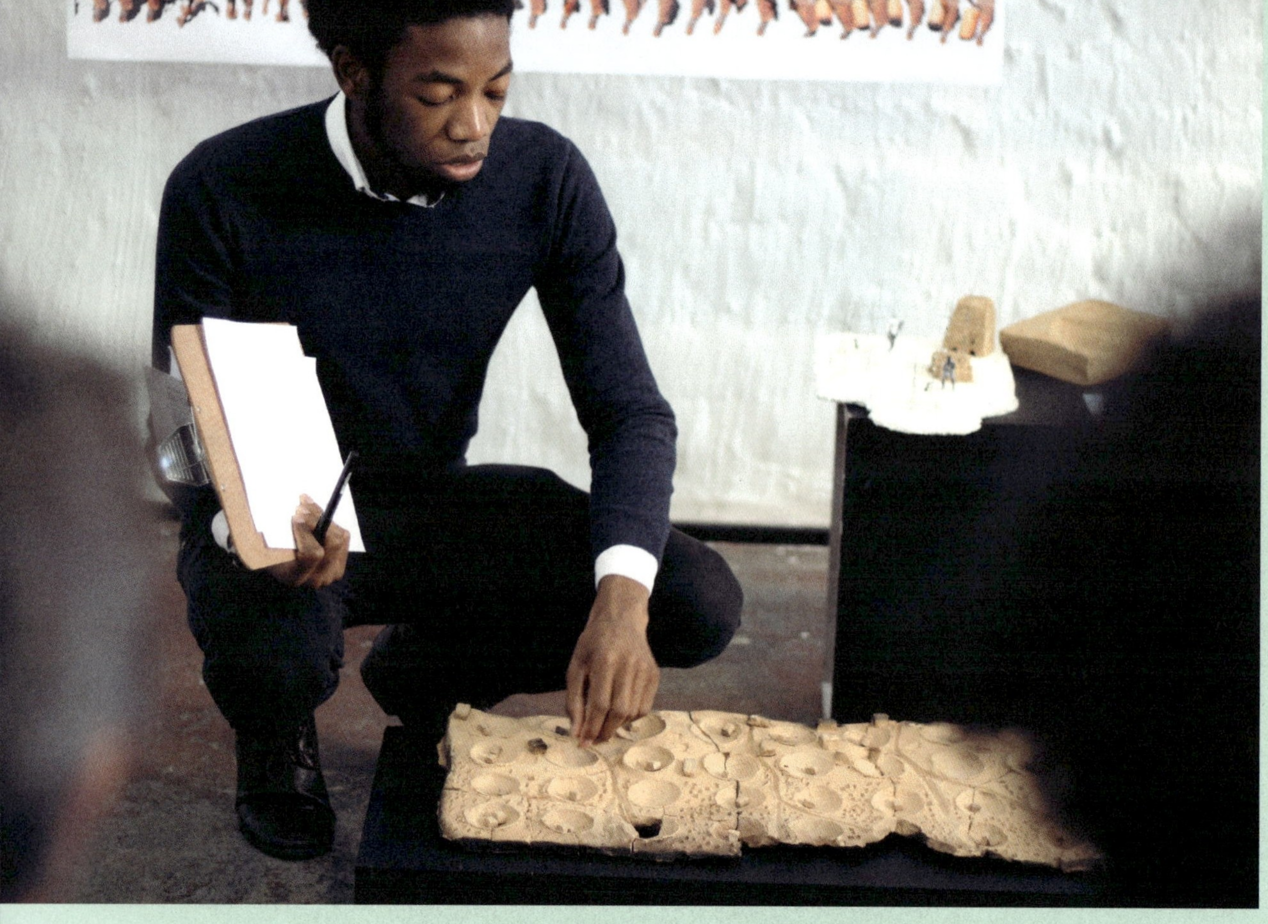

clockwise from top left

Forecasting the future: Students at the Graduate School of Architecture, University of Johannesburg, during International Critics Week, 2018; Lucas Museum of Narrative Art, Los Angeles, USA; Interior view, Museu de Arte de São Paulo Assis Chateaubriand, Brazil; Powerhouse Parramatta, Australia

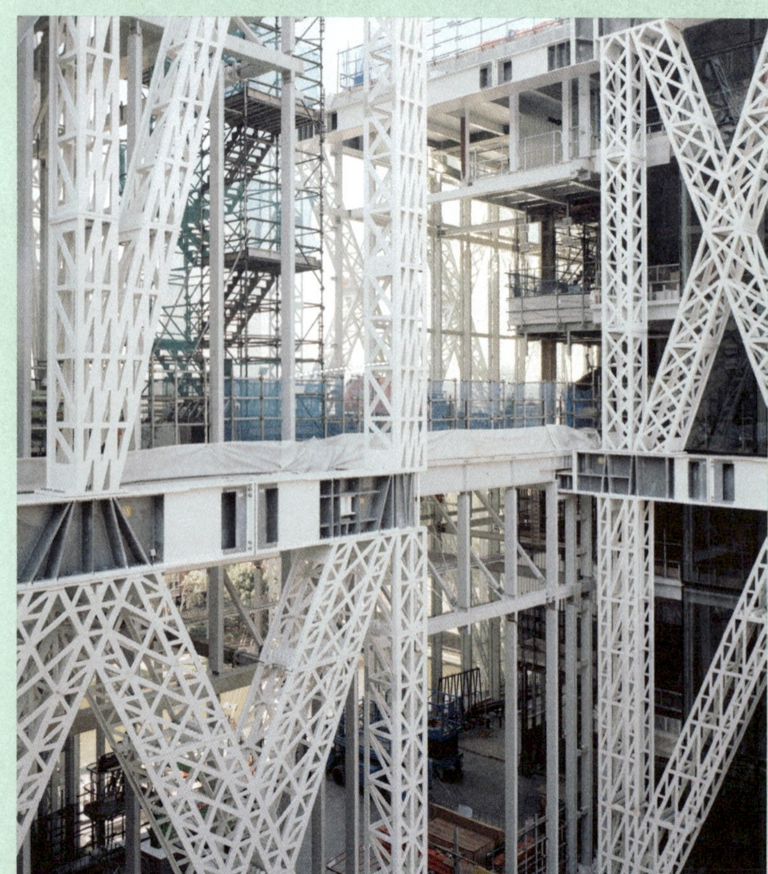

Sandra Jackson-Dumont
Former Director and CEO, Lucas Museum of Narrative Art, USA

I see museums as catalysts for dynamic, timely and rich conversations. I also see them as transgressive and discursive convenors, or gathering spaces, that have the potential to be safer places for nuanced and very difficult conversations. That said, they can only be that if practitioners and cultural custodians rise to the occasion. To live in this work one needs to have the skills and competencies to stand with that which can often be ambiguous, critical, contradictory and/or joyful.

Museums are not necessarily about the buildings. Buildings are a part of them, but so many of us feel like they are just about the buildings, and the collections within those building. Museums are more than that, they are an idea – a narrative construct even – and all the other elements are feeders into that idea. Certainly yes, the objects are important, but above all, museums are about care. Historically, they have been founded for the care of objects, founded for the care of people's histories or the substantiation of personal or national histories. They have been occupied with the business of taking care of specific narratives. We now find ourselves in a place where we are making choices about what we are caring for, who we care about and why anyone should care – but it is still all about care.

The objects in museums are in and of the world in which they were created, and we are in and of that world too. We can't continue acting like museums are hermetically sealed chambers or sanctuaries distinct from fuller social context. While museums can serve as havens and places to lay eyes on the magnificent abilities of artists and curators, they can, at the same time, be tethered to be so much more than a field trip or tourist visit.

Perhaps we have been too dismissive to this point of the more human-centred approach to objects that connects us to each other and to them. Within the museum space, I'm fascinated by this extreme disconnect between how we actually live and act in the world and how we think about the relationship between material culture and fine art objects. Why are some objects considered material culture and others considered art? Some material culture gets categorised as art because someone said so. Who is anointed to make that decision? What I'm interested in is the right to 'say so'. At the Lucas Museum we aim, across everything that we do, to create paths to equity and justice. We believe that working with objects and people has the potential to create a more just society. We are talking about skill-building through visual culture. People always ask me, 'What's the future of museums?' My answer is, 'How about we address the now of museum's since we can do something about that? Then we can talk about the future.'

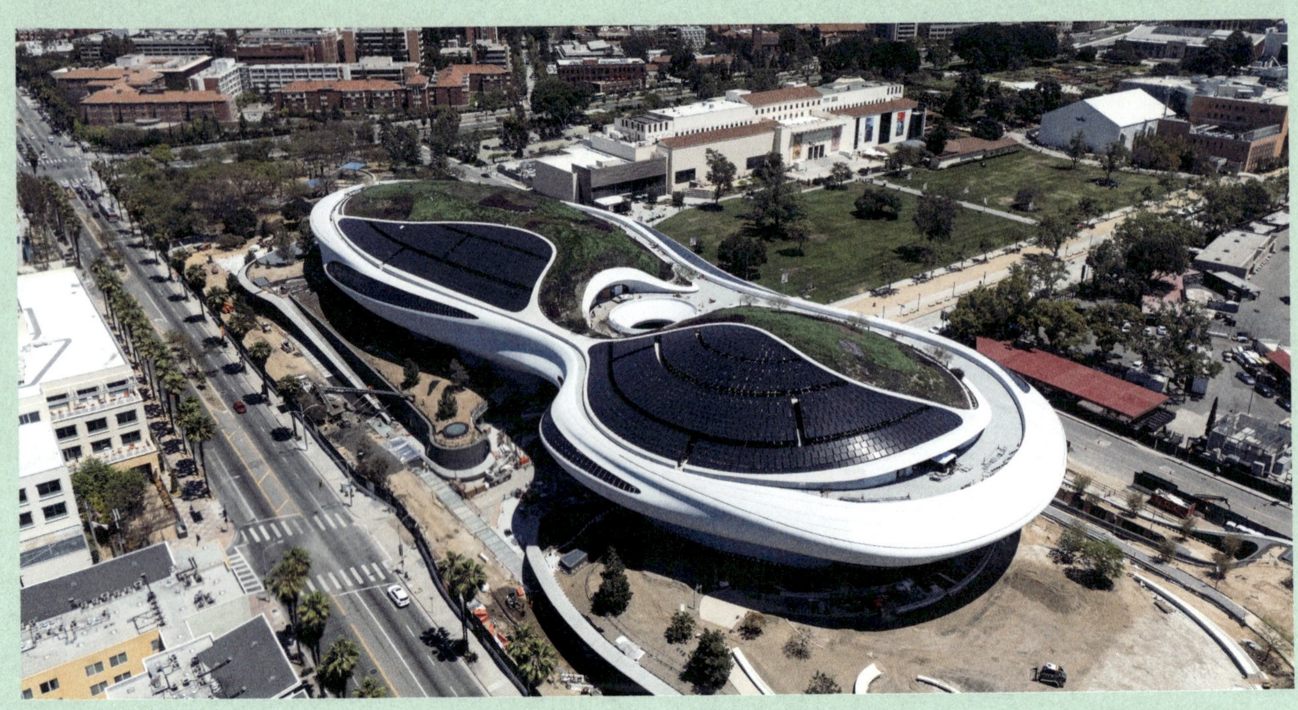

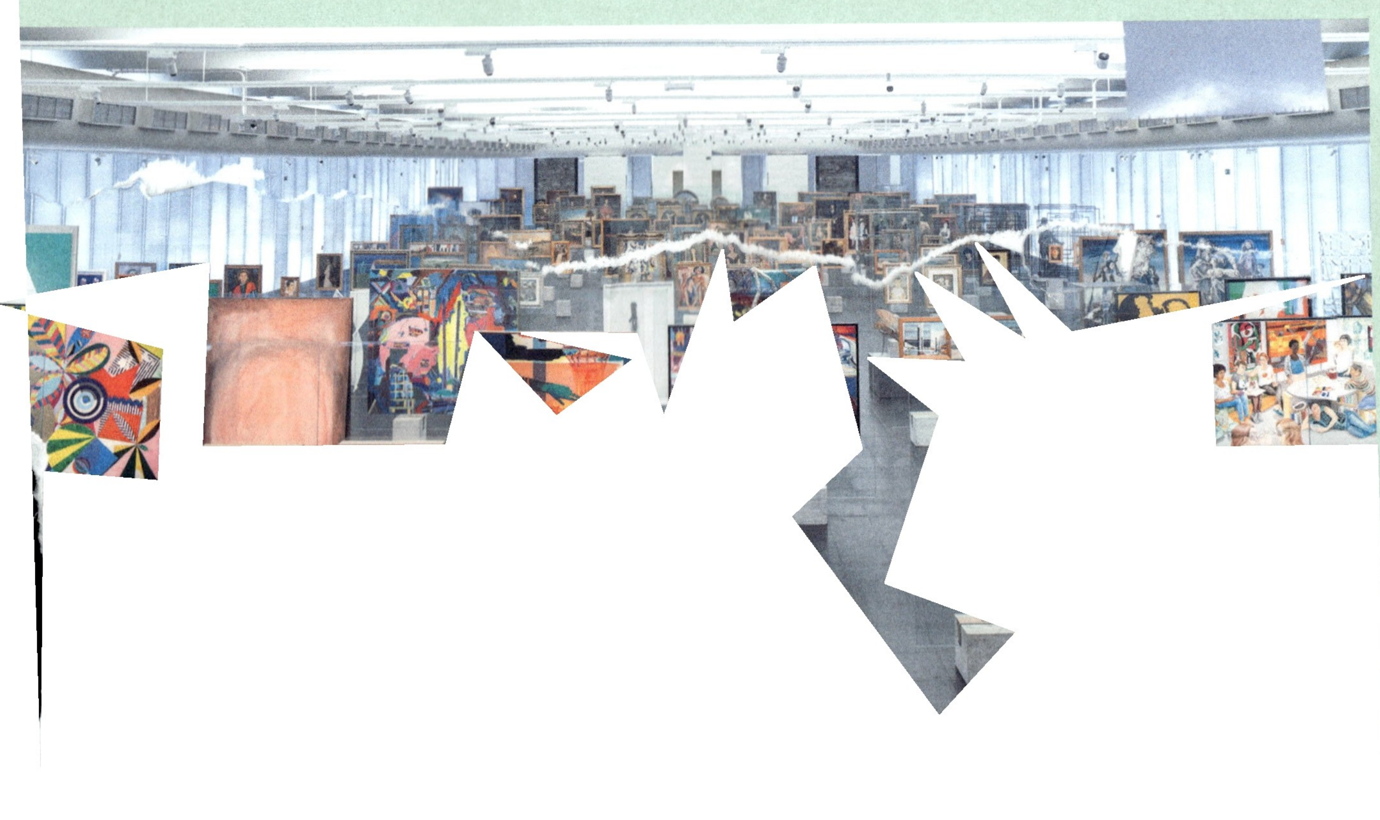

Isabella Rjeille
Curator, Museu de Arte de São Paulo Assis Chateaubriand, Brazil

From my perspective as a curator, a museum is essentially a place of encounters, be it with artworks, objects, histories or people. It is a place where narratives unfold from these encounters, bringing to light important aspects of our society and of art history itself. In a deeper sense, a museum can be a place to learn and unlearn the structures that shape those narratives, and for this reason it should be a place of debate and of active listening to the communities that surround it. Art has the capacity to generate important and, at times, difficult conversations, gathering around it multiple voices from artists, from the audience and from other agents. For this reason, it is important to keep the museum as a space that accommodates diversity and is transformed by it.

The Museu de Arte de São Paulo Assis Chateaubriand (MASP) is located in a central avenue in the city of São Paulo. Avenida Paulista is where many demonstrations start; it is a place of encounter itself, but also a place of dispute. Inaugurated in 1968, MASP's building was designed by the Italian Brazilian architect Lina Bo Bardi and features an open plaza sheltered by a free span, allowing the museum to be literally crossed by the public space. This is not only a physical feature of the architecture, but also a symbolic one, which guides us to the question of how we, as a museum, respond to the social transformations happening around us.

In 2015, under the artistic direction of Adriano Pedrosa, the approach of Lina Bo Bardi was restored, with the renovation and reinstallation of glass easels to display MASP's collection. Without walls, the artworks hang on glass sheets with a concrete base, like a forest of paintings through which the visitor can walk. With this radical display, Bo Bardi sought to break with the logic of the conventionally sacralised space of the museum, seeking to undo hierarchies between artworks such as 'high' and 'low', or 'vernacular' and 'fine' art. The labels of each work are placed behind the glass plates, so you are drawn to a work because what you see interests you and not just because it is by a particular artist. This creates room for encounters with new artworks by a variety of artists, and can help to challenge preconceived notions about a certain artist or artistic production. The material is organised chronologically, so by walking through this forest of paintings the visitor can create their own route, experiencing the various shifts in history and seeing how artists from different backgrounds responded to them.

My advice to museums would be to listen to your surroundings, to the different communities that inhabit the institution daily, both visitors and collaborators. Create a space where they feel welcome and represented by what they find inside and truly embrace diversity at all levels.

M+, Hong Kong, designed by Herzog & de Meuron, 2021

An Interview with Director of M+ Suhanya Raffel

Tim Reeve

Tim Reeve M+ has been one of the places that we've been keeping an eye on as we develop V&A East as part of a post-Olympic district, trying to create a new community and public space with culture and education at its heart. There are obvious similarities with what you've done with M+ and West Kowloon in Hong Kong, so I'm really interested to compare what we're doing in these two amazing places.

What do you feel is important and special about this co-location idea; the idea of creating a new place constructed on the premise that a vibrant community should have culture and education built into it from the beginning? Here we use the fact that 'Albertopolis' is where the V&A has its home in the cultural district born out of the Great Exhibition, and we have a clear idea of what makes it special and what its short-comings are, but what's your view?

Suhanya Raffel It's interesting that you cite the Great Exhibition because, although it was more than 150 years ago, it was initiated by a sense of wanting to share a revolution around lifestyle and crafts from the world, bringing the world to the doorstep of London. What we're seeing now in Asia is museum building at the very forefront of community building, so that relationship between civic institutions and the public is not so very unrelated to that moment so many years ago. How it's expressed in modern, cosmopolitan cities, however, is quite unique and dependent on the location.

If you take Hong Kong, it's very interesting to see how this city – which is a dense but, for China, a relatively small city of 7.5 million local people – decided to invest in cultural infrastructure because they knew that, while they were already a global city and financial hub, the piece of the puzzle around culture was missing. The city decided that museums were crucial and that these institutions would form a relationship with audiences drawn from the local vicinity.

Now the reality of Hong Kong is that it is a city that welcomes over 50 million people annually, which makes it very unique when it comes to visitors that are not Hong Kongers but consider Hong Kong to be a critical part of their everyday lives. These are people who work here, travellers and tourists. This mix of the local and global was interesting when making culture part of our place-making plan.

TR We're having this conversation in 2023 with Covid-19 only just in the rear-view mirror and, despite it being a dreadful and disruptive moment in human history, in some ways it acted as an accelerator for some of the things that you've talked about, particularly the need for West Kowloon and M+ to be for locals. It was one of the very few silver linings that when you opened M+ towards the end of the pandemic, Hong Kong got to experience the district before the world got to see it.

SR I think without question that was a positive thing. What was also interesting was how the institution and its interstitial spaces – not the formal collection spaces but the other kinds of spaces within the institution's umbrella – became completely colonised by the community to do different things, driven by a well-being agenda. That's been wonderful to watch, and it's enlivened the institution in an extraordinary way.

TR What has to happen next for West Kowloon and M+ to be up there as one of the great cultural districts and that keeps Hong Kong at the centre of people's minds when they think about great cities, culture and relationships with local and international audiences?

SR What we are waiting to see is how the rest of the world interacts with us. That's the next step: to welcome a broader mix of audience and to see how that audience works with us, our collections,

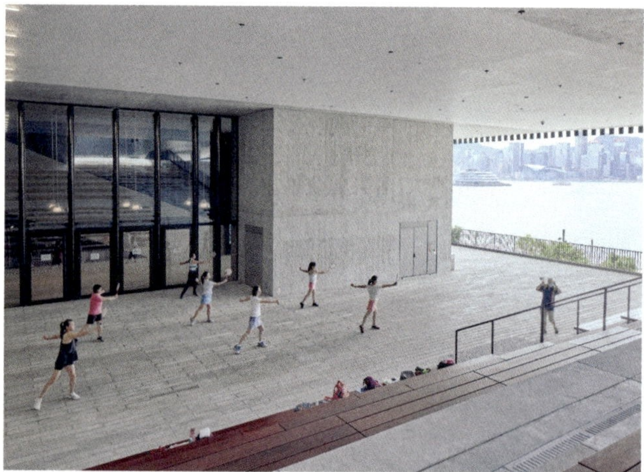

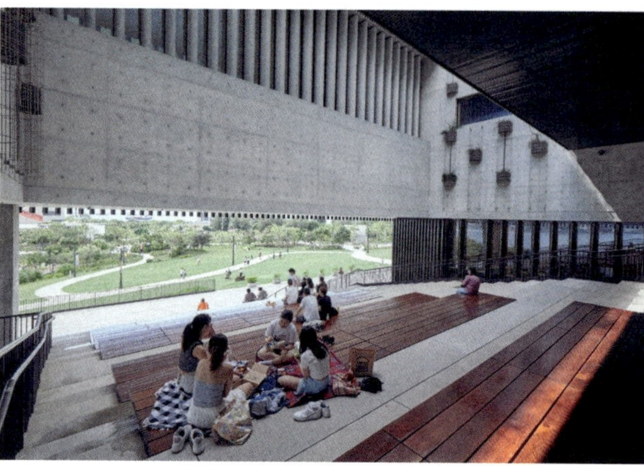

above Exercise on the Horizon Terrace, M+, Hong Kong, 2022
below Socialising on the Horizon Terrace, M+, Hong Kong, 2022

exhibitions and learning programmes. That is key to the work we do now, together with continued sustainability, both financial and structural. We need to respond to a compression in budgets and, at the same time, we have a social responsibility and awareness of the climate crisis, so we need to think about how we respond to and manage those responsibilities.

TR One of the other things we think about in the context of the East Bank, is how London is changing and the population movement from west to east; almost a sense that the future of London is in east London. Time will tell whether that's true and what it means, but it's interesting to think about that in the context of Hong Kong and what West Kowloon means for the rest of Hong Kong, and for the megalopolis that is the Greater Bay Area, as well as what M+ means for partner institutions on the island.

SR It's very clear that the bulk of our audience is actually coming out of the New Territories on the Kowloon side, rather than from Hong Kong Island. Historically the Island has been the financial and political centre, but that's shifting. The Greater Bay Area is clearly an important source of audience, of tourism, of money and influence. We've got the high-speed rail within five minutes walking distance to West Kowloon and this last Sunday we had 20,000 people through the museum coming from the Greater Bay.

TR It's interesting being on the island and looking across to West Kowloon and particularly to M+. It's just staring back at you; it's so ambitious.

SR It's like a beacon. The fact that it also has that screen embedded in the architecture, and the way that the content shown there is cultural in a city that has been so commercially driven in terms of light and moving image at night, it's nice for us to have a counterpoint saying that the city is also a place of culture and creative energy.

TR From that perspective of the architecture, our responsibility as a design museum on the East Bank is to stand out, to be artifact number one for V&A East. I'm imagining with M+ that there is the same kind of responsibility?

SR For us, the conversation with the architects was ongoing. What was important was that it wasn't a design that was set in stone; it was understood that there would be a dialogue with the museum in shaping the design. It became clear that part of the vision for the institution was about it being a public space, and that we needed to have interstitial spaces. Because Hong Kongers live in very small apartments and we don't have great public spaces to relax in, having cultural spaces that are nourishing, that are not the formal exhibition spaces, was important in the evolution of the design.

The emphatically horizontal slab was a design response by the architects to a vertical city, to offer something that you don't normally see, and then to open-up the flow plates inside the museum, to give this fabulous cathedral-like open space, which again nourishes the audience and takes your breath away.

TR What about material choices and the extent to which it is through the materials that you get a local flavour?

SR The vernacular feel of the cladding tiles, made of terracotta, with this deep green/black colour, echoes the structure of bamboo and also the ribbed roof of Chinese architecture. But it's a completely contemporary expression.

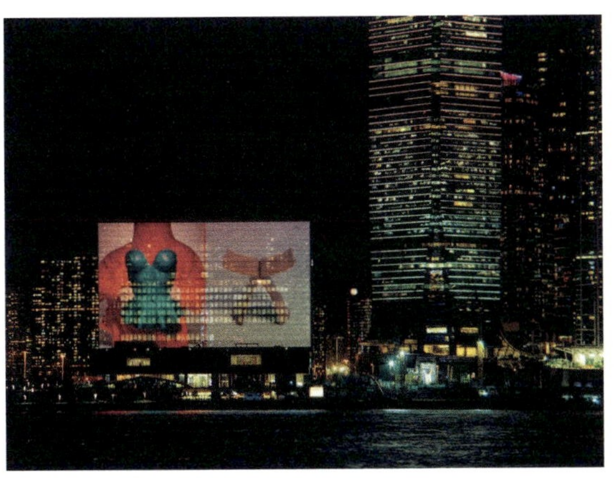

M+ at night, art on the façade, 2021

TR How important was the choice of architect? Herzog & De Meuron are well-known for Tate Modern in the UK, which has always been a point of reference and inspiration.

SR They are practised architects and we benefited from that practise, because I think M+ is their most refined piece of museum architecture to date.

TR You talked about M+ as being a museum for Asia. How important is that responsibility and what do you hope and expect the effect will be, not only on major investment in cultural infrastructure, but also in terms of engagement, audiences, collecting and storytelling?

SR It's very important because M+ stands for 'museum and more'; we encompass a cross-disciplinary approach while also embracing this sense of the transnational. Our collections include design and architecture, as well as moving images, film and art, and there is no other institution like that for Asia. There are comparable institutions, such as the Pompidou for Europe or the Museum of Modern Art for the Americas, and the V&A is one of those institutions for the UK, but Asia doesn't have that. We're the first, and I hope we become a kind of benchmark for other cities within Asia to start establishing similar kinds of institutions, because the cultural histories of the region are huge. We can't encompass the whole story; we can only say parts of it as they intersect with our location. We hope we will act as a catalyst for others.

TR That's such a massive responsibility. M+ represents a paradigm shift for the way that culture investment and cultural organisations work in Asia. That's hugely exciting but also, I would imagine, quite daunting.

SR It is a big responsibility, but at the same time you have to take your first step. And that step has been made. In many ways, Hong Kong was probably the only Asian city that could do it in the first instance, because it doesn't have that burden of nation per se. It has always been porous and open and has that granular dynamism.

TR As you know, we're creating a new V&A, a new institution, in a new place, for a new audience, and of course, you have just finished this kind of journey with M+. It's a beautiful building, but it's also a new culture, a blank sheet of paper. Where do you start?

SR It's been seven years and it's fabulous to look back and see that journey, because we were putting so many things together while acting it and doing it. Building a collection, building a team, building professional staff, building the construction and making a museum culture, all simultaneously and at scale.

I think it was possible because of the many young staff and the youthful energy around the institution, it was unfettered. We also did an enormous amount of work around cultivation of audiences. We went out to the people, we had our M+ rover and established programmes that were about getting to know our neighbourhood, our broader neighbourhood, our region and actively collaborating with regional partners. We also worked with international institutions, helping us on the training end of the work.

There were a lot of scuttlebutts before we opened; years of the Hong Kong press saying that we were going to be irrelevant and nobody was going to come, and the opposite happened. Now that voice has completely gone because it's clear that the city has embraced the institution and recognised the ambition and need. So, when you say, 'How did I do it?' I did it with others, of course, and with a clear sense of purpose for the establishment.

TR We've spent a huge amount of time in east London with schools, community groups and creatives, trying to draw them in to create V&A East with us. We also hope that people who live and work in east London, when they walk into V&A East, will not only see a programme that feels meaningful to them, but that they will also see themselves as part of the museum culture. Do you feel a similar ambition for M+?

SR Absolutely. What's really important is that 65 per cent of our audience is between 18 and 45. That reflects the engagement we undertook in the six years prior to opening. We would do camps for 100 young people every summer, and from that we built alumni. They have become ambassadors who continue to work with us on our learning programmes. We've also worked with schools and teacher groups who we engage with regularly to see where the collections can help as a resource. In that sense, the needs of community are being dealt with as an ongoing conversation.

Digital has been important for us, especially as we move into the mainland where the audiences are in the millions. We've made a very clear decision that social media is the way to reach out, so we have four social media channels that are just for the mainland.

TR Has this collaborative approach posed any particular challenges? You have to be prepared to let go if you're trying to co-create, co-design and give over a sense of ownership, which can be difficult for established institutions. Was it liberating being able to do that, without the traditional legacy of a long-standing museum?

SR There is improvisation happening; there is no road map so we're making it up as we go, and that's very liberating. It's quite exhilarating, but it's also unknown. What anchors us is a more traditional practice around museum collection, building, acquisition, interpretation and research, and that's the known museum world that we all occupy comfortably. At the same time, we're taking that material culture into new areas, and these are collections that are very unique, so that's exciting as well.

TR We are hoping our audience is going to be quite similar to yours: a Gen Z audience at the point they are thinking about life and career choices. We have this incredible opportunity to help young people trying to make sense of the world to look to creative pursuits as part of the answer. There's a huge curiosity but also a huge concern about the direction of the world and an almost activist mentality which, if museums can open themselves up to it, is hugely exciting as a creative challenge and a call to us to evolve.

SR I think we need that, it's a tension that we can draw energy from on both sides.

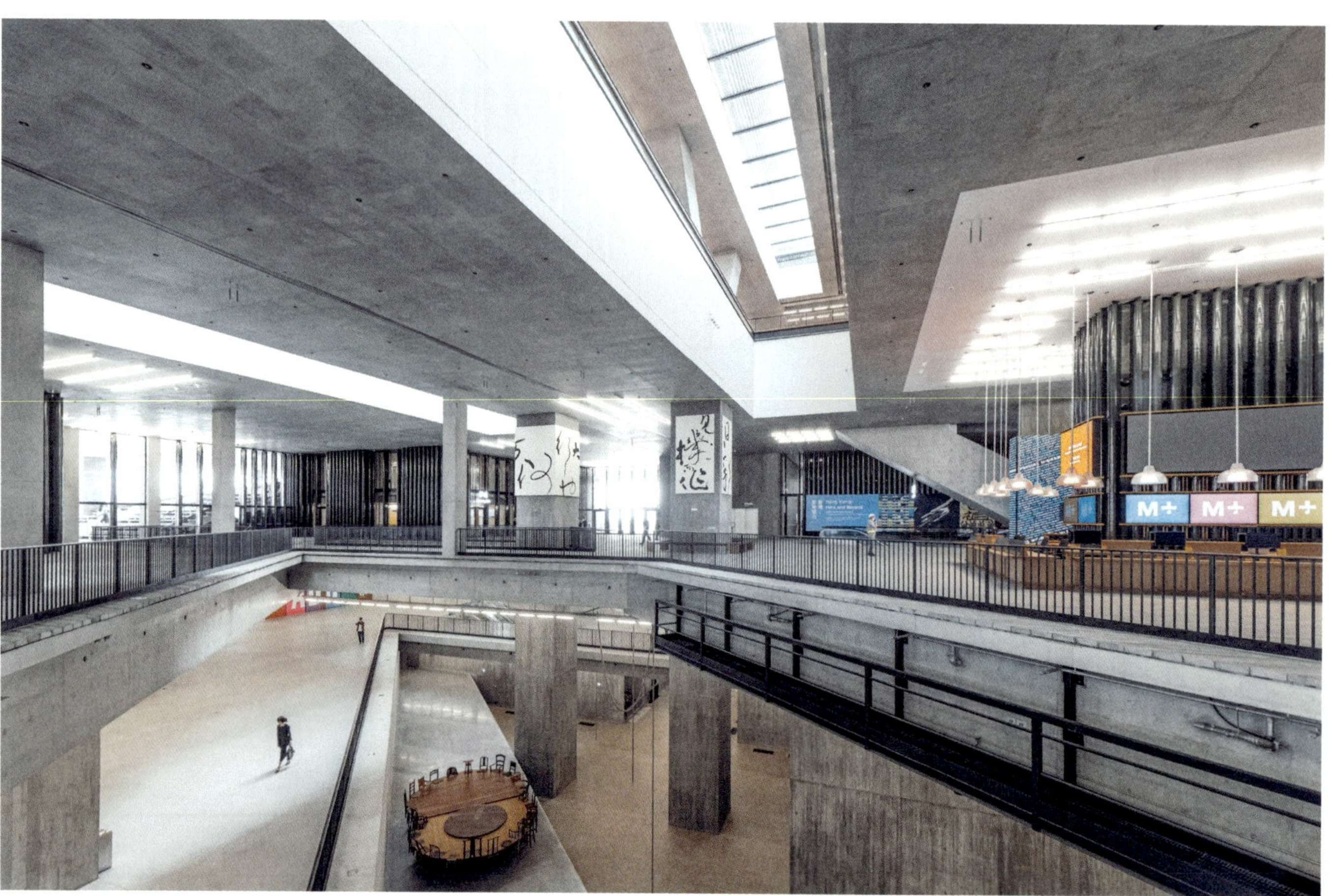

Interior view of M+, 2022

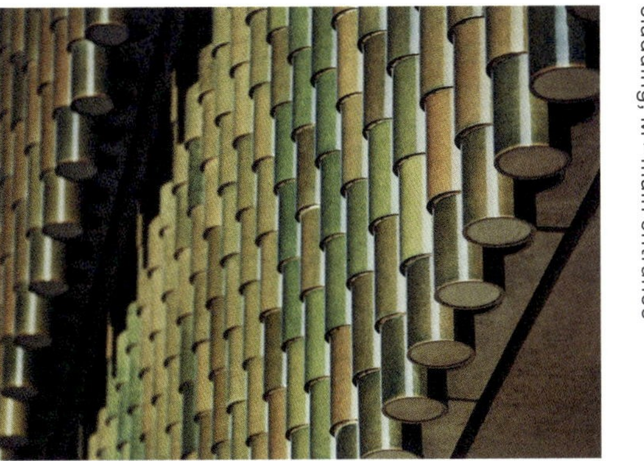

The varying green hues of the terracotta cladding, M+ main entrance

TR How do you imagine the collection and programme developing over time? How important is it for you that emerging creatives from Hong Kong would be inspired to create work for M+? How much will you be providing practitioners with the inspiration and the opportunity to develop their talent and how much will you be acquiring from the local area?

SR The relationship between the local and the international is curatorially driven, with an acquisition policy with a clear strategy. Every acquisition is made with merit in mind; it's an earned place. But it's important for us that we lift Hong Kong creatives and place them with their international colleagues as equals, and by bringing them together we say something that others cannot say. For example, we have the Archigram archive, and it brings the architecture and design collections into a sharp focus because so many Hong Kong architects were trained by those Archigram architects. And this sense of a vertical city, of a walking city, it is as they said, if they built anything, it would have been Hong Kong.

TR I like that idea, that you're placing Hong Kong creativity in its rightful international context. It's actually just reminding people that they are already part of a global tradition and with M+ right on the doorstep there is an opportunity to inspire another generation and to really celebrate that.

SR It's so interesting to see that in relation to, say, Tokyo, or Singapore, or London, or Milan. They're all in there but seen through such a different lens because of our location and the cast of the collection.

TR Is the museum ecosystem now fundamentally changing from something that had a Western focus to something more global? Are we at a tipping point?

SR I certainly think the world is turning and this shift in the museum space, in civic, public, institutional culture is now extremely present and visible. In Asia, it's interesting because the locations form the voices and the expressions that these institutions are making. But it is also clear in the West, and in the more traditional institutions there's a new life flowing in because of those shifts. It's about the relationship to the cities in which these institutions live, the relationship with audiences and the meaning of the collections to people's lives. I think that's a significant shift and, as part of that, the transnational relationships of our collections are being amplified.

TR What would your advice be as we move towards opening V&A East? The reason I'm prompted to ask that question is that I really do think that new institutions have to have that strong anchor, that first and foremost they are local institutions. If they are to be successful nationally and, ultimately, internationally, they must have those roots and be well-nourished in the local context.

SR I think that's true. I would also say that we have to be fearless in how we lead as well. We're taking people on a journey and that journey is not an insular one. It's very important that the local is expressed as outward-looking. I would call it a 'radical parochialism'. That it has a sense of agency around it.

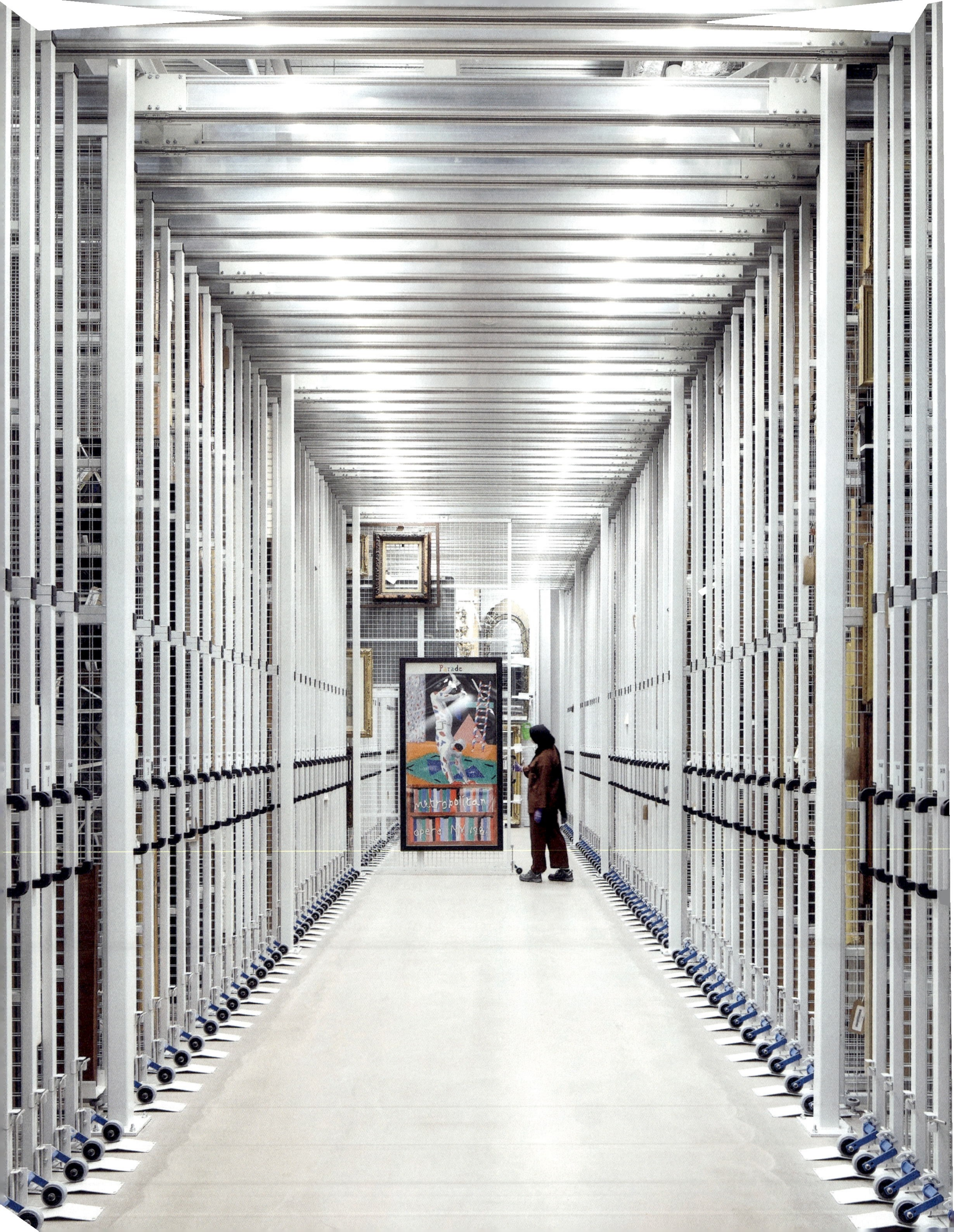
Parade
metropolitan
opera NY

Notes

pp. 42–3
Alison Smithson and Peter Smithson
Robin Hood Gardens
Text by Ben Selig

1 Alison Smithson and Peter Smithson, *Ordinariness and Light* (London 1970).
2 Ibid., p. 57.
3 'Planting Day in Robin Hood Gardens', *Woolmore News*, 29 January 2001.
4 A petition to reverse the listing decision from Building Design and Architects Journal was rejected by English Heritage and the Department for Culture Media and Sport.

pp. 44–5
Tony Minnion and Basement Community Arts Workshop
... get together and get things done, 1984
Text by Ben Selig

1 Tony Minnion in an interview with the author, 1 March 2023.
2 Tower Hamlets Local History Library and Archives: LC7865: Tower Hamlets Federation of Tenants Associations pamphlet, 'Get together and get things done', Annual Report, 1983–4 and 1985–6.
3 Tower Hamlets Local History Library and Archives: LC7863: Tower Hamlets Federation of Tenants Associations, 'Get together and get things done', 1984.
4 Ibid.

pp. 46–7
Kehinde Wiley
Portrait of Melissa Thompson, 2020
Text by Madeleine Haddon

1 Claire Wrathall, 'Kehinde Wiley: "I took the DNA of William Morris and created hybrids"', *Guardian*, 25 January 2020, https://www.theguardian.com/artanddesign/2020/jan/25/kehinde-wiley-william-morris-exhibition-interview [accessed 1 January 2024].
2 Gilman and May Morris (William Morris's youngest daughter) became friends in 1896 after meeting at an International Socialist Conference in London after which Morris invited Gilman to give a lecture at their family home Kelmscott in Hammersmith.
3 Nadja Sayej, 'Kehinde Wiley: "When I first started painting Black women, it was a return home"', *Guardian*, 9 January 2019, https://www.theguardian.com/artanddesign/2019/jan/09/kehinde-wiley-st-louis-when-i-first-started-painting-black-women-it-was-a-return-home [accessed 4 January 2024].

pp. 64–9
New Dialogues with Collections
Text by Zofia Trafas White

1 Further education course leader, V&A East Consultation Workshop, 2019.
2 Okwui Enwezor, 'The State of Things', in *All the World's Futures: 56 International Art Exhibition*. La Biennale di Venezia (Venice 2015), pp. 17–21.
3 Christiana Figueres and Tom Rivett-Carnac, *The Future We Choose: Surviving the Climate Crisis* (London 2020), pp. 1–12.
4 Ibid.
5 Hella Jongerius Louise Schouwenberg, *Beyond the New: A Search for Ideals in Design* (2015), http://beyondthenew.jongeriuslab.com/ [accessed 20 July 2020].
6 Mieke Bal, 'Towards a Relational Inter-Temporality', in Eva Wittocx et al. (eds), *The Transhistorical Museum: Mapping the Field* (Amsterdam 2018), p. 61.
7 Maura Reilly, *Curatorial Activism: Towards an Ethics of Curating* (London 2018), pp. 16–33.
8 Victor Papanek, *Design for the Real World: Human Ecology and Social Change* (New York 1972).
9 Arturo Escobar, *Designs for the Pluriverse: Radical Interdependence, Autonomy and the Making of Worlds* (Durham and London 2018).
10 Julia Watson, 'Introduction. A Mythology of Technology', in *Lo-TEK, Design by Radical Indigenism* (Cologne 2019), pp. 16–27.

pp. 70–79
A Journey Through the Why We Make Galleries
Text by Zofia Trafas White

1 Maud Sulter n.d., quoted in Susannah Thompson, 'Passionate and Political: Centring Black Women in Maud Sulter's "Zabat"', *Art UK*, https://artuk.org/discover/stories/passionate-and-political-centring-black-women-in-maud-sulters-zabat [accessed 15 December 2021].
2 Eileen Gray n.d., quoted in Peter Adam, *Eileen Gray Her Life and Work* (London 2009).
3 Lee Alexander McQueen, quoted in 'Alexander McQueen: Quotes on Past, Present, Future', *AnOther Magazine*, 5 March 2015, https://www.anothermag.com/fashion-beauty/7111/alexander-mcqueen-quotes-on-past-present-future [accessed 16 August 2022].
4 'About | 石巻工房 Ishinomaki Laboratory', n.d., Ishinomaki-Lab.org, https://ishinomaki-lab.org/about/ [accessed 2 June 2022].
5 Lawson Oyekan n.d., quoted in Phillips catalogue, *Design. New York Auction*, 6 June 2019, https://www.phillips.com/detail/lawson-oyekan/NY050119/77 [accessed 23 December 2020].
6 Aaron Koblin, interviewed in Andrew C. Revkin, *Come Fly with Me (and Me and Me and Me ...)*, *New York Times*, 21 November 2007, https://archive.nytimes.com/dotearth.blogs.nytimes.com/2007/11/21/come-fly-with me-and-me-and-me-and-me/ [accessed 16 June 2021].
7 Jerzy Janiszewski, interviewed in Andrzej Brzozowski, 'Znak polskiej wolności', *Biuletyn IPN. Pamięć.pl* (2015), vol. 9, no. 42, p. 16. This is translation from original Polish by the author.
8 Bridget Harvey, 'Repair-Making: Craft, Narratives, Activism', PhD diss. (University of the Arts London 2019), p. 3.
9 Yasmeen Lari, quoted in Shanaz Ramzi, 'Retrospective: Yasmeen Lari', *Architectural Review*, 9 September 2019, https://www.architectural-review.com/buildings/retrospective-yasmeen-lari [accessed 25 September 2020].

10 Sonam Wangchuk, co-founder of the Himalayan Institute of Alternatives Ladakh (HIAL), quoted in Jacopo Prisco, 'The artificial glacier growing in the desert', CNN, 20 July 2017, https://edition.cnn.com/style/article/ice-stupa-sonam-wangchuk/index.html [accessed 29 November 2019].

pp. 110–11
Theaster Gates
Voulkos #1, 2021
Text by Georgia Haseldine

1 Theaster Gates, 'Reflections on Making' in Lydia Yee (ed.), *Theaster Gates: A Clay Sermon* (London 2022), p. 20.
2 Francois Xavier d'Entrecolles, *Lettre du Père d'Entrecolles sur la Porcelaine sur le nouvel établissement de la Mission des Peres Jésuites dans la Krimée* (Paris 1780); George Calfas, 'A Dragon Kiln in the Americas: European-American Innovation and African American Industry', *Journal of African Diaspora Archaeology and Heritage* (2017) vol. 6, no. 2, pp. 133–54, DOI: 10.1080/21619441.2017.1345106.

pp. 112–13
Eileen Gray
Bobadilla rug design, about 1926–9
Text by Zofia Trafas White

1 'Furniture in Bizarre Forms and Styles', *Chicago Tribune*, July 1922.

pp. 114–15
Richard Malone
Ensemble, 2021
Text by Zofia Trafas White

1 Richard Malone interviewed in Edwina Langley, 'How fashion designer Richard Malone is making luxury clothes from ancient skills', *Evening Standard*, 12 September 2019.

pp. 116–17
Circle of Sofonisba Anguissola,
Portrait of Sofonisba Anguissola after a self-portrait, 1530–1620
Text by Madeleine Haddon

1 R. G., 'Account of Sofonisba Anguissola and her Sisters', *Gentleman's Magazine*, October 1801, part II, p. 898.

pp. 122–3
IBUKU Studio
Architectural model for Sharma Springs residence, Bali, 2011
Text by Noel Cheung

1 Mandi Keighran, 'IBUKU's Elora Hardy On Bamboo Architecture and Model Making', *In Design Live Asia,* 3 October 2019, https://www.indesignlive.sg/people/ibuku-elora-hardy-bamboo-architecture [accessed 4 January 2024].

pp. 146–55
A Working Storehouse
Text by Georgia Haseldine

1 See Owen Hatherly on Foster + Partners' glass Reichstag dome: 'The Government of London', *New Left Review* (March/April 2020), no. 122, https://newleftreview.org/issues/ii122/articles/owen-hatherley-the-government-of-london [accessed 9 January 2024].
2 P. J. Proudhorn, *What is Property?* (Cambridge 1994), p. 167.
3 Participant from the first cohort of the Youth Collective, 2021.
4 Sria Chatterjee, 'The Long Shadow of Colonial Science', *Noēma* (March 2021), https://www.noemamag.com/the-long-shadow-of-colonial-science/ [accessed 9 January 2024].
5 Simone de Beauvoir, *The Second Sex*, Contance Borde and Sheila Malovany-Chevallier (trans.) (New York 2011), p. 162.
6 bell hooks, 'The Oppositional Gaze', *Feminism and Tradition in Aesthetics* (Pennsylvania 1995), p. 143.
7 Clémentine Deliss quoted in Mirjam Brusius and Kavita Singh (eds), *Museums Storage and Meaning: Tales from the Crypt* (Oxon 2018), p. 106.
8 Charles Booth, *Life and Labour of the People in London: the trades of East London*, vol. IV (London 1893), p. 161.
9 Interview for CNN *African Voices Changemakers* series, 2015, https://edition.cnn.com/videos/world/2015/03/30/spc-african-voices-sanaa-gateja-a.cnn [accessed October 2023].
10 Yvonne Brewster, https://www.talawa.com/productions/the-black-jacobins [accessed 9 January 2024].
11 'David Bowie on His Favourite Artists', *New York Times*, 14 June 1998, reprinted 14 January 2016, https://www.nytimes.com/2016/01/15/arts/design/david-bowie-on-his-favorite-artists.html [accessed 9 January 2024].
12 adrienne maree brown, *Emergent Strategy: Shaping Change, Changing Worlds* (California 2017), p. 18.

pp. 156–7
Sofia Karim
Turbine Bagh *Samosa Packets*, 2020–21
Text by Miri Ahn

1 https://www.sofiakarim.co.uk/ [accessed 4 January 2024].

pp. 158–9
Unknown maker
Tin-glazed dish, about 1540
Text by Serenella Sessini

1 Timothy Wilson, 'Making Maiolica', *Bulletin of the Detroit Institute of Arts* (2013), vol. 87, nos 1–4, p. 6; see also Alan Caiger-Smith, *Tin-Glaze Pottery in Europe and the Islamic World: The Tradition of 1,000 Years in Maiolica, Faience and Delftware* (London 1973).
2 Ibid., p. 6.
3 Patricia Simons, 'The Cultural Context of Maiolica in Renaissance Italy', *Bulletin of the Detroit Institute of Arts* (2013), vol. 87, nos 1–4, p. 14; Richard A. Goldthwaite, 'The Economic and Social World of Italian Renaissance Maiolica', *Renaissance Quarterly* (Spring 1989), vol. 42, no. 1, p. 13.

pp. 160–61
Rahemur Rahman and Aranya
Suit, 2012
Text by Serenella Sessini

1 Rahemur Rahman, 'Stop using labels like womenswear and menswear', V&A video interview, 15 March 2022, https://www.youtube.com/watch?v=_ECo91X4BHc&t=1s [accessed 8 January 2024].
2 Based on correspondence between Rahemur Rahman and the author, 3 July 2023

pp. 164–5
Alex Moulton (designer), made in Bradford Moulton bicycle, 1962
Text by Kristian Volsing

1 *Earls Court Cycle and Motor Cycle Show* (1962), British Pathé, https://www.youtube.com/watch?v=qxYqgCYmKcQ [accessed 10 November 2023].
2 Joanna Weddell, 'Room 38A and beyond: Post-war British design and the Circulation Department', *V&A Online Journal*, no. 4, 2012, http://www.vam.ac.uk/content/journals/research-journal/issue-no.-4-summer-2012/room-38a-and-beyond-post-war-british-design-and-the-circulation-department [accessed 13 November 2023].

3 Lily Crowther, *Award-winning British Design, 1957–1988* (London 2012), p. 12.

pp. 166–7
Unknown makers
Looted textile fragments, eighteenth to mid-nineteenth century China
Text by Georgia Haseldine

1 Louise Tythacott, 'The Yuanmingyuan and its Objects', in Tythacott (ed.), *Collecting and displaying China's 'Summer Palace' in the West: The Yuanmingyuan in Britain and France* (London 2018), pp. 3–24.
2 Jing Han and Anita Quye, 'Dyes and Dyeing in the Ming and Qing Dynasties in China: Preliminary Evidence Based on Primary Sources of Documented Recipes' (2018) *Textile History*, vol. 49, no. 1, pp. 44–70, https://doi.org/10.1080/00404969.2018.1440099.
3 Garnet Wolseley, *Narrative of the War with China in 1860* (London 1862), p. 236.
4 3.8.17 Letter from Dowager Viscountess Wolseley, Hampton Court Palace, Middlesex, The Viscountess V&A Registry File Loans and Bequests, MA/1/W2680 Wolseley.
5 9.8.17 Letter from Dept of Textiles to DVW, The Viscountess V&A Registry File Loans and Bequests, MA/1/W2680 Wolseley.

pp. 168–9
Various makers
Agra colonnade, about 1637
Text by Revati Mann

1 The Mughals were a powerful dynasty founded by the Central Asian prince, Babur, in 1526. They ruled Hindustan for over 300 years, a vast empire whose geographic extent covered most of modern-day India, Pakistan, and Bangladesh in its heyday.
2 Other components of the dismantled veranda remain in India in the cities of Agra (at Agra Fort, Taj Museum, Circuit House) and Lucknow (at Lucknow State Museum). The eight brackets are made of three double and two single brackets.
3 Hassan Fathy, *Natural Energy and Vernacular Architecture: Principles and Examples with Reference to Hot and Arid Climates* (Chicago 1986), pp. 3–10.
4 Asif Ali, 'Passive Cooling and Vernacularism in Mughal Buildings in North India: A Source of Inspiration for Sustainable Development' *International Transaction Journal of Engineering, Management & Applied Sciences & Technologies* (October 2012) https://www.researchgate.net/publication/267627217 [accessed 9 January 2024]; Vinod Gupta, 'Indigenous Architecture and Natural Cooling' in *Energy and Habitat: Town Planning and Building Design for Energy Conservation* (Michigan 1984), pp. 41–8, https://www.researchgate.net/publication/240619209_INDIGENOUS_ARCHITECTURE_AND_NATURAL_COOLING [accessed 9 January 2024].
5 Daniel Silvernail, 'The Principle of Thermal Mass', 16 May 2015, https://santacruzarchitect.wordpress.com/2015/05/16/the-principle-of-thermal-mass/ [accessed 9 January 2024].
6 See for instance the seventeenth-century Tomb of I'timad-ud Daulah and Asmat Begum in Agra, which was conceived as an earthly paradise.
7 Ebba Koch, *The Complete Taj Mahal and the Riverfront Gardens of Agra* (London 2006), pp. 222–3. Catherine B. Asher, *The New Cambridge History of India: Architecture of Mughal India* (Cambridge 1992), pp. 171–215.
8 Ebba Koch, 'The Mughal Waterfront Garden', in Ebba Koch (ed.), *Mughal Art and Imperial Ideology: Collected Essays* (New Delhi 2001) pp. 183–202.
9 Wheeler M. Thackston (ed. and trans.), *The Baburnama: Memoirs of Babur, Prince and Emperor* (Oxford 1996), p. 360. Asher 1992, p. 30.
10 The fundamental design of a *chahar bagh* is an enclosed quadrilateral divided into four sections by perpendicular irrigation canals or paths converging in a pool or fountain at the centre.

Acknowledgements

With profound thanks to colleagues across the V&A, and to the very many external partners, stakeholders, donors and collaborators – past and present – who made this complex museological fantasy a real-world reality:

V&A East Storehouse was supported by

Blavatnik Family Foundation
Warner Music Group
David Bowie Estate
Garfield Weston Foundation
The Foyle Foundation
Frédéric Jousset
David and Molly Lowell Borthwick

Wolfson Foundation
The Rosalinde and Arthur Gilbert Foundation
Clore Duffield Foundation
The Thompson Family Charitable Trust
Toshiba

V&A Americas Foundation
Frederick Reynolds
John and Hilary Everett
Celia and Edward Atkin CBE
Roderick and Elizabeth Jack
Unwin Charitable Trust
The European Fine Art Foundation
Edmond Weaving
Trevor A. C. Jones
Michael Erik Fredrickson
Sian Richards
The Pilgrim Trust
David and Elizabeth Challen

and many other generous donors

V&A East Project Team

Ali Al-Nakeeb, Charlotte Batts, Amy Bettinson, Manuela Buttiglione, Federica Camisani Calzolari, Isobel Cockburn, Sarah Davies-Goddard, Jasmine Farram, Holly Harris, Karen Hart, Kat Healey, Hannah Hudson, Sally Jennings, Hailee Kukura, Cleo Laskarin, Claire McKeown, Jen McLachlan, Vanessa Meade, Sophia Newton, Martha Norman, Hannah O'Connell, Kristin Panasewicz, Tessa Pierce, Thomas Rhoades, Anna Roza, Pip Simpson, Rosemary Strickland, Nicola Underwood

V&A East Operations and Commercial Team

Phoebe Bitmead-Hill, Josie Bullock, Viktorija Cerkauskaite, Michelle Cook, Tim Gosden, Anne Griffin, Ameena Hashmi, Ian Johnson, Edward May, Ines Mourato, Hazel O'Sullivan, Laura Parker, Amy Poole, Darius Rejaie, Joe Rosslyn, Ella-Marin Scotland-Waters

V&A East Learning and Engagement Team

Sophie Alonso, Bea Burnett, Sarah Green, Rebekah Hundeyin, Kamal Hussain, Sara Ismail, Fazela Khatun, Komal Khetia, Navjot Mangat, Maia Ojerinde-Ardalla, Iqra Rahman, Marijke Steedman, Afia Yeboah

V&A East Curatorial and Interpretation Team

Miri Ahn, Gus Casely-Hayford, Noel Cheung, Brendan Cormier, Amy Davy, Charlotte Flint, Madeleine Haddon, Georgia Haseldine, Sophie Hoffman, Catherine Ince, Alexandra Jones, Chloe Kellow, Rebecca Knott, Yona Lesger, Janice Li, Samantha Manton, Donata Miller-Obebe, Alice Power, Ruben Salgado Perez, Ben Selig, Serenella Sessini, Amanda Stephen, Kristian Volsing, Zofia Trafas White, Tommy Wide

V&A Collections Care and Access Team

Zoe Allen, Sarah Baily, Clair Battisson, Victor Borges, Benjamin Brown, Keara Burr, Victoria Button, Cristina Calvache Quesada, Ana Charriere, Matthew Clarke, Amel Earle, Matthew Fancy, Pedro Gaspar, Elizabeth-Anne Haldane, Hebe Halstead, Simon Hawkes, Tom Haynes, Zoë Hollingworth, Marisa Kalvins, Allen Irvine, Toby Krawczyk, Rachael Lee, Joel Mansfield, Nyssa Mildwaters, Andy Monks, James Parr, Kate Parsons, Panagiota Pozoglou, Katrina Redman, Ben Rubenstein, Ella Siggers, Katy Smith Pam Young, Kira Zumkley

From across other V&A departments

Johanna Agerman Ross, Joseph Ameh, Michael Appouh, Chloe Aspden, Nick Barnard, Eric Bates, Kirstie Beaven, Glenn Benson, Oli Bettesworth, Neil Bingham, Michelle Bolden, Richard Boston, Antonia Bostrom, Stacey Bowles, Victoria Bradley, Sophie Brendel, Katie Burell, Laura Carderera, Lydia Caston, Helen Charman, Marcus Clark, David Daniel, Siria De Silva, Michael Delwiche, Jamie Edmundson, Abigail Francis, Heather Francis, Nathalie Glaser, Andrew Gray, Lizzie Hayes, Bruce Heck, Ruth Hibbard, Mark Hindle, Lizzie Hines, Fiona Hodge, Wen-Sheng Hong, Olivia Horsfall Turner, Daisy Howarth, Nick Humphrey, Tristram Hunt, Lee Hurley, Rory Hyde, Connie Karol Burks, Robyn Kasozi, Madeleine Keinonen, Meneesha Kellay, Zeba Khalid, Jay Khan, Sofia Kyriklidou, Christopher Larner, Jane Lawson, Donna Lea-Dodd, Michael Linington, Jenny Lister, Kieran Long, Adam Lee-Pentelow, Laura MacDonald, Eve MacNeill, Andrew Matthews, Emoke Milton, Laura McKechan, Laura Mitchell, Mark Morris, Sabrina Offord, Richard Palmer, Jen Penfound, Phoebe Pickard, Kati Price, Rhianna Puddifant, Eva Rakhimova, Vernon Rapley, Harriet Reed, Tim Reeve, Catherine Ritman-Smith, Judy Roberts, James Robinson, Mariam Rosser-Owen, Martin Roth, Sophie Rouse, Angelo Russell, Jasmine Sarkodee-Adoo, Laura Searson, Sarah Sevier, Bryony Shepherd, Ivan Shiel, Josephine Small, Margaux Soland, Jacqueline Springer, Holly Stepp, Jessica Strawson, Jo Trapnell, Livia Turnbull, Chris Turner, Florence Tyler, Erik Vieira, Bethany White, Saskia Whitfield, Dom Whooley, Isabel Wilken-Smith, Lucy Wagstaff, Anna White, Christopher Wilk, Abigail Williams, Maude Willaerts, Martin Wong

Blythe House Collection Move

Claire Allen-Johnstone, Beth Arscott, Robert Ashford, Sonia Ashmore, Lilian Baldwin, Osama Barakat, James Barnard, Fahema Begum, Peter Behek, Sarah Belanger, Viktoriya Beshparova, Alasdair Booth-Leigh, Stasia Botwright, Paul Campbell, Paul Caton, Francesca Chappell, Shruti Chhabra, Henrietta Clare, Robin Clark, Alexander Clayton, Andrew Cameron Crawley, Viviane Da Cruz Kawata, Charles Day, Silvia De Vecchi, Ruth De Wynter, Jake Deeble, Candice Dehnavi, Serena Dicks, Gill Disley, Katharine Dorney, Sherrie Eatman, Anna Espanol Costa, Elizabeth Francis, Oliver Gallimore, Claudia Garcia Pereira, Sophie Gibbs, David Gilligan, Victoria Haddock, Isobel Harcourt, Sarah Harrison, Beverley Hart, Rebecca Hayward, Charlotte Hazeldine, Arthur Holmes, Jessica Hook, Guey-Mei Hsu, Claire Hudson, Natalie Ifill, Anne-Margaux Illido, Veronica Isaac, Tabinda Ishaq, Elizabeth Jacklin, Kenneth Jackson, Carolina Jimenez Gray, Jessica Jones, Vannis Jones Rahi, Natalie Keymist, Tomoko Kikawa, Amy King, Eleanor King, Sarah Kingham, Maria Kinti, Andrew Kirk, Natalya Kusel, Chloe Lafferty, Carys Lewis, Sin Ying Joelle Li, Colin Lievens, Margaret Litten, Keith Lodwick, Emma Long, Caitlin Lynch, Giovanna Macelletti, Philippa Mackenzie, Alexandra Marcus, Christopher Marsden, Susan Martin, Katherine Morley, Jamie Mudle, Erin Mullarney, Jessica Murray, Anita Naik, Nika Narkeviciute, Gemma Organ, Amy Ormrod, Yuki Pan, So Yeon Park, Eliane Pineault-Bourgault, Victoria Platt, Poetic Unity, Carly Randall, Paula Reyes Arce, Julia Reynolds, Zoe Richards, Alice Ridgway, Ramona Riedzewski, Christina Ritschel, Juliet Rufford, Ines Satrustegui Hernandez, Jamie Shakespeare,

Lucy Shaw, Nicholas Smith, Suzanne Smith, Emma Snow, Riyaz Somani, Gabriela Somarriba Rocha, Thea Stevenson, Alexandra Strachan, James Sutton, Paul Thomas, Kristian Volsing, Victoria West, Sarah Westbury, Boudewien Westra, Eva White, Jane Wilson, Alice Young

Creative collaborators

A Practice for Everyday Life, Anika Abedin, Larry Achiampong, Naheed Anwar (Subco Trust), Are You Mad, Art Vomit, Arte Conservation, Arup, Alaa Alsaraji, Beam Lighting Design, BG&E, Tim Brogden (Cody Docks), Build Up Foundation, Buro Happold, Chocolate Films, Clay Interactive, CMA Planning, Coda to Coda, Collage Club London, Colliers International, Commissioned By You, Constantine Ltd., Constructive and Co., Creative Technology Systems Integration, Diller Scofidio + Renfro, Tapiwa Dingwiza, Direct Access, E5 Bakehouse, Ede's UK Ltd., Elevate Youth Voice, Elijah, Fieldwork Facility, Klaudia Fior, Florea d.sign GmbH, Fraser Randall, Gardiner & Theobald, Hackney Quest, Hauser & Wirth, Here East, Sahra Hersi, Hoare Lea, Tom Hunter, IDK, Maro Itoje, JA Projects, Suhaiymah Manzor-Khan, Jones Neville, Marcon Fit-Out, Zehra Marikar, Mark + Cristina, Lucy Martin, Andu Masebo, McLaughlin & Harvey, Momart Plc., NinePC, O'Donnell + Tuomey, Orsa, Paul Bramwell Consulting, Hallie Primus, Abiola Remi-Lawal, Rise Contracts Ltd., Robyn Lynch, Sadie St Hilaire, June Sarpong, Sew Social, Soji Sonibare, Solved Workshop, Spotlight Youth Centre, Standard8, Studio Mutt, Studio ZNA, Sysco Productions, Taylor Pearce, Thomas J Price, Tito Mogaji, Melissa Thompson, URGE Collective, Velrada UK, Waymakers Kids, We Not I, Lu Williams, Veselya Yuleva

Agra Colonnade co-production

Aasiyah A-A, Celestine A, Muhammad A, Dina Alsafi, Annie Antony, Rachel Bailey, Romain Beck, Nelly Rouco Castan, Jennifa Chowdhury, Nelufa Chowdhury, Shyam Dattani, Charlotte Diley, Mahika Gautam, Nusraat Gilani, Aysha Goga, Adila H, Emily Hannam, Maha K, Sumayyah M, Revati Mann, Deena Nasaruddin, Herbert-Cristian Panduru, Kanhari Pinge, Rafeya Q, Imad-Uddin R, Rumaysa R, Kavya Iyer Ramalingam, Tim Rayne, Ameerah S, Rosie S, Victor Salander, Sneha Semaleesan, Annika Shamachar, Hashna Sivasothilingam, Subathra Subramaniam, The Creative Dimension Trust, Leah Wallace, Adam Williamson, Tahmila Y

Robin Hood Gardens co-production

Osman Abdi, Nate Agbetu, Mara Ahmed, Jamel Alatise, Hanifa Anam, Sadia Aziza, Asama Begum, Julie Brown, Ikram Choudhury, Sam Elbahja, Sister Christine Frost, Patrisha Galang, Bea Gamblin, Faith Iyobhebhe, Rukaiya Karim, Hoi Long Lai, Serra Luthena, Sophie Mably, Ronnie Norfolk, Cristina Silva, Paul Tandy, Jean Whitelock, Alfie Winslow

External partners

East Bank (Tamsin Ace), A-COLD-WALL, (Samuel Ross), Abba Voyage, (Duncan Sanders), Amillan (Bradley Hilt, Nigel Cowie, Thomas Neale, Finnegan Scott), Badu Sports, Ballymore Plc (Stevan Tennant), BBC (Lorna Clarke, Ahmed Hussain, Sam Jackson, Aled Jones, Faron McKenzie), City Hall (Justine Simons, David Bellamy, Shonagh Manson), Creative Newham (Sanaz Amidi), Creative Wick (William Chamberlain), Delancey (Paul Goswell), Good Growth Hub (Oliver Benjamin), Hawkins Brown (David Bickle), Here East (Mike Magan, Gavin Poole), Jikoni (Ravinder Bhogal, Nadeem Lalani Nanjuwany), London Borough of Hackney (Guy Nicholson, Mayor Caroline Woodley), London Borough of Newham (Mayor Rokhsana Fiaz), London College of Fashion (Professor Andrew Teverson), London Legacy Development Corporation (Mark Camley, Lyn Garner, David Goldstone, Lord Peter Hendy, Shazia Hussain, Rosanna Lawes, Michelle May, Leona Roche, Greg Smith), Manhattan Loft Corporation (Harry Handelsman), Plexal (Andrew Roughan), Sadler's Wells (David Bell, Alistair Spalding, Britannia Morton), UCL East (Helen Fisher, Paola Lettieri), University for the Creative Arts (Magdalene Odundo), University of the Arts London (Nigel Carrington, James Purnell, Mark Farthing), Studio Wayne McGregor (Wayne McGregor, Rebecca Marshall), West Ham United Foundation (Joe Lyons), Yinka Shonibare Foundation

V&A Trustees

Nicholas Coleridge, Paul Ruddock, John Sorrell, Nigel Webb, Kavita Puri, Amanda Levete, Nick Hoffman, Allegra Berman, Professor Polly Blakesley, and co-opted members of the Trustees' V&A East Committee, Mohammed Z Rahman and Zia Zareem Slade

V&A East Youth Collective

Ruwaydah Abidali, Joanna Afroozi, Hafsa Ahmad, Haleema Ahmed, Khizra Ahmed, Saarah Ahmed, Samuel Akolawole, Shirin Al'Rashid, Fahmida Alom, Nuha Irdina Wan Armizi, Miriam Ashon, Ruqaiya Asim, Xaymaca Awoyungbo, Salman Mohd Azhan, Zafirah Badmus, Ayra Bajwa, Reese Campbell, Valentina Hernandez Castrillon, Dani Chamorro, SiQi Sarah Chew, Javier Cornejo, Amelie Crooks, Evelien David, Joshua Dickinson, Maya Egbo, Shardae Eldridge, Dionne Emmerson, Mae Estrada, Victoria Famoriyo, Glenda Gaspard, Chloe Giles, Safiye Hasan, Samiha Hassan, Kairi Hughes, Faizah Hussain, Hafiza Hussain, Maryam Hussain, Amina Yasmin Hussain, Fatheha Hussain, Khadija Yasmin Hussain, Em Hutton, Ariana Islam, Ceylan Ismail, Rameen Jawad, Fahima Khurshed, Ahadi King'Ori, Maya Lewis, Kate Lucas, Ridji Maier, Shai Mitchell, Laula Nassimoldina, Mohammed Noor, Nathan Obiang-Nnang, Damian Osei, Aamina Oughradar, Aniya Sofia Pramanik, Deen Karim Pramanik, Nabiha Qadir, Lukas Rackauskas, Mojisayo Robinson, Zeynep Sahin, Adam Samhan, Jasmine Sarkodee-Adoo, Zoe Scholes, Alina Shafiq, Dhevia Sharma, Maryam Siddique, Maia Szulta, Iguette Tcheko, Talitha Thomas-Kelly, Fatimah Ulghar, Cash Webster, Talia Woodin

Affiliated researchers, residents, interns and fellows

Andrew Adedipe, Freya Fletcher, Liza Fior, Theaster Gates, Cara Gray, Thomas Harding, Rebecca Hundeyin, Jasmine James, Hayley Mardon, Clara De Massol De Rebetz, Adam Moore, Wouter Osterholt, PARAA, Christine Pungong, Matilda Pye, Iqra Rahman, Resolve Collective, Joyoti Roy, Petra Seitz, Aqui Thami, Dani Trew, Eric de Visscher, Kathleen Walter-Meikle, Laura Wilson

And for their work on this publication

Emily Angus, Nina Chang, Sarah Duncan, Rebecca Fortey, Peter Kelleher, Lucy Macmillan, Lizzy Silverton, Andrew Tullis, Tom Windross, Emma Woodiwiss

Finally, particular thanks to Claire McKeown, Catherine Ince, Nigel Webb and Tim Reeve without whom the V&A East project would not have got off the ground during those uncertain early years.

Image Credits

Unless otherwise stated photos © Victoria and Albert Museum, London.

© Hufton + Crow 6, 12, 13, 144, 195, 212, 213, 242; EPW006767 © Historic England 10; © Estate of Maurice Broomfield 18; © 2025 Yinka Shonibare CBE. All Rights Reserved, DACS 20, 21; © The Board of Trustees of the Science Museum 22 (top); Courtesy Alexander McQueen 22 (bottom); Courtesy The Metropolitan Museum of Art, New York 23; Photograph Lewis Jones 24; Photograph courtesy Himalayan Institute of Alternatives, Ladakh (HIAL) 26, 27, 79 (bottom); Photograph Rob Battersby 28; Photograph 鈴木竜一朗 Ryuichiro Suzuki 29; Photograph Sarah Green/V&A 30, 32; Photograph Hallie Primus 34 (top); Photograph Samantha Manton/V&A 34 (bottom); Photograph Navjot Mangat/V&A 38 (top); © Sean Ebsworth Barnes 38 (bottom); Photograph courtesy Rebecca Pierce 39; Photograph Iwan Baan 42, 162, 192, 194, 198; © Tony Minnion 44; © Kehinde Wiley. Courtesy V&A and Stephen Friedman Gallery, London 46; © John Heywood 48; © Estate of Ron Hitchins 50; © Nina Chakrabati 52, 53, 54, 55, 56, 57, 58, 59; © Stephen Gill 64; Courtesy Friends of the Earth 66; © Abbas Akbari 67; Courtesy Ishinomaki Laboratory 68; © JA Projects 70, 102 (bottom) 103 (top and bottom right), 105 (bottom), 106, 107 (bottom and middle); © 2025 Estate of Maud Sulter. All Rights Reserved, DACS 71; © The McNish Trust 72; Courtesy Hussein Chalayan 73 (top); © Yinka Ilori 73 (bottom); © Dee Conway/Bridgeman Images 74 (top); © Aaron Koblin 74 (bottom); Courtesy Granby Workshop 75; © Hany Al-Sayed Ahmad Abd Al-khader 76, 77; Courtesy Issey Miyake and Reality Lab., Tokyo/Artemide, Milan 79 (top); Photograph Abiola Remi-Lawal/Yungbio Photos 80; Photograph Abiola Remi-Lawal/V&A 83, 87, 91, 95, 99; © A Practice for Everyday Life, 103 (bottom right), 104, 105 (middle), 108, 109; Photo: Shahed Saleem 105 (top); © Theaster Gates 110; © 2025 Estate of Eileen Gray. All Rights Reserved, DACS 112; © Richard Malone 114; © Mawuena Kattah 118; Courtesy Takuya Angel 120; © IBUKU Studio 122; © O'Donnell + Tuomey/Ninety90 124; © O'Donnell + Tuomey 126, 128; Courtesy Balenciaga. Photograph Nick Veasey 127; © Nick Kane 138, 139, 140, 141; Photograph Bet Bettencourt 146; Photograph Vicky Grout 148; Photograph Niall Hodson 149; © 2025 Hew Locke. All Rights Reserved, DACS 151; © Lotte Collett 152; Courtesy Lenthall Road Workshop 153; © Sanaa Gateja. Courtesy the Artist 154; © Sofia Karim 156; Courtesy Rahemur Rahman 160; Photograph Sonja Blom/Alamy 170; Photograph Lotte Stekelenburg. Courtesy Museum Boijmans Van Beuningen, Rotterdam 172 (top); Photograph © Tate 172 (bottom); Photograph John Bracegirdle/Alamy 173; Museum Boijmans Van Beuningen, Rotterdam. Photograph Ossip van Duivenbode 175, 176; Photograph David Parry 178; Courtesy Diller Scofidio + Renfro 196, 197; Photograph Mary Ngwu 204 (top), 204 (bottom); Photograph Kemka Ajoku 208, 209; © Adjaye Associates 216; © Carrie Mae Weems. Courtesy the artist and Gladstone Gallery, New York 218; Courtesy PESTS 220 (top); © Guerrilla Girls. Courtesy guerrillagirls.com 220 (bottom); Courtesy Pentagram (Crosby/Fletcher/Forbes) 221; © Thomas J Price. Courtesy the artist and Hauser & Wirth. Photograph V&A 222; Photograph © Migration Museum/Elzbieta Piekacz 226; Concept images by ELEMENTAL © Qatar Museums, 2022 227 (top); Courtesy Nairobi Contemporary Art Institute (NCAI). Photograph Paul Munene 227 (bottom); Photograph Yolisa Nqonqoza 232 (top); Courtesy Powerhouse, Sydney. Photograph Rory Gardiner 232 (bottom); Photograph Myung J. Chun/Los Angeles Times via Getty Images 233 (top); Courtesy MASP, São Paulo. Photograph Eduardo Ortega 233 (bottom); Courtesy Herzog & de Meuron. Photograph Kevin Mak 236, 240; Courtesy M+, Hong Kong. Photograph Dan Leung 238 (top), 238 (bottom), 241; Courtesy M+, Hong Kong. Photograph Andrew Crowe/MetaObjects 239; Photo: Fred Howarth 256

Object Credits

Given by the the artist 18; Purchased with the support of The National Lottery Heritage Fund and the Photographs Acquisition Group 20–21; Given by the Greenwich Mural Workshop 44; Purchased with support from Art Fund and a legacy donation from Dr Philip da Costa 46; Given by John Heywood 48; Purchased through the Cecil Beaton Fund 64; Jameel Acquisition 67; Given by Rupert Faulkner 68; Given by the makers 72; Given by the designer 73 (top); Presented by Art Fund 26–7; Given from the Bloxam Collection 78 (top); Given by Issey Miyake London Ltd. 79; Given by Andrew Baseman 78 (bottom); Acquisition generously supported by Theaster Gates and White Cube 110; Bequeathed by Rev. Alexander Dyce 116; Given by the IBUKU Studio 122; Purchased through the generous support of the Friends of the V&A 151; Given by Lotte Collett and the Hackney Empire 152; Given by the Greenwich Mural Workshop 153; Given by Sofia Karim 156; Gift of the manufacturer 164; Purchased through the generous support of the Friends of the V&A 218; Given by Margaret Timmers 220 (top)

Index

Illustrations are indicated by *italic* page numbers while notes are shown by 'n'.

First published by V&A Publishing
Victoria and Albert Museum,
South Kensington,
London SW7 2RL
vam.ac.uk/publishing

Distributed in North America by
Abrams, an imprint of ABRAMS

V&A Publishing books are
represented in the UK and Europe
by Abrams & Chronicle Books
1 West Smithfield, London, EC1A 9JU,
UK and 57 rue Gaston Tessier, 75166
Paris, France
abramsandchronicle.co.uk
info@abramsandchronicle.co.uk

ISBN 978-1-83851-048-0

10 9 8 7 6 5 4 3 2 1
2030 2029 2028 2027 2026

A catalogue record for this book is
available from the British Library.

Design by A Practice for Everyday Life
Copyediting by Lizzy Silverton, First Pages

New V&A photography by Peter Kelleher and the Photography and Digitisation Dept, with special thanks to Sarah Duncan.

This volume has been produced with four alternative covers, each composed from selected images within the book; image credits on p. 250

Printed in Belgium by Graphius
Reprographics by Dexter PreMedia

V&A Publishing
The power of creativity

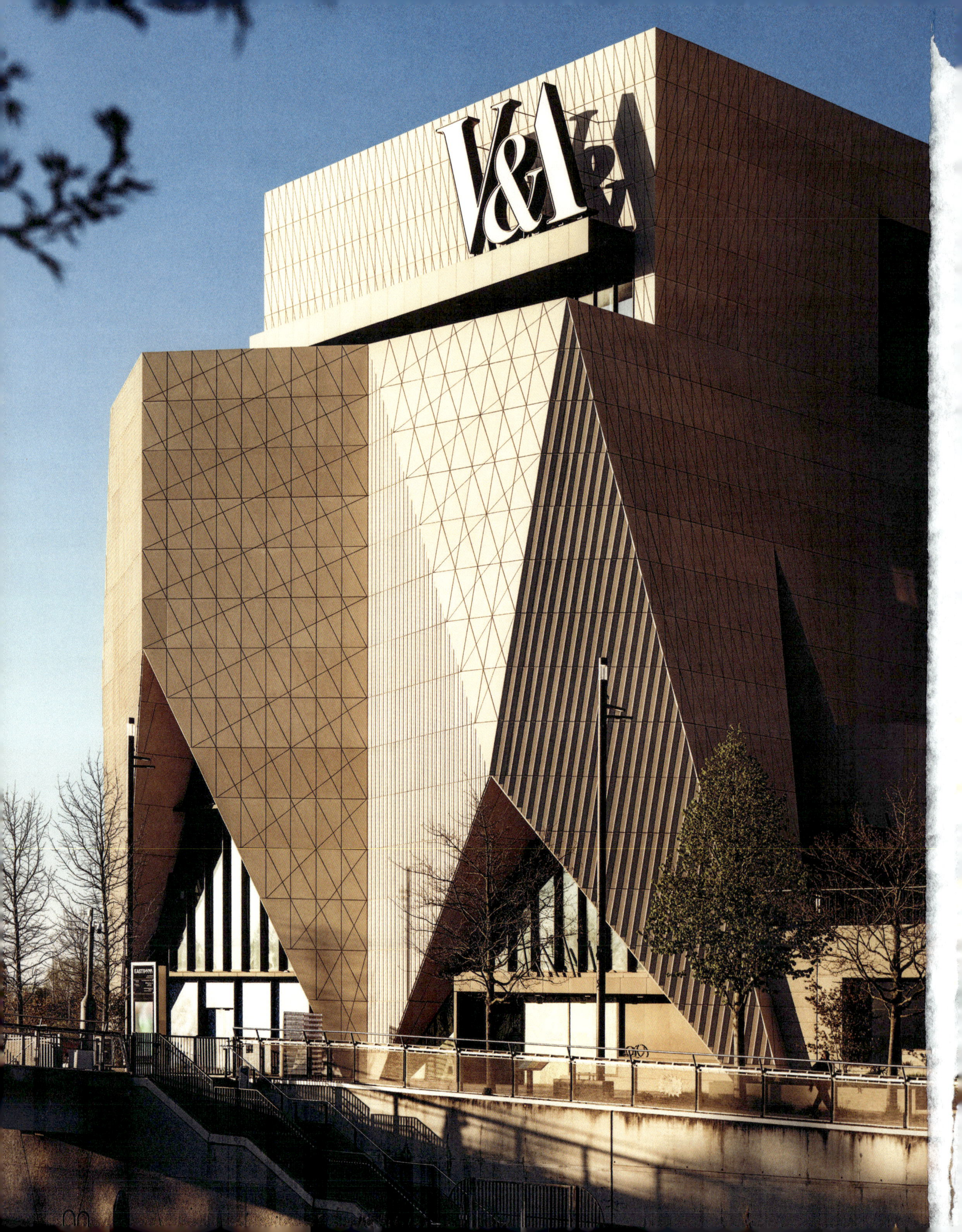
V&A